George B. Clementson

# A Manual relating to Special Verdicts and Special Findings by Juries



Salzwasser

**George B. Clementson**

# A Manual relating to Special Verdicts and Special Findings by Juries

1. Auflage | ISBN: 978-3-84604-698-2

Erscheinungsort: Frankfurt, Deutschland

Erscheinungsjahr: 2020

Salzwasser Verlag GmbH

Reprint of the original, first published in 1940.

# A MANUAL

RELATING TO

# SPECIAL VERDICTS AND SPECIAL FINDINGS BY JURIES

BASED ON THE DECISIONS OF ALL THE STATES

By GEORGE B. CLEMENTSON
OF THE WISCONSIN BAR

ST. PAUL, MINN.
WEST PUBLISHING CO.
1905

# PREFACE.

IT IS hoped that this book on the practice connected with special findings of fact by juries will supply a need which unquestionably exists. Either special verdicts or special findings on particular questions of fact, and in some instances both, are in daily use in more than half of our states and territories, and are highly favored by both bench and bar, by whom they are regarded as legal instruments of precision; yet there is no treatise published covering the subject. In some jurisdictions there is scarcely a damage suit tried in which the defendant, not satisfied with a bare general verdict, does not demand findings on several or all of the controlling facts, either with or without a general verdict, as he may choose or the statute permit, in order to guard against a prejudiced verdict for his adversary. But though most frequently met with in tort actions (notably personal injury cases), the use of special findings is by no means confined thereto, nor is it always the defendant who avails himself of the privilege conferred by the statute, though its benefits and the sense of security it affords are naturally most appreciated by him.

When one studies the reports, and observes the very large number of judgments of trial courts that are sustained, modified, or reversed upon special findings of fact by juries, and in addition perceives the unfamiliarity with this method of procedure which prevails in the profession in spite of its general adoption, he is surprised that the rules of practice relating thereto, embodied in the reports, have not been heretofore collected and published in convenient form. It would seem especially needful that this should be done because of the fact that in matters of practice inferences are most untrustworthy guides. "The law has general principles capable of scientific and methodical statement in condensed form, which shall nevertheless contain the germ from which all of its minutest ramifications may be logically developed. But practice is not general; it is a mass of particulars; nor will logical deduction, even by the strongest reason, be at all sure of its steps from one point to another."[1]

The force of the foregoing quotation has been borne in upon me more than once in preparing this book, which is, in truth, a collection of fragments, but in which nevertheless, as in a mosaic, it is believed there will be found some trace of orderly design. It were too much to hope that it will be considered Mosaic by the profession; yet it will doubtless furnish a guide in practice where many go astray.

The writer originally intended to include in the book the subjects of Agreed Case and Verdict Subject to Opinion of the Court, as being in certain respects related to special verdicts; but the idea was abandoned, after some material had been prepared, because these methods of disposing of a case are not in common use, and especially for the reason that they do not involve the determination of facts by the jury. In Agreed Case, or Case Stated, the jury is dispensed with altogether; while the Verdict Subject to Opinion is required only where there is no dispute as to the facts, the questions involved being purely of law, and is, moreover, directed by the court, whose act it is, and not that of the jury.

In conclusion, the writer wishes to acknowledge his indebtedness to Mr. Ezra R. Thayer, of the Boston bar, for permission to use the work of his father, the late Prof. Thayer, on Evidence at the Common Law, as the basis of the historical account given in chapter 1.

G. B. C.

1 Hon. James T. Mitchell, Chief Justice of Pennsylvania, in an address delivered on invitation of the alumni of the University of Pennsylvania, April 15, 1904: "Hints Upon Practice In Appeals."—American Law Register, June 1904, pp. 337–338.

# TABLE OF CONTENTS.

# TABLE OF CASES CITED.

## A

## B

# C

## D

## E

# F

## G

## H

## I

## J

## K

## L

## M

# N

## O

# P

## Q

## R

## S

## T

## V



## W

## Y



## Z



†

# SPECIAL VERDICTS AND FINDINGS.

## CHAPTER I.

### ORIGIN AND HISTORY OF SPECIAL VERDICTS AND FINDINGS.

The appearance of special verdicts in statutory law dates from the year 1286.

"Sometimes," says Blackstone,[1] "if there arises in the case any difficult matter of law, the jury, for the sake of better information and to avoid the danger of having their verdict attainted, will find a special verdict; which is grounded on the statute of Westm. 2, 13 Edw. I, c. 30, sec. 2. And herein they state the naked facts, as they find them to be proved, and pray the advice of the court thereon; concluding conditionally, that if upon the whole matter the court should be of opinion that the plaintiff had cause of action, they then find for the plaintiff; if otherwise, then for the defendant. This is entered at length on the record, and afterwards argued and determined in the court at Westminster, from whence the issue came to be tried."

The statute referred to was, however, but a recognition and affirmance of the common law.[2]

The attaint had been employed for several centuries as an effective check upon the jury and as the only way of remedying a false verdict. The attaint jury which passed upon the verdict of the trial jury was composed of superior personages—knights of the shire and others of still greater importance—and was a more numerous body. The parties to the original

[1] Com. Bk. III, 77.

[2] So resolved in Dowman's Case, 9 Co. 12.

suit and also the first jury were parties in the second inquiry. If the attaint jury decided contrary to the first finding, the trial jury stood convicted of perjury and was punished, while the judgment was reversed.[3]

The theory upon which the application of this remedy proceeded was that the first jury had willfully falsified. The jury, composed of witnesses summoned by the sheriff, had personal knowledge of the matter in controversy. They were thus independent of the witnesses produced by the parties, who played a very subordinate part. The former might entirely disregard the testimony of the latter, and were under obligation to do so if it was not accordant with what they knew.

"Gradually it was recognized that while the jury might not be bound by the testimony, yet they had the right to believe it, and that they were the only ones to judge of its credibility. It became, then, the chief question whether they had such evidence before them as justified their verdict. If they had, they were not punishable; if they had not, why punish them for what, perhaps, they did not know?"[4]

This idea of the jury's right to believe the witnesses of the parties finally resulted in the attaint becoming unworkable. In 1565, Sir Thomas Smith tells us, "attaints be very seldom put in use, partly because the gentlemen will not meet to slander and deface the honest yeomen, their neighbors; so that of a long time they had rather pay a mean fine than to appear and make enquest. * * * And if the gentlemen do appear, gladlier they will confirm the first sentence, for the cause which I have said, than go against it."[5]

Eventually the courts resorted to new trials to remedy improper verdicts, the Star Chamber, which had been employed for the purpose of supplying the defects of the attaint, having been abolished. By the middle of the seventeenth century the procedure was approved, Glynne, C. J., in Wood v. Gunston

[3] Thayer, Preliminary Treatise on Evidence at the Common Law, c. 4.

[4] Thayer, 137, 138.

[5] Id. 139.

(1655),[6] saying: "If the court do believe that the jury gave a verdict against their direction, they may grant a new trial." Thus modern practice began.

But in the thirteenth and fourteenth centuries, so far at least as statutory provision was concerned, attaints were in a very flourishing condition. They are first mentioned in 1268,[7] and the remedy was extended in 1275 [8] to all matters touching the freehold. In 1326–7,[9] 1331,[10] and 1354 [11] the writ was extended to cases of trespass, and at last, in 1360, the statute of 34 Edw. III, c. 7, provided "against the falsehood of jurors, that every man against whom they shall pass may have the attaint both in pleas real and personal."

The writ of attaint was abolished by 6 Geo. IV, c. 50, § 60. Before the machinery of the attaint became rusty from disuse, the petit jury was exposed, in rendering a general verdict, to a very real danger. Long before we find a statutory blow aimed at perverse jurors, we discover the attaint or its equivalent in operation. Thus, in one of the earliest cases,[12] we have the punishment of a jury who, in their double capacity of witnesses and jurors, had found a verdict which was adjudged to have been false and contrary to their knowledge. In consequence, as a measure of self-protection, the jury in doubtful cases refused to bring in a general verdict, but found the facts only, leaving to the judge the duty of applying the law thereto and rendering judgment thereon. In 1286, as previously stated, the custom was formulated in an enactment, providing that "the justices of assize shall not compel the jurors to say precisely whether it be a disseisin or not, so as they state the truth of the fact, and pray the aid of the justices; but if they will say of their own accord that it is disseisin, their verdict shall be admitted at their own peril."

6 Style, 466.
7 St. Marl. 52 H. III, c. 14.
8 St. West. I, 3 Edw. I, c. 38.
9 St. 1 Edw. III, c. 6.
10 St. 5 Edw. III, c. 7.
11 St. 28 Edw. III, c. 8.
12 Gundulf v. Pichot (1072–1082) Big. Pl. A. N. 34.

The questions which a jury is called upon to decide are commonly denominated "questions of fact." "Ad quæstiones facti non respondent judices; ad quæstiones legis non respondent juratores"—a maxim which Coke was never tired of repeating, and which may have originated with him. But the questions passed upon by the jury are not to-day, nor have they ever been, unmixed questions of fact. They have ever required answers containing elements of opinion and of law. In many cases the "question is mixed, consisting of law and fact, so intimately blended as not to be easily susceptible of separate decision," [13] in fact incapable of separation.

It has never been within the province of the jury to judge of the law, so far as civil cases are concerned, except, according to some early conceptions, in actions for damages for slander and libel.[14] But it is a function of the jury to apply the law under the instructions of the presiding judge; and in this application of the law to the facts found to be established, resulting in a general verdict, the mediæval jury foresaw the likelihood of appeal to the attaint jury and the consequent danger of conviction of perversity and perjury. Inasmuch as, at the outset, the petit jury was composed of witnesses, chosen on account of their supposed knowledge of the matter in dispute, they could not, except at their peril, give credence to the testimony of the witnesses of the parties, however mistaken may have been the supposition upon which the jury had been selected, and however short their personal information may have fallen of affording a satisfactory basis for determination. If they relied upon the testimony of the witnesses sworn before them, in cases where their own knowledge was insufficient, and that testimony proved, upon investigation by the attaint jury, false, they were convicted of contumacious behavior or perjury, and were heavily fined; for, in the theory of the day, their own knowledge was equal to the task of exposing the falsehood. Hence, knowing that the theoretical function of

[13] 1 Greenl. Ev. (12th Ed.) 49.

[14] 1 Thomp. Trials, § 941.

the jury was simply to decide questions of fact arising upon the issue, the jurors refused to group and arrange the facts with a view to returning a general result involving an element of legal and judicial deduction or construction. In doubtful cases, and in some instances undoubtedly distrustful of themselves, they drew well within their province, withholding an opinion, and presenting, as the result of their deliberations, merely the naked facts.

The statute of Edward I recognized this privilege, and later decisions affirmed it. Thus in Dowman's Case it is said: "It was resolved by Sir Ed. Anderson, chief justice, and all of the justices of the bench, that the special verdict was well founded; they held that in all pleas, * * * and upon all issues joined, * * * the jury may find the special matter * * * (and) pray the opinion of the court * * * by the common law, which has ordained that matters in fact shall be tried by the jurors, and matters in law by the judges," etc.[15]

There can be little doubt that fear of attaint was more potent than recognition of their own incompetence in inducing juries to return special verdicts. At no period in its history has the petit jury been noted for modesty or diffidence, when not liable to be called to account. In Martyn v. Jackson,[16] Rainsford, C. J., contended in opposition to his confreres that a new trial should be granted, saying: "Juries are willful enough, and denying a new trial here will but send parties into the chancery." In the same year the Lord Chancellor, upon a motion for an injunction, after a general verdict, granted the same, and remarked that the jury had so misbehaved themselves that he had rather see his house on fire than hear of such another verdict. Other judges, for instance Holt, C. J., in Ash v. Ash,[17] indulged in forcible language anent the behavior and qualifications of juries, and, altogether, it is to be feared that the jury in early days was sadly in need of control.

Lawfully or unlawfully, the judges often compelled special

[15] 9 Co. 12, 13. [16] (1674) 3 Keble, 398. [17] Comb. 357.

verdicts in their endeavor to direct the intelligence of the good men and true who sat in judgment upon suitors. Sometimes special verdicts were ordered, the order being enforced by threats, by punishing the jury, and by granting a new trial.[18] But the jury was in the end victorious. In England its privilege now extends not only to refusal to find generally, but also to refusal to find specially either upon particular points or upon all material facts, in the face of a request or demand for such findings by court or counsel or both. The final clash between court and jury in this connection came in the case of the Mayor and Burgesses of Devizes v. Clark,[19] wherein the corporation alleged that it was possessed of an ancient market on Thursdays; that it was the duty of persons selling butcher's meat at Devizes on market days to expose it for sale in stalls rented by the corporation for that purpose, and not elsewhere; and complained that defendant on divers days sold meat at his own house, and refused to rent and pay for plaintiff's stalls.

Defendant admitted the ancient market, but contended that it did not carry with it the right to prevent townspeople from selling at their own houses on market days.

The judge told the jury that, as it was a matter of legal doubt whether or not the right to an ancient market carried with it the right to prevent parties from selling in their own houses within the town on market days, and as the plaintiff's right to an ancient market was admitted, to find expressly, if they thought the evidence warranted such a finding, whether there was any custom in Devizes to preclude the sale of butcher's meat on market days in any part of the town except on plaintiff's stalls. Upon this some of the jurymen entered into a conversation with the judge, from which it appeared that they understood the effect of his observations as to the point left to them.

18 Chichester's Case, Aleyn, 12 (1644); Gay v. Cross, 7 Mod. 37 (1702); R. v. Bewdley, 1 Peere Williams, 207 (1712).

19 3 Ad. & E. 506.

The jury returned a general verdict for plaintiff, when the following conversation took place: "Williams, B.: Then, gentlemen, you find that in your judgment there has been an immemorial usage for the corporation to demand and receive this stallage for meat in the market, and that there was no right on the part of individuals to sell in a house or shop out of the market? The Foreman: That is not our verdict; our verdict is for the plaintiffs; the right to the market is acknowledged on all hands; of course our verdict is to say that the defendant had not a right to do what he is charged with doing. Williams, B.: Then you further find that the defendant had no right? Foreman: I would rather not add any words." The judge expressed the opinion that a specific finding would prevent further litigation, and the foreman replied that the jury desired to add nothing to its verdict.

The defendant obtained a rule to show cause why the verdict should not be set aside and a new trial had on the ground of uncertainty in the finding of the jury; but it was decided unanimously by the King's Bench that the jury had the right to refuse to speak expressly on the fact, not being bound to find anything except in terms of the issue.

Conforming to this pronouncement, in the comparatively recent case of Reg. v. Jameson, a prosecution for violation of the foreign enlistment act, we find the Lord Chief Justice, against objection of Sir Edward Clark for the defense, propounding to the jury seven questions, but telling them that they are only requested to answer the interrogatories and cannot be compelled to do so; that they can, if they choose, bring in a general verdict of guilty or not guilty, but in refusing to answer the questions will be assuming a grave responsibility, inasmuch as questions of law are involved.[20]

The general tendency in the United States has been to "exalt in some ways the relative functions of the jury beyond all English precedent";[21] but in respect to special verdicts and

[20] See 6 Yale Law J. 32, Prof. Wurts.

[21] Thayer, 219.

findings this is not true. In contrast with the case last referred to are numerous cases in the American reports in which, under statutory provision, questions have been submitted to the jury which they were compelled to answer fully and without evasion before discharge, if a general verdict was agreed upon. And under the code in many of our states the court in its discretion may, and at the request of counsel shall, direct the jury to find a special verdict. Again, the right of the jury of its own motion to return a special verdict is frequently limited, as, e. g., to actions for the recovery of money only or specific real property, and the authority even in this case may depend on there being no direction by the judge to the contrary.

In our country the spectre of absolutism was laid a century ago. It has scarcely crossed the path of our jurisprudence from its very birth. In England, on the other hand, it haunted the public mind during the entire formative period of the Constitution, and left an indelible imprint upon national custom. There (to quote again from Mr. Thayer's valuable treatise), while "logic and neatness of legal theory have always called aloud, at least in recent centuries, for special verdicts, so that the true significance of ascertained facts might be ascertained and declared by the one tribunal fitted to do this finally and with authority, * * * considerations of policy have called louder for leaving to the jury a freer hand. The working out of the jury system has never been shaped merely by legal or theoretical considerations. That body always represented the people, and came to stand as the guardian of their liberties; so that whether the court or the jury should decide a point could not be settled on merely legal grounds; it was a question deeply tinged with practical considerations. While it would have been desirable, from a legal point of view, to require from the jury special verdicts and answers to special questions, that course would have given more power to the King and less to the people." [22]

[22] Thayer, 218, 219.

The passage in more than half of our states and territories of statutes authorizing and regulating special verdicts or interrogatories, or both, and the relaxation in others, which make no express provision on the subject, of the stringent English rule denying the court's right to require answers to questions propounded by it, is perhaps evidence of a widespread belief that control of the jury is as truly and fully the guaranty of liberty as trial by jury. There is no question of the existence in the United States of general dissatisfaction with the administration of justice in the present mode. Beyond doubt the feeling is in large part due to lack of confidence in the jury, and has its root in the general belief (and was opinion ever better founded?) that an uneducated and inexperienced set of men, selected practically at random and certainly without reference to their qualifications, is not competent to decide matters in controversy according to the law and the evidence; is not fit to analyze and weigh the testimony, and (fully as difficult a matter), when a conclusion has been reached as to the real facts established, to apply the law thereto under the instructions of the court. Ordinary intelligence does not qualify a man for the proper performance of these duties. In fact and in short, there is a feeling on the part of the masses that the "time-honored institution" of the jury, this "bulwark of our liberties," is in these modern days more of a clog upon justice than otherwise, while the growing tendency of professional minds is to regard it as an anomaly.

Our people have no fear of dictatorship, imperialism, or the successful encroachments of executive power. They respect and trust the judges they have set over them. They appreciate the fact that the average jury is incompetent intelligently and according to law to decide the questions submitted to it, and that this incapacity is the result not only of defective training, but as well of the heavy handicap which irrational procedure puts upon it. The jury is sadly in need of guidance; yet despite the fact, in our various jurisdictions and with few exceptions, we are more and more withdrawing from it the assistance of "the disciplined mind of an impartial judge." In trial by jury in England, in the federal courts of the United States, and in a few commonwealths of the Union, the desirability and even necessity of aid from the presiding judge is recognized. In Nudd v. Burrows,[23] Swayne, J., says: "It is the right and duty of the court to aid them [the jury] by recalling the testimony to their recollection; by recalling its details; by suggesting grounds of preference where there is a contradiction; by directing their attention to the most important facts; by eliminating the true points of inquiry; by resolving the testimony, however complicated, into its simplest elements; and by showing the bearing of its several parts, and their combined effect, stripped of every consideration which might otherwise mislead or confuse them. How this duty shall be performed depends in every case upon the discretion of the judge. There is none more important resting on those who preside at jury trials. Constituted as juries are, it is frequently impossible for them to discharge their functions wisely and well without this aid. In such cases, chance, mistake or caprice may determine the result."

Going still further, our federal courts have held that even an expression of opinion by the court is permissible.[24] But in many of our states statutes or constitutional provisions prohibit the trial judge from expressing any opinion on questions of fact, or even forbid any comment whatever on the evidence. Not only that, but in those jurisdictions where the court is not explicitly gagged, comment on testimony is at least not commended, and the power must be exercised with such scrupulous care that summing up is felt by the presiding judges to involve scarcely avoidable error, so that, in fact, the evidence is seldom reviewed.

[23] 91 U. S. 439, 23 L. Ed. 286.

[24] Vicksburg & M. R. Co. v. Putnam, 118 U. S. 545, 7 Sup. Ct. 1, 30 L. Ed. 257; California Ins. Co. v. Compress Co., 133 U. S. 387, 10 Sup. Ct. 365, 33 L. Ed. 730; Allis v. U. S., 155 U. S. 117, 15 Sup. Ct. 36, 39 L. Ed. 91; and many others.

Another feature of our jury system which must strike the educated layman as well as the lawyer as absurd is the apportionment of duties between court and jury. Not only is the jury theoretically confined to matters of fact, but actually also to the simplest matters of fact. It cannot be trusted to determine difficult and confusing questions; these must be left to the judge, sitting as a court of equity. "To determine the simple question as to whether or not a promissory note has been paid, twelve men must be called into the jury box because the case happens to be on the law side of the court; while the most complicated questions of fact arising out of alleged fraud, or breaches of trust, or constructive notice, are decided by the judge, because the case happens to be on its equity side;" [25] and this in spite of the adoption of the code, whereby we have but one court for the trial of all cases, legal and equitable, presided over by a single judge.

But not content with simplifying the jury's functions, it has in addition been thought necessary to control its action within the limited but important sphere in which it works. Beyond question this is desirable; but can we stultify ourselves further? Courts are seldom willing to admit the incapacity of juries properly to decide the comparatively simple questions commonly submitted to them; yet such expressions as the following are, in effect, nothing but admissions that the profession has as little confidence as the laity in the jury left to its own devices: "Before the enactment of our statute enabling a party to ask that a jury shall respond to interrogatories, it was difficult to have placed upon the record of a trial the component parts or elements which entered into and formed the verdict of the jury. This was felt and considered as operating injuriously in many instances, because of the current of decisions in this court for many years to the effect that a

[25] See 20 Am. Law Rev. 672, article by Wm. L. Scott favoring abolition of the jury in civil cases.

verdict in a civil case should not be disturbed on the evidence when there was proof tending to sustain it." [26]

One of the main purposes of the interrogatory statute is thus to afford a basis for retrial. Before its passage we felt reasonably certain that the jury had arrived at its verdict in some extraordinary way, whatever the result. Now we can cut away the mantle of mystery in which the general verdict is enveloped, see how the principal facts were determined, and whether the law was applied under the judge's instructions. A perverse verdict may still be returned, granted a jury clever enough to appreciate the effect of its answers, and to shape them to harmonize with its general conclusion. But it is much more difficult to do this than formerly, and by requiring the jury to return the naked facts only we may fairly expect to escape the results of sympathy, prejudice, and passion.

The special verdict and finding, obtainable largely at the option of counsel, is a long step towards removing the cumbrous, expensive, and unsatisfactory machinery of trial by jury. The next step, logically, is for the court to pass upon the facts in all civil cases, or to entirely abolish the general verdict.

The general adoption of the practice of submitting questions to be answered with the general verdict grew out of the prevailing distrust of such verdicts, which, under the rule applied upon appeal, are entitled to every reasonable intendment. It is matter of common knowledge that the general verdict may be the result of anything but the calm deliberation, the weighing of evidence, exchange of impressions and opinions, resolution of doubts, and final intelligent concurrence which, theoretically, produce it. It comes into court unexplained and impenetrable. In many cases it is impossible to tell whether or not the jury has misapplied the law. Let us take a specific instance:

Suppose the verdict must go according as the jury believes one or the other of two witnesses. If A.'s testimony is credited.

[26] Buntin v. Rose, 16 Ind. 209.

the verdict must go for C.; if B.'s testimony is believed, the verdict must be for D. The jury believes the testimony of A. and returns a verdict for D. This may easily occur (and has occurred times innumerable) because of prejudice, compromise, or a "disposition to jump at results upon a general theory of right and wrong, instead of patiently grasping, arranging, and considering details." [27] Upon appeal, the separate facts which the jury found not appearing, the presumptions are all in favor of the verdict. The jury is presumed to have believed the testimony of B. and discarded that of A. If there is any testimony to support the verdict, it will stand. The credibility of the witnesses was entirely for the jury.

Such results are most often due to the failure of juries to intelligently sift and arrange the evidence, and then proceed logically under the instructions of the court. Jurors are seldom men accustomed to orderly thought, and rarely have the special knowledge and training really requisite to the proper performance of their grave duties. They are supposed to take the law from the court and themselves apply it. In some cases they originate it, while in many they neither understand it nor comprehend the significance of the facts before them. It is undoubtedly true that every man on a jury retires to the jury room with an opinion, more or less pronounced, on the merits of the case, and a disposition in favor of one or the other party. This general impression, in the case of an acute mind (close attention during the trial being granted), might be taken as auguring a proper verdict; but it is far more likely, in the average instance, to lead astray, because it is not the idea of a disciplined mind. The opinion of the majority at the outset of the jury's deliberations will generally make the verdict, and if the majority is won over to the opinion of the minority it is less likely to be due to superior reason than to superior will or other influences.

The impenetrable secrecy which once surrounded the pro-

[27] Morrow v. Commissioners, 21 Kan. 484.

cesses by which a general verdict is reached no longer exists in the majority of states. At least, the remedy lies in the interrogatory statute or the special verdict, the benefits of which are at our disposal. The consensus of judicial opinion is that these laws have proven most salutary in operation, and their privileges are daily claimed. Their tendency has been "to dispel the occasional darkness visible of general verdicts." [28] Autocratic power is taken from the twelve good men and true who sit in judgment upon suitors, and they are compelled to do more than flip a copper and keep still about it; that is, if their verdict is to stand. They must justify their return; they must present it as the child of travail, as every good thing is. It must be in larger measure than formerly the result of deliberation and sound conclusion. It is no longer shrouded in night, but exposed to the glare of day, if you will, with all its details revealed; this to the end that the court may decide according to the law, and that justice may be meted out (so far as man can accomplish it) by the only competent umpire, a trained lawyer and honest judge.[29]

[28] Ryan, C. J., in Carroll v. Bohan, 43 Wis. 218, 221.

[29] "Trial by jury in civil causes seems to be declining in public esteem. The expenses necessarily incident to it are naturally increasing, and the delays are greater also from a general tendency, especially in cities, where most judicial business is transacted, to reduce the number of hours a day during which the court is in session. * * * A jury is waived more often than formerly, and there is a growing conviction that, with a capable and independent judiciary, justice can be looked for more confidently from one man than from thirteen." Hon. Simeon E. Baldwin, in Encyclopædia Britannica (10th Ed.) Vol. VI, pp. 163–164, title, "Law—United States." In an address on "The Scope, Uses, and Value of a Special Verdict in the Trial of Civil Causes by Jury," delivered before the Michigan State Bar Association at its fifteenth annual meeting, at Lansing, on June 7, 1904, Hon. Benjamin J. Brown, of Menominee, concludes that "the general verdict in civil causes must go the way of the wooden plow."

He points out that the chief infirmity of the general verdict is that it is quite possible for a jury to come to an entire agreement upon a question which should control the verdict in favor of one party, and yet return a verdict in favor of the other party; while the requirement of a special verdict holds the jury to the line of its duty, and searches the conscience of the individual juror. Such are the contradictions in human nature that many a man who will unite in a general verdict for a large and unwarranted sum of money will shrink from a specific finding against his judgment and sense of right and wrong.

To a student of comparative jurisprudence Mr. Brown regards the general verdict as anomalous. We are unwilling to allow the judge, with his trained and logical mind, to make a general finding of law and fact, yet are willing to allow a jury to return a general verdict.

The general verdict also goes hand in hand with the system of special pleading. Under the relaxation of our practice, the general issue admitting a great variety of defenses, and, the notice under it admitting of every other conceivable legal defense to the case made by the declaration, the issues have become too vague, and too much at large, to consist with a general verdict. The author quotes Judge Metcalfe's assertion that, defective as trial by jury is, it can never be dispensed with in the United States; from which, however, all present force is taken by the concluding sentence, "Still, if special pleading were abolished, we should never desire to see another jury impaneled."

Among the benefits to be derived from general use of special verdicts in civil actions, distinguished in the paper referred to, are the following:

Error committed by the trial judge where a general verdict is rendered will necessarily involve the delay and expense of a new trial. Where a special verdict is taken, time and opportunity on a motion for judgment are afforded to counsel for adequate discussion, and to the court for due deliberation. This is a distinct advantage. And if the case is removed to an appellate court, that court will not send it back for a new trial, but enter judgment as it finds the right to be.

If the jury make a perverse finding, say upon a question of value or amount of damages, it can speedily be corrected by a review of the testimony bearing upon that question alone.

It is true that the opportunity for the display of the highest order of eloquence in civil causes will scarcely survive the adoption of the special verdict, because the advocate naturally deals with a case as a whole, and not in sections. But the special verdict induces simplicity, directness, and brevity in the arguments of counsel, is in line with modern methods, and accords with the business spirit of the age.

# CHAPTER II.

## QUESTIONING THE JURY AS TO GROUNDS OF VERDICT—NEW ENGLAND PRACTICE.

Rhode Island is the only New England state, so far as the writer is aware, which has made specific statutory provision by which the court is authorized to require the jury to return special findings.[1] But for three-quarters of a century before the passage of the act referred to, the settled practice of our Eastern courts permitted the presiding judge to question the jury, after verdict, as to the grounds upon which they had proceeded.[2] Nor was the practice confined to questioning the jury at the time they brought in their verdict, but the judge

1 Gen. Laws 1896, c. 243, § 7; Pub. St. 1882, c. 204, § 34.

2 Johnson v. Higgins, 53 Conn. 236, 1 Atl. 616; Smith v. Putney, 18 Me. 87; Gordon v. Wilkins, 20 Me. (2 App.) 134; Walker v. Bailey, 65 Me. 354; Hix v. Drury, 5 Pick. (Mass.) 296; Pierce v. Woodward, 6 Pick. (Mass.) 206; Parrott v. Thacher, 9 Pick. (Mass.) 426; Dorr v. Fenno, 12 Pick. (Mass.) 521; Roche v. Ladd, 1 Allen (Mass.) 436; Lawler v. Earle, 5 Allen (Mass.) 22; Hamilton Woolen Co. v. Goodrich, 6 Allen (Mass.) 191; Green v. Clay, 10 Allen (Mass.) 90, 87 Am. Dec. 622; Spoor v. Spooner, 12 Metc. (Mass.) 281; Mair v. Bassett, 117 Mass. 356; Spurr v. Inhabitants of Shelburne, 131 Mass. 429; Edwards v. City of Worcester, 172 Mass. 104, 51 N. E. 447; Ellis v. Block, 187 Mass. 408, 73 N. E. 475; Walker v. Sawyer, 13 N. H. 191; Smith v. Powers, 15 N. H. 546; Dearborn v. Newhall, 63 N. H. 301; Norris v. Town of Haverhill, 65 N. H. 89, 18 Atl. 85. See, also, Biggs v. Barry, 2 Curt. 259, Fed. Cas. No. 1,402.

**Questions by Counsel.** Counsel may not examine the jury after general verdict as to the ground of their decision. Houston Electric R. Co. v. Robinson (Tex. Civ. App.) 76 S. W. 209.

Where a verdict is plain and unmistakable, it is error to permit counsel for the unsuccessful party to interrogate the jury, on the reading of the verdict by the clerk, as to what they intended thereby. Anderson v. Green, 46 Ga. 361.

had power as well to submit interrogatories, answers to which were to be returned with the general verdict.[3]

**Early Views.** In adopting the practice of questioning juries, the other New England states, and doubtless New York also, followed the lead of Massachusetts, from whose decisions the following explanations are worth quoting:

In Pierce v. Woodward [4] the court inquired of the jury upon what principle they proceeded in assessing damages. On motion for a new trial it was contended that after a verdict has been recorded the declaration of a juror should not be received to impeach it. On the other hand, it was said that the inquiry was proper, inasmuch as the object was not to prove misbehavior, but merely that the jury had proceeded upon an erroneous principle. A new trial was granted, and the court said: "It is said that we cannot interfere with the verdict upon the declaration of jurors in regard to their proceedings, but that the evidence should come aliunde. The court are not disposed to disturb verdicts by making unnecessary inquiries, but where the judge is surprised by the verdict it is not unusual to ask the jury upon what principle it is found. Here the principle upon which they proceeded was incorrect."

In Parrott v. Thacher [5] the court made inquiry of the jury as to the ground upon which the verdict for plaintiff was rendered, and granted a new trial upon their answers, which showed a disagreement. In the course of the opinion, Parker, C. J., says: "We certainly do not mean to encourage the practice of questioning jurors as to the grounds of their opinions; but where there are distinct grounds upon which the verdict may be given, perhaps it is not improper to ascertain which

[3] Dyer v. Greene, 23 Me. 464; Graves v. Washington Ins. Co., 12 Allen (Mass.) 391; Johnson v. Haverhill, 35 N. H. 74; Wheeler v. Schroeder, 4 R. I. 383; Spaulding v. Robbins, 42 Vt. 90. See, also, Florence Mach. Co. v. Daggett, 135 Mass. 582; Boston Dairy Co. v. Mulliken, 175 Mass. 447, 56 N. E. 711; Wakefield v. Water Co., 182 Mass. 429, 65 N. E. 814.

[4] 6 Pick. (Mass.) 206.

[5] 9 Pick. (Mass.) 426.

they adopted, as there may be little or no evidence on one and sufficient on another; and, if it appears that they did not agree upon either of the grounds, I do not see how their verdict can stand, unanimity being required. If there are three distinct grounds upon which an action can be maintained, all independent of each other, and only four of the jury agree upon each, I do not see how they can amalgamate their opinions and make a legal verdict of them."

In Dorr v. Fenno [6] the court remarked, with reference to the practice of interrogating the jury when they return their verdict: "This practice does not depend upon the consent of the parties. The presiding justice has a discretionary power to make such inquiries of the jury in relation to the business before them as the proper administration of justice may require. Such has ever been the usage of this court. It sometimes happens that the verdict first returned by the jury is not entirely certain, or does not precisely meet the issue joined, or some of the issues do not appear to be definitely found. In such cases, before the verdict can be drawn in form, it is not only proper, but necessary, to ascertain from the jury the real meaning of their finding, that, when the verdict is affirmed, it may with certainty express the true intent of the jury, or that the jury may again be sent out for further deliberation, if any material question appears not to have been determined by them. And, even after the verdict has been affirmed and recorded, it may be important to the due administration of justice, or to prevent unnecessary litigation, to ascertain whether certain points have been determined. It is not uncommon to have several grounds relied upon in a trial, when it cannot be ascertained from the verdict itself upon which ground it was found. In such cases the court will make the proper inquiries of the jury, and if it appear to have been found upon an illegal principle, or if the jury did not agree upon any one ground, the verdict may be set aside. * * * This is, how-

[6] 12 Pick. (Mass.) 521.

ever, a discretionary power, which the court will exercise very sparingly and with great caution. But it is believed to be a power not dangerous or liable to abuse, and one which, if discreetly exercised, will facilitate legal investigation, restrain useless litigation, and promote justice."

In *New York,* in the case of McMasters v. Westchester County Mut. Ins. Co.,[7] the appellate court said: "The course the judge took on the trial, in submitting certain questions to the jury with a view to avoid the necessity of a second trial, was objected to; but such course is not uncommon at the circuits where a doubt is entertained upon the law; it cannot operate to the prejudice of either party, and frequently avoids the trouble and expense of a new trial. It is in the nature of a special verdict, which the jury may always find."

**Object of Questions.** In *Vermont* it is held that the court has power, unless otherwise provided by statute, to require the jury on rendering a general verdict to find specially on particular questions of fact,[8] one reason for the practice being to enable the court to see whether an instruction, for the purposes of the general verdict, if wrong was prejudicial.[9] Similarly, in *Rhode Island,* where two or more grounds of action or defense are taken under the same issue, it is proper for the court, in its discretion, to direct the jury specially to declare upon what ground their verdict is found, in order to ascertain whether a particular direction of the court, in matter of law, affected the result.[10]

7 25 Wend. 382.

8 Spaulding v. Robbins, 42 Vt. 90.

9 McKinstry v. Collins, 74 Vt. 147, 56 Atl. 985.

10 Wheeler v. Schroeder, 4 R. I. 383. See, also, Spencer v. Railroad Co., 62 Conn. 242, 25 Atl. 350. Where findings are conclusive against plaintiff, the ruling of the court on his request for an instruction is immaterial. Spurr v. Inhabitants of Shelburne, 131 Mass. 429. The court may inquire of the jury as to their verdict, for the purpose of ascertaining whether the case has been properly tried. Norris v. Haverhill, 65 N. H. 89, 18 Atl. 85, citing Dearborn v. Newhall, 63 N. H. 301

**Discretion of Court.** Inquiry for the purpose of ascertaining the basis of the jury's decision is discretionary with the court.[11] "As where distinct facts are put in issue, an inquiry may be made for the purpose of correctly stating the questions of law, if any should arise in the case, or for the purpose of terminating the case, if the particular facts found are conclusive as to the matter in issue between the parties." [12] The exercise of such discretion is not subject to exception,[13] where it does not involve a violation of any rule of law or established practice.[14]

The court may inquire of the jury upon what grounds they found their verdict, in the absence and without consent of counsel, and their reply may be considered on appeal in determining the materiality of questions presented by bill of exceptions.[15] Consent of counsel to the submission of questions is unnecessary,[16] except where the court requires special findings without a general verdict.[17]

11 Hamilton Woolen Co. v. Goodrich, 6 Allen (Mass.) 191; Graves v. Insurance Co., 12 Allen (Mass.) 391; Spoor v. Spooner, 12 Metc. (Mass.) 281; Spurr v. Inhabitants of Shelburne, 131 Mass. 429. See, also, Barstow v. Sprague, 40 N. H. 27; Elwell v. Roper, 72 N. H. 585, 58 Atl. 507; Wheeler v. Schroeder, 4 R. I. 383; McKinstry v. Collins, 74 Vt. 147, 56 Atl. 985.

12 Spoor v. Spooner, 12 Metc. (Mass.) 281.

13 Spoor v. Spooner, supra; Spurr v. Inhabitants of Shelburne, 131 Mass. 429, and cases cited.

14 Hamilton Woolen Co. v. Goodrich, 6 Allen (Mass.) 191. Whether special questions requested by a party shall be submitted is a matter in the discretion of the court. Boston Dairy Co. v. Mulliken, 175 Mass. 447, 56 N. E. 711.

Withdrawal of a question is purely discretionary with the court. Florence Mach. Co. v. Daggett, 135 Mass. 582.

15 Lawler v. Earle, 5 Allen (Mass.) 22. The fact that the jury was out twenty-five hours did not make a question by the court improper. Edwards v. City of Worcester, 172 Mass. 104, 51 N. E. 447.

16 Dorr v. Fenno, 12 Pick. (Mass.) 521; Methodist Episcopal Parish v. Clarke, 74 Me. 110; Barstow v. Sprague, 40 N. H. 27. A new

17 Johnson v. Town of Haverhill, 35 N. H. 74.

**Time of Inquiry.** In *Massachusetts* it was held in an early case that inquiry must be made before the separation of the jury, that to permit questions to be put after separation would be unsafe, and that the judge has no power to propound them without consent of both parties.[18]

Whether or not this rule still applies to cases in which the questions are put only after the return, it certainly does not hold where interrogatories are propounded to the jury when they retire, for in a comparatively recent case [19] the Supreme Court of Massachusetts said: "Distinct questions submitted to them [the jury] are in connection with their verdict, and of such nature that the jury cannot properly arrive at a verdict except upon consideration and determination of the specific questions. When, therefore, * * * the verdict has been arrived at, and reduced to writing and signed by the foreman, before the separation of the jury, it is to be inferred that they have before their separation considered the specific questions submitted, and arrived at an agreement as to the answer to be given. If, by mistake or inadvertence, the answer has not been reduced to writing and signed before separation, we think it is still within the power of the court to require the jury to answer the question, and to receive and record the answer in connection with the verdict."

In *Vermont,* in an action for personal injury resulting in death, the jury agreed upon a general verdict for plaintiff, sealed it up, separated for the night, and brought the verdict into court next morning. After they had rendered it the court asked the foreman this question, "Did you find the negligence

trial will not be granted because the jury were directed to find specially material facts in addition to the general verdict. Richardson v. Weare, 62 N. H. 80. Nothing appearing to the contrary, on appeal consent will be presumed. Willard v. Stevens, 24 N. H. 271; Allen v. Aldrich, 29 N. H. 63.

18 Green v. Clay, 10 Allen, 90, 87 Am. Dec. 622. See, also, Smith v. Putney, 18 Me. 87. Contra, Dearborn v. Newhall, 63 N. H. 301.

19 Spencer v. Williams, 160 Mass. 17, 35 N. E. 88.

was in reference to the negligence of the flagman?" The foreman replied, "In reference to the negligence of the flagman." The clerk then, by direction of the court, wrote out the following finding: "The jury on their oaths say that the negligence of the defendant causing the injury arose from the action of the flagman." It was held that this was no error; the jury's answer was authoritative information to the court as to a finding already made.[20]

**Effect of Submission and Answers.** The jury, having been sworn to give a true verdict, are as much bound to make true answers in court touching their verdict as if they had been sworn specifically for that purpose;[21] and an answer stating on what ground the jury found for the defendant is to be given full effect, notwithstanding the judge instructed the jury that if they found for the plaintiff he should ask them to say upon which count, but if for the defendant they need say nothing more.[22]

The court is not required, however, to receive every fact which the jury thinks proper to state; for sometimes statements may be made so irrelevant and foreign to the inquiries put that they would be clearly inadmissible.[23] And as the whole includes all its parts, the power to set aside the entire verdict must carry with it the power to set aside any specific finding upon any separate question submitted to the jury.[24]

Where a special finding is inconsistent with the general ver-

[20] Germond's Adm'r v. Railroad Co., 65 Vt. 126, 26 Atl. 401.

[21] Hix v. Drury, 5 Pick. (Mass.) 296, citing, inter alia, Hackley v. Hastie, 3 Johns. (N. Y.) 252; Taylor v. Greely, 3 Greenl. (Me.) 204; Haskell v. Becket, Id. 92.

[22] Mair v. Bassett, 117 Mass. 356, 359.

[23] Dorr v. Fenno, 12 Pick. (Mass.) 521. Answers cannot be extended by argument to settle a fact beyond that directly covered by them. Ellis v. Block, 187 Mass. 408, 73 N. E. 475. A voluntary finding in the form of an order is a nullity. Billings Slate & Marble Co. v. Hanger, 62 Vt. 160, 19 Atl. 231. See, also, McEldon v. Patton (Neb.) 93 N. W. 938; Levy v. Publishing Co., 65 Hun, 619, 19 N. Y. Supp. 751.

[24] Monies v. City of Lynn, 119 Mass. 273.

dict, the former controls.[25] But a general verdict will not be set aside on account of a special finding in reply to a question of the court, if it does not in terms qualify the verdict, and it appears from the bill of exceptions that it was erroneously recorded through misapprehension.[26]

Where the court inquires of the jury as to the grounds upon which they proceeded in arriving at their verdict, the answers of the foreman, assented to by his fellows, may be made a part of the record, and will have the effect of special findings of the facts so stated by him.[27]

25 Richardson v. Weare, 62 N. H. 80.

26 Roche v. Ladd, 1 Allen (Mass.) 436.

27 Spurr v. Inhabitants of Shelburne, 131 Mass. 429.

# CHAPTER III.

## SYNOPSIS OF STATUTES CONCERNING SPECIAL FINDINGS —OBJECT AND EFFECT—CONSTITUTIONALITY.

At the back of this volume will be found an Appendix, giving the statutory provisions of the several states and territories relating to special verdicts and findings, which may be consulted whenever questions arise which call for examination of the precise terms of particular laws. Such reference will be necessary, however, less often than would at first appear probable, for reasons to be stated at the conclusion of the present chapter, and which may be best appreciated by grouping the laws in question according to their most prominent features.

The statutes of twenty-one states and territories contain, in addition to provisions in regard to general verdicts, specific provisions relating to both special verdicts and special findings.[1] In seven states we find statutory mention or regulation of special verdicts alone,[2] and in seven others of special findings only,[3] while in one the provisions relate to separate-general verdicts,[4] which are not, strictly speaking, either special verdicts or special findings.

Coming first to the consideration of special findings, and leaving the subject of special verdicts to the latter pages of the book:

[1] Arizona, Arkansas, California, Colorado, Idaho, Illinois, Michigan, Minnesota, Montana, Nebraska, Nevada, New York, North Carolina, North Dakota, Ohio, Oregon, South Dakota, Utah, Washington, Wisconsin, Wyoming.

[2] Georgia, Maine, Missouri, New Jersey, South Carolina, Texas, Vermont.

[3] Indiana, Iowa, Kansas, New Mexico, Oklahoma, Rhode Island, West Virginia. The Iowa Code defines the term "special verdict," but contains directions as to practice only in regard to special findings.

[4] Kentucky.

**Submission of Interrogatories Discretionary with Court.** In *Arizona, Arkansas, Colorado, Idaho, Minnesota, Montana, Nebraska, New York, Nevada, North Carolina, North Dakota, Oregon, South Dakota, Utah, Washington, West Virginia, Wisconsin,* and *Wyoming* the submission of interrogatories requiring special findings to be returned with the general verdict, is, by the language of the statute, discretionary with the court.

The *Colorado* statute differs from the others of this group only in providing that the questions "shall be submitted to the attorney of the adverse party before the argument to the jury is commenced."

*West Virginia.* The principal variation of this statute is indicated by italics in the following: "* * * Upon the trial of any issue or issues by a jury, whether under this section or not, the court may *on motion of any party,* direct the jury," etc.

The *Arizona* statute contains no express provision for submission on request of a party, but provides that "in all cases, whether law or chancery, where more than one material issue of fact is joined, interrogatories may, under proper instructions, be submitted to the jury by the court," etc.

—— **What Findings may be Required.** The phraseology of these laws differs, but expresses substantially the following: That in any case in which they render a general verdict, the jury may be required by the court to find specially upon particular questions of fact, to be stated in writing.[5]

The expression, "particular questions of fact," occurs in the

[5] The jury, it would seem, is not at liberty to return special findings in civil cases except by direction of the court.

In an action on a contract of employment stipulating for weekly salary, and also for a commission on sums received by defendant on advertisements secured by plaintiff, who was to devote his entire time to defendant's service, it appeared that plaintiff was discharged for cause. The jury returned a verdict that "the jury finds for the defendant, but that plaintiff is entitled to a commission of 25 per cent. on all advertisements accepted by defendant, to wit, $88.50."

statutes of all of the above states except New York, which employs the words, "one or more questions of fact," and Arizona, which provides that interrogatories "shall be confined to a single question of fact."

—— **Findings to be Written and Recorded.** All of the above statutes require the questions to be stated in writing, the majority specially authorize the court to direct written findings, and all require the findings to be recorded; the provision being, commonly, that they shall be "filed with the clerk and entered upon the minutes."

**Submission Mandatory on Request of Party.** In *California, Illinois, Indiana, Iowa, Kansas,*[6] *Michigan, New Mexico, Ohio,* and *Oklahoma* the statutes are practically identical with the foregoing, except that they oblige the court to instruct the jury to find specially upon particular questions of fact, when the direction is requested by a party. "Must" is the constraining word employed in the enactments of California, Illinois, and Iowa, while in the rest of these states the phrases, "shall direct," "instruct," or "require" are used. †

*Kentucky.* The Kentucky Code provides: "When the evidence is concluded, but before the argument to the jury, either party may require the court to direct the jury to find a separate-general verdict with the general verdict. * * * Unless otherwise directed, the jury may find a general, or a general and separate-general, verdict, or a separate-general verdict; but the court may, without motion, or upon motion of a party, direct the jury to find: (1) A separate-general verdict as to any issue; and with such finding the jury shall also return a general verdict; and, if the separate-general verdict be incon-

Held, that as the verdict is general in favor of the defendant, the qualification in the form of a special finding for plaintiff is unauthorized. Levy v. Publishing Co., 65 Hun, 619, 19 N. Y. Supp. 751.

6 Until 1870 the statute made submission discretionary with the court.

† A similar statute was in force in Maryland 1894–1900. See Appendix.

sistent with the general verdict, judgment shall be rendered pursuant to the former."

The "separate-general verdict" seems to be the equivalent of a finding or findings on particular questions of fact, as the interrogatory statute is interpreted in some states;[7] while the term is not strictly synonymous with "special findings" in states where the latter need not pass upon the issues as entireties, or where it is not necessary that the answers to interrogatories be controlling.

According to the Supreme Court of Kentucky: "The meaning of the expression 'separate-general verdict' is that the verdict is separate as to the particular issue as distinguished from any other issue in the case, and general as to the particular issue. That is, it was intended to apply in cases where there is more than one issue. For instance, an action upon an alleged contract when the issues presented are, first, was the contract procured by fraud or duress? And, second, if it was so procured, and therefore voidable, was it subsequently ratified by the defendant after full knowledge of the fraud and removal of the duress? If, in such case, the jury should find a general verdict for the defendant, the court could not determine whether it was based on the ground that the evidence authorized the conclusion that there was fraud or duress sufficient to invalidate the contract, or upon the ground that there was not evidence sufficient to establish a ratification. The evidence might preponderate in favor of the conclusion that there was fraud or duress sufficient to invalidate the contract, but at the same time the evidence upon the issue of ratification might be such that the preponderance in favor of a ratification should be so

[7] The separate-general verdict upon an issue or issues seems to be strictly synonymous with a special finding upon a "particular question of fact," as the latter term is understood in *Iowa*, and perhaps other states, where the interrogatory statute is construed as in pari materia with that concerning special verdicts, and where the questions of fact to be called for are held to be the ultimate facts presented in a special verdict.

overwhelming that the court should grant a new trial. If a separate-general verdict is asked for, the court should grant it, and with it shall require the jury to return a general verdict. In such cases it is not only proper, but necessary, that the jury should be instructed by the court as to the law applicable to the particular issues to be found by the jury as fully as if there was only one issue in the case, and a jury were required to find a general verdict thereon." [8]

*Rhode Island.* The statute of this state provides that "in any case the common pleas division of the Supreme Court may, and upon request of either party shall, direct the jury to return a special verdict upon any issue submitted to the jury. Such issue may be settled by the justice presiding at the trial, and either party may except to his rulings thereon. In addition to such special findings on the issues submitted, the jury shall in each case return a general verdict, and shall assess such damages, if any, as they may deem just."

There would seem to be a misapplication of terms in this section. In each case a general verdict is to be returned. But a general verdict with a special verdict is unnecessary and improper. A special verdict consists of findings upon all material issues—a determination of facts in such manner that nothing remains for the court but to apply the law thereto. And, formally, the special verdict should conclude conditionally, finding for the one party or the other according as the court may adjudge the law to be in favor of the plaintiff or the defendant, which conclusion is not a general verdict, but is part of the special verdict.

The writer is informed [9] that the special verdict proper is not used in Rhode Island, but that the statute is designed to secure findings upon such material questions of fact as counsel may desire. The rule or practice of the court requires the form of these special findings or issues to be settled prior to

[8] Witty v. Railroad Co., 83 Ky. 21.

[9] Courtesy of W. M. P. Bowen, Esq., master in chancery, Providence.

the closing argument. The special part of the verdict is usually entered in the following form: "The jury further find specially: (1) That," etc.; "(2) that," etc.; different paragraphs being employed to include as many special findings as may have been requested.

—— **Questions to be Submitted to Adversary.** The statutes of *Illinois* and *Iowa* require that the party requesting the submission of interrogatories submit same to the adverse party before the commencement of the argument to the jury.

—— **Other Provisions.** None of the statutes in this group assigns a time for presentation of questions to the court with request for submission.

The *Indiana* law excepts equity cases from the application of its provisions, and the *Michigan* statute applies, by its terms, only to courts of record.

As to statutory requisites of questions, see chapter 5.

**Inconsistency between General Verdict and Special Findings—Latter to Control.** In every state and territory which authorizes the submission of interrogatories calling for special findings, with the exception of *Arizona,* whose statute is silent on the subject, and *Rhode Island* (see, infra, Review), is to be found a section similar to that of Arkansas, which may be taken as the type: "When the special finding of facts is inconsistent with the general verdict, the former controls the latter, and the court may give judgment accordingly." [10]

**Review—*Illinois.*** The Illinois statute provides that "Submitting or refusing to submit a question of fact to the jury, when requested as provided by the first section hereof, may be excepted to and be reviewed on appeal or writ of error as a ruling on a question of law." [11]

*New York.* "When a motion is made to nonsuit the plaintiffs or for the direction of a verdict, the court may, pending

[10] Sand. & H. Dig. 1894, § 5832.

[11] Hurd's Rev. St. 1899, c. 110, § 58b.

the decision of such motion, submit any question of fact raised by the pleadings to the jury, or require the jury to assess the damage. After the jury shall have rendered a special verdict upon such submission or shall have assessed the damage, the court may then pass upon the motion to nonsuit or direct such general verdict as either party may be entitled to. On an appeal from the judgment entered upon such nonsuit or general verdict, such special verdict, or general verdict, shall form a part of the record and the appellate division or the court of appeals may direct such judgment thereon as either party may be entitled to." [12]

*Rhode Island.* "The appellate division of the supreme court may, on motion of any party made and filed, together with a statement of the evidence in such cause at said trial in manner as elsewhere provided in case of petitions for new trial, set aside any general verdict and order judgment to be entered by the common pleas division in favor of either party upon any special verdict found in any cause; or it may order a new trial generally, or upon any issue submitted at such trial, as, upon an inspection of all the evidence adduced, and the general or special verdicts found therein, to it shall seem just." [13]

**Uniformity of Statutes and Decisions.** It is apparent from this brief survey of the enactments relating to interrogatories and special findings in response, that these statutes present sufficient uniformity on their face to justify a somewhat general treatment of the subject in the body of the text.

They are readily grouped in two broad classes: (1) Those making the submission of interrogatories, to be answered with the general verdict, discretionary with the court; (2) those requiring the court to submit interrogatories upon request of a party. Points of difference in other respects are not marked,

[12] Code Civ. Proc. § 1187.

[13] Judiciary Act, c. 23, § 7. See appendix, Court and Practice Act, 1905.

and resemblances are accentuated by the common provision for control of the general verdict by the special finding or findings in cases where the two are inconsistent, and for judgment accordingly, and by the uniform provision for recording the answers.

But upon examination of the decisions we observe that, even as to the main distinction between these groups, there is more difference in phraseology than in construction and practice. Under statutes of both groups the court may submit questions of its own motion, where no request is made. Where request is made under statutes of the first class the judge may comply in his discretion; but this discretion is not to be arbitrarily exercised. It is unnecessary to supply citations here. For the present let the statement suffice that the discretion is not absolute and may not be capriciously used. It must be sound, guarded, judicious, and its exercise may be reviewed as in other cases.

The writer agrees with Senator Tracy that "as a matter of faith, we can assent to the theological dogma of 'an overruled free agency,' but in a matter of legal reasoning we are justified in asking for pretty strong evidence to convince us that a judicial discretion can exist independently of the right or power of exercising it"; [14] but the fact remains that the majority of courts hold judicial discretion in the matter of submitting questions to juries reviewable for abuse. And, to be plain, "abuse" will be found, on appeal, to have occurred when the appellate court is of opinion that it would not have done the same thing under the same circumstances had it been sitting at nisi prius. It thus appears that the appellate court, regarded as a Snark, is of the species Boojum, in whose presence judicial discretion vanishes as softly and suddenly as did the Baker in the poem.

The gist of the decisions upon statutes of the first or discretionary class is, really, that if the interrogatories requested

[14] Oneida Common Pleas v. People, 18 Wend. 79, 99.

are proper and seasonably presented, they should be submitted, though there are a few cases which attach a more absolute character to the discretion of the court.

On the other hand, under statutes of the second or mandatory class, a party's right to demand submission is not unconditional. He may require the court to submit interrogatories only when they are in proper form, of proper substance, and properly presented.

These constructions all but wipe away the dividing line between the discretionary and mandatory groups, and give the practice and procedure in any state of either group authority in any other of that group and no little weight in jurisdictions whose laws fall within the remaining class.

But further, and more important, the statutes of either group do little more than sanction a certain practice. They are skeletons and prescribe practically nothing of procedure, and in a sense are merely declaratory of an old American custom. Upon trial a multitude of questions arise that cannot be resolved by reference to substantive law. Questions as to the time and manner of request for interrogatories; their preparation and form; their number, alteration, requisities; the time for their submission; the instructions to be given with them; the result of failure to answer, return of evasive or insufficient answers, of answers without a general verdict; the construction of findings, etc.—to few, if any, of these questions (which constitute only part of those likely to arise) can the statute give definite answer.

It is upon inquiries connected with such matters that the decisions of any state where the practice of submitting interrogatories prevails are of general value.

It is difficult in any book to handle a subject regulated by statute, in a general way, where the effort is made to include all jurisdictions having laws upon the matter discussed. In most cases it is, in fact, impossible. The present subject, however, lends itself fairly well to such treatment, and it is believed that substantial uniformity in decisions as well as statutes will be discovered.

**Object and Effect of Statutes.** The decisions which seek to define the objects of these statutory provisions naturally adduce reasons for their enactment similar to those given by the Massachusetts courts in regard to the early practice existing there independent of statute. The lead of Massachusetts has been followed, and more extensive control has been provided as requirements dictated.

The need of such control over the jury has been increasingly felt from the day when the jury ceased to be considered the last barrier of popular liberty against despotic executive and judicial encroachment. When the long English struggle with Stuart prerogative ended in the Revolution and the flight of James, the jury had outlived its most important function in the evolution of free institutions, and it has since come to need some of the restraint it formerly imposed. Under Tudor and Stuart it combated, with varying spirit and success, the absolutism for which those monarchs stood, and helped ward off or broke the force of kingly blows at ancient liberties. Each year thereafter witnessed a dwindling of executive and an increase of popular power, so that to-day in England there is practically but one estate.

The function of the jury as a buffer has long disappeared, but in proportion as the necessity for independence has diminished its autocracy has, in fact, increased. Its action very often has been arbitrary or ignorant, and by reason of the halo with which political superstition had invested it in days of peril its judgments have been held in too much sanctity by both trial and appellate courts. The general verdict has always been highly indulged, and presumptions which the reason and method which produced it would rarely sustain have been entertained in its favor. It is true that the special verdict now and then enlightened the court as to the path which surefooted justice should tread; but as the return of facts only could not be required at common law, but was entirely discretionary with the jury, the judges were rarely afforded that insight into the jury's view of the weight of the evidence so often needed to do right between the parties and to save time and expense.

The New England states, as has been seen, early broke away from English custom and tradition, and assumed the right to question juries concerning the grounds of their verdicts when such inquiry was deemed expedient. New York followed the practice, and incorporated it in her Code, and other states, with various modifications, adopted a similar course. Most of them also prescribed that special verdicts might be compelled; but the special verdict is a more cumbrous instrument, and seems to be less commonly used in a number of jurisdictions, while in a few it has been entirely discarded.

Referring to Elizabethan coercion and restraint of the jury, Hallam indulges in glowing language: "That primeval institution, those inquests by twelve men, the unadulterated voice of the people, responsible alone to God and their consciences, which should have been heard in the sanctuaries of justice, as fountains springing from the lap of earth, became, like waters constrained in their course, stagnant and impure." [15]

Whether or not this panegyric is justified by the part played by the jury in the period when the British constitution was with difficulty acquiring stability, it certainly does not appeal (as eminently descriptive) to the lawyer who nowadays defends a corporation in a damage suit—at least some parts do not. It is apparent, on looking over the reported cases, that the American tendency is to demand something more than responsibility to heaven and the juror's conscience, and it would seem that the "unadulterated voice" emanating from the jury-box is occasionally too raucous for judicial and legislative ears.

The statutes under consideration were adopted for a number of reasons, but, primarily, for the control of juries as a result

[15] Const. Hist. Eng. Vol. 1, p. 234.

of widespread distrust of the methods by which the average general verdict is reached. These enactments are the best proof of lack of faith on the part of those well informed on the subject, in the intelligence, candor, and honesty of juries, especially in civil cases. They emphasize the decline of the jury in public estimation, and hint at its supersession, since they afford the spectacle of an arbiter who cannot be trusted to exercise his functions, but who must be circumscribed and circumvented in the interest of justice.

For the general verdict too often covers a multitude of transgressions. Instructions are ignored, and the strongest testimony disregarded, not, perhaps, because the average jury is so ignorant that it should not know better, but because it is inclined to take everything into its own hands and make its own law. The tendency is seen where the jury brings in a verdict for a party, with evasive or equivocal answers to special interrogatories which could be easily answered fully and definitely under the evidence by men of ordinary intelligence. The reason of the evasion is not far to seek. It indicates simply that the jury has formed its general verdict because of sympathy, prejudice, or other improper influence, and fears that definite findings on the interrogatories submitted would defeat the judgment the jurors wish to see rendered. Such occurrences are not uncommon. They show how arbitrary the jury's action often would be, were it left to its own devices, and in how salutary a manner the check provided by statute operates.

It is probably true that in the great majority of cases the general verdict, however surprising, is a conclusion upon general ideas of right and wrong, and that the jury think they are doing justice between the parties. It is the result of sympathy. It is said that no nobler virtue warms the human heart than sympathy; but here it ceases to be a virtue. To deem otherwise would be an intolerable reflection upon the law and its administration. It is not for inexperienced and uneducated men to upset established legal principles to which the best minds of centuries have given assent. Willful verdicts are impertinent and insulting. They are in direct violation of the jurors' oaths. They bring courts into contempt and make for anarchy.

One of the best explanations of the legislative purpose in authorizing special interrogatories is to be found in Morrow v. Commissioners of Saline County,[16] in which the court said: "The main object of special questions is to bring out the various facts separately, in order to enable the court to apply the law correctly, and to guard against misapplication of the law by the jury. It is matter of common knowledge that a jury influenced by a general feeling that one side ought to recover will bring in a verdict accordingly, when at the same time it will find a certain fact to have been proved which in law is an insuperable barrier to a recovery in accord with the general verdict. And this does not imply intentional dishonesty in the jury, or a failure on the part of the court to instruct correctly, but rather a disposition to jump at results upon a general theory of right and wrong, instead of patiently grasping, arranging, and considering details. Scarcely any jury will, when questioned as to a single fact, respond that it exists without some sufficient evidence of its existence. Its response will as a rule be correct, if direct, and, if not correct, then evasive and equivocal. And such evasive and equivocal answers always cast suspicion upon the verdict. The suggestion springs almost involuntarily that the answers are thus evasive and equivocal from an unwillingness on the part of the jury to stultify themselves so far as to say that the facts were or were not proved, mingled with a fear that a direct and positive answer will avoid the effect of the general verdict they have returned."

And, similarly, in *Wisconsin:* "The purpose of submitting particular controverted questions of fact is to secure a direct

16 21 Kan. 484. See, also, Union Pac. R. Co. v. Shannon, 33 Kan. 446, 6 Pac. 564; Southern Kan. Ry. Co. v. Gorsuch, 47 Kan. 583, 28 Pac. 703.

answer free from any bias or prejudice in favor of or against either party. It is a wise provision in certain cases when properly administered. It has often been demonstrated in the trial of causes that the nonexpert juryman is more liable than the experienced lawyer or judge to be led away from material issues of fact involved by some collateral circumstance of little or no significance, or by sympathy, bias, or prejudice; and hence it is common practice for courts, in the submission of such particular questions and special verdicts, to charge the jury, in effect, that they must have nothing to do with, and must not consider the effect which their answers may have upon, the controversy or the parties. * * * It is certainly a very proper thing to do when the business or reputation of either party is such as to naturally stimulate a bias in favor of the one party or the other."[17]

A few of the numerous decisions in which the object of the statutes under consideration is discussed are given below. The list is by no means complete, but the cases cited state the main reasons given by the courts. They are of interest as indicating the theories and conclusions upon which practice has proceeded, and, it will be noticed, give about equal prominence to the functions of control and assistance.

*Idaho.* "In cases where the number and nature of the issues are such as likely to confuse the jury, the court can greatly aid it by formulating such issues into distinct propositions, and thus have them submitted in logical, concise questions instead of one confused mass. Through a general verdict, a jury is more likely to jump to a conclusion, or yield to its impulse or sympathy, than when special issues are submitted, to which the facts can be directly applied. Certainly the court must submit only those material, and in such number and form as will aid, and not bewilder, the jury. Is this a matter left entirely to the discretion of the court? It might be so held if

[17] Ryan v. Insurance Co., 77 Wis. 611, 615, 46 N. W. 885; Coats v. Town of Stanton, 90 Wis. 130, 62 N. W. 619.

the statute were designed alone for the convenience of the court, but it is not. On the contrary, its object is to aid the jury to the proper conclusions, and to promote justice in the administration of the law. It is a discretion that must be soundly exercised by the court, and subject to review as any other discretionary power when not properly exercised."[18]

*Illinois.* The case of Chicago & N. W. R. Co. v. Dunleavy[19] contains a lengthy discussion as to the meaning of "particular questions of fact," and the distinction between special verdicts and special findings, and strongly disapproves the practice, permitted by certain courts, of submitting a great number of interrogatories, as tending to confuse the jury, where the aim should be to assist it.

*Indiana.* "The main purpose that the interrogatories and answers serve is to test the correctness of the general verdict."[20]

"The statute was designed to elicit material facts, not items of evidence. It was not intended that the interrogatories should be employed to harass or confuse jurors, but the purpose of the statute is to elicit the facts so that the court may pronounce judgment upon them."[21]

"Before the enactment of our statute enabling a party to ask that a jury shall respond to interrogatories, it was difficult to have placed upon the record of a trial the component parts of, or elements which entered into and formed, the verdict of a jury. This was felt, and considered as operating injuriously in many instances, because of the current of decisions in this court for many years to the effect that a verdict in a civil case should not be disturbed on the evidence, where there was proof tending to sustain it."[22]

18 Burke v. McDonald, 2 Idaho (Hasb.) 679, 33 Pac. 49.

19 129 Ill. 132, 22 N. E. 15.

20 Evansville & T. H. R. Co. v. Marohn, 6 Ind. App. 646, 34 N. E. 27; McCullough v. Martin, 12 Ind. App. 165, 35 N. E. 719, 39 N. E.

21 Louisville, N. A. & C. Ry. Co. v. Kane, 120 Ind. 140, 22 N. E. 80.

22 Buntin v. Rose, 16 Ind. 209.

*Iowa.* Special findings are designed to exhibit the grounds upon which the general conclusion is based.[23]

"The design of special interrogatories is to point out the controlling questions in the case, exact for them separate consideration, and thereby guard against misapprehension of what are the vital issues to be determined. When the answers cover all the ultimate facts, these furnish a full explanation of the general verdict and a safe test of its accuracy. Their use, however, should never be perverted to the purpose of confusing and misleading jurors, nor to that of merely satisfying the curiosity of parties. Yet this might, and no doubt would, often be the result if, upon the request of either party, the jury must be required to find specially upon any particular question of fact, regardless of whether it inhered in or affected the general verdict." [24]

*Michigan.* "The statute authorizing special questions contemplates that they shall be put in explanation of the general verdict." [25]

"Special questions to the jury are to enable the court to learn what view the jury take of the material issues, and to correct their possibly wrong inferences from the facts which they find to exist." [26]

"The purpose of having special findings is to know what the rights of the parties are and to have them spread upon the record." [27]

The object of the statute is "to ascertain whether the jury had, in making up their verdict, properly applied the law, as given by the court, to the facts of the case." [28]

905; Manning v. Gasharie, 27 Ind. 399, 409; Maple v. Vestal, 114 Ind. 325, 16 N. E. 620.

23 Ford v. Railroad Co., 69 Iowa, 627, 29 N. W. 755.

24 Morbey v. Railroad Co., 116 Iowa, 84, 89 N. W. 105.

25 Hendrickson v. Walker, 32 Mich. 68.

26 Cole v. Boyd, 47 Mich. 98, 10 N. W. 124; Harbaugh v. Cicott, 33 Mich. 241; Mechanics' Bank v. Barnes, 86 Mich. 632, 49 N. W. 475.

27 Durfee v. Abbott, 50 Mich. 479, 15 N. W. 559.

28 Beecher v. Galvin, 71 Mich. 391, 39 N. W. 469.

"The statute gives the right to put specific questions to the jury for the very purpose of enabling the court to know whether in finding generally they have properly considered the necessary elements of the finding." [29]

*Missouri.* The object of the statute is to obtain an explanation of the general verdict.[30]

In this state the statute permitting special questions to be put was in force only a short time.[31]

*Nevada.* By submitting special interrogatories, the expense and delay of a second trial may be often avoided, and by this practice the law is much more effectually separated from the fact than by giving hypothetical instructions.[32]

*New York.* "The object of the provision in regard to special findings was to enable the court to leave the case to the jury generally, but to control their verdict by findings, which would render a second trial unnecessary, in cases where no exceptions were taken, or rather to prevent the necessity of exceptions to the charge. If, in such cases, the court instruct the jury to find for either party, provided they find in a certain way upon certain questions of fact, such instructions would be subject to exceptions, and error in any of them would send the case back for a new trial." [33]

*North Carolina.* The purpose of the provision is to settle some important leading questions of fact, arising in the case, that are not made issuable facts in the pleadings, but are deemed by the court material to a just determination of the cause.[34]

*Ohio.* The statute is intended to elicit from the jury such special findings of fact as shall test the correctness of the gen-

[29] International Wrecking & Transportation Co. v. McMorran, 73 Mich. 467, 41 N. W. 510.

[30] Benton v. Railroad Co., 25 Mo. App. 155.

[31] Anderson v. McPike, 41 Mo. App. 328.

[32] Lambert v. McFarland, 7 Nev. 159.

[33] Moss v. Priest, 1 Rob. 632, 19 Abb. Prac. 314.

[34] Porter v. Railroad Co., 97 N. C. 66, 2 S. E. 581, 2 Am. St. Rep. 272.

eral verdict, and does not require the submission of questions whose only purpose is to ascertain the mental processes by which the jury arrived at the conclusions of facts.[35]

*Washington.* "That the provision of our statute in relation to special verdicts (sic) is a wise one we have no doubt. The object thereof was to enable the parties, by the aid of the court, to confine jurors to their sphere, and require them to find facts, and, having done so, to apply the law as given them by the court." [36]

*West Virginia.* "Before this statute allowing special questions to a jury, the essential matters of fact involved in a trial were wrapped up in the general verdict, and it could not be told whether each and all of these essential facts were, in fact, in the opinion of the jury, found for the party prevailing; and as the province of the court to set aside the verdict was narrow, the losing party could not have the benefit of a fact which the jury, had they passed separately, would have found for him. * * * This statute I regard as a salutary instrument to enable the parties to have the jury, as the triers of the facts under the evidence, to say what is their finding separately upon the controlling facts in the case." [37]

**Constitutionality.** In Walker v. New Mexico & S. Pac. R. Co.[38] the question was raised of the constitutionality of the New Mexico statute authorizing special findings, and providing for judgment on the special findings, if inconsistent with the general verdict.

[35] Gale v. Priddy, 66 Ohio St. 400, 64 N. E. 437; Schweinfurth v. Railroad Co., 60 Ohio St. 215, 54 N. E. 89; Cleveland & E. Electric R. Co. v. Hawkins, 64 Ohio St. 391, 60 N. E. 558.

[36] Redford v. Railroad Co., 9 Wash. 55, 36 Pac. 1085.

[37] Bess v. Railroad Co., 35 W. Va. 492, 14 S. E. 234, 29 Am. St. Rep. 820; Peninsular Land Transp. & Mfg. Co. v. Insurance Co., 35 W. Va. 666, 14 S. E. 237; Veith v. Salt Co., 51 W. Va. 96, 41 S. E. 187, 57 L. R. A. 410.

[38] 165 U. S. 593, 17 Sup. Ct. 421, 41 L. Ed. 837.

Justice Brewer, in delivering the opinion of the court, said in part:

"The putting of special interrogatories to a jury and asking for specific responses thereto in addition to a general verdict is not a thing unknown to the common law, and has been recognized independently of any statute. Beyond this, we cannot shut our eyes to the fact that in many states in the Union, in whose Constitutions is found in the most emphatic language an assertion of the inviolability of trial by jury, are statutes similar to the one enacted by the territorial Legislature of New Mexico; that these statutes have been uniformly recognized as valid; and that a large amount of the litigation in the courts is carried through in obedience to the provisions of such statutes. It would certainly startle the profession to be told that such statutes contravene a constitutional requirement of the inviolability of jury trials.

"Indeed, the very argument of counsel for plaintiff in error is an admission that up to a certain extent these statutes are undoubtedly valid. That argument is practically that, when the specific findings are returned and found to be conflicting with the general verdict, the court is authorized to grant a new trial, but can do no more. But why should the power of the court be thus limited? If the facts as specially found compel a judgment in one way, why should not the court be permitted to apply the law to the facts thus found? It certainly does so when a special verdict is returned. When a general verdict is returned, and the court determines that the jury have either misinterpreted or misapplied the law, the only remedy is the award of a new trial, because the constitutional provision forbids it to find the facts. But when the facts are found, and it is obvious from the inconsistency between the facts as found and the general verdict that in the latter the jury have misinterpreted or misapplied the law, what constitutional mandate requires that all should be set aside and a new inquiry made of another jury? Of what significance is a question as to a specific fact? Of what avail are special interrogatories and special findings, if all that is to result therefrom is a new trial, which the court might grant if it were of opinion that the general verdict contained a wrong interpretation or application of the rules of law? Indeed, the very thought and value of special interrogatories is to avoid the necessity of setting aside a verdict and a new trial—to end the controversy so far as the trial court is concerned upon that single response from the jury.

"We are clearly of opinion that this territorial statute does not infringe any constitutional provision, and that it is within the power of the Legislature of a territory to provide that on a trial of a common law action the court may, in addition to the general verdict, require specific answers to special interrogatories, and, when a conflict is found between the two, render such judgment as the answers to the special questions compel."

# CHAPTER IV.

## DISTINCTION BETWEEN SPECIAL VERDICT AND FINDINGS IN RESPONSE TO INTERROGATORIES—IN WHAT CASES SPECIAL FINDINGS MAY BE REQUIRED—DISCRETION OF COURT.

It is necessary for the practitioner to bear in mind the distinction between special verdicts and findings in response to special interrogatories. They are not the same thing,[1] though they to some extent subserve the same purpose [2] and are in pari materia.[3] Notwithstanding the fact that many rules of practice are applicable to questions and answers in either form, the ends they were designed to serve are immediately, if not ultimately, different, and appreciation of this difference will enable counsel to avoid errors which have frequently proved disastrous.

The ideas of the profession upon this distinction, and upon matters generally connected with special verdicts and findings, are apparently confused, and it must be admitted that the decisions, to which we are wont to go for assistance, in many instances do little to dissipate, if they do not actually thicken, the fog. About as often as not we find that opinions denominate answers to questions upon particular matters of fact (answers perhaps not at all determinative) "special verdicts"; and this not only in jurisdictions where such interrogatories are rarely put, but as well in states whose statutes expressly provide for both modes of controlling the jury, and even in jurisdictions where special verdicts have been abolished.

1 Manning v. Gasharie, 27 Ind. 399; Todd v. Fenton, 66 Ind. 25; Chicago & N. W. Ry. Co. v. Dunleavy, 129 Ill. 132, 22 N. E. 15; Tourtelotte v. Brown, 1 Colo. App. 408, 29 Pac. 132; Carroll v. Railroad Co., 99 Wis. 399, 75 N. W. 176, 67 Am. St. Rep. 872.

2 Manning v. Gasharie, supra.

3 Chicago & N. W. Ry. Co. v. Dunleavy, supra.

In a way, any response by a jury to a question which seeks to uncover the jury's view of the weight of the evidence, and the jurors' opinions as to the existence or nonexistence of a fact or facts, is a "special verdict." It is special inasmuch as it is not the usual form. So, too, any return the jury may make which departs from the ordinary formulæ may be said to be a "special verdict." In strictness, however, by a special verdict the jury, instead of finding for either party, find and state all the facts at issue, and conclude conditionally that if, upon the whole matter, the court should be of the opinion that the plaintiff has good cause of action, they find for the plaintiff, and assess his damages; if otherwise, then for the defendant.

The want of a formal conclusion will not, according to present views, vitiate the verdict; but, generally speaking, failure to find upon any material issue made by the pleadings will render it incapable of supporting a judgment.

Herein is the main distinction between the special verdict and special findings in response to interrogatories: The special verdict is the sole basis of judgment. It finds the facts only, leaving it for the court to apply the law thereto, and is never properly rendered with a general verdict. It must be complete and consistent in and with itself, without aider by intendment or reference to the evidence. If it does not find all the facts essential to sustain (or defeat, as the case may be) the cause of action, it will not support a judgment. If, contrary to proper practice, a general verdict be returned with it, the latter neither helps nor harms either party. It is a mere conclusion of law by the jury from the facts specially found. Judgment must still be rendered, if at all, upon the special verdict.

On the other hand, the special findings embrace answers to one or more questions pertinent to but not necessarily covering any of the issues, though they may be controlling. They are never required except when a general verdict is returned, and are designed to explain and test the latter. The submission of interrogatories under the statute is a sort of "exploratory opening" into the abdominal cavity of the general verdict (if I may be pardoned a surgical metaphor), by which the court determines whether the organs are sound and in place and the proper treatment to be pursued. The general verdict and special findings are considered together, and anything necessary to the right to judgment of the party in whose favor the general verdict is rendered, which is not found in the answers, is presumed to be included in the general verdict. There is therefore no necessity that the answers should cover all the issues, nor does the statute contemplate that they should. The general verdict is controlled by the special findings only when the two are irreconcilable. The latter furnish a basis for judgment only when it is apparent that upon no conceivable hypothesis under the pleadings and evidence admissible thereunder can the findings be true and the party in whose favor the general verdict is rendered have ground left to stand upon.[4]

From these distinctions arise differences in procedure, and the application of diverse rules as to the request for, requisites, submission, construction, etc., of, interrogatories and findings, ignorance of which is apt to result detrimentally, whether to him who seeks or to him who opposes either kind of special

[4] The following are some of the cases in which the distinction between special verdicts and findings under the statute is discussed or indicated: McCormack v. Phillips, 4 Dak. 506, 34 N. W. 39; Chicago & N. W. Ry. Co. v. Dunleavy, 129 Ill. 132, 22 N. E. 15; Manning v. Gasharie, 27 Ind. 409; Toledo, W. & W. Ry. Co. v. Hammond, 33 Ind. 379, 5 Am. Rep. 221; Sage v. Brown, 34 Ind. 464; White v. Adams, 77 Iowa, 295, 42 N. W. 199; Hazard Powder Co. v. Viergutz, 6 Kan. 471; First Nat. Bank of Sturgis v. Peck, 8 Kan. 660; Louisville & N. R. Co. v. Brice, 84 Ky. 298, 1 S. W. 483; Tarbox v. Gotzian, 20 Minn. 139 (Gil. 122); Coleman v. Railway Co., 38 Minn. 260, 36 N. W. 638; Carr v. Carr, 4 Lans. (N. Y.) 314; Dray v. Crich, 3 Or. 298; Cronk v. Railway Co., 3 S. D. 93, 52 N. W. 420; Carroll v. Railroad Co., 99 Wis. 399, 75 N. W. 176, 67 Am. St. Rep. 872; Ward v. Railroad Co., 102 Wis. 215, 78 N. W. 442.

return. They affect the instructions of the judge, the awarding of new trials, and review upon appeal.

Similarities, as well as differences, are naturally to be found in the two modes of obtaining express findings of fact by the jury. Thus, in both cases the jury must find facts, and not mere items of evidence; the facts found should be controlling, and should not contain conclusions of law; the court may not look to the evidence in construing findings of either kind; with other points of likeness.

**In What Cases Court may Require Special Findings.** As has been noticed, the request for findings in answer to special interrogatories must be conditioned upon the return of a general verdict. This is so because in all states where a verdict other than general is permissible the statute provides that the special findings may be required only in that contingency. Such was the early New England rule, independent of statute.

The findings are not designed to cover all the controverted facts and the entire issue, and cannot stand alone [5] unless they are so full, clear, and consistent that the proper judgment can be rendered thereon as a legal conclusion from the facts found, in which case they really constitute a special verdict.[6]

**—— May be Required in All Cases Where a General Verdict is Returned.** In Moline Plow Co. v. Gilbert,[7] the meaning of section 261 of the Dakota Code of Civil Procedure was in question.[8] Said section was as follows: "In an action for the recovery of money only, or specific real property, the jury, in their discretion, may render a general or special verdict. In all other cases the court may direct the jury to find a special verdict in writing upon all or any of the issues, and in all cases

5 Eudaly v. Eudaly, 37 Ind. 440; Blacker v. Slown, 114 Ind. 322, 16 N. E. 621; Montgomery v. Sayre, 91 Cal. 206, 27 Pac. 648; Id. (Cal.) 25 Pac. 552.

6 Cotzhausen v. Simon, 47 Wis. 103, 1 N. W. 473; Pea v. Pea, 35 Ind. 387; Crich v. Insurance Co., 45 Minn. 441, 48 N. W. 198.

7 3 Dak. 239, 15 N. W. 1.

8 Above section same as Rev. Code Civ. Proc. S. D. 1903, § 271.

may instruct them, if they render a general verdict, to find upon particular questions of fact, to be stated in writing, and may direct a written finding thereon." [9]

Counsel conceded that in all cases other than those for the recovery of money only or specific real property the court might direct the jury to find upon particular questions of fact, but contended that the language of the statute excluded the idea of direction in cases for the recovery of money only, etc. It was held, however, that the word "all" in the clause relating to special findings did not mean "all other," and that in any case in which a general verdict was returned the court might instruct the jury to find upon particular questions of fact.[10]

**—— May be Required in All Cases Where All Issues Covered.** Under section 5380, Gen. St. Minn. 1894, in the case of Morrow v. Railway Co.,[11] it is held that the judge may in every case require findings on specific questions of fact, which will cover every issue in the case and amount to a special verdict. And if this is done, it is immaterial whether the jury are required to render a general verdict or not, as the special findings will control and supersede such general verdict. "The different parts of the section may be reconciled by interpreting the first part to mean that in an action for the recovery of money or specific real property the judge may, in his discretion, instruct the jury that they may, in their discretion, render a general or special verdict. We adopt this interpretation."

**—— Special Proceedings.** It is held in *Michigan* that the statute [12] does not apply to condemnation cases.[13] But in

[9] Similar to Idaho, Minnesota, Nebraska, Nevada, North Carolina, Oregon, Washington, Wyoming.

[10] See Olmstead v. Dauphiny, 104 Cal. 635, 38 Pac. 505; Thompson v. Gregor, 11 Colo. 531, 19 Pac. 461; Marx v. Kilpatrick, 25 Neb. 107, 41 N. W. 111; Webb v. Railway Co., 7 Utah, 17, 24 Pac. 616.

[11] 74 Minn. 480, 77 N. W. 303.

[12] How. Ann. St. § 7606.

[13] City of Grand Rapids v. Luce, 92 Mich. 92, 52 N. W. 635; Toledo S. & M. R. Co. v. Campau, 83 Mich. 31, 46 N. W. 1026.

*California* and *Kansas* special findings seem to be required in these as in other proceedings.[14]

It is doubtful whether the *Michigan* law providing for submission of interrogatories applies to the trial of an issue of fact in the supreme court in a mandamus case, and sent down to the circuit court for trial. The circuit judge cannot restrict the scope of the inquiry, and it is not certain that he can enlarge it.[15]

—— **Equity Cases.** (See "Discretion of Court," infra.)

—— **Criminal Cases.** Statutes permitting findings to be required in response to interrogatories are held not to apply to criminal cases,[16] for the reason that so to apply them would be to impair the right of trial by jury secured by the Constitution. It is one of the most essential features of the right of trial by jury that no jury should be compelled to find any but a general verdict in criminal cases, and the removal of this safeguard would violate its design and destroy its spirit.[17]

But though the jury cannot be compelled to answer specially, it is undoubtedly at liberty to include special findings in its verdict.[18]

### Discretion of Court.

It has been seen that the statutes authorizing the submission of special interrogatories naturally fall into two classes: (1)

[14] St. Louis, Ft. S. & W. R. Co. v. McAuliff, 43 Kan. 185, 23 Pac. 102, where judgment was directed on special findings inconsistent with general verdict. See, also, Ellsworth, M. N. & S. E. Ry. Co. v. Maxwell, 39 Kan. 651, 18 Pac. 819; San Jose & A. R. Co. v. Mayne, 83 Cal. 566, 23 Pac. 522.

[15] Miner v. Vedder, 66 Mich. 101, 33 N. W. 47.

[16] State v. Ridley, 48 Iowa, 370; People v. Marion, 29 Mich. 32; Underwood v. People, 32 Mich. 2, 20 Am. Rep. 633; State v. Nagle, 14 R. I. 331.

[17] People v. Marion, supra.

[18] Underwood v. People, supra.

Those making the submission discretionary with the court;[19] and (2) those requiring the court to submit upon request of a party.[20]

**Under Statutes of Discretionary Class.** Under statutes of this group is to be found a great mass of decisions, reference to which would be of little assistance in ascertaining what construction the courts put upon the language of the law, inasmuch as they simply reiterate the general principle that "submission is discretionary with the court," without attempting to define the limits of such discretion. In other words, they are cases in which there is no question of abuse of discretion raised. But in these same jurisdictions are to be found numerous decisions which do define the discretion expressly or impliedly conferred by the statute, which limit it, or give it unrestricted scope.

**—— Discretion Absolute.** In *Oregon* and *Washington*, whose statutes are similar to others of the group, and provide that the court "may" instruct the jury, if they render a general verdict, to find upon particular questions of fact, the courts have held the submission of interrogatories to be entirely in the discretion of the trial judge.[21] Refusal to submit cannot be regarded as error,[22] and the discretion will not be re-

[19] Arizona, Arkansas, Colorado, Idaho, Minnesota, Montana, Nebraska, Nevada, New York, North Carolina, North Dakota, Oregon, South Dakota, Utah, Washington, West Virginia, Wisconsin, Wyoming.

[20] California, Illinois, Indiana, Iowa, Kansas, Kentucky, Michigan, New Mexico, Ohio, Oklahoma, Rhode Island.

[21] Pencil v. Insurance Co., 3 Wash. St. 485, 28 Pac. 1031; Bailey v. Traction Co., 16 Wash. 48, 47 Pac. 241; Walker v. McNeill, 17 Wash. 582, 50 Pac. 518; Columbia & P. S. R. Co. v. Hawthorne, 3 Wash. T. 353, 19 Pac. 25; Morrison v. Railroad Co., 34 Wash. 70, 74 Pac. 1064; Knahtla v. Railway Co., 21 Or. 136, 27 Pac. 91; Wild v. Railway Co., 21 Or. 159, 27 Pac. 954. See, also, Prosser v. Railway Co., 17 Mont. 372, 43 Pac. 81, 30 L. R. A. 814.

[22] Pencil v. Insurance Co., Walker v. McNeill, Columbia & P. S. R. Co. v. Hawthorne, supra. See, also, Elwell v. Roper, 72 N. H. 585, 58 Atl. 507; Smith v. Steamship Co., 99 Cal. 462, 34 Pac. 84.

viewed,[23] no matter how proper or pertinent the questions may be in substance or sufficient in form.[24]

In White v. White [25] we have the first case in Oregon in which the court had to consider questions submitted under objection, and therein it is said that "the nature and form of the particular question are largely within the discretion of the trial judge, and unless it is apparent that there was a clear abuse of discretion, or unless the question submitted, even upon immaterial or inconclusive matters, was palpably misleading as to the main issue, or could not be answered without danger of confusion or misrepresentation," the submission will not be ground for reversal.

—— **Discretion Subject to Review.** But according to the weight of opinion, the discretion is reviewable either as to submission or refusal.[26] The power conferred upon the court must be soundly exercised,[27] and error can be maintained by showing its abuse.[28]

23 Knahtla v. Railway Co., Bailey v. Traction Co., supra.

24 See Knahtla v. Railway Co., supra; Swift v. Mulkey, 14 Or. 59, 12 Pac. 76.

25 34 Or. 141, 55 Pac. 645.

26 Olmstead v. Dauphiny, 104 Cal. 635, 38 Pac. 505; Burke v. McDonald, 2 Idaho (Hasb. 679), 33 Pac. 49; Jones v. Annis, 47 Kan. 478, 28 Pac. 156; Iltis v. Railway Co., 40 Minn. 273, 41 N. W. 1040; Floaten v. Ferrell, 24 Neb. 347, 38 N. W. 732; Missouri Pac. Ry. Co. v. Baier, 37 Neb. 235, 55 N. W. 913; Atchison, T. & S. F. R. Co. v. Lawler, 40 Neb. 356, 58 N. W. 968; Murphy v. Gould, 40 Neb. 728, 59 N. W. 383; Reed v. McRill, 41 Neb. 206, 59 N. W. 775; Hedrick v. Strauss, 42 Neb. 485, 60 N. W. 928; American Fire Ins. Co. v. Landfare, 56 Neb. 482, 76 N. W. 1068; Chicago, St. P., M. & O. R. Co. v. Lagerkrans, 65 Neb. 566, 91 N. W. 358, 95 N. W. 2; Mangum v. Mining Co., 15 Utah, 534, 50 Pac. 834; Kerr v. Lunsford, 31 W. Va. 659, 8 S. E. 493, 2 L. R. A. 668.

Submission is within the "reasonable" discretion of court. City of Crete v. Hendricks, 2 Neb. (Unof.) 847, 90 N. W. 215.

27 St. Louis & S. F. Ry. Co. v. Jones, 59 Ark. 105, 26 S. W. 595; Burke v. McDonald, 2 Idaho (Hasb. 679), 33 Pac. 49; Atchi-

28 See footnote 28 on following page.

In general it may be said that questions seasonably presented, and proper in form and substance, should be submitted, and that refusal to submit them constitutes abuse of discretion. But the trial judge determines the necessity for submission upon all the facts and circumstances of the case before him, the procedure therein, and the nature of the issues involved, and it may happen that refusal to submit is justified upon the ground, not that the interrogatories are in themselves defective or inopportune, but that the issues are not complicated, and the submission of the questions would tend to confuse rather than assist the jury; [29] that they have been substantially included in those already submitted; [30] or for other reasons which suggest themselves to the court in the exercise of its general function of shaping and controlling the trial in furtherance of justice.

**Under Statutes of Mandatory Class.** In this group the statutes provide that the court, at the request of a party, "must" or "shall" direct the jury to find upon particular questions of fact. It is held thereunder that it is error to deny either party the right to have special findings made by the jury as to any material fact within the issues.[31] But it is not counsel's privilege to require submission regardless of the form or substance

son, T. & S. F. R. Co. v. Lawler, 40 Neb. 356, 58 N. W. 968; Murphy v. Gould, 40 Neb. 728, 59 N. W. 383; Phœnix Ins. Co. v. King, 52 Neb. 562, 72 N. W. 855; Gila Valley, G. & N. R. Co. v. Lyon (Ariz.) 80 Pac. 337.

28 Olmstead v. Dauphiny, 104 Cal. 635, 38 Pac. 505; Floaten v. Ferrell, 24 Neb. 347, 38 N. W. 732; Mangum v. Mining Co., 15 Utah, 534, 50 Pac. 834.

The abuse must be "evident and apparent." Denver & R. G. R. Co. v. Nye, 9 Colo. App. 94, 47 Pac. 654.

29 Giffen v. City of Lewiston, 6 Idaho, 231, 55 Pac. 545.

30 Powell v. Chittick, 89 Iowa, 513, 56 N. W. 652; Russell v. Gregg, 49 Kan. 89, 30 Pac. 185; Hamilton v. Buchanan, 112 N. C. 463, 17 S. E. 159.

31 Clegg v. Waterbury, 88 Ind. 21; Bower v. Bower, 142 Ind. 194, 41 N. E. 523; McCoy v. Insurance Co., 107 Iowa, 80, 77 N. W. 529; Trumble v. Happy, 114 Iowa, 624, 87 N. W. 678; City of Wyandotte

of the interrogatories;[32] the questions must be material,[33] and call for ultimate facts inhering in, and necessary to be determined in reaching, a verdict.[34]

In general, to refuse submission under mandatory statutes is error only where the questions presented are proper in form and substance, and, of course, the demand is seasonably made.[35]

It is thus seen that the distinction as to discretion of the court, which seems to arise from the difference in the terms of the laws of the several jurisdictions, in reality amounts to little or nothing.

**When Interrogatories Asked Covered by Others Submitted.** Counsel may not insist on submission of the precise questions presented, in identical language. What questions should be submitted to the jury is a matter in the discretion of the court.[36] No prejudice arises from refusal to submit interrogatories when the court submits others covering sub-

v. White, 13 Kan. 196; Elliott v. Reynolds, 38 Kan. 274, 16 Pac. 698; Jones v. Annis, 47 Kan. 478, 28 Pac. 156; Bickford v. Champlin, 3 Kan. App. 681, 44 Pac. 901; Spencer v. Mortgage Co., 6 Kan. App. 378, 50 Pac. 1094; Stephens v. Creamery Co., 9 Kan. App. 883, 57 Pac. 1058; Baltimore & O. R. Co. v. Cain, 81 Md. 87, 31 Atl. 801, 28 L. R. A. 688; Babbitt v. Bumpus, 73 Mich. 331, 41 N. W. 417, 16 Am. St. Rep. 585; Zucker v. Karpeles, 88 Mich. 413, 50 N. W. 373; Hemenway v. Burnham, 90 Mich. 227, 51 N. W. 276; Robinson v. Insurance Co. (N. M.) 66 Pac. 535; City of Oklahoma City v. Hill, 4 Okl. 521, 46 Pac. 568.

32 Robinson v. Insurance Co. (N. M.) 66 Pac. 535.

33 Bickford v. Champlin, 3 Kan. App. 681, 44 Pac. 901.

34 Decatur v. Simpson, 115 Iowa, 348, 88 N. W. 839; Hemenway v. Burnham, 90 Mich. 227, 51 N. W. 276.

35 Clegg v. Waterbury, 88 Ind. 21; Bower v. Bower, 142 Ind. 194, 41 N. E. 523; Jones v. Annis, 47 Kan. 478, 28 Pac. 156; Zucker v. Karpeles, 88 Mich. 413, 50 N. W. 373.

It is generally error to refuse to submit questions of fact, drawn in proper form, material to the case, and based upon the evidence. Atchison, T. & S. F. R. Co. v. Ayers, 56 Kan. 176, 42 Pac. 722.

36 McDougall v. Sulphite-Fibre Co., 97 Wis. 382, 73 N. W. 327.

stantially the same ground.[37] If error there be, it is harmless where the information sought is contained in the answers to interrogatories so submitted.[38]

**Right to Submit as Affected by Provisions Concerning Special Verdicts and Discretion of Jury.** The statutes of many states permit the jury, in certain classes of cases, to return a special verdict, in its discretion. In a few jurisdictions the jury may, in any case, render a general or special verdict. In any case in which it is within the discretion of the jury to render either a general or special verdict, it would seem proper to refuse a request for special findings, where the answers thereto would be decisive of the whole issue and in effect a special verdict.[39] But the Supreme Court of *Minnesota* has taken opposite ground, and has nullified the discretion conferred on the jury by "reconciling" the different parts of the section, and construing it to mean that, "in an action for the recovery of money only, or specific real property, the judge may, in his discretion, instruct the jury that they may, in their discretion, render a general or special verdict." [40]

The general rule may be stated to be that where by statute the jury may, in all or certain classes of cases, in their discretion render a general or special verdict, the court has no power

[37] Joy v. Bitzer, 77 Iowa, 73, 41 N. W. 575, 3 L. R. A. 184; Livingston v. Heck, 122 Iowa, 74, 94 N. W. 1098; Russell v. Gregg, 49 Kan. 89, 30 Pac. 185; Green v. Brown & Manzanares Co. (N. M.) 72 Pac. 17.

It is not error to refuse to submit special interrogatories to the jury, when requested by either party, when the jury are required by the court of its own motion to answer particular questions embracing every material fact arising in the case. Warden v. Reser, 38 Kan. 86, 16 Pac. 60.

See, also, Wilson v. Onstott, 121 Iowa, 263, 96 N. W. 779; Coley v. City of Statesville, 121 N. C. 301, 28 S. E. 482; Pretzfelder v. Merchants' Ins. Co., 123 N. C. 164, 31 S. E. 470, 44 L. R. A. 424; Hocutt v. Railroad Co., 124 N. C. 214, 32 S. E. 681.

[38] Joy v. Bitzer, supra.

[39] White v. Adams, 77 Iowa, 295, 42 N. W. 199.

[40] Morrow v. Railroad Co., 74 Minn. 480, 77 N. W. 303.

to order special findings.[41] By this, however, is meant merely that to require a jury in such cases to return answers to questions would be error. So long as the direction is conditioned upon the return of a general verdict, there is no deprivation of the jury's right under the statute to choose the form of its return.

**Discretion Absolute When Jury Trial not of Right.** It is proper to submit questions for special findings in equity cases, as in divorce,[42] will contests,[43] accounting,[44] etc. In these and many other instances, where trial by jury is not matter of right, the court's discretion as to submission is absolute.[45] The right of counsel to put questions and require answers depends upon whether or not the answers would be conclusive.[46] In equity cases the findings are merely advisory to the court and do not meet the test.

If the court in an equity suit has submitted questions, one view is that it is in no way bound by the findings made, but may substitute its own findings, and such action is not reviewable.[47] In *Minnesota*, on the other hand, a verdict of a jury upon specific questions of fact submitted to them in an equity action is as binding on the court as a general verdict, and is

41 Meyers v. Hart, 3 Colo. App. 392, 33 Pac. 647; Hall v. Carter, 74 Iowa, 364, 37 N. W. 956.

42 Morrison v. Morrison, 14 Mont. 8, 35 Pac. 1.

43 Carroll's Will, 50 Wis. 437, 7 N. W. 434; Jackman's Will, 26 Wis. 104; Orchardson v. Cofield, 171 Ill. 14, 49 N. E. 197, 40 L. R. A. 256, 63 Am. St. Rep. 211; Thompson v. Thompson, 49 Neb. 157, 68 N. W. 372; Gwin v. Gwin, 5 Idaho, 271, 48 Pac. 295.

44 Loomis v. Armstrong, 63 Mich. 357, 29 N. W. 867.

**Cancellation**—Tucker v. Roach, 139 Ind. 275, 38 N. E. 822.

45 Reddick v. Keesling, 129 Ind. 128, 28 N. E. 316; Banning v. Hall, 70 Minn. 89, 72 N. W. 817.

46 Finch v. Green, 16 Minn. 355 (Gil. 315); Loomis v. Armstrong, supra.

47 Idaho & Ore. Land Imp. Co. v. Bradbury, 132 U. S. 509, 10 S. Ct. 177, 33 L. Ed. 433. See, also, Hall v. Linn, 8 Colo. 264, 5 Pac. 641; Taylor v. Collins, 51 Wis. 123, 8 N. W. 22.

subject to the same rules as to setting it aside for insufficiency of the evidence.[48]

**Rule as to Discretion of Court—Missouri.** In this state, where the practice of submitting interrogatories for special findings existed for but a short time, it has been held that such interrogatories are governed by the same rules as questions put to witnesses, and that the allowance or refusal of an interrogatory, e. g., which is leading and suggestive of the answer desired, is in the discretion of the court.[49]

**"May" in Statute Confers Discretion.** Under a not unusual construction of the word "may," it was contended in McLean v. Burbank,[50] that the provision that the court "may instruct" the jury to make special findings conferred power, but not discretion, making the word synonymous with "shall" or "must," and bringing the statute within the mandatory group. The court held, however, that the statute employed the word in its ordinary and permissive sense.

**Statutes not Applicable to Federal Courts.** A state law, making the submission of interrogatories on request a matter of right, does not apply to United States courts.[51]

48 Reider v. Walz (Minn.) 101 N. W. 601; Marvin v. Dutcher, 26 Minn. 391, 4 N. W. 685; Pinney's Will, 27 Minn. 280, 6 N. W. 791, 7 N. W. 144; Niggeler v. Maurin, 34 Minn. 118, 24 N. W. 369.

The *Indiana* statute expressly excludes equity cases from the scope of its provisions; while the *Arizona* law applies to "all cases, whether law or chancery, where more than one material issue is joined," but is not mandatory in form.

As to special verdicts in equity cases, see chapter 11.

49 Anderson v. McPike, 41 Mo. App. 328.

50 12 Minn. 530 (Gil. 438).

51 Indianapolis & St. L. R. Co. v. Horst, 93 U. S. 291, 23 L. Ed. 898. See, also, Dwyer v. Railroad Co. (C. C.) 52 Fed. 87; United States Mut. Acc. Ass'n v. Barry, 131 U. S. 100, 9 Sup. Ct. 755, 33 L. Ed. 60; Grimes Dry Goods Co. v. Malcolm, 7 C. C. A. 426, 58 Fed. 670.

# CHAPTER V.

## REQUEST FOR INTERROGATORIES—PREPARATION, FORM, AND REQUISITES—MATERIALITY—WITHDRAWAL.

**Necessity for Request.** It is generally held that the court may, of its own motion, submit interrogatories to the jury and require special findings thereon.[1] Such submission, though discretionary, is nevertheless reviewable. On the other hand, in no case can error be predicated upon failure to submit questions, in the absence of a proper request by counsel. A party wishing special findings must ask for them,[2] and as presented to the court they must cover all the facts upon which findings are desired. A request for special findings upon certain facts does not constrain the court, in submitting the questions presented, to include, of its own motion, others which it may be desirable or necessary to have answered.[3]

Decisions asserting the necessity of a request are not numerous, for the reason that the matter is self-evident. It probably also comes within the general rule pertaining to instructions upon particular points. Courts are agreed that "partial nondirection, or omission to charge as to a particular issue, or mere generalization, indefiniteness, ambiguousness, and the like, constitute no reversible error in the absence of a specific request

[1] See post, p. 68.

[2] Bagley v. Grand Lodge, 131 Ill. 498, 22 N. E. 487; Chicago & A. R. Co. v. Elmore, 32 Ill. App. 418; Stevens v. Rose, 69 Mich. 259, 37 N. W. 205; Town v. Railroad Co., 50 Neb. 768, 70 N. W. 402; Schwabeland v. Holahan, 6 Misc. Rep. 623, 26 N. Y. Supp. 880. He cannot avail himself of his adversary's request for a special finding in a case where the request is denied. Bingham v. Stage, 123 Ind. 281, 23 N. E. 756.

The court is not bound to call for questions, nor to request them to be handed up at the proper time. Miller v. Voss, 40 Ind. 307.

[3] Town v. Railroad Co., 50 Neb. 768, 70 N. W. 402; Atkinson v. Saltsman, 3 Ind. App. 139, 29 N. E. 435.

for more specific and comprehensive instructions."[4] "The failure of a judge to charge upon any material point usually results from inadvertence, and the law casts upon the parties the duty of calling the judge's attention to the matter. If he then refuses to give a proper requested instruction, such refusal is ground of error; but a party cannot, in a court of error, avail himself of an omission which he made no effort to have supplied at the time. The court cannot be presumed to do more, in ordinary cases, than express its opinion upon the questions which the parties themselves have raised on the trial."[5]

**Request Must be Specific.** It follows from the above that a party asking to have questions of fact arising on the evidence submitted to the jury must state in his request or motion the precise questions he desires submitted, if he would render his exception to the ruling denying the request of any avail.[6]

**Time of Request.** Most of the statutes regulating special findings fix no time for presenting interrogatories to the court, thus leaving it to a great extent discretionary with the trial judge as to when they should be received.[7]

It is important that special interrogatories should be subjected to the examination of the court, and that the opposite party should have an opportunity to submit objections, and this cannot be done unless a reasonable time is allowed between their delivery to the court and the retirement of the jury.[8] They should not be submitted at such a stage as to work surprise or be manifestly unfair to the other side.[9]

[4] Abb. Tr. Brief (2d Ed.) 408, note 2 and cases cited.

[5] 11 Enc. Pl. & Prac. 217–222.

[6] Flandreau v. Elsworth, 151 N. Y. 473, 45 N. E. 853.

[7] Fleetwood v. Machine Co., 95 Ind. 491; Kopelke v. Kopelke, 112 Ind. 435, 13 N. E. 695; Hartlep v. Cole, 120 Ind. 253, 22 N. E. 130; Sherfey v. Railroad Co., 121 Ind. 427, 23 N. E. 273; Baltimore Traction Co. v. Appel, 80 Md. 603, 31 Atl. 964; Jaspers v. Lano, 17 Minn. 296 (Gil. 273); Lambert v. McFarland, 7 Nev. 159; Peninsular Land Transp. & Mfg. Co. v. Insurance Co., 35 W. Va. 666, 14 S. E. 237.

[8] Ollam v. Shaw, 27 Ind. 388.

[9] Peninsular Land Transp. & Mfg. Co. v. Insurance Co., supra.

—— **Before Argument.** Under the statutes of certain states, providing for submission of proposed questions to adverse counsel and fixing the time of such submission, the courts have commonly held that the questions should be presented before argument, and the tendency elsewhere is to approve the rule.[10]

The statute of *Kentucky* fixes the time for presenting the request for a separate-general verdict as "when the evidence is concluded, but before the argument to the jury," etc.

Upon review appellate courts are inclined to allow the trial court wide latitude, and to refuse to reverse for error in the submission of interrogatories not presented at the most approved season,[11] in cases where substantial justice appears to have been done.

The distinction has been made between requiring submission as of right (which may be only when the questions are presented before argument) and by grace of the court (at a subsequent period).[12]

—— **During Argument.** It has been held in *Indiana* that it is no cause for reversal that counsel, after argument begun, prepared interrogatories, and, without submitting them to adverse counsel, gave them to the court, who submitted them, as it was not necessary to submit them to opposing counsel, and the time for presenting them was within the discretion

10 Glasgow v. Hobbs, 52 Ind. 239; Wabash, St. L. & P. Ry. Co. v. Tretts, 96 Ind. 450; Kopelke v. Kopelke, 112 Ind. 435, 13 N. E. 695; Sherfey v. Railroad Co., 121 Ind. 427, 23 N. E. 273; Cleveland Stone Co. v. Stone Co., 11 Ind. App. 423, 39 N. E. 172; Hamline v. Engle, 14 Ind. App. 685, 42 N. E. 760; McKelvey v. Railroad Co., 35 W. Va. 500, 14 S. E. 261; Baltimore Traction Co. v. Appel, 80 Md. 603, 31 Atl. 964; Caledonian Fire Ins. Co. v. Traub, 86 Md. 86, 37 Atl. 782.

The last two cases require refusal of questions presented after argument begun.

11 Fleetwood v. Machine Co., 95 Ind. 491. But see Maryland cases cited in note 5.

12 Sherfey v. Railroad Co., 121 Ind. 427, 23 N. E. 273.

of the court;[13] while in the same state refusal to submit questions presented, without inspection by opposing counsel, after argument begun, has been upheld.[14]

In *Kansas* it has been held that it is error to refuse to submit proper interrogatories requested by defendant after the opening argument by plaintiff, though the attention of opposing counsel had not been called to the proposed questions.[15]

—— **After Argument.** In *Michigan* it is held that counsel are not obliged to furnish special questions until after the arguments are closed.[16]

In *Kansas* it is said that the prevailing practice is to make the request either before argument or at its conclusion.[17]

—— **During Instructions.** After the evidence and arguments of counsel are closed, and the court has begun to instruct the jury, a request for submission of interrogatories is properly refused.[18]

—— **After Instructions.** The court may properly refuse to submit interrogatories not requested until the close of the charge, and to which the opposite party had no opportunity to object, but it is not reversible error to submit them.[19]

13 Id.

14 Wabash, St. L. & P. Ry. Co. v. Tretts, 96 Ind. 450, citing Glasgow v. Hobbs, 52 Ind. 239; Hamline v. Engle, 14 Ind. App. 685, 42 N. E. 760, 43 N. E. 463. See, also, Fleetwood v. Machine Co., 95 Ind. 491; Cleveland Stone Co. v. Stone Co., 11 Ind. App. 423, 39 N. E. 172; Hopper v. Moore, 42 Iowa, 563.

15 City of Topeka v. Boutwell, 53 Kan. 20, 35 Pac. 819, 27 L. R. A. 593, citing Bent v. Philbrick, 16 Kan. 190; Atchison, T. & S. F. R. Co. v. Plunkett, 25 Kan. 198; City of Wyandotte v. Gibson, Id. 236; Wichita & W. R. Co. v. Fechheimer, 36 Kan. 45, 12 Pac. 362.

16 Zucker v. Karpeles, 88 Mich. 413, 50 N. W. 373.

17 Wilcox v. Byington, 36 Kan. 212, 12 Pac. 826.

18 Malady v. McEnary, 30 Ind. 273; Miller v. Voss, 40 Ind. 307.

19 Truitt v. Truitt, 37 Ind. 514. The court may submit interrogatories after argument and instructions. Fresno Canal & Irrigation Co. v. Warner, 72 Cal. 379, 14 Pac. 37.

—— **After Verdict Directed.** After a verdict for one party has been directed, it is too late for the other to request the submission of questions for special findings.[20]

—— **After Jury Retires and After Verdict.** It is not error to refuse to submit questions offered after agreement of the jury, but before the verdict is returned;[21] and, as a rule, after the return of the general verdict it is too late to request special findings.[22] But the contrary has been held in *Minnesota,* where it was said that "if the jury had already agreed in a general verdict * * * it could not embarrass them, however late the hour or however fatigued they might be, to be required to answer any question material to the issue, for they must already have passed upon it."[23]

—— **Court May Not Fix Time.** In *Ohio* it is held that, as the statute fixes no time when the interrogatories shall be submitted, the court cannot add to the statute by fixing the time.[24] Requests are submitted in time before the jury retires.[25]

—— **Record Must Show Time.** An objection that the court erred in refusing to submit special interrogatories cannot be sustained where the record does not show when the

[20] Robbins v. Insurance Co., 79 Hun, 117, 29 N. Y. Supp. 513.

[21] Lambert v. McFarland, 7 Nev. 159.

[22] Hairgrove v. Millington, 8 Kan. 480; Smythe v. Parsons, 37 Kan. 79, 14 Pac. 444; Allen v. Dodson, 39 Kan. 226, 17 Pac. 667; Lambert v. McFarland, 7 Nev. 159. See, also, Everson v. Graves, 26 Neb. 262, 41 N. W. 994; Burleson v. Burleson, 28 Tex. 383.

[23] Jaspers v. Lano, 17 Minn. 296 (Gil. 273). (Is it possible the court waxes gently sarcastic?) And see, Germond's Adm'r v. Railroad Co., 65 Vt. 126, 26 Atl. 401.

[24] Baltimore & O. R. Co. v. McCamey, 12 Ohio Cir. Ct. R. 543, 5 Ohio Dec. 631.

[25] Toledo & O. C. Ry. Co. v. Beard, 11 O. C. D. 406, 20 Ohio Cir. Ct. R. 681; Baltimore & O. R. Co. v. McCamey, supra.

interrogatories were presented to the court.[26] It will not be assumed that they were presented in due season.[27]

**Submission to Adversary.** The statutes of *Colorado, Illinois,* and *Iowa* provide that the particular questions on which findings are desired must be submitted to the attorney of the adverse party before the argument to the jury is commenced.

These provisions are imperative,[28] and submission to the court alone is insufficient.[29]

The requirement does not apply to chancery cases.[30]

Where the time for referring questions to adverse counsel has gone by, and an emergency for submission arises, the court may meet the difficulty by submitting questions suo motu.[31]

Where no such statutory requirement exists, submission to the opposing party is not necessary,[32] though it may be desirable. Where, however, the request for findings comes after the charge, and the adversary asks time to examine the proposed interrogatories, refusal to grant the opportunity is just cause for complaint.[33]

According to one view, interrogatories by the court suo motu do not come within the purview of the statute, and may be

[26] American Fire Ins. Co. v. Sisk, 9 Ind. App. 305, 36 N. E. 659; Cleveland Stone Co. v. Stone Co., 11 Ind. App. 423, 39 N. E. 172; Morris v. Morris, 119 Ind. 341, 21 N. E. 918.

[27] Caledonian Fire Ins. Co. v. Traub, 86 Md. 86, 37 Atl. 782.

[28] McMahon v. Sankey, 133 Ill. 636, 24 N. E. 1027; Pittsburg, C., C. & St. L. R. Co. v. Smith, 207 Ill. 486, 69 N. E. 873; St. Louis, A. & T. H. R. Co. v. Ellis, 58 Ill. App. 110; Petrie v. Boyle, 56 Iowa, 163, 9 N. W. 114; Crosby v. Hungerford, 59 Iowa, 712, 12 N. W. 582; Humbert v. Larson, 89 Iowa, 258, 56 N. W. 454; Barnes v. Town of Marcus, 96 Iowa, 675, 65 N. W. 984.

[29] Crosby v. Hungerford, supra.

[30] Harp v. Parr, 168 Ill. 459, 48 N. E. 113.

[31] Humbert v. Larson, 89 Iowa, 258, 56 N. W. 454.

[32] Sherfey v. Railroad Co., 121 Ind. 427, 23 N. E. 273; City of Topeka v. Boutwell, 53 Kan. 20, 35 Pac. 819, 27 L. R. A. 593.

[33] Truitt v. Truitt, 37 Ind. 514.

submitted to the jury without first referring them to counsel.[34] But according to another, while there may be cases where the submission of questions by the court without notice would not be ground for reversal [35] (where it is plain that there was no injurious effect), as a rule it is error not to submit questions so propounded to the party to whom they are adverse.

In Pittsburg, C., C. & St. L. R. Co. v. Smith [36] the court says: "It is true that the Legislature did not see fit to command the court; but every reason which could have moved them to require the adverse party to submit an interrogatory applies with equal force where the same interrogatory is propounded by the court without a request, and we would scarcely adopt a rule of practice that a court might be less fair and just to a litigant than the statute requires his adversary to be."

**Request Should be Written.** *California* and *Michigan* are the only states whose statutes require the request for submission to be in writing; but the common provision being that the interrogatories shall be stated in writing, and the request and questions presented together constituting the motion upon which the court rules, it is better and safer practice to put the request also in definite, written form. The exact nature of the demand is thus placed beyond dispute. Moreover, in many jurisdictions the statute requires requests for instructions to be in writing, and the request for submission of interrogatories is, in a way, a request for instructions.[37]

**Request Must be Conditional.** A uniform condition of the right to require special findings is that the jury return a general verdict. Every statute (with exceptions hereinafter noted) permitting interrogatories to be put provides that the court may (or "shall") "instruct" or "require" the jury to find spe-

[34] Clark v. Ralls, 71 Iowa, 189, 32 N. W. 327; Briggs v. McEwen, 77 Iowa, 305, 42 N. W. 303.

[35] See Chicago, B. & Q. R. Co. v. Burton, 53 Ill. App. 69.

[36] 207 Ill. 486, 69 N. E. 873.

[37] But see McCallister v. Mount, 73 Ind. 559. "The request may be made orally or in writing." 2 Thomp. Trials, § 2675.

cially upon particular questions of fact, "if" or "when" or "in any case in which," etc., "they render a general verdict" (or equivalent expression). The conditional clause is not found in the statutes of *Indiana, Kansas,*[38] *Oklahoma,* and *Rhode Island* for the reason that in these jurisdictions a general verdict is required in all cases.

In *Indiana,* where we find the fullest exposition of the law and practice relating to interrogatories and findings, the statute requiring a general verdict in all cases is of recent enactment.[39] Under the old law, in all actions it was within the discretion of the jury, unless otherwise directed by the court, to render a general or special verdict.[40]

In general, then, the request should be that the court instruct the jury to answer the interrogatories "if they render a general verdict," and an unconditional demand is properly refused.[41] That the request for special findings shall contain such a condition is not a matter of mere form, but one of substance.[42]

[38] Special verdicts were abolished in Kansas by Laws 1874, c. 91, § 1, amendatory of Gen. St. 1868, c. 80, § 286.

[39] Act approved and in force March 4, 1897; Thornton's Rev. St. 1897, § 560; Burns' Rev. St. 1901, § 555.

[40] Burns' Rev. St. 1894, § 555; Rev. St. 1888, §§ 546, 547.

[41] Bird v. Lanius, 7 Ind. 615; La Grange County v. Kromer, 8 Ind. 446; Crassen v. Swoveland, 22 Ind. 427; Morse v. Morse, 25 Ind. 156; Schenck v. Butsch, 32 Ind. 338; Otter Creek Block Coal Co. v. Raney, 34 Ind. 329; Hopkins v. Stanley, 43 Ind. 553; Adams v. Holmes, 48 Ind. 299; Hodgson v. Jeffries, 52 Ind. 334; Killian v. Eigenmann, 57 Ind. 481; Ogle v. Dill, 61 Ind. 438; Todd v. Fenton, 66 Ind. 25; McIlvain v. State, 80 Ind. 69; Taylor v. Burk, 91 Ind. 252; Louisville, N. A. & C. Ry. Co. v. Worley, 107 Ind. 320, 7 N. E. 215.

[42] Gale v. Priddy, 66 Ohio St. 400, 64 N. E. 437. In this case the court states that the Ohio statute was adopted from Indiana, where it has received a settled construction, which was presumably adopted with it. See, also, Sun Oil Co. v. Insurance Co., 8 O. C. D. 145, 15 Ohio Cir. Ct. R. 355.

Error in unconditionally directing a return of answers is cured by return with general verdict. Woollen v. Whitacre, 91 Ind. 502.

**Form of Request.** It is not only necessary that the request be conditional, but compliance with the statute in other respects is essential. The request should not specify that the court require answers in case a verdict is found for a certain party. The demand must be for answers in case a general verdict (for either party) is returned. Submission upon a request such as is first above mentioned would be error.[43]

It is also necessary to request that the court instruct the jury to find specially upon particular questions of fact. In Gale v. Priddy [44] questions were prepared and submitted to the court for the purpose of securing special findings, but the request was not properly made. The record showed that defendant requested the court "to direct the jury to give a special verdict in writing upon certain issues" which the appellate court held to be a "very different thing" from findings upon "particular questions of fact." The appellant could not, therefore, complain of refusal to require special findings which he may have intended to call for under the statute, but which, in fact, he did not demand.

It has also been held that where a party requests the court to propound all or none of a series of interrogatories, some of which are proper and some of which are improper, it is not error to refuse to submit the whole or any part of such series.[45]

**Additional Interrogatories and Amendments.** Where interrogatories are submitted to a jury, if additional ones are desired they should be prepared and submitted to the court, with

[43] Hadley v. Hadley, 82 Ind. 75; Wood v. Ostram, 29 Ind. 177. "If you find a general verdict for the plaintiff in this case, you will also answer and return with your general verdict the following questions" (submitted by the court), held proper, as the answers could have had no effect in controlling a general verdict for the defendant. Chicago & A. R. Co. v. Harrington, 192 Ill. 9, 61 N. E. 622.

[44] 66 Ohio St. 400, 64 N. E. 437. See, also, Ætna Life Ins. Co. v. Dorney, 68 Ohio St. 151, 67 N. E. 254.

[45] Sun Oil Co. v. Insurance Co., 8 O. C. D. 145, 15 Ohio Cir. Ct. R. 355.

request that they be submitted to the jury.[46] "The court should, at the time the jury are instructed, determine for itself whether or not the special requests are such as should be submitted; and, if the requests as presented are not in such form that it is reasonable and necessary to require an answer to each of them, the court should so decide, and give opportunity to the party presenting such requests to amend them until satisfactory to the court." [47]

**Waiver of Rights.** A party who obtains from a jury findings in answer to questions propounded by him is not thereby precluded from questioning the correctness of the replies.[48] He is no more bound by them than by the general verdict.

### PREPARATION, FORM, AND REQUISITES.

It is the duty of counsel to present, with the request for special findings, the questions to which answers are desired, and, if proper, the court should submit them.

**Substitution and Amendment by Court.** The court is not obliged, however, to submit interrogatories in the precise form in which they are asked by counsel. It rests largely in the sound discretion of the judge as to how generally or how particularly the question to be submitted shall be stated,[49] and he may revise interrogatories proposed by the parties to fit the facts involved.[50] Substitution by the court of a question in different form, but relating to the same ultimate fact, is not error,[51] even though unnecessary,[52] and a modification where-

46 Bradley v. Bradley, 45 Ind. 67; Atkinson v. Saltsman, 3 Ind. App. 139, 29 N. E. 435.

47 Redford v. Railway Co., 9 Wash. 55, 36 Pac. 1085.

48 Illinois Steel Co. v. Mann, 197 Ill. 186, 64 N. E. 328.

49 Foster v. Turner, 31 Kan. 58, 1 Pac. 145; Southern Kan. Ry. Co. v. Walsh, 45 Kan. 653, 26 Pac. 45.

50 Taylor v. Wootan, 1 Ind. App. 188, 27 N. E. 502, 50 Am. St. Rep. 200; Life Assur. Co. v. Haughton, 31 Ind. App. 626, 67 N. E. 950, and cases cited; Terre Haute & I. R. Co. v. Voelker, 31 Ill. App. 314.

51 Chicago & A. R. Co. v. Pearson, 184 Ill. 386, 56 N. E. 633; Pratt v. Railroad Co., 107 Iowa, 287, 77 N. W. 1064.

52 Gardner v. Meeker, 169 Ill. 40, 48 N. E. 307.

by a question, as presented referring to an evidentiary, is changed to one referring to an ultimate fact, is certainly proper.[53]

But where the question propounded by counsel is controlling, substitution by the court of another and quite different one is error. Thus, the defendant asked the court to submit to the jury a special question, which was, "Was the sidewalk in question unsafe or unfit for travel October 14, 1901?" In lieu thereof the judge substituted the question, "Did the city up to and including October 14, 1901, use ordinary care and diligence to keep the sidewalk in question in reasonable repair for reasonably safe and convenient travel?" The question propounded in the case was one the answer to which if in the negative would have controlled the general verdict, and should have been given. The question substituted was essentially different, and the refusal to submit the requested interrogatory was held damaging error.[54]

It is the duty of the court to submit to the jury only such interrogatories as are pertinent to the issues, or some of them, involved in the case. If interrogatories are prepared by counsel and submitted to the court which are not pertinent to the issues or not in proper form, the court may refuse to submit them, or may change them, or prepare others as substitutes.[55] The court should revise the questions, strike out or amend those improper in form or equivocal in meaning, or which are outside of or immaterial to the issues, as also such as are not based on any evidence in the case.[56] "The court is not a mere

[53] Chicago & N. W. Ry. Co. v. Dunleavy, 129 Ill. 132, 22 N. E. 15.

[54] Beaudin v. Bay City (Mich.) 99 N. W. 285.

[55] Maxwell v. Boyne, 36 Ind. 120; Allen v. Davison, 16 Ind. 416; Norton v. Volzke, 158 Ill. 402, 41 N. E. 1085, 49 Am. St. Rep. 167; Chicago & A. R. Co. v. Pearson, 184 Ill. 386, 56 N. E. 633; Chicago & A. R. Co. v. Harrington, 192 Ill. 9, 61 N. E. 622; Southern Kan. Ry. Co. v. Walsh, 45 Kan. 653, 26 Pac. 45; Louisville City Ry. Co. v. Weams, 80 Ky. 420; Chilson v. Wilson, 38 Mich. 267; Cole v. Laws, 104 N. C. 651, 10 S. E. 172; Redmon v. Chandley, 119 N. C. 575, 26 S. E. 255.

[56] Atchison, T. & S. F. R. Co. v. Ayers, 56 Kan. 176, 42 Pac. 722.

mouthpiece through which the party interrogates the jury. The jury is not, as it were, placed on the witness stand to be cross-examined by counsel. It is the duty of the court to supervise the questions presented—to select the most important, and arrange them in a clear and natural manner. Thus a symmetry and order will be preserved which will tend to secure truth and justice. The case will go clearly to the jury, and the answers will be more apt to be harmonious and consistent. * * * We do not mean that the court is called upon to write out questions, or that it should be particular or precise about the phraseology of counsel, for it is the party, and not the court, that is seeking answers as to particular facts; but only this, that the court should require the parties to present an orderly arrangement of questions, should strike out the trifling and unimportant, and should not permit the jury to be confused and the case lumbered up with useless matter." [57]

**Submission by Court Suo Motu.** The court may, of its own motion, prepare and submit to the jury interrogatories for special findings,[58] either with [59] or without others submitted

[57] Brewer, J., in Missouri Pac. Ry. Co. v. Holley, 30 Kan. 465, 473, 1 Pac. 130.

[58] Chicago, B. & Q. R. Co. v. Burton, 53 Ill. App. 69; Bryan v. Lamson, 88 Ill. App. 261; Killian v. Eigenmann, 57 Ind. 480; Senhenn v. City of Evansville, 140 Ind. 675, 40 N. E. 69; Lauter v. Duckworth, 19 Ind. App. 535, 48 N. E. 864; Life Assur. Co. v. Haughton, 31 Ind. App. 626, 67 N. E. 950; Clark v. Ralls, 71 Iowa, 189, 32 N. W. 327; Briggs v. McEwen, 77 Iowa, 303, 42 N. W. 303; Waggoner v. Oursler, 54 Kan. 141, 37 Pac. 973; Mannen v. Stebbins, 1 Kan. App. 261, 40 Pac. 1085; Oliver v. Morawetz, 97 Wis. 332, 72 N. W. 877; Carroll v. Railroad Co., 99 Wis. 399, 75 N. W. 176, 67 Am. St. Rep. 872.

Not error for the court, of its own motion, to submit interrogatories after the opening argument of plaintiff was finished and at the end of the argument for the defendant. Oliver v. Morawetz, 97 Wis. 332, 72 N. W. 877.

[59] Norton v. Volzke, 158 Ill. 402, 41 N. E. 1085, 49 Am. St. Rep. 167.

upon request of counsel. Its right to propound questions on its own motion is comparable with the right to give instructions.[60]

**Objections.** If the questions asked are defective, the court's attention should be called to the fact before they are submitted; otherwise they will not be closely criticised on appeal.[61] But if questions are omitted which a party thinks should be submitted, he cannot raise the question by objecting to the submission of the draft. His remedy is by submitting an additional draft containing the facts on which he desires findings.[62]

Where objection is made to all the special questions submitted, but no specific objection is made to any separate question, and some of the questions are proper, the objection is properly overruled.[63]

After an answer has been returned, it is too late to object that the submission was improper.[64]

**Number of Interrogatories.** Good practice requires that the questions put be few and simple,[65] and adapted to aid, not confuse, the jury.[66] A party is not entitled to a special finding

[60] Norton v. Volzke, supra; Chicago & A. R. Co. v. Harrington, 192 Ill. 9, 61 N. E. 622.

[61] Dupont v. Starring, 42 Mich. 492, 4 N. W. 190.

Though a special interrogatory is defective in form, if submitted to the jury and answered without objection it is not necessarily to be disregarded. Van Hook v. Young's Estate, 29 Ind. App. 471, 64 N. E. 670.

[62] Lake Shore & M. S. Ry. Co. v. Stupak, 123 Ind. 210, 23 N. E. 246.

[63] Hartman v. Hosmer, 65 Kan. 595, 70 Pac. 598. And a general exception to a refusal to submit to the jury a number of special interrogatories is insufficient if one of them is improper. Coffeyville Vitrified Brick & Tile Co. v. Shanks, 69 Kan. 306, 76 Pac. 856.

[64] Brooker v. Weber, 41 Ind. 426.

[65] Fowler v. Hoffman, 31 Mich. 220.

[66] Burke v. McDonald, 2 Idaho (Hasb.) 679, 33 Pac. 49; Butterfield v. Kirtley, 115 Iowa, 207, 88 N. W. 371; Morbey v. Railroad Co., 116 Iowa, 84, 89 N. W. 105.

upon every circumstance which may have a bearing on the case.[67]

*Michigan's* is the only statute expressly limiting the number of questions that may be asked, which it provides shall not exceed five;[68] but while the statutes with this exception do not impose a definite limit as to the number and character of the special findings that may be called for, yet it must be implied that there shall be a reasonable limit in every case, and unless it appears that the limit imposed by the trial court probably affected the party complaining in some material degree such ruling ought not to be ground for reversal.[69]

"However natural the curiosity parties may have to know the precise course of reasoning by which jurors may arrive at verdicts either for or against them, they have no right, under guise of submitting questions of fact, to require them to give their views upon each item of evidence, and thus practically subject them to a cross-examination as to the entire case. Such practice would subserve no useful purpose, and would only tend to embarrass and obstruct the administration of justice." [70]

Where particular questions of fact are submitted to a jury, they need not, as where a special verdict is required, cover all the issues.[71] They are designed to test the general verdict, and not to elicit all the material facts in the case.

[67] Hawley v. Railway Co., 71 Iowa, 720, 29 N. W. 787; Scagel v. Railroad Co., 83 Iowa, 380, 49 N. W. 990.

[68] Laws 1885, No. 15; Comp. Laws, § 10,237.

[69] Toledo, St. L. & K. C. R. Co. v. Kid, 29 Ill. App. 353; Saint v. Guerrerio, 17 Colo. 448, 30 Pac. 338, 31 Am. St. Rep. 320.

[70] Chicago & N. W. Ry. Co. v. Dunleavy, 129 Ill. 132, 22 N. E. 15, criticising Atchison, T. & S. F. R. Co. v. Cone, 37 Kan. 567, 15 Pac. 499, in which 136 questions were submitted without remark by the appellate court upon the abuse of the statute.

The right to ask special interrogatories does not go to the extent of permitting a party to cross-examine the jury on the processes employed by them in reaching their verdict. Haney-Campbell Co. v. Association, 119 Iowa, 188, 93 N. W. 297.

[71] Carroll v. Railroad Co., 99 Wis. 399, 75 N. W. 176, 67 Am. St.

**To be Stated in Writing.** It is uniformly provided that the questions submitted for special findings be stated in writing, and it is customary for the court to read them in connection with the charge, and deliver them to the jury when they retire.

**Interrogatories should be Single, Direct, and Definite.** The *Arizona* law requires that the "interrogatories shall be plain, terse, direct, and simple, shall each be confined to a single question of fact, and shall be so framed as to be answered by yes or no, and shall be so answered." [72]

The *Michigan* statute provides that the special questions "shall be each in single, short sentences, readily answered by yes or no." [73]

A special interrogatory should call for a finding of but one material fact involved in the issue.[74] It should be clear and distinct, and capable of being answered briefly.[75] Compound interrogatories, calling for findings on several distinct propositions, are properly refused,[76] and questions disjunctive in

Rep. 872; George v. Railroad Co., 126 Cal. 357, 58 Pac. 819, 46 L. R. A. 829, 77 Am. St. Rep. 184.

72 Rev. St. 1901, § 218, par. 1427.

73 Comp. Laws, § 10,237.

74 Wolff Mfg. Co. v. Wilson, 152 Ill. 9, 38 N. E. 694, 26 L. R. A. 229; Illinois Steel Co. v. Mann, 197 Ill. 186, 64 N. E. 328; Rosser v. Barnes, 16 Ind. 502; Chicago & E. I. R. Co. v. Ostrander, 116 Ind. 259, 15 N. E. 227, 19 N. E. 110; New York, C. & St. L. R. Co. v. Grossman, 17 Ind. App. 652, 46 N. E. 546; Bettman v. Shadle, 22 Ind. App. 542, 53 N. E. 662; Pope v. Bank, 23 Ind. App. 210, 54 N. E. 835; Wabash R. Co. v. Schultz, 30 Ind. App. 495, 64 N. E. 481; Powell v. Chittick, 89 Iowa, 513, 56 N. W. 652; Atchison, T. & S. F. R. Co. v. Aderhold, 58 Kan. 293, 49 Pac. 83. Should not cover the whole issue. Todd v. Fenton, 66 Ind. 25.

An interrogatory inquiring whether the "preponderance of the evidence" establishes a certain fact, disapproved as to form. Wabash R. Co. v. Schultz, supra.

75 Scagel v. Railroad Co., 83 Iowa, 380, 49 N. W. 990; Marshall v. Blackshire, 44 Iowa, 476.

76 Brier v. Davis, 122 Iowa, 59, 96 N. W. 983; Jones v. Shelby Co.

form are objectionable, as tending to produce ambiguous answers.[77]

Questions should be clear and concise, and in such form that the jury may give direct answers thereto.[78] They should be so framed that all minds would understand them alike,[79] should not be broader than the issue,[80] and their order should be such as not to confuse the jury.[81]

Indefinite interrogatories are properly refused,[82] as are also such as are frivolous, immaterial, repetitious, and run to minor and subdivided facts, into which the principal fact may be resolved.[83]

**Negative or Leading Form.** It is proper to refuse interrogatories which are propounded in negative or leading form.[84] or which assume as true material facts in issue.[85] But it has been held that where questions relate to the issues on which the case turns, and call for answers either "Yes" or "No," it

(Iowa) 100 N. W. 520. But a question is not double where it contains two antagonistic propositions, and where the answer to one in the affirmative answers the other in the negative. Noakes v. Morey, 30 Ind. 103.

77 Chicago City R. Co. v. Considine, 50 Ill. App. 471.

78 City of Guthrie v. Shaffer, 7 Okl. 459, 54 Pac. 698; Redford v. Railroad Co., 9 Wash. 55, 36 Pac. 1085.

79 Wilkie v. Chandon, 1 Wash. St. 355, 25 Pac. 464.

80 People v. City of Alton, 193 Ill. 309, 61 N. E. 1077, 56 L. R. A. 95.

81 Wesson v. Car-Wheel Co., 154 Mass. 514, 28 N. E. 679.

82 Powell v. Chittick, 89 Iowa, 513, 56 N. W. 652; Caledonian Fire Ins. Co. v. Traub, 86 Md. 86, 37 Atl. 782.

83 Burr v. Honeywell, 6 Kan. App. 783, 51 Pac. 235.

84 Atchison, T. & S. F. R. Co. v. Ayers, 56 Kan. 176, 42 Pac. 722; Same v. Butler, 56 Kan. 433, 43 Pac. 767; Riley v. Wolfley, 60 Kan. 855, 55 Pac. 461; Benton v. Railway Co., 25 Mo. App. 155. But see Chicago City Ry. Co. v. Bucholz, 90 Ill. App. 440; Rice v. Rice, 6 Ind. 100; Morbey v. Railroad Co., 116 Iowa, 84, 89 N. W. 105; Stat. Arizona, Michigan, Appendix. As a matter of fact, there is much less danger of obscurity in the answers if the questions are leading.

85 Elliott v. Reynolds, 38 Kan. 274, 16 Pac. 698.

is no objection that they are so framed that no other answers can be given.[86]

Special interrogatories are not improperly leading and suggestive merely because their form indicates to the jury how to find in order to authorize a judgment for one party or the other.[87]

The rule applicable to leading questions to witnesses would seem to be equally applicable to interrogatories propounded to juries. In the latter as in the former case, objection to questions as leading is addressed to the discretion of the court, and the court's ruling is not reviewable except where abuse of discretion is apparent. This was the rule as early stated in *Missouri,* where at the same time it was intimated that it is better practice to avoid questions leading in form.[88]

**"Particular Questions of Fact."** Almost without exception statutes regulating special interrogatories permit or require the court to instruct the jury to find upon "particular questions of fact," the meaning of which phrase has been frequently passed upon by the courts.

In *Illinois* it is held that the word "material" (which is employed in place of "particular") refers to ultimate and not to evidentiary facts.[89]

Requests for special findings which require the jury to answer merely as to acts or omissions which may or may not, in their opinion, be evidence of care or negligence, and from their answers to which, either way, the court cannot say, as matter of law, whether care or negligence is the result, are not "material." [90]

86 Denver & R. G. R. Co. v. Sipes, 26 Colo. 17, 55 Pac. 1093. See, also, Redford v. Railway Co., 9 Wash. 55, 36 Pac. 1085.

87 Louisville & N. R. Co. v. Mitchell, 87 Ky. 327, 8 S. W. 706; Rice v. Rice, 6 Ind. 100.

88 Anderson v. McPike, 41 Mo. App. 328.

89 Chicago & N. W. Ry. Co. v. Dunleavy, 129 Ill. 132, 22 N. E. 15; Chicago, R. I. & P. Ry. Co. v. Clough, 134 Ill. 586, 25 N. E. 664; Pike v. City of Chicago, 155 Ill. 656, 40 N. E. 567.

90 Chicago & N. W. Ry. Co. v. Dunleavy, supra. And see Chicago Exch. Bdg. Co. v. Nelson, 197 Ill. 334, 64 N. E. 369.

*Indiana.* The facts must be pertinent and involved in the issue,[91] and the questions must not call for conclusions of law.[92]

Interrogatories submitted asking the jury to state specially under which paragraph of the complaint they find for the plaintiff, and, if under more than one, to state how they found under each, and to state what they found to be the immediate and proximate cause of the accident, are improper, since neither of such interrogatories calls for a fact presented by the issues, but requires conclusions drawn from all the evidence submitted.[93]

A "particular fact" does not mean a conclusion drawn from all the evidence submitted to the jury, and means something less than the whole issue.[94] But the jury may be compelled to find the particular facts covering the whole issue.[95]

*Iowa.* The facts must be material and pertinent to the matter in controversy, and the interrogatories must ask a response as to the existence of some particular fact, and not embrace a series of facts which are necessarily included in and determined by the general verdict.[96]

91 Blacker v. Slown, 114 Ind. 322, 16 N. E. 621.

92 Ohio & M. Ry. Co. v. Stansberry, 132 Ind. 533, 32 N. E. 218.

93 Salem-Bedford Stone Co. v. Hilt, 26 Ind. App. 543, 59 N. E. 97; Clear Creek Stone Co. v. Dearmin, 160 Ind. 162, 66 N. E. 609; Consolidated Stone Co. v. Morgan, 160 Ind. 241, 66 N. E. 696; Farmers' Ins. Ass'n v. Reavis (Ind. Sup.) 70 N. E. 518.

The Supreme Court cannot consider an answer to an interrogatory submitted to the jury, stating on what paragraph of the complaint their verdict is based. Muncie Pulp Co. v. Davis, 162 Ind. 568, 70 N. E. 875.

It is proper to refuse to require the jury to itemize the elements of damages. Southern Indiana R. Co. v. Moore (Ind. App.) 72 N. E. 479.

94 Blacker v. Slown, 114 Ind. 322, 16 N. E. 621. See, also, Morrow v. Association (Iowa) 101 N. W. 468; White v. Adams, 77 Iowa, 298, 42 N. W. 199.

95 Salem-Bedford Stone Co. v. Hilt, 26 Ind. App. 543, 59 N. E. 97.

96 Whalen v. Railway Co., 75 Iowa, 563, 39 N. W. 894; Lewis v. Railroad Co., 57 Iowa, 127, 10 N. W. 336.

If the facts called for by the interrogatories are material, it is not reversible error to submit them, though they be not ultimate in nature.[97]

Interrogatories should, whenever possible, be so framed as to call for categorical answers.[98]

There is no error in refusing to submit an interrogatory an answer to which either in the affirmative or in the negative would be a complete determination of the case, and amount to a special verdict.[99]

Section 3727 of the Code, relating to special interrogatories, has uniformly been construed as pari materia with section 3726, concerning special verdicts. The particular questions of fact to be called for in answer to interrogatories are held to be the ultimate facts presented in a special verdict.[100]

*Michigan.* Questions must be such as involve legal consequences and have some controlling force in reaching a conclusion.[101]

*Ohio.* "Particular questions of fact" are held to be those the answers to which will establish ultimate and determinative facts, and not such as are only of a probative character.[102]

*Oregon.* The questions referred to by the statute must be material and pertinent, and in general relate to ultimate rather than evidentiary facts.[103]

**Immaterial Facts—Facts Not in Issue.** It is not error to refuse to submit interrogatories calling for facts not within the issues.[104]

97 Manatt v. Scott, 106 Iowa, 203, 76 N. W. 717, 68 Am. St. Rep. 293.

98 Morbey v. Railroad Co., 116 Iowa, 84, 89 N. W. 105.

99 White v. Adams, 77 Iowa, 295, 42 N. W. 199.

100 Morbey v. Railroad Co., 116 Iowa, 84, 89 N. W. 105, citing: German Sav. Bank v. Bank, 101 Iowa, 530, 70 N. W. 769, 63 Am. St. Rep. 399; Nodle v. Hawthorn, 107 Iowa, 383, 77 N. W. 1062; Thompson v. Brown, 106 Iowa, 367, 76 N. W. 819.

101 Dubois v. Campau, 28 Mich. 304; John Hancock Mut. Ins. Co. v. Moore, 34 Mich. 41.

102 Schweinfurth v. Railway Co., 60 Ohio St. 215, 54 N. E. 89.

103 White v. White, 34 Or. 141, 55 Pac. 645.

104 Powell v. Bank, 125 Cal. 468, 58 Pac. 83; Ohio & M. Ry. Co.

—— **Questions Requiring Speculation.** Interrogatories requiring the jury to speculate as to what might have happened in a certain contingency should not be submitted.[105]

—— **Facts Not in Evidence.** It is the duty of the trial court to submit special questions requested by a party when such questions are pertinent under the issues and evidence; but where no evidence has been given upon which the jury could intelligently answer the questions, it is proper to refuse to submit them.[106]

A special interrogatory that assumes as a fact that which is neither proved nor admitted is properly refused.[107] But the objection that there was no evidence on which to submit a question cannot be urged by one who has, in a requested instruction, sought the submission of the same question;[108] and

v. Trapp, 4 Ind. App. 69, 30 N. E. 812; Maybin v. Webster, 8 Ind. App. 547, 35 N. E. 194; McCullough v. Martin, 12 Ind. App. 165, 39 N. E. 905; Keller v. Gaskill, 20 Ind. App. 502, 50 N. E. 363; Lukin v. Halderson, 24 Ind. App. 645, 57 N. E. 254; Bellows v. West Fork Tp., 70 Iowa, 320, 30 N. W. 582; Cormac v. Bronze Co., 77 Iowa, 32, 41 N. W. 480; White v. Adams, 77 Iowa, 295, 42 N. W. 199; Atchison, T. & S. F. R. Co. v. Dickerson, 4 Kan. App. 345, 45 Pac. 975; Missouri Pac. Ry. Co. v. Brown, 5 Kan. App. 880, 47 Pac. 553; Pierce v. Brennan, 88 Minn. 50, 92 N. W. 507. It is error to submit a finding as to whether defendant guarantied the quantity of land sold, when plaintiff made no claim of guaranty but relied on fraudulent representations. Boddy v. Henry (Iowa) 101 N. W. 447.

105 Atchison, T. & S. F. R. Co. v. Lannigan, 56 Kan. 109, 42 Pac. 343.

106 Consolidated Coal Co. v. Maehl, 130 Ill. 551, 22 N. E. 715; Cormac v. Bronze Co., 77 Iowa, 32, 41 N. W. 480; Willson v. Phelps, 86 Iowa, 735, 53 N. W. 115; German Sav. Bank v. Bank, 101 Iowa, 530, 70 N. W. 769, 63 Am. St. Rep. 399; Leroy & W. Ry. Co. v. Anderson, 41 Kan. 528, 21 Pac. 588; Parkinson Sugar Co. v. Riley, 50 Kan. 401, 31 Pac. 1090, 34 Am. St. Rep. 123; Daniel v. Robinson, 66 Mich. 299, 42 N. W. 61; Swarthout v. Lucas, 102 Mich. 492, 60 N. W. 973; Solomon v. Yrisarri, 9 N. M. 480, 54 Pac. 752.

107 Scagel v. Railway Co., 83 Iowa, 380, 49 N. W. 990. See, also, Toledo & W. Ry. Co. v. Goddard, 25 Ind. 185.

108 McDonald v. Railway Co., 105 Mich. 659, 63 N. W. 966.

where issues not based upon the pleadings are submitted without objection, objection cannot be made to them for the first time on appeal.[109]

Submission of an interrogatory as to a fact concerning which there is total absence of proof naturally has the tendency to induce the inexperienced minds of the jurors to conclude that there is proof, and may well constitute reversible error.[110]

—— **Uncontroverted Facts.** Questions as to facts not in dispute are properly refused.[111] Where the parties have agreed on the facts the court may decline to submit interrogatories for findings thereon, but not unless the agreement is made matter of record.[112]

When a fact is established by the undisputed evidence it is as much a verity in the case as though it were admitted by the pleadings, and it would be absurd to submit the question of its existence to the jury.[113]

—— **Evidentiary Facts.** Interrogatories calling for special findings upon merely evidentiary facts should be refused.[114]

[109] Porter v. Railroad Co., 97 N. C. 66, 2 S. E. 581, 2 Am. St. Rep. 272.

[110] Kay v. Noll, 20 Neb. 380, 30 N. W. 269; Willson v. Phelps, 86 Iowa, 735, 53 N. W. 115.

[111] Powell v. Chittick, 89 Iowa, 513, 56 N. W. 652; Citizens' State Bank v. Fuel Co., 89 Iowa, 618, 57 N. W. 444; Fleishman v. Ver Does, 111 Iowa, 322, 82 N. W. 757; Livingston v. Stevens, 122 Iowa, 62, 94 N. W. 925; Russell v. Gregg, 49 Kan. 89, 30 Pac. 185; Bickford v. Champlin, 3 Kan. App. 681, 44 Pac. 901; Daniells v. Aldrich, 42 Mich. 58, 3 N. W. 253; Pigott v. Engle, 60 Mich. 221, 27 N. W. 3; Wilkie v. Chandon, 1 Wash. St. 355, 25 Pac. 464.

[112] Durfee v. Abbott, 50 Mich. 479, 15 N. W. 559. The admission of a fact upon the trial does not preclude the opposite party from putting a special question requiring the jury specifically to find the fact. Harbaugh v. People, 33 Mich 241.

A fact admitted on the trial is one of the facts in the case as much as the finding of the special verdict, and should be incorporated in the bill of exceptions. Murphey v. Weil, 86 Wis. 643, 57 N. W. 1112.

[113] Berg v. Railway Co., 50 Wis. 419, 7 N. W. 347.

[114] Chicago & N. W. Ry. Co. v. Dunleavy, 129 Ill. 132, 22 N. E. 15;

But interrogatories need not be confined to issuable facts.[115] If they are pertinent to the issues it is sufficient; one cannot, however, have a finding upon every circumstance having some bearing on the case.[116]

Findings of fact should not be recitals of the testimony, but statements of fact proved by the testimony.[117] "It would be clearly of no avail to require the jury to find mere matters of evidence, because, after being found, they would in no way aid the court in determining what judgment to render. Doubtless a probative fact from which the ultimate fact necessarily results would be material, for there the court could infer such ultimate fact as a matter of law. But where the probative fact is merely prima facie evidence of the fact to be proved, the proper deductions to be drawn from the probative fact presents a question of fact and not of law, requiring further action by the jury, and it cannot, therefore, be made the basis of any action by the court." [118]

Lake Erie & W. R. Co. v. Morain, 140 Ill. 117, 29 N. E. 869; Terre Haute & I. R. Co. v. Eggmann, 159 Ill. 550, 42 N. E. 970; Chicago City R. Co. v. Taylor, 170 Ill. 49, 48 N. E. 831; Chicago & A. R. Co. v. Winters, 175 Ill. 293, 51 N. E. 901; Watson v. Roth, 191 Ill. 382, 61 N. E. 65; Chicago & A. R. Co. v. Harrington, 192 Ill. 9, 61 N. E. 622; Nelson v. Fehd, 203 Ill. 120, 67 N. E. 828; Lloyd v. Kelly, 48 Ill. App. 554; Cleveland, C., C. & St. L. R. Co. v. Monks, 52 Ill. App. 627; Louisville, N. A. & C. Ry. Co. v. Wood, 113 Ind. 544, 14 N. E. 572; Same v. Hubbard, 116 Ind. 193, 18 N. E. 611; Same v. Cauley, 119 Ind. 142, 21 N. E. 546; Board of Com'rs of Huntington County v. Bonebrake, 146 Ind. 311, 45 N. E. 470; Heiney v. Garretson, 1 Ind. App. 548, 27 N. E. 989; Banning v. Railway Co., 89 Iowa, 74, 56 N. W. 277; Jenkins v. Beachy (Kan. Sup.) 80 Pac. 947. An interrogatory, "In what did the negligence consist?" calls for evidentiary matters. Illinois Cent. R. Co. v. Scheffner, 209 Ill. 9, 70 N. E. 619.

115 Porter v. Railroad Co., 97 N. C. 66, 2 S. E. 581, 2 Am. St. Rep. 272; Bean v. Railroad Co., 107 N. C. 731, 12 S. E. 600; Manatt v. Scott, 106 Iowa, 203, 76 N. W. 717, 68 Am. St. Rep. 293.

116 Hawley v. Railway Co., 71 Iowa, 717, 29 N. W. 787.

117 Oliphant v. Commissioners, 18 Kan. 386; Dull v. Dumbauld, 7 Kan. App. 376, 51 Pac. 936.

118 Chicago & N. W. Ry. Co. v. Dunleavy, 129 Ill. 132, 22 N. E. 15; Same v. Bouck, 33 Ill. App. 123.

It is said that questions the answers to which will establish probative facts from which ultimate material facts may be inferred as matter of law should not be excluded, especially in cases which involve what are called "mixed questions of law and fact," and, in general, that the court should exercise great deliberation and caution in the matter of excluding interrogatories from the jury; for, while permitting immaterial questions is not likely to work injury after verdict, the exclusion of material questions may be fatal to the rights of the party requesting them.[119]

—— **Conclusions as to Veracity of Witness, etc.** In an action against a railroad company for killing plaintiff's intestate, there being evidence that deceased was on the street crossing when struck by defendant's engine, and the jury having been instructed to find for plaintiff only in case deceased was on the street, the court will not weigh the evidence, though the jury answer affirmatively to a request for a finding as to whether certain witnesses found blood on the track south of the street, there being evidence that might explain that fact, and the request being objectionable as calling for conclusions as to the truthfulness or accuracy of the witnesses.[120]

On the trial of a cause the jury were instructed at request of plaintiff if they found a general verdict to answer the following interrogatory: "Are there any facts alleged in the complaint which are not true? If so, state what they are." Held, that the interrogatory was impertinent, and should not have been submitted to the jury, and, having been submitted, there was no error in the refusal of the court to require the jury to make their answer more specific.[121]

—— **Conclusions of Law.** Interrogatories calling for conclusions of law are objectionable.[122] But error in submitting

119 Gale v. Priddy, 66 Ohio St. 400, 64 N. E. 437; Louisville, N. A. & C. Ry. Co. v. Miller, 141 Ind. 550, 37 N. E. 348.

120 Balch v. Railroad Co., 78 Mich. 654, 44 N. W. 151.

121 Morse v. Morse, 25 Ind. 156.

122 Board of Com'rs of Huntington County v. Bonebrake, 146 Ind.

such questions is harmless where the answers are not conclusive, and there are others supporting the general verdict.[123]

Where an interrogatory submits to the jury the question whether there is any evidence tending to prove an alleged fact, the answer will be disregarded, the question being one of law for the court.[124]

Whether the question submitted calls for a legal conclusion may depend on the instructions given therewith. Thus, the

311, 45 N. E. 470; Indiana Bituminous Coal Co. v. Buffey, 28 Ind. App. 108, 62 N. E. 279; Fire Ass'n v. Yeagley (Ind. App.) 72 N. E. 1035; Bowen v. Railroad Co., 95 Mo. 268, 8 S. W. 230. As are also interrogatories embracing questions both of law and fact. Korrady v. Railway Co., 131 Ind. 261, 29 N. E. 1069.

The submission of an interrogatory which calls only for a legal conclusion "is always at least an abstract error, which is calculated to confuse, if not mislead, the jury." Chicago & E. I. Ry. Co. v. Ostrander, 116 Ind. 259, 15 N. E. 227, 19 N. E. 110.

A question whether transactions by a partner were within the scope of the partnership business held to involve more of law than of fact, and not a subject of special finding by jury. Banner Tobacco Co. v. Jenison, 48 Mich. 459, 12 N. W. 655.

An interrogatory, "Was defendant guilty of negligence causing the injury in this case, and, if so, in what did such negligence consist?" properly refused as not restricted to ultimate facts, but seeking an opinion on probative facts. Chicago Exchange Bdg. Co. v. Nelson, 197 Ill. 334, 64 N. E. 369. An interrogatory calling for construction of an instrument is improper. The question is for the court. Symmes v Brown, 13 Ind. 318.

Question, "Did the defendants, or either of them, guaranty to plaintiff that there was 17,000 acres of land," etc., is objectionable as calling for a conclusion of law. Boddy v. Henry (Iowa) 101 N. W. 447, citing Thomas v. Schee, 80 Iowa, 237, 45 N. W. 539; Home Ins. Co. v. Packet Co., 32 Iowa, 246, 7 Am. Rep. 183; O'Leary v. Insurance Co., 100 Iowa, 399, 69 N. W. 686.

123 Chicago & E. I. R. Co. v. Ostrander, 116 Ind. 259, 15 N. E. 227, 19 N. E. 110; Lautmann v. Miller, 158 Ind. 382, 63 N. E. 761. It is not error to submit an interrogatory which calls for a legal conclusion, if the finding necessarily inheres in the general verdict. Taylor v. Railway Co., 112 Iowa, 157, 83 N. W. 892.

124 Bowen v. Railway Co., 95 Mo. 268, 8 S. W. 230.

jury having been charged, in an action on a note given for a scale, that if the scale was worthless when delivered there was failure of consideration, an interrogatory as to whether or not there was consideration is not objectionable as calling for a conclusion of law.[125]

**Materiality—Tests.** In preceding paragraphs the materiality required in interrogatories has been somewhat negatively defined. From criteria found in the decisions we may deduce the following rules:

What is a material fact is to be determined by the court;[126] but the determination is not to be arbitrarily reached, and should result from the application of the following test:

Would answers to the interrogatories requested most favorable to the party requesting them be inconsistent with a general verdict for his adversary?

If so, the questions are material;[127] otherwise not.

125 Toledo Sav. Bank v. Rathmann, 78 Iowa, 288, 43 N. W. 193.

The question to which the minds of the jury were directed all through the trial was whether or not the defendant was bound by the contract in view of the alleged fraud in procuring his signature. One of the special interrogatories was, "Is the defendant bound by the written contract in question?" The jury answered, "No." Held, that the question should have been more specific, but its submission was not error under the circumstances. Esterly v. Eppelsheimer, 73 Iowa, 260, 34 N. W. 846.

126 City of Wier v. Herbert, 6 Kan. App. 596, 51 Pac. 582.

127 Chicago Anderson Pressed Brick Co. v. Reinneiger, 140 Ill. 334, 29 N. E. 1106, 33 Am. St. Rep. 249; Illinois Cent. R. Co. v. Scheffner, 209 Ill. 9, 70 N. E. 619; Fortune v. Jones, 30 Ill. App. 116; John S. Metcalf Co. v. Nystedt, 102 Ill. App. 71; Id., 203 Ill. 333, 67 N. E. 674; City of Beardstown v. Clark, 104 Ill. App. 568; Id., 204 Ill. 524, 68 N. E. 378; Chicago, P. & St. L. Ry. Co. v. Willard, 111 Ill. App. 225; Thompson v. Brown, 106 Iowa, 367, 76 N. W. 819; First Nat. Bank v. Miltonberger, 33 Neb. 847, 51 N. W. 232; Benson v. Townsend, 54 Hun, 634, 7 N. Y. Supp. 162; Veith v. Salt Co., 51 W. Va. 96, 41 S. E. 187, 57 L. R. A. 410.

It has been held, on the other hand, that when special questions are in proper form within the issues, and not repetitious, they should be submitted on request, though answers most favorable to the re-

The rule is found stated in a variety of ways, but all conveying the same idea.

Questions the answers to which would be inconclusive, and which, no matter how answered, would not be inconsistent with a general verdict, should be withheld from the jury.[128] The

questing party may not be sufficient to overthrow a verdict for the adverse party. Atchison, T. & S. F. R. Co. v. Ayers, 56 Kan. 176, 42 Pac. 722; Hawley v. Railway Co., 71 Iowa, 717, 29 N. W. 787. But this seems contrary both to the weight of authority and the purpose of the law.

In Denver & R. G. R. Co. v. Nye, 9 Colo. App. 94, 47 Pac. 654, and O'Leary v. Insurance Co., 100 Iowa, 399, 69 N. W. 686, it was held that where answers must of necessity be embraced in the general verdict it is not error to refuse the interrogatories. This would seem exactly wrong. If the questions were not such as must necessarily be determined by the jury in reaching their verdict, they would certainly be immaterial.

The judge is not bound to submit any questions which if answered in favor of the party proposing them could not benefit him in the action. Partridge v. Gilbert, 3 Duer (N. Y.) 184.

[128] Jacksonville S. E. Ry. Co. v. Southworth, 135 Ill. 250, 25 N. E. 1093; Norton v. Volzke, 54 Ill. App. 545; Chicago & A. R. Co. v. Reilly, 75 Ill. App. 125; Ohio & M. Ry. Co. v. Trapp, 4 Ind. App. 69, 30 N. E. 812; Bonham v. Insurance Co., 25 Iowa, 335; Mickey v. Insurance Co., 35 Iowa, 183; Lawson v. Railroad Co., 57 Iowa, 674, 11 N. W. 633; Liston v. Railway Co., 70 Iowa, 716, 29 N. W. 445; Van Horn v. Overman, 75 Iowa, 421, 39 N. W. 679; Hablichtel v. Yambert, 75 Iowa, 539, 39 N. W. 877; Whalen v. Railway Co., 75 Iowa, 563, 39 N. W. 894; Cormac v. Bronze Co., 77 Iowa, 32, 41 N. W. 480; Barnes v. Town of Marcus, 96 Iowa, 675, 65 N. W. 984; Swift v. Wyatt, 2 Kan. App. 554, 43 Pac. 984; Sheahan v. Barry, 27 Mich 217; Fowler v. Hoffman, 31 Mich. 215; Frankenberg v. Bank, 33 Mich. 46; Harbaugh v. People, 33 Mich. 241; Foster v. Gaffield, 34 Mich. 356; Brooks v. Fairchild, 36 Mich. 231; Michigan Paneling Mach. & Mfg. Co. v. Parsell, 38 Mich. 475; Johnson v. Insurance Co., 39 Mich. 33; Swift v. Plessner, 39 Mich. 178; Daniells v. Aldrich, 42 Mich. 58, 3 N. W. 253; Castner v. Insurance Co., 50 Mich. 273, 15 N. W. 452; Cousins v. Railway Co., 96 Mich. 386, 56 N. W. 14; Pierce v. Brennan, 88 Minn. 50, 92 N. W. 507; First Nat. Bank v. Miltonberger, 33 Neb. 847, 51 N. W. 232; Sloan v. Manufacturing Co., 58 Neb. 713, 79 N. W. 728; Bentley v. Insurance Co., 40 W. Va. 729, 23 S. E. 584.

facts sought to be elicited by interrogatories should be such as to "control" the general verdict.[129] In general, they should be "ultimate" facts [130]—that is, should relate to facts that the jury must find in arriving at their verdict; [131] facts upon which the rights of the parties ultimately depend.[132] There may, however, be facts material to be determined which are not ulti-

[129] St. Louis, A. & T. H. R. Co. v. Winkelmann, 47 Ill. App. 276; Chicago City Ry. Co. v. Olis, 94 Ill. App. 323; Id., 192 Ill. 514, 61 N. E. 459; Nelson v. Richardson, 108 Ill. App. 121; Dreher v. Railroad Co., 59 Iowa, 599, 13 N. W. 754; Van Horn v. Overman, 75 Iowa, 421, 39 N. W. 679; Clifton v. Granger, 86 Iowa, 573, 53 N. W. 316; Spaulding v. Railway Co., 98 Iowa, 205, 67 N. W. 227; Germaine v. City of Muskegon, 105 Mich. 213, 63 N. W. 78; Davis v. Teachout's Estate, 126 Mich. 135, 85 N. W. 475, 86 Am. St. Rep. 531; Kerr v. Lunsford, 31 W. Va. 659, 8 S. E. 493, 2 L. R. A. 668; Peninsular Land Transp. & Mfg. Co. v. Insurance Co., 35 W. Va. 666, 14 S. E. 237; Andrews v. Mundy, 36 W. Va. 22, 14 S. E. 414; Veith v. Salt Co., 51 W. Va. 96, 41 S. E. 187, 57 L. R. A. 410.

[130] Judy v. Sterrett, 153 Ill. 94, 38 N. E. 633; Firemen's Ins. Co. v. Paper Co., 161 Ill. 9, 43 N. E. 713; Gundlach v. Schott, 192 Ill. 509, 61 N. E. 332, 85 Am. St. Rep. 348; Chicago Exch. Bdg. Co. v. Nelson, 197 Ill. 334, 64 N. E. 369; Chicago & A. R. Co. v. Gore, 202 Ill. 188, 66 N. E. 1063, 95 Am. St. Rep. 224; City of Pekin v. Egger, 104 Ill. App. 546; City of Beardstown v. Clark, Id. 568; Chicago, P. & St. L. Ry. Co. v. Willard, 111 Ill. App. 225; Chicago & A. Ry. Co. v. Bell, Id. 280; Thomas v. Schee, 80 Iowa, 237, 45 N. W. 539; Cawker City State Bank v. Jennings, 89 Iowa, 230, 56 N. W. 494; Aultman & Taylor Co. v. Shelton, 90 Iowa, 288, 57 N. W. 857; Fleishman v. Ver Does, 111 Iowa, 322, 82 N. W. 757; Trumble v. Happy, 114 Iowa, 624, 87 N. W. 678; Greenlee v. Mosnat (Iowa) 101 N. W. 1122.

The court may properly refuse to submit questions which relate indirectly to ultimate facts, but are evidentiary and do not call for direct answers as to the ultimate facts. Illinois Steel Co. v. Mann, 197 Ill. 186, 64 N. E. 328.

[131] Rouse v. Osborne, 3 Kan. App. 139, 42 Pac. 843; Read v. Insurance Co., 103 Iowa, 307, 72 N. W. 665, 64 Am. St. Rep. 180; Klos v. Zahorik, 113 Iowa, 161, 84 N. W. 1046, 53 L. R. A. 235; Dickerson v. Dickerson, 50 Mich. 37, 14 N. W. 691.

[132] Elgin City Ry. Co. v. Salisbury, 162 Ill. 187, 44 N. E. 407; Chicago Exch. Bdg. Co. v. Nelson, 197 Ill. 334, 64 N. E. 369; Kletzing v. Armstrong, 119 Iowa, 505, 93 N. W. 500.

mate, and in such case it is not reversible error to submit them.[133]

[133] Manatt v. Scott, 106 Iowa, 203, 76 N. W. 717, 68 Am. St. Rep. 293.

The opinion in Atchison, T. & S. F. R. Co. v. Plunkett contains the following philosophical disquisition: "There can be no such thing as reaching ultimate facts. And this is true, whether we are attempting in the line of causes and effects to reach first or original facts, or are attempting by division and subdivision to reach simple and primary facts. All facts are caused by antecedent and pre-existing facts, and all facts in turn become the prolific source and origin, the potent and efficient causes, of still other and succeeding facts. No fact springs into existence of itself, and no fact is wholly isolated from other facts. All facts constitute a chain, or rather network, of causes and effects, from the creation down to the present time, and as we cannot by any possibility reach to the beginning of creation we therefore cannot by any possibility reach first or original facts or isolated facts. Nor can we by any possibility reach ultimate simple facts. Whether, indeed, there are any such things as ultimate simple facts is as much a debatable question as whether there are ultimate atoms of matter or ultimate portions or divisions of time or space. Facts, when brought into existence, must in the nature of things occupy time and space in coming into existence and in having an existence. Hence they must in the nature of things be as endlessly divisible into smaller portions as the time and space which they occupy, which are generally believed to be infinitely divisible. Hence the minutest fact that comes within our comprehension must necessarily be composed of an infinite number of still smaller facts, and hence we cannot know anything of ultimate simple facts. Our knowledge really extends only to comprehending (and that obscurely) compound facts, or complex facts. And as all facts are connected more or less intimately with other facts—being first effects, then causes—they may all be used as proof of these other facts with which they are connected, or may in turn be proved by them. They may be the probative facts, the evidential facts, or the final facts to be proved. They may be the evidence of the facts, or the facts to be finally found or proved. All findings of fact, whether of a court or a jury or a referee, are necessarily mere conclusions or inferences drawn from the evidence; that is, drawn from other facts. It is therefore not a valid objection to a finding of a jury that it is the finding of a compound fact, or a complex fact, or a comprehensive fact including many minor and subordinate facts, or that it is a conclusion, or an inference

—— **Improper Submission, When Not Error.** The verdict will not be disturbed because immaterial interrogatories were submitted to the jury, where the findings in answer thereto are not in conflict with the general verdict, and the general verdict could not have been influenced thereby.[134] And, as has been seen, it is not error to submit interrogatories calling for probative facts, if the ultimate facts necessarily result therefrom and may be inferred as matter of law.[135]

It would seem that error could not, in any case, be predicated upon submission of immaterial questions, unless thereby the jury was improperly influenced in answering proper questions submitted or was misled as to the general verdict. If questions are immaterial, findings thereon cannot be in conflict

from the evidence or from other facts; for all findings must necessarily be subject to these same objections. The jury's findings are always conclusions. They cannot be otherwise, and the jury cannot in any case, or in any sense, find ultimate facts. They can find the facts in great detail, or they can find them in very general or comprehensive terms. And where they find the facts both in detail and in general terms, we may disregard the general findings. If the findings in detail contradict the general findings, we may order the judgment to be rendered in accordance with the findings in detail, and wholly ignore the general findings. For instance: Where a question of negligence arises in a case, the jury cannot be allowed to say conclusively, after finding certain special facts, that these facts constitute negligence, when in fact and manifestly they do not constitute negligence. But in order to disregard the general conclusion of the jury, it is necessary that it may be seen that they are only general conclusions from special facts which have already been sufficiently ascertained or found. Otherwise it would be necessary to regard such general conclusions as general findings of fact." 25 Kan. 188, 196-198.

134 Sage v. Haines, 76 Iowa, 581, 41 N. W. 366; Pettingill v. Jones, 30 Mo. App. 280.

The submission may be irregular under the Code, but is not sufficient to sustain a motion for a new trial. Petrie v. Boyle, 56 Iowa, 163, 9 N. W. 114.

135 Chicago & N. W. Ry. Co. v. Dunleavy, 129 Ill. 132, 22 N. E. 15; Gale v. Priddy, 66 Ohio St. 400, 64 N. E. 437. See Guernsey v. Fulmer, 66 Kan. 767, 71 Pac. 578.

with the general verdict or inconsistent with others upon controlling facts, and should simply be disregarded.

### Withdrawal of Interrogatories.

It would seem that in the few states where the discretion of the court as to submission of interrogatories is of an absolute character it cannot be error for the judge to withdraw interrogatories from the consideration of the jury. In *Massachusetts* it is said: "The submission of special questions to the jury, to be answered by them in addition to the general verdict, is often a highly convenient practice, but it is a matter within the discretion of the court, and to the exercise of it no exception lies. When, therefore, the court determines to withdraw such questions before the finding thereon is rendered, or to accept the verdict, even if the jury has failed to pass upon them, it may do so. If a verdict has been rendered which completely decides the issue immediately before the jury, neither party can object to its reception, because the jury has failed to pass specially upon inquiries which it would be advantageous to have had answered by reason of their relation to other stages of the controversy." [136] No vested right is acquired by either party to have the findings made because the court has once so directed.[137]

But in *Washington*, where the court's discretion as to refusal is unlimited, it is held that, once having submitted questions to the jury, the court should require an answer thereto, and that to receive a general verdict without answers (the equivalent of withdrawal) is reversible error.[138]

Where the statute is imperative in form, making the submission of interrogatories matter of right upon proper request, it is error to withdraw them formally, or in effect (as by refus-

[136] Florence Mach. Co. v. Daggett, 135 Mass. 582, 585.

[137] Moss v. Priest, 19 Abb. Prac. (N. Y.) 314. To same effect, Taylor v. Ketchum, 5 Rob. (N. Y.) 507; National Refining Co. v. Miller, 1 S. D. 548, 47 N. W. 962.

[138] Redford v. Railway Co., 9 Wash. 55, 36 Pac. 1085.

ing to require answers).[139] And even where the statute is discretionary in form, it has been held that where the court calls upon the jury to answer an interrogatory going to the very gist of the cause of action it cannot withdraw it, and so remove the obstacle which prevents the jury agreeing.[140] It makes no difference that the question withdrawn was not requested by counsel, but was submitted by the court of its own motion. The fact that it was so submitted indicates that there were very good reasons therefor, and the presumption is that the jury did not answer because they could not do so in a manner that would sustain their verdict.[141] Nor does it excuse withdrawal that the interrogatories were offered, under objection, after argument and instructions, and so late that the court would have been justified in declining to submit them, if they relate to material questions of fact.[142]

The question of the propriety of withdrawal most frequently resolves itself into this: Would an answer to the question or questions favorable to the defendant be conclusive against plaintiff's right to recover? If so, withdrawal is error; [143] otherwise not.[144]

139 See Otter Creek Block Coal Co. v. Raney, 34 Ind. 329; Sage v. Brown, Id. 464; Summers v. Greathouse, 87 Ind. 205; Groscop v. Rainier, 111 Ind. 361, 12 N. E. 694; Kansas Pac. Ry. Co. v. Reynolds, 8 Kan. 623; Union Pac. Ry. Co. v. Fray, 35 Kan. 708, 12 Pac. 98; American Cent. Ins. Co. v. Hathaway, 43 Kan. 403, 23 Pac. 428.

140 Ermentraut v. Insurance Co., 67 Minn. 451, 70 N. W. 572.

141 Eischen v. Railway Co., 81 Minn. 59, 83 N. W. 490.

142 McKelvey v. Railway Co., 35 W. Va. 500, 14 S. E. 261.

143 See Sun Mut. Ins. Co. v. Dudley, 65 Ark. 240, 45 S. W. 539.

But it is just as much error to accept a general verdict for defendant, without answers to material interrogatories requested by defendant, as it is to withdraw questions proposed by defendant and accept a general verdict for plaintiff. In either case the disagreement as to answers shows that the jury have not determined a matter essential to be determined in arriving at the verdict. See Ermentraut v. Insurance Co., 67 Minn. 451, 70 N. W. 572.

144 Schneider v. Railroad Co., 42 Minn. 68, 43 N. W. 783.

—— **Right of Party Proposing Questions.** Where material interrogatories have been submitted, and the jury have returned a general verdict without answers, the court cannot allow the interrogatories to be withdrawn by the party proposing them.[145] The adversary becomes equally entitled to answers, and therefore the questions may not be withdrawn over the latter's objection.[146] However, a few cases hold, by implication at least, that where a party has not requested the questions,[147] or framed his own with reference to them, [148] it is not error for the court to withdraw them on motion of the adversary.

—— **Withdrawal Proper.** In any case there is no abuse of discretion in withdrawing a purely hypothetical question, such as none but men skilled in the subject can answer,[149] or questions embodied in others already passed upon by the jury; [150] and where the interrogatories permitted to be withdrawn are not in the record, the apppellate court will presume, in the absence of any showing to the contrary, that they were withdrawn because impertinent or immaterial.[151]

Of course, too, questions may be withdrawn by consent of both parties, and exceptions to the submission are thereby waived.[152]

Under the great majority of statutes the discretion of the court as to submission of questions must be soundly exercised.

145 Duesterberg v. State, 116 Ind. 144, 17 N. E. 624.

146 See Wood v. Ostram, 29 Ind. 177; Noakes v. Morey, 30 Ind. 103; Otter Creek Block Coal Co. v. Raney, 34 Ind. 329; Maxwell v. Boyne, 36 Ind. 120; Peters v. Lane, 55 Ind. 391; Pitzer v. Railway Co., 80 Ind. 569; Summers v. Greathouse, 87 Ind. 205.

147 Cook v. Clinton, 64 Mich. 310, 31 N. W. 317, 8 Am. St. Rep. 816.

148 Missouri Pac. Ry. Co. v. Moffatt, 60 Kan. 113, 55 Pac. 837, 72 Am. St. Rep. 343.

149 Continental Life Ins. Co. v. Yung, 113 Ind. 159, 15 N. E. 220, 3 Am. St. Rep. 630.

150 Smith v. Wilson, 5 Kan. App. 379, 48 Pac. 436.

151 Groscop v. Rainier, 111 Ind. 361, 12 N. E. 694.

152 Read v. Nichols, 118 N. Y. 224, 23 N. E. 468, 7 L. R. A. 130.

In such jurisdictions the question upon appeal, where error is assigned upon the withdrawal of interrogatories, evidently is, did the withdrawal constitute an abuse of discretion, did it operate prejudicially to the party complaining? The mere fact of withdrawal does not furnish ground for reversal, apart from the consequences. The court's discretion cannot logically be limited to submission alone, leaving it without power thereafter to assist the jury by taking from its consideration questions improper in substance or form, which may be calculated to confuse or mislead (as the court may conclude upon reflection), or which have become immaterial since their submission.

# CHAPTER VI.

## INSTRUCTIONS—ARGUMENT.

Where a special verdict is submitted to a jury, the court is not required to give instructions as to the general rules of law applicable to the case. Indeed, it is not good practice to do so, and frequently results in reversal. In such case the instructions are properly confined to the questions submitted.

On the other hand, findings upon particular questions of fact may be required under the statute only when and in case a general verdict is returned, and it is as proper, and, in most cases as necessary, to charge the jury regarding the law by which they are to be guided when interrogatories are submitted as when they are not. The main object of the charge is to assist the jury in arriving at a general verdict in conformity to the law and the evidence; the findings are merely incidental. The submission of special interrogatories does not relieve the jury from the necessity of applying the law, which must, therefore, be laid down by the court,[1] whereas, in the case of a special verdict, the jury finds the facts only, leaving the application of the law to the judge.

**Instructions as to General Verdict.** It is error for the court to refuse to instruct the jury, and, without requiring a general verdict, to submit only a portion of the facts, rendering judgment upon the answers and other facts found by itself.[2]

When a court, submitting questions to a jury, instructs them if they answer such questions in one manner to return a general verdict for plaintiff, and if in another to return such a verdict

[1] Witty v. Railroad Co., 83 Ky. 21. Statutes requiring instructions to be in writing do not necessarily apply to direction to find specially. McCallister v. Mount, 73 Ind. 559. See, also, Atchison, T. & S. F. R. Co. v. Johnson, 3 Okl. 41, 41 Pac. 641.

[2] Pickett v. Handy, 5 Colo. App. 295, 38 Pac. 606.

for the defendant,[3] it is not error when thereafter the jury return the questions with their answers, but without any general verdict, to direct them to incorporate therewith a general verdict, and to state for whom the verdict should be.[4]

**Instructions as to Answers—Absence of Evidence.** Where special questions of fact are submitted to the jury for answer, it is erroneous for the court to instruct the jury that, "In case no evidence can be found bearing upon the question required to be answered, the jury will say 'Don't know' or 'Cannot answer from the evidence' ";[5] and it is also error where the court, at the request of a party, has instructed the jury to find specially as to certain facts, to instruct them that, if the evidence is too uncertain to enable them to answer the interrogatories, they may so report in the way of a special verdict.[6] When requests for special findings are made, the court should instruct the jury to answer each of them, and the general verdict should not be received until such requests have been answered without evasion.[7]

In Crane v. Reeder[8] the court instructed the jury that they were not obliged to answer absolutely the questions submitted to them, and that if they were of opinion that there was not evidence sufficient to satisfy their minds, in one way or the other, in regard to any particular question, they might so state in answer to any specific question.

The instruction was criticised as follows on appeal: "Now this instruction * * * cannot be true at all, unless the particular question upon which the jury should fail to find was ir-

[3] Bad practice. See succeeding paragraphs.

[4] Mooney v. Olsen, 22 Kan. 69.

[5] Union Pac. Ry. Co. v. Fray, 35 Kan. 700, 12 Pac. 98; Maxwell v. Boyne, 36 Ind. 120; Clark v. Railroad Co., 35 Kan. 350, 11 Pac. 134. But see Williamson v. Yingling, 80 Ind. 379.

[6] Chicago, B. & Q. R. Co. v. Van Patten, 74 Ill. 91.

[7] Redford v. Railroad Co., 9 Wash. 55, 36 Pac. 1085.

[8] 25 Mich. 303. See, also, Wilson v. Railroad Co., 57 Mich. 155, 23 N. W. 627.

relevant to the issue; and if it was, the court should not have allowed it to be put. No question should have been put to the jury that was not material to the inquiry upon which they were about to enter, and upon every material question one party or the other would have held the affirmative, and unless he made out his case upon it by the evidence should have had a finding against him upon it. Every fact essential to a party's case which he fails to prove is considered as not established, and must be negatived in the conclusions of the jury; it will not do to ignore it."

—— **Answering Question After General Verdict Found.** It is said not to be error for the court to seal interrogatories in an envelope and deliver them to the jury with the instruction that they are not to open the envelope and consider the questions until they have agreed upon a general verdict, as the statute (*Indiana*) regulating special findings provides that interrogatories are only to be answered after a general verdict has been agreed to.[9]

The objections raised by the *Wisconsin* court in Ryan v. Rockford Ins. Co.[10] seem applicable to the above procedure. Its natural tendency is to cause the jury to answer questions in such a way as to harmonize them with the general verdict rather than with the evidence, which they might be tempted to disregard. Moreover, the Indiana statute apparently did not, at the time this decision was rendered, and does not now, provide that the questions submitted be answered after a general verdict had been agreed upon. The language of the statute was, "if they render a general verdict," [11] i. e., in any case in which a general verdict is, in fact, returned, which would seem not to be equivalent to a requirement that the findings should not be made until a general verdict had been found.

—— **Suggesting Answers.** It is error for the court to instruct the jury what answers shall be made to interrogatories, in

[9] Summers v. Tarney, 123 Ind. 560, 24 N. E. 678.

[10] 77 Wis. 611, 46 N. W. 885.

[11] 1 Rev. St. 1888, §§ 546, 547.

case the general verdict goes a certain way.[12] The jury are the sole and exclusive judges of the facts from the testimony in the case, and the court has no right, upon controverted questions, where there is a conflict of evidence, to suggest or dictate to the jury answers to particular questions of fact submitted to them for findings.[13]

Where an interrogatory is submitted as to a fact essential to plaintiff's right of recovery, and the jury return a general verdict for plaintiff, but answer that they are unable to agree upon any of the special questions, a direction by the court that, having found a general verdict, they are bound to answer the special questions in harmony with it, and instructing them how to frame such replies, is error, as its effect is that the court, and not the jury, decides the material issues.[14]

—— **Effect of Answers.** It is error for the court to inform the jury as to the effect their answers would have upon the general verdict. "The jury has no right to be informed how any particular answer to a special question would affect the case, or what judgment would follow in consequence of it; for to impart such information would almost necessarily defeat the object intended to be secured by a special verdict or answers to particular questions in connection with a general verdict." [15]

Not only should the court not suggest to the jury the possible effect of their answers upon the general verdict, but, where the business or reputation of either party is such as to naturally stimulate a bias in favor of the one party or the other, it is a very proper thing to charge the jury, in effect, that they have nothing to do with, and must not consider the effect which their answers may have upon, the controversy or the parties.[16]

12 Beecher v. Galvin, 71 Mich. 391, 39 N. W. 469; Maclean v. Scripps, 52 Mich. 214, 17 N. W. 815, 18 N. W. 209.

13 Usher v. Hiatt, 18 Kan. 195.

14 Cole v. Boyd, 47 Mich. 98, 10 N. W. 124.

15 Coats v. Town of Stanton, 90 Wis. 130, 136, 62 N. W. 619.

16 Ryan v. Insurance Co., 77 Wis. 611, 46 N. W. 885.

**—— Harmonizing Answers with General Verdict and Each Other.** There seems to be a difference of opinion as to the propriety of instructions requesting the jury to secure harmony between their findings and the general verdict.

In *Iowa* it has been held that such a caution was "timely, and tended to direct the jury to a careful consideration of the facts," [17] and that the instruction, "You will be careful * * * that these answers are in harmony with and support your general verdict," was proper, and did not require the jury to answer the interrogatories with reference to the general verdict rather than the facts of the cause.[18]

In *Oklahoma* the court declared that it was proper to refuse an instruction that the jury should answer the special questions "without regard to the general verdict" ; [19] but the decision is based upon the view that such an instruction would amount to a requirement that the jury return answers to the interrogatories whether they elected to return a general verdict or not, whereas the statute requires interrogatories to be proposed in connection with a general verdict.

In *Michigan* it is held that it is error to instruct the jury that their answers must be consistent with the general verdict,[20] and in *Kansas* that it is improper to charge the jury that their answers should be consistent with the general verdict [21] or with each other.[22]

17 Des Moines & D. Land & Tree Co. v. Trust Co., 82 Iowa, 663, 45 N. W. 773.

18 Capital City Bank v. Wakefield, 83 Iowa, 46, 48 N. W. 1059.

19 Atchison, T. & S. F. R. Co. v. Johnson, 3 Okl. 41, 41 Pac. 641, citing Killian v. Eigenmann, 57 Ind. 480; Lake Erie & W. Ry. Co. v. Fix, 88 Ind. 381, 45 Am. Rep. 464; Hadley v. Hadley, 82 Ind. 75; Taylor v. Burk, 91 Ind. 253.

20 Mechanics' Bank v. Barnes, 86 Mich. 632, 49 N. W. 475; Cole v. Boyd, 47 Mich. 98, 10 N. W. 124. But see People v. Murray, 52 Mich. 288, 17 N. W. 843.

21 Coffeyville Vitrified Brick Co. v. Zimmerman, 61 Kan. 750, 60 Pac. 1064. To same effect, Coats v. Town of Stanton, 90 Wis. 130, 62 N. W. 619.

22 McCook v. Kemp, 10 Kan. App. 381, 59 Pac. 1100; Dry-Goods Co.

In a *Wisconsin* case, in submitting a question to the jury the court said: "If you answer that question 'Yes,' it would be in accordance with a general verdict for plaintiff. If you answer it 'No,' it would be inconsistent with a general verdict for plaintiff. You can see you will answer that question 'Yes' or 'No.'" Held error. "This was peculiarly calculated to secure special answers that would be consistent with a general verdict rather than in accordance with the weight of the evidence upon each of such particular questions. The effect of such instructions was very much the same as though the court had charged the jury that they should answer the particular questions in the way they had thus been informed would be consistent with such general verdict. This was misleading, and well calculated to defeat the very object of the statute authorizing such submissions." [23]

Objection to an instruction that the answers to special interrogatories submitted must be consistent with the general verdict should be made while there is still opportunity to correct the error. If made after the jury retires, it comes too late.[24]

**Cure of Errors—Erroneous Instructions.** Errors in giving or refusing instructions may be cured by the jury's findings, without which the effect of the court's action would not be known and would be presumptively prejudicial.

Judgment will not be reversed, notwithstanding an erroneous instruction, if from the jury's findings it affirmatively appears that the verdict was not reached upon the facts to which the instruction applied, or that the instruction was without influence.[25]

v. Kahn, 53 Kan. 274, 36 Pac. 327; Coats v. Town of Stanton, supra. But see Atchison, T. & S. F. R. Co. v. Woodcock, 42 Kan. 344, 22 Pac. 421.

23 Ryan v. Insurance Co., 77 Wis. 611, 616, 46 N. W. 885.

24 Maclean v. Scripps, 52 Mich. 214, 17 N. W. 815, 18 N. W. 209.

25 Lemmon v. Moore, 94 Ind. 40; Worley v. Moore, 97 Ind. 15; Bedford S., O. & B. R. Co. v. Rainbolt, 99 Ind. 551; Cleveland, C., C. & I. R. Co. v. Newell, 104 Ind. 264, 3 N. E. 836, 54 Am. Rep. 312;

So, if the answers show that correct instructions which were refused could not have changed the verdict, the error is harmless.[26]

The instructions may also themselves cure error in the form of interrogatories submitted. Thus, where counsel for appellant asked the court to submit to the jury the question, "What *was* the value per acre of the lands permanently flowed at the

Morgan v. Jackson, 32 Ind. App. 169, 69 N. E. 410; Clark v. Ralls, 71 Iowa, 189, 32 N. W. 327; Fisk v. Railroad Co., 83 Iowa, 253, 48 N. W. 1081; Ft. Scott, W. & W. R. Co. v. Karracker, 46 Kan. 511, 26 Pac. 1027; Marcott v. Railroad Co., 49 Mich. 99, 13 N. W. 374; Elwood v. Saterlie, 68 Minn. 173, 71 N. W. 13; Davis v. Guarnieri, 45 Ohio St. 470, 15 N. E. 350, 4 Am. St. Rep. 548; Brasen v. Railway, 4 Wash. 754, 31 Pac. 34; Eicholtz v. Holmes, 8 Wash. 71, 35 Pac. 607; Wright v. Mulvaney, 78 Wis. 89, 46 N. W. 1045, 9 L. R. A. 807, 23 Am. St. Rep. 393; Daly v. City of Milwaukee, 103 Wis. 588, 79 N. W. 752; Tesch v. Railway & Light Co., 108 Wis. 593, 84 N. W. 823, 53 L. R. A. 618; Hodges v. Nalty, 113 Wis. 567, 89 N. W. 535; Gordon v. Sullivan, 116 Wis. 543, 93 N. W. 457.

Where it appears from the special findings that an instruction, which construed alone might be faulty, has not influenced the verdict, the giving of it is not sufficient cause for reversal. Ft. Scott, W. & W. Ry. Co. v. Jones, 48 Kan. 51, 28 Pac. 978.

Erroneous omission of the element of malice from an instruction with reference to exemplary damages in an action for slander is harmless, where the jury specially find that defendant was actuated by malice. Walker v. Wickens, 49 Kan. 42, 30 Pac. 181.

Error in instructing the jury that the burden was on defendant to prove the set-off pleaded by him, when such set-off consisted of judgments which were admitted and of which proof was not required, was without prejudice, the jury having specially found that the judgments had been paid. Keairnes v. Durst, 110 Iowa, 114, 81 N. W. 238.

[26] Moore v. Lynn, 79 Ind. 299; Trentman v. Wiley, 85 Ind. 33; Kuhns v. Gates, 92 Ind. 66; Dickey v. Shirk, 128 Ind. 278, 27 N. E. 733; Seekel v. Norman, 78 Iowa, 254, 43 N. W. 190; Leavenworth, T. & S. W. Ry. Co. v. Paul, 28 Kan. 816; Pearl v. Benton Tp. (Mich.) 100 N. W. 188; New Omaha Thomson-Houston Electric Light Co. v. Dent (Neb.) 94 N. W. 819; Knowlton v. Railway Co., 59 Wis. 278, 18 N. W. 17; Harriman v. Insurance Co., 49 Wis. 71, 5 N. W. 12. See, also, Spurr v. Inhabitants of Shelburne, 131 Mass. 429.

time they were so permanently flowed?" and the court submitted the question, "What *is* the value of the lands, if any, permanently flowed?" the apparent error was cured by an instruction, in connection with the question, that "you will ascertain from the evidence what *was* the value of the land at the time of the taking, and that will be the damages, with interest added, for such lands." [27]

Where the jury make a special finding, which conclusively disposes of the case, an erroneous instruction given in the general charge of the court, and not excepted to, and under which the jury return a general verdict inconsistent with the special finding, is not the law of the case so as to prevent the court from rendering judgment on the special finding, notwithstanding the general verdict.[28]

An appellate court will apply the rules and principles of law to facts found by the jury in its special findings; and, if the general verdict is the same that the law would pronounce on the facts, the fact that erroneous instructions were given is harmless, provided the court can see that the error did not contribute to lead the jury to the special finding of facts.[29]

**Discussion of Interrogatories in Argument.** It has been held in *Michigan* that it is improper for counsel in the course of argument to instruct the jury how to answer interrogatories submitted,[30] and in *Indiana* that the privilege of reading to the jury either the original interrogatories or copies thereof is purely a matter of favor with the court, which may grant or deny the privilege.[31]

In other states it is said to be entirely competent for an attorney to read special questions to the jury, discuss the evi-

[27] Velte v. United States, 76 Wis. 278, 45 N. W. 119.

[28] Maceman v. Society, 69 Minn. 285, 72 N. W. 111. See chapter 8, "Effect of Erroneous Instructions."

[29] Tuller v. Fox, 46 Ill. App. 97.

[30] Zucker v. Karpeles, 88 Mich. 413, 50 N. W. 373.

[31] Chestnut v. Railroad Co., 157 Ind. 509, 62 N. E. 32.

dence applicable thereto, and suggest answers which in his judgment ought to be returned.[32] He may state that the general verdict and special findings should be consistent, and what the findings should be to support a general verdict.[33]

[32] Timins v. Railroad Co., 72 Iowa, 94, 33 N. W. 379; Chicago & A. R. Co. v. Gore, 202 Ill. 188, 66 N. E. 1063, 95 Am. St. Rep. 224.

[33] Powell v. Chittick, 89 Iowa, 513, 56 N. W. 652.

# CHAPTER VII.

## FINDINGS.

Where Made—Signing—Answers Without General Verdict—Failure to Answer—Indefinite and Evasive Answers—Evidentiary Facts—Conclusions of Law—Findings Contrary to Evidence—Correction and Addition.

**Findings, Where Made, to be in Writing.** Special findings must, like the general verdict, be pronounced in open court.[1] It is never necessary to require the jury to withdraw, unless they desire to do so. Hence special interrogatories may be put and answered in the courtroom.[2]

It seems that oral answers by the foreman are of no effect. Failure of counsel to object to such replies is a waiver of the right to have written answers, while by receiving the general verdict without insisting on written answers the court is deemed to have withdrawn the instruction to answer the questions. The general verdict then stands as though no questions had been propounded.[3]

**Signing Answers.** *California.* Where answers to special interrogatories are not signed by the jury as a whole, nor by their foreman, as provided by Code Civ. Proc. § 618, they are not effective for any purpose;[4] and the same rule exists in *Oklahoma.*[5]

1 Egmann v. Railway Co., 65 Ill. App. 345.

2 Bottomley v. Goldsmith, 36 Mich. 27.

3 Moss v. Priest, 19 Abb. Prac. (N. Y.) 314. The fact that the trial judge wrote the findings of the jury does not vitiate them if they agreed to them as their verdict. Aiken v. Lyon, 127 N. C. 171, 37 S. E. 199.

4 Greenberg v. Hoff, 80 Cal. 81, 22 Pac. 69.

5 Under St. 1893, § 4174; City of Kingfisher v. Altizer, 13 Okl. 121, 74 Pac. 107.

*Indiana.* Answers to interrogatories put to the jury are in the nature and have the same force and effect as a special verdict, and under the statute,[6] which provides that the verdict of the jury "must be reduced to writing and signed by the foreman," a failure on the part of the foreman to sign the answers to interrogatories propounded to the jury is good ground for granting a new trial.[7] The statute does not require that the answers to special interrogatories shall be each signed by the foreman, but that is the better practice.[8]

The neglect of the foreman so to designate himself in signing is no ground for not accepting the verdict, where it appears from the signature of the general verdict that the person signing the answers was in fact the foreman.[9]

*Rhode Island.* A special finding by a jury, which is neither signed by the foreman of the jury, nor read to them by the clerk as their verdict, cannot be entered by him as such, after the discharge of the jury.[10]

—— **Waiver of Objection.** Where answers are returned and recorded with the general verdict, without objection, it cannot afterwards be objected by the party propounding the questions that they were not signed by the foreman of the jury.[11]

**Answers Without General Verdict.** If a jury find on special questions of fact, without a general verdict, the findings are

6 2 Gav. & H. p. 203, § 334.

7 Sage v. Brown, 34 Ind. 464. "The answers to the interrogatories, not being signed, were no part of the verdict; hence, a motion for judgment for the defendant thereon, notwithstanding the general verdict, was properly overruled." Vater v. Lewis, 36 Ind. 288, 10 Am. Rep. 29.

8 Louisville & N. R. Co. v. Kemper, 153 Ind. 618, 53 N. E. 931: Sage v. Brown, 34 Ind. 464.

9 Norwich Union Fire Ins. Soc. v. Girton, 124 Ind. 217, 24 N. E. 984.

10 Rose v. Harvey, 18 R. I. 527, 30 Atl. 459. *Polling Jury.*—The jury, having been polled as to their general verdict, may be polled en masse as to their special findings. Norman v. Hopper (Wash.) 80 Pac. 551.

11 Vater v. Lewis, 36 Ind. 288, 10 Am. Rep. 29, citing Noble v. Enos,

of no weight or force,[12] and judgment cannot be rendered thereon [13] unless the findings determine all the material issues in the case, and can be regarded in the light of a special verdict.[14] To have this effect the findings must be so full, clear, and consistent that the proper judgment can be rendered thereon as a legal conclusion from the facts found.[15]

Where specific interrogatories are propounded to a jury, to be answered by them unconditionally, and they seem to be so framed as to cover what appears to be the substance of the whole case, and are fully answered, but the jury makes no general verdict, the court may well render judgment in accordance with such answers, because the course of the parties would fairly indicate an intention or consent to waive a general verdict.[16] So, too, a party waives his right to a general verdict by stipulating that certain questions of fact be submitted to the jury, and that the remaining questions be decided by the court.[17]

To be available on appeal, the objection to failure to return a general verdict must be made when the findings are returned.[18]

19 Ind. 72; McElfresh v. Guard, 32 Ind. 408. See, also, Menne v. Neumeister, 25 Mo. App. 300; Thompson v. Thompson, 49 Neb. 157, 68 N. W. 372.

12 Pickett v. Handy, 5 Colo. App. 295, 38 Pac. 606; Eudaly v. Eudaly, 37 Ind. 440.

13 Kiel v. Reay, 50 Cal. 61; Hopkins v. Shull (Logan Com. Pl.) 3 West. Law Month. (Ohio) 609; Manning v. Monaghan, 23 N. Y. 539.

14 Montgomery v. Sayre, 91 Cal. 206, 27 Pac. 648; Paine v. Railroad Co., 31 Ind. 283; Toledo, W. & W. Ry. Co. v. Hammond, 33 Ind. 379, 5 Am. Rep. 221; Hopkins v. Stanley, 43 Ind. 553; Kealing v. Voss, 61 Ind. 466; Coleman v. Railroad Co., 38 Minn. 260, 36 N. W. 638; Crich v. Insurance Co., 45 Minn. 441, 48 N. W. 198.

15 Pea v. Pea, 35 Ind. 387; McIlvain v. State, 80 Ind. 69; Woollen v. Whitacre, 91 Ind. 502; Coleman v. Railroad Co., supra; Cotzhausen v. Simon, 47 Wis. 103, 1 N. W. 473.

16 Crassen v. Swoveland, 22 Ind. 427; and see Carr v. Carr, 4 Lans. (N. Y.) 314.

17 State Ins. Co. v. Gray, 44 Kan. 731, 25 Pac. 197.

18 Id.; National Horse Importing Co. v. Novak, 95 Iowa, 596, 64 N. W. 616.

**Failure to Answer—When Material.** It is the duty of the jury to answer special interrogatories fully, where the evidence enables them to do so; but failure to make a special finding is of consequence only when the answer thereto might have been of controlling force. If a finding most favorable to the adverse party upon the questions left unanswered would not have been inconsistent with the general verdict, the omission is immaterial.[19]

Failure to return a special finding will not necessitate reversal unless, because of the failure, it is manifest from the record that the jury has not found the facts necessary to authorize its general verdict.[20]

The right of a party to have the jury answer special interrogatories submitted at his request is not absolute; it is sufficient if they are answered in so far as they are material [21]—that is, relate to ultimate facts.[22] If immaterial, the failure to answer is not prejudicial,[23] and will furnish no ground for reversal of the judgment rendered on the general verdict.[24]

The following are a few examples of cases where omission to find has been held without effect on the general verdict:

When the questions have become immaterial by reason of

19 Chicago & N. W. Ry. Co. v. Dunleavy, 129 Ill. 132, 22 N. E. 15; Ohio & M. Ry. Co. v. Ramey, 139 Ill. 9, 28 N. E. 1087, 32 Am. St. Rep. 176; Dreher v. Railroad Co., 59 Iowa, 599, 13 N. W. 754; Osborne v. Pennsylvania Co., 10 Ky. Law Rep. 970, 11 S. W. 207; Schneider v. Railroad Co., 42 Minn. 68, 43 N. W. 783; McClary v. Stull, 44 Neb. 175, 62 N. W. 501; Town v. Railroad Co., 50 Neb. 768, 70 N. W. 402; Doane v. Loan & Trust Co., 51 Neb. 280, 70 N. W. 909. See, also, Dyer v. Taylor, 50 Ark. 314, 7 S. W. 258.

20 Sutherland v. Insurance Co., 87 Iowa, 505, 54 N. W. 453, citing Dively v. City of Cedar Falls, 27 Iowa, 227; Hatfield v. Lockwood, 18 Iowa, 296; Hardin v. Branner, 25 Iowa, 364.

21 Buetzier v. Jones, 85 Iowa, 721, 51 N. W. 242.

22 Andrews v. Railroad Co., 77 Iowa, 669, 42 N. W. 513.

23 Miles v. Wikel, 74 Iowa, 712, 39 N. W. 95.

24 Pettibone v. Maclem, 45 Mich. 381, 8 N. W. 84; Missouri Pac. Ry. Co. v. Vandeventer, 26 Neb. 222, 41 N. W. 998, 3 L. R. A. 129; Town v. Railroad Co., 50 Neb. 768, 70 N. W. 402.

plaintiff having abandoned the action as to the particular items embraced therein;[25]

Where the questions have been answered in other responses;[26]

Where proof of the facts suggested is not required;[27]

Where, by agreement, the questions were to be answered only in case of verdict for plaintiff, and the verdict was for defendant;[28]

Where no evidence has been introduced on which answers could be given.[29]

But where material questions have been submitted, it is error, against objection, to receive a general verdict without answers to the interrogatories, and judgment rendered on the general verdict under such circumstances will be reversed.[30]

The court is not at liberty, without the consent of the parties, to withdraw or disregard the interrogatories, and if not finally answered it will be held equivalent, as to the matters involved therein, to a finding against the party having the burden of proof.[31] The general verdict should be set aside and a new trial granted.[32]

[25] Pioneer Mfg. Co. v. Assurance Co., 110 N. C. 176, 14 S. E. 731, 28 Am. St. Rep. 673.

[26] Osborne v. Pennsylvania Co., 10 Ky. Law Rep. 970, 11 S. W. 207.

[27] Andrews v. Railway Co., 77 Iowa, 669, 42 N. W. 513.

[28] Bagley v. Grand Lodge, 31 Ill. App. 618.

[29] Ft. Scott, W. & W. R. Co. v. Karracker, 46 Kan. 511, 26 Pac. 1027; Missouri Pac. Ry. Co. v. Vandeventer, 26 Neb. 222, 41 N. W. 998, 3 L. R. A. 129.

[30] Tourtelotte v. Brown, 1 Colo. App. 408, 29 Pac. 132; Perry, Matthews-Buskirk Stone Co. v. Wilson, 160 Ind. 435, 67 N. E. 183; Rathbun v. Parker, 113 Mich. 594, 72 N. W. 31; Doom v. Walker, 15 Neb. 339, 18 N. W. 138; Sandwich Enterprise Co. v. West, 42 Neb. 722, 60 N. W. 1012; Redford v. Railway Co., 9 Wash. 55, 36 Pac. 1085; Carrico v. Railway Co., 39 W. Va. 86, 19 S. E. 571, 24 L. R. A. 50. But see McCormack v. Phillips, 4 Dak. 506, 34 N. W. 39.

[31] Nichols, Shepard & Co. v. Wadsworth, 40 Minn. 547, 42 N. W. 541; Eischen v. Railway Co., 81 Minn. 59, 83 N. W. 490.

[32] Id.

—— **Compelling Answers.** It is generally held that it is the duty of the jury to answer fully and without evasion, and that it is proper to send the jury back to make findings which they have omitted,[33] which may be done even where they have returned a sealed verdict and separated.[34]

The question then arises as to the effect of failure to compel the jury to answer. Necessarily it cannot be error to neglect or refuse to require the jury to answer immaterial and improper interrogatories.[35] It is only fair and pertinent questions that can be truthfully answered under the testimony that a party may insist on having answered as of right.[36] If the questions are immaterial they should never have been submitted in the first instance, and the omission to answer them does not affect the right to judgment of the party in whose favor the general verdict is rendered;[37] or the questions may have become immaterial by reason of answers to preceding questions.[38]

[33] Consolidated Coal Co. v. Maehl, 130 Ill. 551, 22 N. E. 715; Noakes v. Morey, 30 Ind. 103; McElfresh v. Guard, 32 Ind. 408; Maxwell v. Boyne, 36 Ind. 120; Reeves v. Plough, 41 Ind. 204; Rowell v. Klein, 44 Ind. 290, 15 Am. Rep. 235; Bradley v. Bradley, 45 Ind. 67; Summers v. Greathouse, 87 Ind. 207; Bank of Monroe v. Gifford, 79 Iowa, 300, 44 N. W. 558, and cases cited; Judge v. Jordan, 81 Iowa, 519, 46 N. W. 1077; Roberts v. Roberts, 91 Iowa, 228, 59 N. W. 25; Clark v. Railway Co., 35 Kan. 350, 11 Pac. 134; Tarbox v. Gotzian, 20 Minn. 139 (Gil. 122); Nichols, Shepard & Co. v. Wadsworth, supra. But see Harbaugh v. People, 33 Mich. 241.

Mandamus will not lie to compel the court to receive the verdict until the jury have found upon all the special issues submitted. Rose v. Harvey, 18 R. I. 527, 30 Atl. 459.

[34] Consolidated Coal Co. v. Maehl, supra; Chicago & A. R. Co. v. Reilly, 75 Ill. App. 125; and see Roberts v. Roberts, 91 Iowa, 228, 59 N. W. 25; Spencer v. Williams, 160 Mass. 17, 35 N. E. 88; Dailey v. Douglass, 40 Mich. 557.

[35] Town v. Railroad Co., 50 Neb. 768, 70 N. W. 402; Robinson v. Insurance Co. (N. M.) 66 Pac. 535; Noakes v. Morey, 30 Ind. 103; Porter v. Waltz, 108 Ind. 40, 8 N. E. 705.

[36] Atchison, T. & S. F. R. Co. v. Shaw, 56 Kan. 519, 43 Pac. 1129.

[37] Dyer v. Taylor, 50 Ark. 314, 7 S. W. 258; Johnson v. Insurance Co., 39 Mich. 33; McClary v. Stull, 44 Neb. 175, 62 N. W. 501.

[38] City of Wyandotte v. Gibson, 25 Kan. 236.

The rule seems to be that failure to compel answer to questions which the jury have ignored is equivalent to withdrawal of the questions, and that the effect is the same as though the court had refused to submit them in the first instance.[39] This means that if the interrogatories call for material facts which the jury must determine in reaching a general verdict it is error to refuse to compel answers, whether under statutes of the mandatory or discretionary groups;[40] and this is so as well where the interrogatories are submitted by the court sua sponte[41] as where they are submitted on request of counsel.

The right of a party to have specific questions submitted "is not one which enables him to determine what are material facts and what questions must be answered. He may present any number of questions for submission, as any number of instructions, but it is the duty of the court to determine what in the one case shall be submitted, as in the other what shall be given. And the court, by declining to compel the answer to any specific questions, in effect withdraws them from the jury. And this the court may do, if in so doing no material question is deprived of a specific answer."[42]

39 Cleveland, C., C. & St. L. Ry. Co. v. Doerr, 41 Ill. App. 530; City of Wyandotte v. Gibson, supra; Burr v. Honeywell, 6 Kan. App. 783, 51 Pac. 235; Johnson v. Husband, 22 Kan. 277; Florence Mach. Co. v. Daggett, 135 Mass. 582; Robinson v. Insurance Co. (N. M.) 66 Pac. 535; Moss v. Priest, 19 Abb. Prac. (N. Y.) 314. See, also, Cronin v. City of Holyoke, 162 Mass. 257, 38 N. E. 445; Banner Tobacco Co. v. Jenison, 48 Mich. 459, 12 N. W. 655; National Refining Co. v. Miller, 1 S. D. 548, 47 N. W. 962.

Logically the result is that in states where the discretion of the court as to submission of interrogatories is absolute it cannot be error to refuse to compel answers on motion or to neglect to do so. In fact, however, it has been held in *Washington* that the court, having decided that the requests for special findings were in proper form and having submitted them to the jury, should require an answer thereto before receiving the general verdict, and that it is reversible error not to do so. Redford v. Railway Co., 9 Wash. 55, 36 Pac. 1085. See, also, Eischen v. Railway Co., 81 Minn. 59, 83 N. W. 490.

40 Rathbun v. Parker, 113 Mich. 594, 72 N. W. 31.

41 Eischen v. Railway Co., 81 Minn. 59, 83 N. W. 490.

42 City of Wyandotte v. Gibson, 25 Kan. 236, 243–245.

—— **Waiver of Objection.** It seems that in any case a party cannot complain unless he moves the court to require the jury to supply omissions. Error cannot be maintained unless the party desiring answers insists upon getting them. The objection that the jury returned a general verdict without making the special findings called for cannot be made for the first time on appeal.[43] Consent of a party to the discharge of the jury is a waiver of the objection that they have failed to answer specific questions[44] and a waiver of the request for the special findings.[45]

—— **Who may Object to Omission.** It has been held in *Illinois* that a party not submitting questions has no right to complain of the jury's failure to answer questions submitted by his adversary, the statute, it was said, giving a party the right to put questions solely for his own benefit.[46] But a more liberal construction has been adopted elsewhere. In many cases a party may refrain from submitting interrogatories because those he would propound have already been requested by his adversary. He has a right to assume that the jury will discharge its duty, and would be prejudiced if the court refused to compel it to do so if there is evidence on which findings could be made. For these and other reasons courts, upon request of either party, should instruct the jury fully and explicitly to answer the interrogatories submitted.[47]

43 Mack v. Leedle, 78 Iowa, 164, 42 N. W. 636; Mayo v. Halley, 124 Iowa, 675, 100 N. W. 529; Dickey v. Shirk, 128 Ind. 278, 27 N. E. 733.

44 McCormack v. Phillips, 4 Dak. 506, 34 N. W. 39; Bagley v. Grand Lodge, 31 Ill. App. 618; Id., 131 Ill. 498, 22 N. E. 487; Caldwell v. Brown, 9 Ohio Cir. Ct. R. 691; City of Guthrie v. Thistle, 5 Okl. 517, 49 Pac. 1003; Carrico v. Railway Co., 39 W. Va. 86, 19 S. E. 571, 24 L. R. A. 50.

45 Brown v. Railroad Co. (Cal.) 12 Pac. 512; Id., 72 Cal. 523, 14 Pac. 138. See, also, Long v. Duncan, 10 Kan. 294; Bradley v. Bradley, 45 Ind. 67.

46 Bagley v. Grand Lodge, 31 Ill. App. 618; Id., 131 Ill. 498, 22 N. E. 487. Compare Cleveland, C., C. & St. L. Ry. Co. v. Doerr, 41 Ill. App. 530.

47 American Cent. Ins. Co. v. Hathaway, 43 Kan. 399, 23 Pac. 428;

—— **Excuse of Want of or Conflicting Evidence.** When the jury fail to answer interrogatories calling for ultimate facts, they should, the court being moved thereto, be sent back to answer them. They will not be allowed to evade their duty in this respect,[48] and the attempt to do so may be construed as an admission of inability to make special findings under the evidence that would be consistent with the general verdict returned.[49] But jurors cannot be expected to answer questions without evidence before them to enable them to do so.[50] In cases where there is no evidence upon which answers could be given, it is proper for the jury so to state.[51] Such a return is to be construed against the party having the burden of proof of the facts sought to be elicited.[52]

Where, however, there is evidence upon which to base find-

McClaren v. Railroad Co., 83 Ind. 319; Duesterberg v. State, 116 Ind. 144, 17 N. E. 624; Dickey v. Shirk, 128 Ind. 278, 27 N. E. 733.

[48] Summers v. Greathouse, 87 Ind. 207.

[49] Eischen v. Railway Co., 81 Minn. 59, 83 N. W. 490.

[50] Ft. Scott, W. & W. R. Co. v. Karracker, 46 Kan. 511, 26 Pac. 1027; Kay v. Noll, 20 Neb. 380, 30 N. W. 269.

[51] Maxwell v. Boyne, 36 Ind. 120; Williamson v. Yingling, 80 Ind. 379; Louisville, N. A. & C. Ry. Co. v. Thompson, 107 Ind. 442, 8 N. E. 18, 9 N. E. 357, 57 Am. Rep. 120, and cases cited; Cleveland, C., C. & I. Ry. Co. v. Asbury, 120 Ind. 289, 22 N. E. 140; Cincinnati, H. & I. R. Co. v. Cregor, 150 Ind. 625, 50 N. E. 760; Terre Haute & P. R. Co. v. Barr, 31 Ill. App. 57.

[52] Indianapolis Abattoir Co. v. Temperly, 159 Ind. 651, 64 N. E. 906, 95 Am. St. Rep. 330; Bryson v. Railway Co., 89 Iowa, 677, 57 N. W. 430; Clark v. Railway Co., 35 Kan. 350, 11 Pac. 134; Heyman v. Simmons, 4 Kan. App. 1, 45 Pac. 728; Watson v. Railway Co., 46 Minn. 321, 48 N. W. 1129. See Crane v. Reeder, 25 Mich. 303.

Where the answer "No evidence" is given to an interrogatory calling for a fact necessary to be found to entitle plaintiff to judgment, a verdict for plaintiff and judgment thereon cannot stand, and defendant is entitled to judgment on the answer. Cleveland, C., C. & St. L. Ry. Co. v. Heine, 28 Ind. App. 163, 62 N. E. 455. The general verdict is not vitiated where the absence of evidence is immaterial. See Chicago & E. I. R. Co. v. Goyette, 32 Ill. App. 574; McMarshall v. Railroad Co., 80 Iowa, 757, 45 N. W. 1065, 20 Am. St. Rep. 445.

ings, the answer that there is no evidence is false, and should not be received,[53] but the court should compel the jury to answer truthfully, or, in the event of their failure to agree, should discharge them, as in the case of a disagreement on a general verdict.[54]

It must be comparatively seldom that the answer of "No evidence" is justified, since, if true, both court and counsel have been at fault in allowing the questions to be submitted, and it may be taken for granted that in the average case the jury either needs tonic treatment for "that tired feeling," or but too well realizes that its general verdict cannot meet the test which the special findings are designed to supply.

Refusal to require specific answers, where the jury answer "No evidence," is not reversible error where no answers that might have been given under the evidence would necessarily have controlled the general verdict.[55]

Failure to answer for the reason, as expressed by the jury, that the evidence is too conflicting, has been held equivalent to a finding that the facts concerning which they are asked to make findings do not exist or are not proved.[56] Such an answer ought not, however, to be accepted. The jury may answer "No evidence" when in fact there is none, but if there is a conflict of evidence it is the duty of the jury to answer according to the preponderance of the evidence. If there is no preponderance either way, then the jury should answer against the party having the burden of proof as to the fact inquired about.[57] If the jury is unable to agree, it is their duty to re-

[53] Kansas Pac. Ry. Co. v. Peavey, 34 Kan. 472, 8 Pac. 780.

[54] Perry, Matthews-Buskirk Stone Co. v. Wilson, 160 Ind. 435, 67 N. E. 183.

[55] Citizens' St. R. Co. v. Batley, 159 Ind. 368, 65 N. E. 2; American Tin Plate Co. v. Williams, 30 Ind. App. 46, 65 N. E. 304; Frank Bird Transfer Co. v. Krug, 30 Ind. App. 602, 65 N. E. 309.

[56] Atchison, T. & S. F. R. Co. v. McCandliss, 33 Kan. 366, 6 Pac. 587.

[57] Perry, Matthews-Buskirk Stone Co. v. Wilson, 160 Ind. 435, 67 N. E. 183. See, also, Crane v. Reeder, 25 Mich. 303.

port the fact to the court, and if finally unable to agree the court should discharge them on account of such disagreement.

—— **Failure to Agree.** Failure to agree upon a material question is equivalent to failure to find and agree upon any verdict in the case.[58] Upon such failure a general verdict cannot be received against objection.[59] The result is a mistrial. The jury should be discharged, and the case submitted to a new jury precisely as in the case of disagreement on the general verdict.[60]

Failure to agree upon the special questions stultifies the general verdict, if one is returned. None but interrogatories relating to ultimate facts are properly submitted. Assuming that such facts only have been called for, it is apparent, in case of failure to agree on answers, that the jury have not found the facts necessary to authorize judgment for either party. The peculiar office and restraining effect of special interrogatories is here excellently illustrated. Without them actual disagreement as to vital matters would be completely disguised by the superficial unanimity of the general verdict, which needs must be accepted as evidencing the proper discharge of the jury's duty, though in fact it has been misconceived or evaded.

But failure to agree upon specific questions can nullify the effect of the general verdict only where findings in favor of the adverse party would be conclusive against the right of the party in whose favor the verdict is rendered.[61] If the facts

[58] Hardin v. Branner, 25 Iowa, 364.

[59] Tourtelotte v. Brown, 1 Colo. App. 408, 29 Pac. 130; Doom v. Walker, 15 Neb. 339, 18 N. W. 138; Redford v. Railway Co., 9 Wash. 55, 36 Pac. 1085.

It is error for the court to direct the jury to answer a special question by saying that they do not agree. Clark v. Weir, 37 Kan. 98, 14 Pac. 533.

[60] Kansas Pac. Ry. Co. v. Reynolds, 8 Kan. 623; Clark v. Weir, 37 Kan. 98, 14 Pac. 533; Redford v. Railway Co., 9 Wash. 55, 36 Pac. 1085; Elliott v. Village of Graceville, 76 Minn. 430, 79 N. W. 503.

[61] Schneider v. Railroad Co., 42 Minn. 68, 43 N. W. 783. See, also, Darling v. West, 51 Iowa, 259, 1 N. W. 531; Kellow v. Railway Co.,

are not essential for the support of the general verdict, it is not error to instruct the jury that, if it can agree as to other interrogatories, to do so, and return the findings with the general verdict.[62]

If the verdict is sustained by any one of the two or more interpretations of the evidence, it is not necessary that the jury should concur in a special finding; but if they must necessarily agree on the answer to some particular question before they can find the verdict, and their answer shows that they cannot agree, the general verdict should be disregarded.[63]

Failure to agree on a general verdict will, of course, excuse the jury from answering the interrogatories.[64]

**Indefinite and Evasive Answers.** Where questions of fact submitted to a jury are not fully answered, the court, on application of either party,[65] should instruct the jury to fully and explicitly answer them,[66] and it is error to refuse to do so.[67]

68 Iowa, 470, 23 N. W. 745, 27 N. W. 466, 56 Am. Rep. 858; Andrews v. Railway Co., 77 Iowa, 669, 42 N. W. 513; Town of Wakefield v. Wakefield Water Co., 182 Mass. 429, 65 N. E. 814.

62 Sutherland v. Insurance Co., 87 Iowa, 505, 54 N. W. 453.

63 Arkansas M. Ry. Co. v. Canman, 52 Ark. 517, 13 S. W. 280.

64 Leffel v. Leffel, 35 Ind. 76.

65 Cleveland, C., C. & St. L. Ry. Co. v. Doerr, 41 Ill. App. 530; American Cent. Ins. Co. v. Hathaway, 43 Kan. 399, 23 Pac. 428.

66 Bradley v. Bradley, 45 Ind. 67; Bowman v. Phillips, 47 Ind. 341; Hammond, Whiting & E. C. Electric Ry. Co. v. Spyzchalski, 17 Ind. App. 7, 46 N. E. 47; Hazard Powder Co. v. Viergutz, 6 Kan. 471; Arthur v. Wallace, 8 Kan. 267; Leavenworth, T. & S. W. Ry. Co. v. Jacobs, 39 Kan. 204, 17 Pac. 791; Baltimore & O. R. Co. v. McPeek, 16 Ohio Cir. Ct. R. 87; Coats v. Town of Stanton, 90 Wis. 130, 62 N. W. 619.

67 Chicago, B. & Q. R. Co. v. Greenfield, 53 Ill. App. 424; Cleveland, C., C. & I. Ry. Co. v. Asbury, 120 Ind. 289, 22 N. E. 140; Johnson v. Husband, 22 Kan. 277; Atchison, T. & S. F. R. Co. v. Cone, 37 Kan. 567, 15 Pac. 499.

Where an interrogatory is requested to be submitted to the jury, within the issues joined by the pleadings and the evidence introduced, asking for a more explicit answer to another interrogatory submitted, it is error for the court to refuse to submit it to the jury. American

The duty of the jury is to give direct and positive answers.[68] Where there is evidence bearing upon every fact covered by the interrogatories to the jury, and the latter return evasive answers thereto, it is error to receive such answers; and where direct answers might change the general verdict, the court should require the jury to answer definitely, and in direct language, or to inform it of their disagreement, if any.[69]

But that answers to interrogatories are not supported by the evidence is no reason for returning them to the jury for further answers. That fact can be taken advantage of only upon motion for a new trial. It is not within the province of the trial court to require juries to make answers that are strictly within the evidence. That is a matter within the conscience of the jury. Further answers may be required where those returned are uncertain or evasive, but not because they are untrue.[70]

The court need not require the jury to answer more definitely an interrogatory not pertinent to any material issue or of controlling force. It is not error to refuse to do so;[71] nor is it error to refuse to require a more explicit answer to a ques-

Cent. Ins. Co. v. Hathaway, 43 Kan. 399, 23 Pac. 428. Overruling a motion to require the jury to return to their room, and make fuller answer, is not a good assignment of error, but is properly a cause for a new trial. Knight v. Knight, 6 Ind. App. 268, 33 N. E. 456.

68 Winfield Nat. Bank v. McWilliams, 9 Okl. 493, 60 Pac. 229.

69 Cleveland, C., C. & I. Ry. Co. v. Asbury, 120 Ind. 289, 22 N. E. 140.

70 Board of Com'rs of Jackson County v. Nichols, 139 Ind. 611, 38 N. E. 526, citing Indianapolis & St. L. R. Co. v. Stout, 53 Ind. 143.

71 Chicago, B. & Q. R. Co. v. Greenfield, 53 Ill. App. 424; Elgin, J. & E. Ry. Co. v. Raymond, 148 Ill. 241, 35 N. E. 729; Morse v. Morse, 25 Ind. 156; Indiana Stone Co. v. Stewart, 7 Ind. App. 563, 34 N. E. 1019; Green v. Eden, 24 Ind. App. 583, 56 N. E. 240; Atchison, T. & S. F. R. Co. v. Campbell, 16 Kan. 200. Where defendant was not entitled to judgment on the answers to special interrogatories, refusal of the court to require an answer to be made more specific was harmless. Lake Erie & W. R. Co. v. McFall (Ind.) 72 N. E. 552.

tion which has become immaterial by reason of answers to other questions.[72]

If instead of answering the interrogatories "Yes" or "No," as they could do, the jury give answers from which it cannot be determined whether they accord or conflict with the general verdict, a new trial should be granted.[73]

—— **Particular Answers.** Answers expressing only the inclination of the jury, as "We think not," etc., are insufficient and too uncertain to base a judgment upon;[74] and so are conditional answers, as e. g., where the question was whether a person had notice, and the jury answered, "Yes, if possession is notice."[75]

Where there is no evidence on which to base an affirmative or negative answer to interrogatories, an answer, "Evidence don't show," is sufficient, and its acceptance is not error.[76]

[72] Taylor v. Wootan, 1 Ind. App. 188, 27 N. E. 502, 50 Am. St. Rep. 200; City of Wyandotte v. Gibson, 25 Kan. 236.

[73] Fisk v. Railway Co., 74 Iowa, 424, 38 N. W. 132; Comer v. Himes, 49 Ind. 482; Scheible v. Law, 65 Ind. 332; Sanders v. Weelburg, 107 Ind. 266, 7 N. E. 573.

[74] Hopkins v. Stanley, 43 Ind. 553; but see Martin v. Railway Co., 59 Iowa, 411, 13 N. W. 424, in which the court instructed the jury that if they could not answer the questions by "Yes" or "No" they might answer them in some other manner, and the jury's answers that they "think" and "have reason to believe" are held sufficient.

See, also, McGuire v. Railway Co., 23 Mo. App. 325. Where the jury is asked to find specially whether a particular fact exists, and answers "Probably not," this is a finding that for the purposes of the case the fact does not exist. Davis v. Guarnieri, 45 Ohio St. 470, 15 N. E. 350, 4 Am. St. Rep. 548.

The answer, "In our judgment," etc., held sufficiently certain; but answer, "Can't say definitely," held insufficient. Peters v. Lane, 55 Ind. 391.

"We think not," held an answer in the negative. Guernsey v. Fulmer, 66 Kan. 767, 71 Pac. 578.

[75] Woodson v. McCune, 17 Cal. 304; Garfield v. Water Co., Id. 510.

[76] Terre Haute & P. R. Co. v. Barr, 31 Ill. App. 57; Cincinnati, H. & I. R. Co. v. Cregor, 150 Ind. 625, 50 N. E. 760; Atchison, T. & S. F. R. Co. v. Campbell, 16 Kan. 200; and see Caldwell v. Brown, 11 Ohio

The answer of a jury to an interrogatory as to the existence of certain supposed facts was, "The weight of the evidence justifies the jury in answering, 'No.'" Held, that no error was committed in refusing to require the jury to answer more explicitly. It was the duty of the jury to answer the interrogatory according to the weight of the evidence.[77]

—— **Answer "Don't Know," or Equivalent.** It is error to instruct the jury that in case no evidence can be found bearing upon the question they may answer "Don't know," [78] and where the jury return a general verdict, and in answer to certain special interrogatories state that they "do not know" (or equivalent expression), the verdict cannot be sustained.[79] But the answer is harmless if the questions asked are immaterial,[80] and is proper where the evidence does not warrant

Cir. Ct. R. 485. "Evidence not conclusive," treated as no answer. Albany Land Co. v. Rickel, 162 Ind. 222, 70 N. E. 158.

[77] Mutual Ben. Life Ins. Co. v. Cannon, 48 Ind. 264.

[78] Union Pac. Ry. Co. v. Fray, 35 Kan. 700, 12 Pac. 98; Kansas Pass. Ry. Co. v. Peavey, 34 Kan. 472, 8 Pac. 780; Atchison, T. & S. F. Ry. Co. v. Cone, 37 Kan. 567, 15 Pac. 499; Same v. Lannigan, 56 Kan. 109, 42 Pac. 343. See, also, Crane v. Reeder, 25 Mich. 303; Wilson v. Railroad Co., 57 Mich. 155, 23 N. W. 627.

[79] Darling v. West, 51 Iowa, 259, 1 N. W. 531; Lytton v. Railroad Co., 69 Iowa, 338, 28 N. W. 628; Morrow v. Commissioners, 21 Kan. 484; Baehler v. Ranch Co., 31 Kan. 502, 3 Pac. 343; Kansas Pac. Ry. Co. v. Peavey, 34 Kan. 472, 8 Pac. 780; Leavenworth, T. & S. W. Ry. Co. v. Jacobs, 39 Kan. 204, 17 Pac. 791; Atchison, T. & S. F. Ry. Co. v. Hale, 64 Kan. 751, 68 Pac. 612; Mechanics' Bank v. Barnes, 86 Mich. 632, 49 N. W. 475.

The answer, "Can't say," is equivalent to no answer at all. Hawley v. City of Atlantic, 92 Iowa, 172, 60 N. W. 519.

[80] Elgin, J. & E. Ry. Co. v. Raymond, 148 Ill. 241, 35 N. E. 729; Andrews v. Railroad Co., 77 Iowa, 669, 42 N. W. 513; Seekel v. Norman, 78 Iowa, 254, 43 N. W. 190; Patterson v. Bridge Co., 90 Iowa, 247, 57 N. W. 880; Saar v. Railroad Co., 119 Iowa, 60, 93 N. W. 66. See, also, Atchison, T. & S. F. Ry. Co. v. McCandliss, 33 Kan. 366, 6 Pac. 587.

Answers, "We cannot say," and "Do not know," do not vitiate the general verdict. They are to be understood as a reply to the effect

any other finding,[81] or where, after an honest endeavor on the part of the jury, the court is satisfied that they cannot answer in any other manner.[82]

Where there is evidence bearing on the facts covered by the interrogatories to the jury, who return evasive answers thereto, such as "So stated," "Don't know," etc., while if the interrogatories were answered in the affirmative, as warranted by the evidence, the general verdict would be overthrown, the court should require the jury to answer definitely, unless they cannot agree.[83] The answer "Don't know" may sometimes be accepted where the question is not as to one of the principal facts, but runs to one of the minor and subdivided facts, but never when the determination of the fact is essential to the conclusion reached in the general verdict.[84]

Where evidence has been given pertinent to any fact to which an interrogatory has been addressed, and the jury answer "Don't know," the special findings are imperfect and insufficient; and it is the duty of the trial court, upon objection and

that there is no evidence upon the points, and the failure to find cannot render the findings and verdict contradictory, where no answer that could be given would be controlling. McMarshall v. Railway Co., 80 Iowa, 757, 45 N. W. 1065, 20 Am. St. Rep. 445.

In an action against a city for allowing garbage, which emitted noxious odors, to be dumped in a street adjacent to plaintiff's premises, interfering with her enjoyment thereof, where the evidence disclosed that plaintiff also permitted garbage to accumulate on her lot, an answer by the jury to a special interrogatory, as to whether or not noxious odors were emitted from the garbage on plaintiff's lot, that they did not know, is not reversible error, since plaintiff could recover for defendant's wrongful maintenance of a nuisance irrespective of whether or not she herself maintained one on her own land. Correll v. City of Cedar Rapids, 110 Iowa, 333, 81 N. W. 724.

81 Terre Haute & P. R. Co. v. Barr, 31 Ill. App. 57; Guernsey v. Fulmer, 66 Kan. 767, 71 Pac. 578.

82 Kansas Pac. Ry. Co. v. Peavey, 34 Kan. 472, 8 Pac. 780.

83 Life Assur. Co. of America v. Haughton, 31 Ind. App. 626, 67 N. E. 950.

84 Atchison, T. & S. F. R. Co. v. Campbell, 16 Kan. 200; Laverenz v. Railroad Co., 56 Iowa, 689, 10 N. W. 268.

proper motion, to require the jury, under instructions, to retire and answer such interrogatory, if they can agree upon an answer or answers. If they cannot agree, they should so report to the court. The same rule applies where the jury answer "Evidence not sufficient." It is reversible error to accept such answers against objection.[85]

Where the jury say they "do not know" in answer to special questions that under the charge and the evidence are material to the issue, the result is a mistrial.[86] It is also held that the answer "Don't know" is a finding in the negative on the question asked;[87] a finding against the party whose case needs the support of the alleged facts;[88] a finding unfavorable to the party having the burden of proving the affirmative of the question.[89] If, from the testimony, the jurors do not know whether an alleged fact exists, it follows that the testimony does not show that it exists, and, therefore, for the purposes of the case, it does not exist.[90] The finding then fairly operates against him who had the burden of proving its existence.[91]

[85] Life Assur. Co. of America v. Haughton, 31 Ind. App. 626, 67 N. E. 950, and cases cited; Cleveland, C., C. & I. Ry. Co. v. Asbury, 120 Ind. 289, 22 N. E. 140; Atchison, T. & S. F. Ry. Co. v. Hale, 64 Kan. 751, 68 Pac. 612. But see City of Topeka v. Noble, 9 Kan. App. 171, 58 Pac. 1015, in which it was held that the court did not err in refusing to require the answer, "Don't know," to be made more definite. "These answers were equivalent to a finding in the negative. Therefore such answers are specific, definite, and certain."

[86] Wilson v. Railroad Co., 57 Mich. 155, 23 N. W. 627; Lytton v. Railroad Co., 69 Iowa, 338, 28 N. W. 628; Atchison, T. & S. F. R. Co. v. Cone, 37 Kan. 567, 15 Pac. 499.

[87] Atchison, T. & S. F. R. Co. v. Swarts, 58 Kan. 235, 48 Pac. 953; City of Topeka v. Noble, 9 Kan. App. 171, 58 Pac. 1015; Maclean v. Scripps, 52 Mich. 214, 17 N. W. 815, 18 N. W. 209; Atchison, T. & S. F. R. Co. v. Johnson, 3 Okl. 41, 41 Pac. 641.

[88] Allen v. Lizer, 9 Kan. App. 548, 58 Pac. 238.

[89] Atchison, T. & S. F. R. Co. v. Lannigan, 56 Kan. 109, 42 Pac. 343; Heyman v. Simmons, 4 Kan. App. 1, 45 Pac. 728; Kalina v. Railroad Co., 69 Kan. 172, 76 Pac. 438.

[90] Morrow v. Commissioners, 21 Kan. 484.

[91] Flannery v. Railway Co., 23 Mo. App. 120.

—— **Objections.** Objection that special findings are not sufficiently definite and direct is waived unless taken when the verdict is rendered,[92] when motion should be made to have them sent back to the jury to be more fully answered.

**Evidentiary Facts.** While the special findings need not cover all the ultimate facts, they should be only of ultimate facts essential to the decision of the case.[93] They must state facts, not evidence thereof.[94] Thus, e. g., where fraud is an issuable fact, the jury should find it as an ultimate fact, and not merely the badges of it.[95] If the answers returned relate merely to evidentiary matters, they will be ignored;[96] they cannot control the general verdict.[97]

But a finding of probative facts is sufficient, if the ultimate facts necessarily result therefrom.[98]

**Conclusions of Law.** To permit the jury to return conclusions of law rather than statements of fact would defeat the manifest purpose of the statute.[99] Such conclusions are to be disregarded.[100] They cannot be considered in determining the

92 Elgin, J. & E. Ry. Co. v. Raymond, 148 Ill. 241, 35 N. E. 729; Reeves v. Plough, 41 Ind. 204; Bradley v. Bradley, 45 Ind. 67; Huss v. Railway Co., 113 Iowa, 343, 85 N. W. 627; Arthur v. Wallace, 8 Kan. 267; Kansas Pac. Ry. Co. v. Pointer, 14 Kan. 37; Johnson v. Husband, 22 Kan. 277; Manny v. Griswold, 21 Minn. 506; Crandall v. McIlrath, 24 Minn. 127; Varco v. Railroad Co., 30 Minn. 18, 13 N. W. 921; Moss v. Priest, 1 Rob. (N. Y.) 632, 19 Abb. Prac. 314.

93 Morbey v. Railroad Co., 116 Iowa, 84, 89 N. W. 105.

94 Wilson v. Campbell, 119 Ind. 286, 21 N. E. 893. See Chapter V.

95 Voris v. Association, 20 Ind. App. 630, 50 N. E. 779; John H. Hibben Dry Goods Co. v. Hicks, 26 Ind. App. 646, 59 N. E. 938.

96 Rowley v. Sanns, 141 Ind. 179, 40 N. E. 674; Kirkpatrick v. Reeves, 121 Ind. 280, 22 N. E. 139.

97 Baltimore & O. & C. R. Co. v. Rowan, 104 Ind. 88, 3 N. E. 627.

98 Miller v. Luco, 80 Cal. 257, 22 Pac. 195; Chicago & N. W. Ry. Co. v. Dunleavy, 129 Ill. 132, 22 N. E. 15; Rowley v. Sanns, 141 Ind. 179, 40 N. E. 674; Severy v. Railroad Co., 6 Okl. 153, 50 Pac. 162.

99 Louisville, N. A. & C. Ry. Co. v. Worley, 107 Ind. 320, 7 N. E. 215.

100 Pittsburgh, C., C. & St. L. Ry. Co. v. Gray, 28 Ind. App. 588, 64

sufficiency of the verdict.[101] For example, where, in an action to recover for fires set by a locomotive, the jury found that the plaintiff was free from negligence, without finding the facts, it was held that a verdict in his favor was unsupported; [102] and a special finding in these words, "We, the jury, find that the plaintiff had a right to replevy the mill," amounted to no more than a conclusion of law, which the jury could not decide, and would not authorize judgment for possession of the property.[103]

Conclusions of law are ineffective. They cannot control the general verdict.[104]

—— **Examples of Sufficient Findings.** Where the answer was that the cause of action was barred by certain sections of the Code, a finding that the action was barred by such sections is not insufficient on the ground that it states mere conclusions of law.[105]

On the contest of a will, a special finding that the testator

N. E. 39; Aultman & Co. v. Richardson, 21 Ind. App. 211, 52 N. E. 86; Hodges v. Standard Wheel Co., 152 Ind. 680, 54 N. E. 383.

101 Peirce v. Oliver, 18 Ind. App. 87, 47 N. E. 485; Bechdolt v. Railroad Co., 113 Ind. 343, 15 N. E. 686; Board of Com'rs of Huntington Co. v. Bonebrake, 146 Ind. 311, 45 N. E. 470; New York, C. & St. L. Ry. Co. v. Grossman, 17 Ind. App. 652, 46 N. E. 546.

102 Cleveland, C., C. & St. L. Ry. Co. v. Hadley, 12 Ind. App. 516, 40 N. E. 760. See, also, Toledo & W. Ry. Co. v. Goddard, 25 Ind. 185; City of Elwood v. Carpenter, 12 Ind. App. 459, 40 N. E. 548; Gaston v. Bailey, 14 Ind. App. 581, 43 N. E. 254.

A finding that deceased exercised ordinary care is the statement of a conclusion. Wabash R. Co. v. Keister (Ind. Sup.) 67 N. E. 521; Avery v. Nordyke & Marmon Co. (Ind. App.) 70 N. E. 888.

As to findings on the question of negligence, see, particularly, post, chapter 12.

103 Keller v. Boatman, 49 Ind. 104.

104 Board of Com'rs Hamilton County v. Newlin, 132 Ind. 27, 31 N. E. 465; Fishbaugh v. Spunaugle, 118 Iowa, 337, 92 N. W. 58. See, also, Silsby v. Frost, 3 Wash. T. 388, 17 Pac. 887.

105 Luco v. Toro (Cal.) 18 Pac. 866; Id., 88 Cal. 26, 25 Pac. 983, 11 L. R. A. 543.

was not of sound mind is a finding of an ultimate fact, and not a mere conclusion of law.[106]

A finding that a note was paid before action brought was not a finding of a conclusion of law, since payment is a question of fact.[107]

**Responsiveness.** Findings must respond to the issues submitted. A special finding which clearly shows that the jury must have based their verdict on a theory of the case radically different from that contended for by the prevailing party, and not involved in the issues submitted for their determination, will authorize a reversal of the judgment.[108]

**Findings Contrary to Evidence, or Where Evidence Lacking.** When special findings on material questions are contrary to the evidence, the general verdict based thereon should be set aside [109] and a new trial granted on motion assigning such improper findings as a basis.[110] But to justify the court in thus setting aside the general verdict, the fact or facts found by the jury contrary to, or without warrant by, the evidence, must be indispensable to the support of the general verdict.[111] Though a special finding is not warranted by the testimony, the judgment will not be disturbed if the general verdict is sustained by the evidence.[112]

—— **Striking Out Part of Findings.** A new trial will be granted for want of evidence to support special findings only

[106] Clements v. McGinn (Cal.) 33 Pac. 920.

[107] Wipperman v. Hardy, 17 Ind. App. 142, 46 N. E. 537.

[108] Aultman & Taylor Mach. Co. v. Wier, 67 Kan. 674, 74 Pac. 227.

[109] Chicago, K. & N. Ry. Co. v. Muncie, 56 Kan. 210, 42 Pac. 710; St. Louis Bridge Co. v. Fellows, 31 Ill. App. 282.

[110] Avery v. Moore, 133 Ill. 74, 24 N. E. 606. See Dixon v. Bausman, 17 Wash. 304, 49 Pac. 540, in which it was held that defendant, who had submitted interrogatories, could not complain that there was no testimony to support the answers. Post, chapter 9.

[111] New York, C. & St. L. R. Co. v. Baltz, 141 Ind. 661, 36 N. E. 414, 38 N. E. 402.

[112] Phœnix v. Lamb, 29 Iowa, 352.

when it would be granted for insufficiency of the evidence to support the general verdict,[113] and motion for a new trial is the only way in which advantage can be taken of the failure of the jury to find according to the evidence. It is not proper to move to strike out the findings, without asking to have a new trial, either of the whole issue or of the particular question of fact.[114] "Possibly, if a special finding were incumbered with facts outside of the issues, or mere statements of evidence, or other extraneous matter which could have no proper place in a finding of facts, a motion to strike out might be entertained with propriety. But even then the refusal of the court to strike out parts of the special findings would hardly be ground for reversal." [115] But to strike out a finding on matter properly in the case, leaving the general verdict and other special findings to stand, might require a judgment different from that which would be required if the objectionable finding were retained, and the effect would be that of trial by the court without a jury.[116]

**Setting Aside Findings.** Special findings are seldom set aside independently of the general verdict. If inconsistent with the general verdict, they control it, and judgment should be rendered upon them unless the verdict is set aside as not sustained by the evidence. In the latter case it is necessary merely to move "to set aside the verdict and grant a new trial." Nothing need be said in the motion about the answers returned by the jury. When the verdict is set aside and a new trial granted, everything appertaining to the verdict falls, and the case stands for trial as though no trial had ever been had.[117]

113 Indianapolis & St. L. R. Co. v. Stout, 53 Ind. 143.

114 Jordan v. Railway Co., 42 Minn. 172, 43 N. W. 849, 6 L. R. A. 573.

115 Tarkington v. Purvis, 128 Ind. 188, 25 N. E. 879, 9 L. R. A. 607.

116 Jordan v. Railroad Co., supra; and see Noakes v. Morey, 30 Ind. 103. See, also, Crynes v. City of Independence, 115 Iowa, 448, 88 N. W. 937.

117 McCrum v. Corby, 15 Kan. 112, 117. If the general verdict is

There is no error in setting aside findings not in conflict with the general verdict, and therefore not controlling,[118] for the general verdict remains, and judgment must be rendered on it; but for that reason it can rarely be of advantage to the party against whom the general verdict is returned to have the findings set aside, though it may occasionally profit him to have this done. Thus, in Geraghty v. Randall,[119] the court set aside a special finding of fraud on the part of defendant, which was not in conflict with the general verdict for plaintiff, because a statute provided that upon a finding of malice, fraud, or willful deceit plaintiff might have execution against the body of the defendant upon the judgment, and the court thought that while fraud was proved yet it was not of the intentional and premeditated character contemplated by the statute.

Findings cannot be set aside upon the motion for judgment, for here they are to be taken as verities. The question of the sufficiency of the evidence to support them can be raised only by motion for a new trial.[120]

**Correction and Addition—By Jury.** It has been seen that it is proper, when the jury omit to find upon material questions, or return evasive answers, to send them back to supply or properly frame findings;[121] and the court may instruct them to answer fully, even if it requires a re-examination of the whole case and has the effect to change their verdict.[122]

Exception lies to an error in requiring corrections;[123] but overruling a motion to have the jury retire and make fuller an-

not set aside, the motion as to the findings will be overruled. Ohio & M. Ry. Co. v. Selby, 47 Ind. 471, 17 Am. Rep. 719.

118 See Arndt v. Hosford, 82 Iowa, 499, 48 N. W. 981; Geraghty v. Randall, 18 Colo. App. 194, 70 Pac. 767. As to power of court where there is no statutory provision as to control, see Monies v. City of Lynn, 119 Mass. 273.

119 18 Colo. App. 194, 70 Pac. 767.

120 See chapter 8.

121 Ante, pp. 104–108.

122 Hyatt v. Clements, 65 Ind. 12; Rush v. Pedigo, 63 Ind. 479.

123 Chittenden v. Evans, 48 Ill. 52.

swer is not a good assignment of error. It is properly cause for a new trial.[124]

When the jury are sent back to complete their general verdict, they may change the answer to an interrogatory previously brought in, since they are entitled to change their verdict or special findings at any time before they are received.[125]

It was held in Southern Kansas Ry. Co. v. Gorsuch,[126] where the jury, after answering certain special interrogatories and being sent back to answer other questions upon which they had omitted to find, or to return more specific answers, brought in answers contradictory to the former ones, and by their verdict showed want either of intelligence or fairness, that the verdict should have been set aside and a new trial granted. It admits of no doubt, however, that until the general verdict has been received the jury has the whole case before it. The practice is to object to the reception of the general verdict on the ground that the jury have not properly responded to the interrogatories, and to request the court to send the jury back to amend its answers and supply omissions. It seems that the power of the jury over both verdict and findings must be as great upon reconsideration as it was when they were first sent out, and that it is not to be considered that the general verdict and the explicit answers are accepted, while the jury takes back with it for further consideration and action simply the unanswered or defectively answered questions. "A verdict is a declaration of the truth as to the matters of fact submitted to the jury. However many questions it may have determined, yet it should be returned as a whole unit. From its very nature, separate parts of it should not be determined and returned at different times and in separate fractions." [127]

After discharge it is too late to send the jury back to make further answer or to change its findings.[128] In this respect a

[124] Knight v. Knight, 6 Ind. App. 268, 33 N. E. 456.

[125] Saterlee v. Saterlee, 28 Colo. 290, 64 Pac. 189.

[126] 47 Kan. 583, 28 Pac. 703.

[127] Ryan v. Insurance Co., 77 Wis. 611, 618, 46 N. W. 885.

[128] Columbus, C. & I. C. Ry. Co. v. Powell, 40 Ind. 37; Kansas Pac.

verdict with special findings does not differ from one without. The reason of the rule is twofold: (1) The existence of the particular jury has terminated, and they cannot reassemble. (2) By failure to object to the reception of the verdict before the jury is discharged, the parties have accepted the verdict as it is; they have waived the right to more specific findings.[129]

Sealed verdicts are required to be opened in the presence of the jury in open court, unless the parties stipulate that it shall be otherwise, and in a legal sense the verdict is not returned until this is done. Previous thereto its substance is unknown; it has not been entered upon the minutes, nor has the jury been discharged. Even though the jury have separated after bringing such verdict into court, if they are present when it is opened they may be required on motion to supply answers to questions.[130]

It is probable that after discharge the jury may be recalled to correct their findings (as it is held they may their general verdict) as to a mere matter of form which might have been corrected by the court, but not to alter the substance of their verdict, nor will the affidavits of jurors be received to impeach their verdict by asserting that they meant to answer a special interrogatory in a manner directly opposite to the answer returned, which would be equivalent to permitting them to change their verdict.[131]

—— **By Court.** The court has power to correct an informality in the verdict, and, if instructions properly given are disregarded, may (if the case affords means of so doing without further finding upon a question which ought to be deter-

Ry. Co. v. Pointer, 14 Kan. 37; Mitchell v. Mitchell, 122 N. C. 332, 29 S. E. 367. See, however, Dailey v. Douglass, 40 Mich. 557.

129 Vater v. Lewis, 36 Ind. 288, 10 Am. Rep. 29; Long v. Duncan, 10 Kan. 294; Kansas Pac. Ry. Co. v. Pointer, supra.

130 Tarbox v. Gotzian, 20 Minn. 139 (Gil. 122); and see Roberts v. Roberts, 91 Iowa, 228, 59 N. W. 25; Olwell v. Railway Co., 92 Wis. 330, 66 N. W. 362.

131 McKinley v. Bank, 118 Ind. 375, 21 N. E. 36. See, also, Spencer v. Spencer (Mont.) 79 Pac. 320.

mined only by the jury) correct the verdict so that it shall substantially conform to the instructions.[132] "In the correction of a general verdict the court cannot take into consideration and determine questions of fact which the jury should pass upon, and which might affect the result. He must take their actual or necessary findings upon the facts. But where, from the record, it appears what the findings were, or must legally have been, they are to be considered with the pleadings and verdict in determining what the judgment upon special questions and answers should be." Thus, in an action for a bill of merchandise, the defendants admitted liability on all but one item, which they claimed the right to return. The jury found specially against the right, but returned a general verdict only for the amount admitted. On motion the court amended the verdict by adding the amount of said item, and its action was held proper.[133] So where, in an action to recover for the conversion of a span of horses and a cutter, the jury find all the issuable facts in favor of plaintiff, but in the general verdict assess the damages only at the interest on the amount claimed, the court may instruct the jury to assess plaintiff's damages, and add the interest, and may direct the form of their verdict.[134]

The verdict may be amended in matter of form, after the discharge of the jury. Where the verdict is, on its face, good in substance, the authority to put it in form rests with the court, and does not depend on the assent of the jury.[135]

In an action properly triable by the court, but in which a jury is impaneled to find upon particular questions submitted, the court may, after the discharge of the jury, make additional findings of essential facts; for the duty to make the findings complete rests upon the court.[136] And in an action where spe-

[132] Abb. Tr. Brief (2 Ed.) 538.

[133] Trevor v. Hawley, 99 Mich. 504, 58 N. W. 466.

[134] Doran v. Ryan, 81 Wis. 63, 51 N. W. 259.

[135] Italian-Swiss Agricultural Colony v. Pease, 194 Ill. 98, 62 N. E. 317.

[136] Schmitt v. Schmitt, 31 Minn. 106, 16 N. W. 543.

cial questions are submitted, and one of the parties asks the court to make additional findings, such party cannot complain, though the subsequent findings of the court set aside a part of the special findings of the jury, where the judgment is based on the findings of the court, and those of the jury approved by the court.[137]

But in an action properly triable before a jury, where the parties waive a jury, but one is nevertheless impaneled by the court, in his discretion, to whom are submitted questions for special findings, the court cannot disregard the findings made by the jury, substitute his own, and render judgment thereon. If the verdict and findings of the jury are not supported by the evidence, or for any other reason should not be permitted to stand, it is the duty of the court to set them aside and award a new trial;[138] and in an action triable to a jury, additional findings of fact made by the court at plaintiff's request cannot operate to control the findings of the jury to defendant's prejudice.[139]

Special findings by the jury cannot be changed or set aside by the court on the ground of mistake on the part of the jurors.[140]

—— **Discussion of Defective Answers before Jury.** It may be error for the court to permit counsel to argue the matter of correcting answers or making fuller return, in the presence of the jury, as, e. g., to suggest that the verdict practically covers the necessary answers, in a case where the jury evidently evaded their duty for fear of undermining their general verdict, and where, being remanded, they returned answers sup-

137 Franks v. Jones, 39 Kan. 236, 17 Pac. 663.

138 Hill v. Ellis, 5 Kan. App. 532, 48 Pac. 204; and see McCanlass v. Flinchum, 98 N. C. 358, 4 S. E. 359.

139 Round Lake Ass'n v. Kellogg, 58 Hun, 605, 11 N. Y. Supp. 859.

140 Kennedy v. Ball & Wood Co., 91 Hun, 197, 36 N. Y. Supp. 325. It is error for the court to change special findings so as to make them agree with the general verdict. Usher v. Hiatt, 18 Kan. 195.

porting the general verdict.[141] It is also error to allow counsel to discuss, in the presence of the jury, the probability of their having misunderstood a special question to which they returned an answer inconsistent with the general verdict, and to recall them after being discharged, and send them back to reconsider the question, after a juror has dissented upon a poll of the jury.[142]

141 Brassel v. Railway Co., 101 Mich. 5, 59 N. W. 426.
142 Zimmerman v. Fibre Co., 113 Mich. 1, 71 N. W. 321.

# CHAPTER VIII.

## JUDGMENT ON FINDINGS NOTWITHSTANDING GENERAL VERDICT.

Motion—General Rules of Construction—Inconsistency Between Findings—Nature of Inconsistency Necessary to Control—Sufficiency of Findings—Judgment Where Damages Not Found or Found Only in Findings—Inconsistency Between Findings and Verdict as to Damages—Effect of Erroneous Instructions.

By reference to the Appendix it will be seen that the statutes authorizing special findings upon particular questions of fact uniformly provide that when the special finding of facts is inconsistent with the general verdict the former controls the latter, and the court may give judgment accordingly. This rule of control also exists elsewhere, apart from statutory requirement.[1]

Hundreds of cases are to be found in the reports in which the rule is mentioned and applied to the facts in hand. Some of the more important are given below,[2] and others are dis-

[1] Richardson v. Weare, 62 N. H. 80. If in the finding of a jury special matter follows or is followed by general matter, the verdict will be judged according to the special matter. Fraschieris v. Henriques, 6 Abb. Prac. N. S. (N. Y.) 251.

[2] *Arkansas.* Arkansas Midland R. Co. v. Cauman, 52 Ark. 517, 13 S. W. 280.

*California.* Leese v. Clark, 20 Cal. 387; McDermott v. Higby, 23 Cal. 489; Blood v. Light, 31 Cal. 115; Vaughn v. Railroad Co., 83 Cal. 18, 23 Pac. 215; Cox v. Delmas, 99 Cal. 104, 33 Pac. 836; Portland Cracker Co. v. Murphy, 130 Cal. 649, 63 Pac. 70.

*Colorado.* Londoner v. People, 15 Colo. 557, 26 Pac. 140; Rio Grande Southern R. Co. v. Deasey, 3 Colo. App. 196, 32 Pac. 725; Pickett v. Handy, 5 Colo. App. 295, 38 Pac. 606.

*Dakota.* Everett v. Buchanan, 2 Dak. 249, 6 N. W. 439.

*Idaho.* Bradbury v. Land Imp. Co., 2 Idaho (Hasb.) 239, 10 Pac. 620.

*Illinois.* Chicago & N. W. R. Co. v. Dunleavy, 129 Ill. 132, 22 N. E. 15; Lake Shore & M. S. Ry. Co. v. Johnsen, 135 Ill. 641, 26 N. E. 510;

tributed in appropriate connections throughout the chapter; while a few, which afford no new light, but are mere reiterations of established principles, have been omitted.

Barnes v. Rembarz, 150 Ill. 192, 37 N. E. 239; Chicago & N. W. Ry. Co. v. Johnson, 27 Ill. App. 351; Treffert v. Railroad Co., 36 Ill. App. 93; Egmann v. Railway Co., 65 Ill. App. 345; Toledo, St. L. & W. R. Co. v. Valodin, 109 Ill. App. 132.

*Indiana.* Fromm v. Leonard, 21 Ind. 243; Manning v. Gasharie, 27 Ind. 399; Campbell v. Dutch, 36 Ind. 504; Wisler v. Holderman, 40 Ind. 106; Skillen v. Jones, 44 Ind. 137; Shanks v. Albert, 47 Ind. 461; Murray v. Phillips, 59 Ind. 56; Monroe v. Adams Exp. Co., 65 Ind. 60; Cook v. Howe, 77 Ind. 442; Hill v. Perry, 82 Ind. 28; Growcock v. Hall, Id. 202; Northwestern Mut. Fire Ins. Co. v. Blankenship, 94 Ind. 535, 48 Am. Rep. 185; Croy v. Railroad Co., 97 Ind. 126; Frank v. Grimes, 105 Ind. 346, 4 N. E. 414; Rice v. City of Evansville, 108 Ind. 7, 9 N. E. 139, 58 Am. Rep. 22; Bechdolt v. Railroad Co., 113 Ind. 343, 15 N. E. 686; Indianapolis & V. R. Co. v. Lewis, 119 Ind. 218, 21 N. E. 660; Cadwallader v. Railroad Co., 128 Ind. 518, 27 N. E. 161; Ft. Wayne Traction Co. v. Hardendorf (Ind. Sup.) 72 N. E. 593; Stewart v. Patrick, 5 Ind. App. 50, 30 N. E. 814; Wilson v. Evers, 15 Ind. App. 46, 43 N. E. 572; Moody v. Standard Wheel Co., 20 Ind. App. 422, 50 N. E. 890; Lawrence v. Leathers, 31 Ind. App. 414, 68 N. E. 179; Roots Co. v. Meeker (Ind. Sup.) 73 N. E. 253.

*Iowa.* Hardin v. Branner, 25 Iowa, 364; Aldrich v. Price, 57 Iowa, 151, 9 N. W. 376; Kemper v. City of Burlington, 81 Iowa, 354, 47 N. W. 72; Capital City Bank v. Wakefield, 83 Iowa, 46, 48 N. W. 1059; Martin v. Widner, 91 Iowa, 459, 59 N. W. 345; Schulte v. Railway Co., 114 Iowa, 89, 86 N. W. 63; Saar v. Railway Co., 119 Iowa, 60, 93 N. W. 66.

*Kansas.* Nichols v. Weaver, 7 Kan. 373; Kansas Pac. R. Co. v. Reynolds, 8 Kan. 623; Tobie v. Commissioners, 20 Kan. 14; Partonier v. Pretz, 24 Kan. 238; Gripton v. Thompson, 32 Kan. 367, 4 Pac. 698; Clark v. Railroad Co., 35 Kan. 350, 11 Pac. 134; Leavenworth, N. & S. Ry. Co. v. Wilkins, 45 Kan. 674, 26 Pac. 16; School Dist. v. Lund, 51 Kan. 731, 33 Pac. 595; City of Kansas City v. Brady, 52 Kan. 297, 34 Pac. 884, 39 Am. St. Rep. 349; Missouri, K. & T. R. Co. v. Bussey, 66 Kan. 735, 71 Pac. 261; Heyman v. Simmons, 4 Kan. App. 1, 45 Pac. 728; Missouri Pac. R. Co. v. Wren, 10 Kan. App. 408, 62 Pac. 7; National Brass Mfg. Co. v. Rawlings (Kan.) 80 Pac. 628.

*Kentucky.* Louisville & N. R. Co. v. Brice, 84 Ky. 298, 1 S. W. 483.

*Michigan.* Swift v. Plessner, 39 Mich. 178; Cole v. Boyd, 47 Mich.

Motion. The party in whose favor the general verdict is rendered is entitled to judgment thereon as a matter of course, without motion. If, therefore, the opposing party wishes to urge his right to judgment, he must move for judgment on the

98, 10 N. W. 124; International Wrecking & Transp. Co. v. McMorran, 73 Mich. 467, 41 N. W. 510; Cortland Mfg. Co. v. Platt, 83 Mich. 419, 47 N. W. 330.

*Minnesota.* Twist v. Railroad Co., 39 Minn. 164, 39 N. W. 402, 12 Am. St. Rep. 626; Vogt v. Honstain, 85 Minn. 160, 88 N. W. 443; Roe v. Winston, 86 Minn. 80, 90 N. W. 122.

*Missouri.* Benton v. Railroad Co., 25 Mo. App. 155; Rand v. Grubbs, 26 Mo. App. 591.

*Montana.* Febes v. Tiernan, 1 Mont. 179; Woolman v. Garringer, 2 Mont. 407; Neimick v. Am. Ins. Co., 16 Mont. 318, 40 Pac. 597.

*Nebraska.* Ogg v. Shehan, 17 Neb. 323, 22 N. W. 556; Williams v. Eikenberry, 22 Neb. 210, 34 N. W. 373; Culbertson Irrigating & Water Power Co. v. Olander, 51 Neb. 539, 71 N. W. 298; Norfolk Beet-Sugar Co. v. Preuner, 55 Neb. 656, 75 N. W. 1097.

*New York.* Moss v. Priest, 1 Rob. 632, 19 Abb. Prac. 314; Dempsey v. New York, 10 Daly, 417.

*Ohio.* Harsh v. Klepper, 28 Ohio St. 200; City of Troy v. Brady, 67 Ohio St. 65, 65 N. E. 616; Clark v. Bradshaw, 2 Ohio Cir. Ct. R. 56, 1 O. C. D. 359.

*Oklahoma.* Severy v. Railway Co., 6 Okl. 163, 50 Pac. 162.

*Oregon.* Rolfes v. Russell, 5 Or. 400; Loewenberg v. Rosenthal, 18 Or. 178, 22 Pac. 601.

*South Dakota.* Cronk v. Railroad Co., 3 S. D. 93, 52 N. W. 420.

*Utah.* Warner v. Association, 8 Utah, 431, 32 Pac. 696.

*Washington.* Willey v. Morrow, 1 Wash. T. 474; Stewart v. Publishing Co., 1 Wash. St. 521, 20 Pac. 605; Pepperall v. Transit Co., 15 Wash. 176, 45 Pac. 407; Ottison v. Edmonds, 15 Wash. 362, 46 Pac. 398; Hobert v. City of Seattle, 32 Wash. 330, 73 Pac. 383.

*West Virginia.* Peninsular Land Transp. & Mfg. Co. v. Insurance Co., 35 W. Va. 666, 14 S. E. 237; Andrews v. Mundy, 36 W. Va. 22, 14 S. E. 414.

*Wisconsin.* Lemke v. Railway Co., 39 Wis. 449; Davis v. Town of Farmington, 42 Wis. 425; Ryan v. Insurance Co., 46 Wis. 671, 1 N. W. 426; Kelley v. Railroad Co., 53 Wis. 74, 9 N. W. 816.

**Setting General Verdict Aside.** The court may not set a general verdict for defendant aside, and give judgment for plaintiff, on the ground of inconsistency between the verdict and the special findings. The general verdict must stand, and the plaintiff can have judgment

special findings [3] on the ground that they are inconsistent with the general verdict.[4] This he may do either orally or in writing.[5]

The motion is not a waiver of the right to complain in other particulars.[6] The right to move for a new trial is not lost if the motion is overruled;[7] nor does moving for a new trial preclude this motion.[8] The two may even be filed simultaneously, though proper practice requires the motion for judgment to be first filed, and, if refused, then the motion for a new trial.[9]

in his favor only if entitled thereto upon the facts found in answers to the questions. U. S. Trust Co. v. Harris, 2 Bosw. (N. Y.) 75, 87. See, also, Dempsey v. New York, 10 Daly (N. Y.) 417.

Verdict for plaintiff set aside and judgment rendered for defendant on the findings. Blevins v. Railroad Co., 3 Okl. 512, 41 Pac. 92; Jordan v. Railroad Co., 42 Minn. 172, 43 N. W. 849, 6 L. R. A. 573.

3 Leese v. Clark, 20 Cal. 387; Drake v. Mining Co., 32 Colo. 259, 75 Pac. 913; Truitt v. Truitt, 37 Ind. 514; Tritlipo v. Lacy, 55 Ind. 287; Bartlett v. Railway Co., 94 Ind. 281; Newell v. Houlton, 22 Minn. 19; Carter v. Lumber Co., 6 Okl. 11, 41 Pac. 356. But see Egmann v. Railway Co., 65 Ill. App. 345.

4 Farley v. Eller, 40 Ind. 319.

5 Salander v. Lockwood, 66 Ind. 285; Atchison, T. & S. F. Ry. Co. v. Holland, 58 Kan. 317, 49 Pac. 71.

6 Cullison v. Lindsay, 108 Iowa, 124, 78 N. W. 847, and cases cited.

7 Brannon v. May, 42 Ind. 92; Murray v. Phillips, 59 Ind. 56; Nichols v. State, 65 Ind. 512. The mere fact that a motion for judgment on the findings is designated in the judgment as a motion for a new trial does not authorize the conclusion that it was treated as a motion for a new trial in the lower court. Hooker v. Chittenden, 106 Iowa, 321, 76 N. W. 706.

8 Leslie v. Merrick, 99 Ind. 180.

9 Davis v. Turner, 69 Ohio St. 101, 68 N. E. 819. Compare Stein v. Railroad Co., 41 Ill. App. 38.

The presumption is that the motions were ruled upon in their proper order. Diamond Plate Glass Co. v. De Hority, 143 Ind. 381, 40 N. E. 681.

If the motion for judgment is overruled, the motion for new trial may be insisted upon, and, if sustained, that is a waiver of any errors in overruling the motion for judgment; but if both motions are

The motion for judgment on the special findings must be made before judgment is entered on the general verdict. Otherwise it comes too late. But motion for a new trial might be proper even after entry of judgment on the general verdict, and if granted would vacate the judgment.[10]

As to form, the motion must cover all, and not merely a part, of the findings,[11] and it is improper to ask judgment both "on the general verdict and on the special findings." [12] But where justice requires, and neither court nor counsel can be misled by its irregular form, the motion may be sustained. Thus, in a case where the general verdict was for plaintiff, but the answers to interrogatories were clearly inconsistent therewith and sustained the answer, the defendant moved for judgment "upon the interrogatories notwithstanding the general verdict," and it was held on appeal that the objection that the motion should have been for judgment on the answers to the interrogatories was too technical.[13]

In a case where the special findings were inconsistent with the general verdict for plaintiff, the defendant moved in arrest of judgment that the findings entitled him to judgment, and the court granted the motion. On appeal it was objected that the motion in arrest of judgment in civil cases is abrogated by the Code. It was held, however, that by arresting judgment the court merely refused to give judgment for the plaintiff on the general verdict in his favor, and there stopped. "If the court took the correct view of the special finding of facts, the defendant asked for and obtained only a portion of the relief

overruled, the moving party has a right to be heard on both on appeal. Picart v. Railroad Co., 82 Iowa, 148, 47 N. W. 1017.

Motions for a new trial and for judgment on the special findings are inconsistent, but the latter will be considered an alternative motion. Owens v. Railroad Co. (U. S. Cir. Ct., Ohio) 35 Fed. 715, 1 L. R. A. 75.

10 Citizens' St. R. Co. v. Reed, 28 Ind. App. 629, 63 N. E. 770.

11 Byram v. Galbraith, 75 Ind. 134.

12 Northwestern Mut. Fire Ins. Co. v. Blankenship, 94 Ind. 535, 538, 48 Am. Rep. 185, citing Mitchell v. Geisendorf, 44 Ind. 358.

13 Shanks v. Albert, 47 Ind. 461.

to which it was entitled, and was entitled to all that it obtained. Hence, conceding, for the purposes of the case, what counsel for plaintiff claim, that under the Code it is irregular to arrest judgment in a civil action, * * * it is apparent that the plaintiff was not injured by the practice adopted * * * if the court determined correctly the effect of the special finding." [14]

—— **Appeal.** The ruling on the motion for judgment upon the answers notwithstanding the general verdict may be determined by inspection of the record without bill of exceptions, as in the case of demurrer to a pleading.[15] All that is necessary to present the question on appeal is that the record show the ground of the application and an exception noted to the ruling.[16] No motion for a new trial is necessary, for the error, if any there be, is apparent "on the face of the judgment." [17] But if a party moves for a new trial and obtains it he cannot complain on appeal of error in overruling his motion for judgment on the findings. By procuring the new trial he waives the error.[18]

**Construction.** Special findings should, if possible, be so construed as to harmonize them with each other and with the general verdict.[19] With this object it is the duty of the court

[14] Lemke v. Railroad Co., 39 Wis. 449, 453, 454. See, also, Hooker v. Chittenden, 106 Iowa, 321, 76 N. W. 706.

[15] Cargar v. Fee, 140 Ind. 572, 39 N. E. 93, and cases cited; Schaffner v. Kober, 2 Ind. App. 409, 28 N. E. 871; Conners v. Railroad Co., 71 Iowa, 490, 32 N. W. 465, 60 Am. Rep. 814.

[16] Horn v. Eberhart, 17 Ind. 118; Campbell v. Dutch, 36 Ind. 504; Monroe v. Express Co., 65 Ind. 60; Terre Haute & I. R. Co. v. Clark, 73 Ind. 168; Bartlett v. Railroad Co., 94 Ind. 281.

[17] Phelps & Bigelow Windmill Co. v. Buchanan, 46 Kan. 314, 26 Pac. 708.

[18] Williams v. Frick, 71 Iowa, 362, 32 N. W. 382. See, also, Hollenbeck v. City of Marshalltown, 62 Iowa, 21, 17 N. W. 155; Fitzpatrick v. Papa, 89 Ind. 17; McInnes v. Sutton, 35 Wash. 384, 77 Pac. 736; Pieart v. Railroad Co., 82 Iowa, 148, 47 N. W. 1017.

[19] Chicago Anderson Pressed Brick Co. v. Rembarz, 150 Ill. 192,

to interpret the findings liberally,[20] and where, upon any reasonable inference or fair and sensible view of their terms, they can be reconciled with the general verdict, this course should be adopted and the general verdict upheld.[21] They should be construed in the light of the pleadings and instructions [22] and as a whole.[23] Though there be apparent inconsistency between some of the special findings and the general verdict, yet if, taking the findings as a whole, such inconsistency is not necessarily to be implied, the verdict must stand.[24] A party

37 N. E. 239; Bonham v. Insurance Co., 25 Iowa, 328; St. Louis & S. F. R. Co. v. Ritz, 33 Kan. 404, 6 Pac. 533; Union Pac. Ry. Co. v. Fray, 43 Kan. 750, 23 Pac. 1039; Drinkwater v. Sauble, 46 Kan. 170, 26 Pac. 433; Jackson v. Linnington, 47 Kan. 396, 28 Pac. 173, 27 Am. St. Rep. 300; City of Kansas City v. Slangstrom, 53 Kan. 431, 36 Pac. 706; MacElree v. Wolfersberger, 59 Kan. 105, 52 Pac. 69; Anderson v. Pierce, 62 Kan. 756, 64 Pac. 633; Missouri, K. & T. Ry. Co. v. Bussey, 66 Kan. 735, 71 Pac. 261; Benz v. Geissell, 24 Minn. 169; Ready v. Elevator Co., 89 Minn. 154, 94 N. W. 442; Krumdick v. Railroad Co., 90 Minn. 260, 95 N. W. 1122.

The jury found that the wire broke as plaintiff was passing under it, "without warning." Held that, as the term "warned" would apply rather to plaintiff than to the company, which might rather be said to be "advised" of the danger, the answer would not be construed as negativing notice to the company, and therefore would not overthrow the general verdict. Citizens' St. R. Co. v. Batley, 159 Ind. 368, 65 N. E. 2.

20 Bevens v. Smith, 42 Kan. 250, 21 Pac. 1064.

21 Krumdick v. Railroad Co., 90 Minn. 260, 95 N. W. 1122.

22 Cullison v. Lindsay, 108 Iowa, 124, 78 N. W. 847; Goltz v. Railroad Co., 22 Minn. 55. The findings must be considered together in the light of the pleadings. Fishbaugh v. Spunaugle, 118 Iowa, 337, 92 N. W. 58.

23 Alhambra Addition Water Co. v. Richardson, 72 Cal. 598, 14 Pac. 379; Byram v. Galbraith, 75 Ind. 134; Growcock v. Hall, 82 Ind. 202; Baltimore & O. & C. R. Co. v. Rowan, 104 Ind. 88, 3 N. E. 627; Rice v. Manford, 110 Ind. 596, 11 N. E. 283; Schaffner v. Kober, 2 Ind. App. 409, 28 N. E. 871; Seekel v. Norman, 78 Iowa, 254, 43 N. W. 190; City of Kansas City v. Slangstrom, 53 Kan. 431, 36 Pac. 706; Dupont v. Starring, 42 Mich. 492, 4 N. W. 190.

24 Fishbaugh v. Spunaugle, 118 Iowa, 337, 92 N. W. 58; Bills v.

is not at liberty to select such findings as suit his purpose and reject such as are against him.[25]

Obscurities and apparent inconsistencies are to be given weight in favor of rather than against the general verdict.[26] If the findings are open to double construction, that construction will be adopted which upholds the general verdict.[27] Thus, where an interrogatory improperly contains more than one question, and the answer of the jury may be applied to each question, one of which would be consistent with the general verdict, while the other would not, the answer will be given the construction which sustains the verdict.[28]

The rule to be applied in construing special findings of a jury, as announced by the Supreme Court of *Kansas,* is as follows: (1) It is the duty of the court to harmonize the same with one another and the general verdict if possible. (2) If found to be inconsistent with each other, or consistent with each other and inconsistent with the general finding, but not destructive of plaintiff's right of recovery, the court should order a new trial. (3) If consistent with one another, and both inconsistent with the general finding and destructive of plaintiff's right of recovery, judgment should be entered thereon for defendant.[29]

City of Ottumwa, 35 Iowa, 110; Davis v. Reamer, 105 Ind. 318, 4 N. E. 857; Chambers v. Butcher, 82 Ind. 508.

[25] Shuck v. State, 136 Ind. 63, 35 N. E. 993, and cases cited; Ohio & M. Ry. Co. v. Heaton, 137 Ind. 1, 35 N. E. 687.

[26] Jones v. Austin, 26 Ind. App. 399, 59 N. E. 1082; Kerr v. Goetz, 88 Ill. App. 41; Stevens v. Matthewson, 45 Kan. 594, 26 Pac. 38.

[27] Warner v. Association, 8 Utah, 431, 32 Pac. 696; Larkin v. Upton, 144 U. S. 19, 12 Sup. Ct. 614, 36 L. Ed. 330; McCorkle v. Mallory, 30 Wash. 632, 71 Pac. 186.

[28] Indiana Bituminous Coal Co. v. Buffey, 28 Ind. App. 108, 62 N. E. 279.

[29] Anderson v. Pierce, 62 Kan. 756, 64 Pac. 633; Citizens' Nat. Bank v. Larabee, 64 Kan. 158, 67 Pac. 546. See, post, "Inconsistency Between Findings."

—— **Aider by Intendment Not Permitted.** The answers to interrogatories cannot be aided by intendment, as such intendments are all in favor of the general verdict.[30]

A general verdict upon issues and evidence properly submitted is presumed to have decided every fact or deduction therefrom essential to support it, while a special finding must be limited and controlled by its specific terms.[31] The general verdict

[30] Independent Dryer Co. v. Machine Co., 60 Ill. App. 390; Rice v. Manford, 110 Ind. 596, 11 N. E. 283; Cincinnati, H. & I. R. Co. v. Clifford, 113 Ind. 460, 15 N. E. 524; City of Greenfield v. State, 113 Ind. 597, 15 N. E. 241; Town of Poseyville v. Lewis, 126 Ind. 80, 25 N. E. 593; Consolidated Stone Co. v. Summit, 152 Ind. 297, 53 N. E. 235, and cases cited; Louisville & N. R. Co. v. Kemper, 153 Ind. 618, 53 N. E. 931; Roush v. Roush, 154 Ind. 562, 55 N. E. 1017; Morford v. Railroad Co., 158 Ind. 494, 63 N. E. 857; Johnson v. Gebhauer, 159 Ind. 271, 64 N. E. 855; Wright v. Railroad Co., 160 Ind. 583, 66 N. E. 454; Wabash R. Co. v. Keister (Ind. Sup.) 67 N. E. 521; Indianapolis St. R. Co. v. Johnson (Ind. Sup.) 72 N. E. 571; Chicago, L. & L. R. Co. v. Woodward (Ind. Sup.) 72 N. E. 558; Hoffman v. Toll, 2 Ind. App. 287, 28 N. E. 557; Schaffner v. Kober, 2 Ind. App. 409, 28 N. E. 871; Burke v. Gardner, 11 Ind. App. 475, 39 N. E. 290; City of Huntington v. McClurg, 22 Ind. App. 261, 53 N. E. 658; City of Bluffton v. McAfee, 23 Ind. App. 112, 53 N. E. 1058; American Tin Plate Co. v. Williams, 30 Ind. App. 46, 65 N. E. 304; Mitchell v. Joyce, 76 Iowa, 449, 41 N. W. 161; Johnson v. Miller, 82 Iowa, 693, 47 N. W. 903, 31 Am. St. Rep. 514; Foster v. Gaffield, 34 Mich. 356; Folsom v. Railroad Co., 68 N. H. 178, 44 Atl. 134; Andros v. Childers, 14 Or. 447, 13 Pac. 65; Warner v. Association, 8 Utah, 431, 32 Pac. 696; Peninsular Land Transp. & Mfg. Co. v. Insurance Co., 35 W. Va. 666, 14 S. E. 237.

Nothing will be presumed in favor of the answer of the jury to special interrogatories, and where, in an action against a railroad for negligently causing the death of plaintiff's minor child, employed by defendant against plaintiff's consent, the answers are addressed solely to questions of negligence, and do not touch upon the question of employment of plaintiff's son against his consent, they will not defeat recovery for the value of the son's services. Ft. Wayne, C. & L. R. Co. v. Beyerle, 110 Ind. 100, 11 N. E. 6.

[31] Krumdick v. Railroad Co., 90 Minn. 260, 95 N. W. 1122; Nettersheim v. Railroad Co., 58 Minn. 10, 59 N. W. 632. But though all presumptions must be indulged in support of a general verdict as against

must be understood as establishing the truth of every material averment of the complaint, except in so far as such averments are contradicted or modified by the answers to the interrogatories.[32] Therefore, where interrogatories are confined to one or more of several paragraphs of the complaint, and the answers of the jury are inconsistent with the general verdict for plaintiff as to the issues covered by such paragraphs, but are not inconsistent with the verdict as to the issues included in other paragraphs, defendant is not entitled to judgment.[33] The presumption is that the general verdict covers findings in plaintiff's favor upon all facts necessary to be proved under the issues not covered by the findings.[34] No presumption will be indulged in favor of the answers. If they are to control the case and otherthrow the general verdict, they must be consistent with each other and free from any obscurity. If they are contradictory within themselves or uncertain when taken together, they cannot control. They must destroy the general verdict, if at all, only by their own inherent clearness and strength.[35]

In ruling on the motion for judgment on the special findings non obstante veredicto, "the court ought not to assume

the answers to interrogatories, the party in whose favor the general verdict is rendered can invoke no fact in his favor under such presumptions that he would not have been allowed to prove. Lake Shore & M. S. R. Co. v. Graham, 162 Ind. 374, 70 N. E. 484.

32 Indianapolis St. R. Co. v. Hockett, 161 Ind. 196, 67 N. E. 106; Ohio & M. Ry. Co. v. Trowbridge, 126 Ind. 391, 26 N. E. 64; Chicago & E. I. R. Co. v. Hedges, 105 Ind. 398, 7 N. E. 801; U. S. Trust Co. v. Harris, 2 Bosw. (N. Y.) 75, 87. See, also, Johnson v. Miller, 82 Iowa, 693, 47 N. W. 903, 48 N. W. 1081, 31 Am. St. Rep. 514, and cases cited.

33 Toledo, W. & W. R. Co. v. Milligan, 52 Ind. 505; Frazer v. Boss, 66 Ind. 1; Tucker v. Roach, 139 Ind. 275, 38 N. E. 822.

34 To ascertain the issues, if any, settled by the general verdict, other than those specially decided in answer to special interrogatories, the pleadings are necessarily examined. Schulte v. Railroad Co., 114 Iowa, 89, 86 N. W. 63.

35 Citizens' St. R. Co. v. Hoop, 22 Ind. App. 78, 53 N. E. 244.

an attitude of unreason, * * * because that would be to abridge the operation of the interrogatory statute. To the end, however, that, unless clearly entitled to it, a party may not obtain a judgment to whom the jury evidently did not intend that a judgment should be awarded, and because of the presumption against the jury having been inconsistent in its findings, it is required that every reasonable intendment shall be indulged in favor of the general verdict, and that, on the other hand, the court shall strictly and without favorable intendment construe the answers to the interrogatories against the moving party." [36]

**What may be Considered.** In determining whether the special findings are inconsistent with the general verdict, so that the latter must be held to be controlled by the former, the court is not permitted to regard the evidence introduced on the trial.[37] Ordinarily resort can be had only to the findings and verdict and to the pleadings.[38] The question to be decided is not whether, in the light of the evidence adduced, the general verdict is inconsistent with the facts found, the remedy in case of

[36] McCoy v. Railroad Co., 158 Ind. 662, 64 N. E. 92.

[37] Chicago & N. W. R. Co. v. Dunleavy, 129 Ill. 132, 22 N. E. 15; Schulte v. Railroad Co., 114 Iowa, 89, 86 N. W. 63; Higgins v. Kendall, 73 Ind. 522; Stevens v. City of Logansport, 76 Ind. 498; Shaffer v. Ryan, 84 Ind. 140; Pennsylvania Co. v. Smith, 98 Ind. 42; Cox v. Ratcliffe, 105 Ind. 374, 5 N. E. 5; Shoner v. Pennsylvania Co., 130 Ind. 170, 28 N. E. 616, 29 N. E. 775; British-American Assur. Co. v. Wilson, 132 Ind. 278, 31 N. E. 938; McCoy v. Railroad Co., 158 Ind. 662, 64 N. E. 92; City of Evansville v. Thacker, 2 Ind. App. 373, 28 N. E. 559; Schaffner v. Kober, 2 Ind. App. 409, 28 N. E. 871; City of Ft. Wayne v. Patterson, 3 Ind. App. 36, 29 N. E. 167; City of Huntington v. Burke, 21 Ind. App. 655, 52 N. E. 415; Chicago & E. R. Co. v. Lee, 29 Ind. App. 480, 64 N. E. 675; Schulte v. Railroad Co., 114 Iowa, 89, 86 N. W. 63. But see Newman v. Railroad Co., 80 Iowa, 678, 45 N. W. 1054; Wilson v. Onstott, 121 Iowa, 263, 96 N. W. 779.

[38] Higgins v. Kendall, supra; City of Indianapolis v. Kollman, 79 Ind. 504; Louthain v. Miller, 85 Ind. 161; Consolidated Stone Co. v. Summit, 152 Ind. 297, 53 N. E. 235; Indiana R. Co. v. Maurer, 160 Ind. 25, 66 N. E. 156; Hazard Powder Co. v. Viergutz, 6 Kan. 471.

such inconsistency being a new trial,[39] but whether, accepting the facts found, within the issues, as verities,[40] there is irreconcilable conflict between them and the general verdict.

In *Iowa* it has been said to be proper to consider admissions of the parties, whether made by the pleadings or by other means;[41] but, except as to the pleadings, this rule has since been disapproved.[42] Certainly, to be considered admitted facts must be set forth on the record. Courts cannot act upon supposed or actual understandings or admissions made in the presence of the jury, but not settled by being declared on the record,[43] and must regard the facts stated, and not items of evidence improperly thrust into the findings,[44] whether documentary or otherwise,[45] and even though uncontroverted.[46]

**Inconsistency Between Findings.** When special findings are inconsistent with each other, the general verdict cannot be controlled by them.[47] According to one view, they merely

[39] Stevens v. City of Logansport, 76 Ind. 498.

[40] Porter v. Waltz, 108 Ind. 40, 8 N. E. 705; citing, Cox v. Ratcliffe, 105 Ind. 374, 5 N. E. 5; Pennsylvania Co. v. Smith, 98 Ind. 42; Baltimore & O. & C. R. Co. v. Rowan, 104 Ind. 88, 3 N. E. 627; Wilson v. Evers, 15 Ind. App. 46, 43 N. E. 572.

[41] Coffman v. Railroad Co., 90 Iowa, 462, 57 N. W. 955; Martin v. Widner, 91 Iowa, 459, 59 N. W. 345.

[42] Kerr v. Waterworks Co., 95 Iowa, 513, 64 N. W. 596.

[43] See Durfee v. Abbott, 50 Mich. 479, 15 N. W. 559.

[44] Kirkpatrick v. Reeves, 121 Ind. 280, 22 N. E. 139.

[45] Cox v. Ratcliffe, 105 Ind. 374, 5 N. E. 5; Pennsylvania Co. v. Smith, 98 Ind. 42; Shuck v. State, 136 Ind. 63, 35 N. E. 993.

[46] Shuck v. State, supra.

[47] Smith v. Heller, 119 Ind. 212, 21 N. E. 657; Kirkpatrick v. Reeves, 121 Ind. 280, 22 N. E. 139; Gates v. Scott, 123 Ind. 459, 24 N. E. 257; Heltonville Mfg. Co. v. Fields, 138 Ind. 58, 36 N. E. 529; Board Com'rs of Parke Co. v. Wagner, 138 Ind. 609, 38 N. E. 171; McCoy v. Ry. & Light Co., 158 Ind. 662, 64 N. E. 92; Indianapolis Abattoir Co. v. Temperly, 159 Ind. 651, 64 N. E. 906, 95 Am. St. Rep. 330; Phillips v. Michaels, 11 Ind. App. 672, 39 N. E. 669; Fireman's Fund Ins. Co. v. Dunn, 22 Ind. App. 332, 53 N. E. 251; Chicago & E. R. Co. v. Kreig, 22 Ind. App. 393, 53 N. E. 1033; Sloan v. Lowder, 23 Ind. App. 118, 54 N. E. 135; Indiana Natural Gas Co. v. McMath, 26

neutralize each other and do not impair the general verdict,[48] and judgment should be rendered thereon.

But in *Idaho,*[49] *Kansas,*[50] *Oklahoma,*[51] and perhaps in *Rhode*

Ind. App. 154, 57 N. E. 593; American Car & Foundry Co. v. Clark, 32 Ind. App. 644, 70 N. E. 828; Bills v. Ottumwa, 35 Iowa, 107; Fishbaugh v. Spunaugle, 118 Iowa, 337, 92 N. W. 58.

48 Chambers v. Butcher, 82 Ind. 50; Keesling v. Ryan, 84 Ind. 89; Grand Rapids & I. R. Co. v. McAnnally, 98 Ind. 412; Davis v. Reamer, 105 Ind. 318, 4 N. E. 857; Redelsheimer v. Miller, 107 Ind. 485, 8 N. E. 447; Rice v. Manford, 110 Ind. 596, 11 N. E. 283; Chicago & E. I. R. Co. v. Ostrander, 116 Ind. 259, 15 N. E. 227, 19 N. E. 110; Gates v. Scott, 123 Ind. 459, 24 N. E. 257; Dickey v. Shirk, 128 Ind. 278, 27 N. E. 733; City of Huntington v. McClurg, 22 Ind. App. 261, 53 N. E. 658; Wabash R. Co. v. Biddle, 27 Ind. App. 161, 59 N. E. 284; Chicago & E. R. Co. v. Lee, 29 Ind. App. 480, 64 N. E. 675; Foster v. Gaffield, 34 Mich. 356. See, also, Drake v. Justice Gold Min. Co., 32 Colo. 259, 75 Pac. 913.

In an action against a railroad company for injuries to a brakeman caused by a defective brake, a special finding that the defect could have been readily discovered by plaintiff, and another that it was not shown whether the defect could have been discovered had an examination been made, negative each other so as to leave a general verdict for plaintiff decisive that he was not guilty of contributory negligence. Matchett v. Railroad Co., 132 Ind. 334, 31 N. E. 792.

Where the first paragraph of a complaint seeks recovery of $500 as the reasonable value of services, and the second seeks recovery of such sum as the amount specially agreed to be paid, and an answer to a special interrogatory is that the amount found due plaintiff ($500) was not by reason of a contract to pay same, but was the reasonable value of the services, and the answer to another interrogatory is that the general verdict is based on the second paragraph of the complaint, the latter answer will be disregarded. Vermillion v. Mustard, 15 Ind. App. 293, 43 N. E. 1012.

49 A new trial will be granted when findings are contradictory, as where one finding declares that decedent was competent to make a will, and another finds that he had an insane delusion and was not of sound and disposing mind. Gwin v. Gwin, 5 Idaho, 271, 48 Pac. 295.

50 Shoemaker v. Railroad Co., 30 Kan. 359, 2 Pac. 517; Aultman, Miller & Co. v. Mickey, 41 Kan. 348, 21 Pac. 254; Parkinson Sugar

51 See footnote 51 on following page.

*Island*,[52] the rule is that where the answers of the jury to special questions are not only inconsistent with the general verdict, but also with each other as to material matters, no judgment can be entered, and a new trial should be granted.

**Absolute Inconsistency Requisite to Control.** The special findings must exclude every theory which will sustain the verdict,[53] and are inconsistent only when, as a matter of law, they

Co. v. Riley, 50 Kan. 401, 31 Pac. 1090, 34 Am. St. Rep. 123; Berry v. Railroad Co., 52 Kan. 759, 34 Pac. 805, 39 Am. St. Rep. 371; Latshaw v. Moore, 53 Kan. 234, 36 Pac. 342; City of Kansas City v. Brady, 53 Kan. 312, 36 Pac. 726; Union Pac. R. Co. v. Sternbergh, 54 Kan. 410, 38 Pac. 486; Atchison, T. & S. F. R. Co. v. Holland, 58 Kan. 317, 49 Pac. 71; St. Louis & S. F. Ry. Co. v. Bricker, 61 Kan. 224, 59 Pac. 268; Atchison, T. & S. F. R. Co. v. Hamlin, 67 Kan. 476, 73 Pac. 58; Chase v. Bank of Horton, 9 Kan. App. 186, 59 Pac. 39. See, also, Atchison & S. F. R. Co. v. Maher, 23 Kan. 163; Same v. Harvey, 31 Kan. 750, 3 Pac. 568; Manhattan, A. & B. R. Co. v. Keeler, 32 Kan. 163, 4 Pac. 143; St. Louis & S. F. Ry. Co. v. Ritz, 33 Kan. 404, 6 Pac. 533; Union Pac. Ry. Co. v. Shannon, 33 Kan. 446, 6 Pac. 564; Atchison, T. & S. F. R. Co. v. Weber, 33 Kan. 543, 6 Pac. 877, 52 Am. Rep. 543; Same v. Wagner, 33 Kan. 660, 7 Pac. 204; Same v. Brown, 33 Kan. 757, 7 Pac. 571; Chicago, I. & K. R. Co. v. Townsdin, 38 Kan. 78, 15 Pac. 889.

[51] Special findings being inconsistent with each other, and some of them with the general verdict, neither party is entitled to judgment upon the verdict or findings, and it is the duty of the court to grant a new trial. Dickerson v. Waldo, 13 Okl. 189, 74 Pac. 505.

In this case the court refers to the rule in *Indiana*, and remarks: "In our opinion the doctrine announced by the Kansas court is the better and safer practice."

[52] See Healey v. Railroad Co., 20 R. I. 136, 37 Atl. 676.

[53] Stein v. Railroad Co., 41 Ill. App. 38; Snyder v. Robinson, 35 Ind. 311, 9 Am. Rep. 738; Indianapolis & St. L. R. Co. v. Stout, 53 Ind. 147; Peninsular Land Transp. & Mfg. Co. v. Insurance Co., 35 W. Va. 666, 14 S. E. 237.

Where there are several paragraphs of the complaint, and the interrogatories do not cover the issues under all of them, the findings are not inconsistent with a general verdict for plaintiff, though they show that plaintiff is not entitled to judgment upon the issues covered. The conclusion is that the verdict was rendered upon the paragraph or paragraphs not covered by the interrogatories and findings. To-

will authorize a judgment different from that which the verdict will permit.[54] To have this effect all the issues upon which the verdict might be sustained must be adversely covered.[55]

ledo, W. & W. Ry. Co. v. Milligan, 52 Ind. 505; Frazer v. Boss, 66 Ind. 1; Tucker v. Roach, 139 Ind. 275, 38 N. E. 822; Cleveland, C., C. & St. L. Ry. Co. v. Berry, 152 Ind. 607, 53 N. E. 415, 46 L. R. A. 33. See, also, Lake Erie & W. Ry. Co. v. Fishback, 5 Ind. App. 403, 32 N. E. 346.

[54] Loewenberg v. Rosenthal, 18 Or. 178, 22 Pac. 601. See, also, Delawter v. Ditching Co., 26 Ind. 407.

They should be sufficient, when strictly construed, to warrant, in view of the issues, a judgment in favor of the moving party. Campbell v. Dutch, 36 Ind. 504; Rice v. City of Evansville, 108 Ind. 7, 9 N. E. 139, 58 Am. Rep. 22; McKinley v. Bank, 118 Ind. 375, 21 N. E. 36; Louisville & N. R. Co. v. Crunk, 119 Ind. 542, 21 N. E. 31, 12 Am. St. Rep. 443; Dickey v. Shirk, 128 Ind. 278, 27 N. E. 733; McCoy v. Railroad Co., 158 Ind. 662, 64 N. E. 92; Gaar, Scott & Co. v. Rose, 3 Ind. App. 269, 29 N. E. 616; Hobert v. City of Seattle, 32 Wash. 330, 73 Pac. 383.

To justify the court in rendering judgment upon a special finding of facts against the general verdict, such findings must be inconsistent with the general verdict, and, when taken together with the facts admitted by the pleadings, must be sufficient to establish or defeat the right to recover. Lamb v. Society, 20 Iowa, 127; Hardin v. Branner, 25 Iowa, 364; Bills v. City of Ottumwa, 35 Iowa, 107; Crouch v. Deremore, 59 Iowa, 45, 12 N. W. 759; Hammer v. Railroad Co., 61 Iowa, 56, 15 N. W. 597; Hawley v. City of Atlantic, 92 Iowa, 174, 60 N. W. 519; Case v. Railroad Co., 100 Iowa, 490, 69 N. W. 538; Kerr v. Waterworks Co., 95 Iowa, 513, 64 N. W. 596; Schulte v. Railroad Co., 114 Iowa, 89, 86 N. W. 63.

[55] McDermott v. Higby, 23 Cal. 490; Gall v. Beckstein, 66 Ill. App. 478; Delawter v. Ditching Co., 26 Ind. 407; Snyder v. Robinson, 35 Ind. 311, 9 Am. Rep. 738; Pea v. Pea, 35 Ind. 387; Campbell v. Dutch, 36 Ind. 504; Kealing v. Voss, 61 Ind. 466; West v. Cavins, 74 Ind. 265; Byram v. Galbraith, 75 Ind. 134; Rice v. City of Evansville, 108 Ind. 7, 9 N. E. 139, 58 Am. Rep. 22; McKinley v. Bank, 118 Ind. 375, 21 N. E. 36; Shuck v. State, 136 Ind. 63, 35 N. E. 993; Cincinnati, R. & M. R. Co. v. Miller (Ind. App.) 72 N. E. 827; Cleveland, C., C. & St. L. Ry. Co. v. Johnson, 7 Ind. App. 441, 33 N. E. 1004; Lake Erie & W. R. Co. v. Graver, 23 Ind. App. 678, 55 N. E. 968; Lamb v. Society, 20 Iowa, 127; Hardin v. Branner, 25 Iowa, 364; Phoenix v. Lamb, 29 Iowa, 352; Schulte v. Railroad Co., 114 Iowa, 89,

Where the special findings do not embrace and cover all of the issues, and are not inconsistent with a general verdict for plaintiff as to issues not covered by them, defendant is not entitled to judgment thereon, though they be inconsistent with the general verdict as to the issues covered.[56]

The findings need not, however, in all cases cover all the issues in the sense of all the issues raised by the pleadings. For instance, a single finding that defendant was not negligent would defeat an action grounded on negligence, and would entitle defendant to judgment, notwithstanding other issues raised

86 N. W. 63; Seeds v. Bridge Co., 68 Kan. 522, 75 Pac. 480; Reed v. Lammel, 40 Minn. 397, 42 N. W. 202.

Where a complaint against a city for personal injuries alleged that defendant had notice that the sidewalk was decayed and unsafe, and also that it was broken and dangerous, and the jury found a general verdict for plaintiff, but found, in answer to a special interrogatory, that there was no evidence that defendant had "actual notice" of the broken condition of the walk, it was not error to refuse to give judgment for defendant on such answer, as it did not touch the question of "constructive notice" nor negative notice of the "decayed, unsafe, and dangerous" condition of the walk. City of Indianapolis v. Tansel, 157 Ind. 463, 62 N. E. 35.

Suit was brought for necessaries and attendance furnished to defendant's minor son in his last sickness, for funeral expenses, etc., which were alleged to have been rendered at defendant's request, etc., with the averment that defendant promised, etc. The verdict was for plaintiff, with special findings that (1) the minor left his home voluntarily; (2) that when he left he was 20 years of age; and (3) that when he left he was in good health and capable of supporting himself. Held, that defendant could not claim judgment on the special findings, because they did not negative the alleged fact that the services were rendered at his request. Horn v. Eberhart, 17 Ind. 118. See post, "Sufficiency of Findings to Support Judgment."

56 Toledo, W. & W. Ry. Co. v. Milligan, 52 Ind. 505.

Where the general verdict is in favor of one party, and the findings on the special issues are in favor of the other, the court should render judgment in accordance with the special findings, if they embrace all the issues raised by the pleadings; if not, then judgment should be rendered on the general verdict. McDermott v. Higby, 23 Cal. 489.

by the pleadings were not passed upon. The one finding would render all other issues immaterial.[57]

The record must show on its face that the findings and verdict are repugnant and that both cannot stand.[58] A mere presumption of inconsistency is insufficient;[59] it must appear affirmatively.[60] The antagonism must be absolute and incapable of being removed by any conceivable evidence legitimately admissible under the issues.[61]

[57] See Ebsery v. Railroad Co., 61 Ill. App. 265; Cleveland, C., C. & St. L. R. Co. v. Johnson, 7 Ind. App. 441, 33 N. E. 1004; Schulte v. Railroad Co., 114 Iowa, 89, 86 N. W. 63; Cronk v. Railroad Co., 3 S. D. 93, 52 N. W. 420.

A special finding that a person killed on the railroad track failed to look and listen for an approaching train shows him guilty of contributory negligence, and controls a general verdict in favor of his administrator, and the railroad company is entitled to judgment notwithstanding the general verdict. Pennsylvania Co. v. Meyers, 136 Ind. 242, 36 N. E. 32; Hill v. Railroad Co., 31 Ind. App. 98, 67 N. E. 276. See, also, Chicago & E. I. Ry. Co. v. Hedges, 118 Ind. 5, 20 N. E. 530; Republic Iron & Steel Co. v. Jones, 32 Ind. App. 189, 69 N. E. 191; Morford v. Railroad Co., 158 Ind. 494, 63 N. E. 857.

[58] Amidon v. Gaff, 24 Ind. 128; Ridgeway v. Dearinger, 42 Ind. 157; McCallister v. Mount, 73 Ind. 559; Cook v. Howe, 77 Ind. 442; Baldwin v. Shuter, 82 Ind. 560; Indianapolis & V. Ry. Co. v. Lewis, 119 Ind. 218, 21 N. E. 660; Graham v. Payne. 122 Ind. 403, 24 N. E. 216; Consolidated Stone Co. v. Summit, 152 Ind. 297, 53 N. E. 235; Evansville & I. R. Co. v. Gilmore, 1 Ind. App. 468, 27 N. E. 992; Schaffner v. Kober, 2 Ind. App. 409, 28 N. E. 871; Block v. Haseltine, 3 Ind. App. 491, 29 N. E. 937; Muncie St. Ry. Co. v. Maynard, 5 Ind. App. 372, 32 N. E. 343; Keeley Brewing Co. v. Parnin, 13 Ind. App. 588, 41 N. E. 471.

[59] Close v. Atkins, 39 Iowa, 521.

[60] Cox v. Ratcliffe, 105 Ind. 374, 5 N. E. 5; Lake Erie & W. R. Co. v. Graver, 23 Ind. App. 678, 55 N. E. 968.

[61] Pahlman v. Taylor, 75 Ill. 629; Smith v. McCarthy, 33 Ill. App. 176; John Matthews Apparatus Co. v. Neal, 71 Ill. App. 363; Kerr v. Goetz, 88 Ill. App. 41; Chicago City R. Co. v. White, 110 Ill. App. 23; Amidon v. Gaff, 24 Ind. 128; Adams v. Cosby, 48 Ind. 153; Higgins v. Kendall, 73 Ind. 522; Stevens v. City of Logansport, 76 Ind. 498; Cook v. Howe, 77 Ind. 442; Louthain v. Miller, 85 Ind. 161; Brown v. Searle, 104 Ind. 218, 3 N. E. 871; Lockwood v. Rose, 125

The reason of the rule last stated is that "the jury is required to pronounce upon all the issuable facts proved in the case, while the court, in testing the force of the isolated facts disclosed by answers to interrogatories, does not know and can-

Ind. 588, 25 N. E. 710; Town of Poseyville v. Lewis, 126 Ind. 80, 25 N. E. 593; Louisville, N. A. & C. Ry. Co. v. Creek, 130 Ind. 139, 29 N. E. 481, 14 L. R. A. 733; Shoner v. Railroad Co., 130 Ind. 170, 28 N. E. 616, 29 N. E. 775; Chicago, St. L. & P. R. Co. v. Spilker, 134 Ind. 380, 33 N. E. 280; Shuck v. State, 136 Ind. 71, 35 N. E. 993; Sievers v. Lumber Co., 151 Ind. 642, 50 N. E. 877; Southern Ind. R. Co. v. Peyton, 157 Ind. 690, 61 N. E. 722; McCoy v. Railroad Co., 158 Ind. 662, 64 N. E. 92; Indiana R. Co. v. Maurer, 160 Ind. 25, 66 N. E. 156; Stoy v. Railroad Co., 160 Ind. 144, 66 N. E. 615; Wright v. Railroad Co., 160 Ind. 583, 66 N. E. 454; Weller v. Bectell, 2 Ind. App. 228, 28 N. E. 333; Hoffman v. Toll, 2 Ind. App. 287, 28 N. E. 557; City of Ft. Wayne v. Patterson, 3 Ind. App. 36, 29 N. E. 167; Gaar, Scott & Co. v. Rose, 3 Ind. App. 269, 29 N. E. 616; Hoggatt v. Railroad Co., 3 Ind. App. 437, 29 N. E. 941; Muncie St. R. Co. v. Maynard, 5 Ind. App. 372, 32 N. E. 343; Jewell v. Town of Sullivan, 5 Ind. App. 188, 31 N. E. 829; Evansville & T. H. R. Co. v. Weikle, 6 Ind. App. 340, 33 N. E. 639; Rittenhause v. Knoop, 9 Ind. App. 126, 36 N. E. 384; Lake Erie & W. R. Co. v. McHenry, 10 Ind. App. 525, 37 N. E. 186; Fitzmaurice v. Puterbaugh, 17 Ind. App. 318, 45 N. E. 524; Sponhaur v. Malloy, 21 Ind. App. 287, 52 N. E. 245; City of Huntington v. McClurg, 22 Ind. App. 261, 53 N. E. 658; Chicago & E. R. Co. v. Kreig, 22 Ind. App. 393, 53 N. E. 1033; Hobbs v. Stone Co., 22 Ind. App. 436, 53 N. E. 1063; Lake Erie & W. R. Co. v. Graver, 23 Ind. App. 678, 55 N. E. 968; Rhodius v. Johnson, 24 Ind. App. 406, 56 N. E. 942; City of Mishawaka v. Kirby, 32 Ind. App. 233, 69 N. E. 481; Smith v. Railroad Co. (Ind. App.) 73 N. E. 928; Farmers' Ins. Ass'n v. Reavis (Ind. Sup.) 70 N. E. 518; Bonham v. Insurance Co., 25 Iowa, 328; Toledo Electric St. Ry. Co. v. Bateman, 16 Ohio Cir. Ct. R. 162, 8 O. C. D. 220.

Plaintiff sued on a promissory note. Answer, non est factum. The jury returned a general verdict for plaintiff, assessing his damages for the full amount of the note, principal and interest. They also returned their answer to an interrogatory, as follows: "Q. Did Herman Brems sign said note? A. No." Defendant moved for judgment in his favor non obstante veredicto, which was denied. On appeal the judgment was sustained. The answer was not in irreconcilable conflict with the general verdict, because to say that defendant did not

not know what other facts touching the same matters were rightfully before the jury to justify their verdict. Therefore, in conceding to the jury the presumption of right judgment, to

"sign" the note was not saying that he did not execute it, e. g., by authorizing another to sign it, which, in fact, was what the testimony showed to be the case. Brems v. Sherman, 158 Ind. 300, 63 N. E. 571.

In an action by a servant to recover for injuries received while crossing a field under the master's direction, a general verdict for the servant is not superseded by a special finding that the servant, by going at an angle, would have avoided the hole into which he fell; that the hole was newly made, and, before going to it, he first had to cross the dirt taken out of the hole; that at the time he was looking at the light in a distant house eight feet higher than the ground; and that there was no public or private way leading to the hole—since, under Horner's Ann. St. 1897, § 546, the servant was not required to submit special interrogatories eliciting all pertinent facts, and under the general issue he might have shown that he did not know of a safe way of crossing the field, or that he was directed by the master to take the route that he did take, or told that it was safe, and that the night was dark, and the hole, which was unknown to him, could not be seen; thereby avoiding an irreconcilable conflict between the general and special verdicts. Indiana Pipe-Line & Refining Co. v. Neusbaum, 21 Ind. App. 361, 52 N. E. 471.

In an action against a railroad company for forcibly ejecting him from its train, the plaintiff alleged that he was ejected because he refused to pay the fare demanded, and that the ejecting was done with unnecessary violence. The jury returned a general verdict for plaintiff, and specially found that plaintiff had no ticket, and that he was put off the train because he refused to pay the regular fare. Held, that the special findings were not inconsistent with the general verdict, since they did not negative the allegation that unnecessary violence was used. Evansville & I. R. Co. v. Gilmore, 1 Ind. App. 468, 27 N. E. 992.

When, in an action on a promissory note brought by a purchaser for value after maturity, facts are alleged in the answer which defendant claims show lack of consideration, and issue is joined thereon, and on the question of the plaintiff's ownership, and the jury bring in as a special finding that at the beginning of the action the plaintiff was and now is the owner and holder of the note, and find generally for the defendant, it will be presumed that they found the allegations as to lack of consideration to be true, and judgment non

overthrow the general verdict the special facts returned must be of such a nature as to exclude the possible existence of other controlling facts, provable under the issues, relating to the

obstante veredicto will not be rendered. Andros v. Childers, 14 Or. 447, 13 Pac. 65.

In an action for injuries at a railroad crossing, a special finding that plaintiff stopped and stood upon the track where he was struck, that before stopping he looked for approaching cars, and that there was nothing to prevent his seeing the cars which struck him, is not inconsistent with a general verdict for plaintiff, where the cars that struck him might have been on a different track from the one on which he stood. Lake Shore & M. S. Ry. Co. v. Johnsen, 135 Ill. 641, 26 N. E. 510.

In an action against a railroad company for personal injuries received by the derailment of the car in which plaintiff was a passenger, the complaint alleged numerous defects in defendant's cars and tracks as the cause of the derailment. By answers to interrogatories the jury negatived all the alleged defects except that, at a place where such car was derailed, the embankment was insufficiently ballasted, the ties were rotten, and the rails imperfectly fastened thereto, whereby the car was thrown from the embankment and turned partially over, as to which there was no special finding. Held, that a general verdict for plaintiff should not be set aside on the ground that it is contrary to the findings, since it will be presumed that the jury based such general verdict on that branch of the case on which no facts were found inconsistent therewith. Cleveland, C., C. & St. L. Ry. Co. v. Johnson, 7 Ind. App. 441, 33 N. E. 1004.

A special finding that plaintiff, in a suit for personal injuries, knew of the defect in the street that caused the injuries six or eight months before the accident, is not inconsistent with a general verdict for plaintiff, as such knowledge is consistent with the exercise of reasonable care on plaintiff's part. City of Evansville v. Thacker, 2 Ind. App. 370, 28 N. E. 559.

Where one count of a declaration charges the defendant with mere negligence, and another count charges it with injuring plaintiff wilfully and recklessly, a special finding that plaintiff did not exercise ordinary care is not inconsistent with a general verdict for plaintiff, since, under the latter count, contributory negligence is no defense. Wabash R. Co. v. Speer, 156 Ill. 244, 40 N. E. 835.

"Authorities need not be cited in support of the proposition that the general verdict determines all material issues in appellee's favor;

same subject."[62] The rule is also said to be "rooted in the theory that the general verdict is the jury's deduction from all the facts proved in the case, and in its support it will be presumed that isolated adverse facts specially found were overcome by other proved facts, if such facts might have been properly proved under the issues."[63]

In a recent *Iowa* case it is doubted whether the rule above mentioned exists in that state as broadly as recognized by the *Indiana* courts.[64]

In defining the nature of the conflict which must exist to enable the findings to control the general verdict, it is also said that it must be irreconcilable;[65] that is, it must be so great that no reasonable hypothesis or inference can remove it.[66]

that all reasonable presumptions will be indulged in favor of the general verdict, and none indulged in favor of the answers to the interrogatories; that if the answers are to control, they must be in irreconcilable conflict with the general verdict; that, if the answers are antagonistic or inconsistent, they neutralize each other and will be disregarded; and that the answers override the general verdict only when both cannot stand, the conflict being such as to be beyond the possibility of being removed by any evidence admissible under the issues." Union Traction Co. v. Vandercook, 32 Ind. App. 621, 69 N. E. 486.

[62] City of South Bend v. Turner, 156 Ind. 418, 60 N. E. 271, 54 L. R. A. 396, 83 Am. St. Rep. 200.

[63] Chicago, I. & L. R. Co. v. Leachman, 161 Ind. 512, 69 N. E. 253.

[64] Fishbaugh v. Spunaugle, 118 Iowa, 337, 92 N. W. 58; and see Newman v. Railroad Co., 80 Iowa, 678, 45 N. W. 1054, in which, in determining whether judgment notwithstanding the general verdict should be rendered, the findings are construed "in the light of the evidence." See, also, Benz v. Geissell, 24 Minn. 169.

[65] Pahlman v. Taylor, 75 Ill. 629; Stein v. Railroad Co., 41 Ill. App. 38; Independent Dryer Co. v. Machine Co., 60 Ill. App. 390; Starrett v. Gault, 62 Ill. App. 209; Gall v. Beckstein, 66 Ill. App. 478; Kerr v. Goetz, 88 Ill. App. 41; Detroit, E. R. & I. R. Co. v. Barton, 61 Ind. 293; Woollen v. Wishmier, 70 Ind. 108; Baldwin v. Shuter, 82 Ind. 560; Grand Rapids & I. R. Co. v. McAnnally, 98 Ind. 412; Stringer v. Frost, 116 Ind. 477, 19 N. E. 331, 2 L. R. A. 614, 9 Am. St. Rep. 875; Graham v. Payne, 122 Ind.

[66] See footnote 66 on following page.

A finding of a legal conclusion will not vitiate the general verdict, where there are facts properly found consistent with

403, 24 N. E. 216; Rogers v. Leyden, 127 Ind. 50, 26 N. E. 210; Chicago, St. L. & P. R. Co. v. Spilker, 134 Ind. 380, 33 N. E. 280; Todd v. Badger, 134 Ind. 204, 33 N. E. 963; Consolidated Stone Co. v. Summit, 152 Ind. 297, 53 N. E. 235; Louisville & N. R. Co. v. Kemper, 153 Ind. 618, 53 N. E. 931; Roush v. Roush, 154 Ind. 562, 55 N. E. 1017; City of South Bend v. Turner, 156 Ind. 418, 60 N. E. 271, 54 L. R. A. 396, 83 Am. St. Rep. 200; Grand Rapids & I. R. Co. v. Cox, 8 Ind. App. 29, 35 N. E. 183; Walter A. Wood Mowing & Reaping Mach. Co. v. Irons, 10 Ind. App. 454, 36 N. E. 862; Lake Shore & M. S. R. Co. v. Wilson, 11 Ind. App. 488, 38 N. E. 343; Phillips v. Michaels, 11 Ind. App. 672, 39 N. E. 669; Bower v. Thomas, 22 Ind. App. 505, 54 N. E. 142; Rogers v. City of Bloomington, 22 Ind. App. 601, 52 N. E. 242; Miller v. Stevens, 23 Ind. App. 365, 55 N. E. 262; Lukin v. Halderson, 24 Ind. App. 645, 57 N. E. 254; Wicker v. Messinger, 12 O. C. D. 425, 22 Ohio Cir. Ct. R. 712.

[66] Ridgeway v. Dearinger, 42 Ind. 157; Redelsheimer v. Miller, 107 Ind. 485, 8 N. E. 447; New York, C. & St. L. R. Co. v. Railroad Co., 116 Ind. 60, 18 N. E. 182; Stringer v. Frost, 116 Ind. 477, 19 N. E. 331, 2 L. R. A. 614, 9 Am. St. Rep. 875; Grand Rapids & I. R. Co. v. Ellison, 117 Ind. 234, 20 N. E. 135; Indianapolis & V. R. Co. v. Lewis, 119 Ind. 218, 21 N. E. 660; Louisville, E. & St. L. Consol. R. Co. v. Summers, 131 Ind. 241, 30 N. E. 873; Princeton Coal & Mining Co. v. Roll, 162 Ind. 115, 66 N. E. 169; Evansville & T. H. R. Co. v. Marohn, 6 Ind. App. 646, 34 N. E. 27; Board of Com'rs of De Kalb Co. v. Machine Works, 14 Ind. App. 214, 42 N. E. 689; Bevens v. Smith, 42 Kan. 250, 21 Pac. 1064.

On the trial of a claim against an estate for money collected by decedent on a note in his hands for collection, there was a general verdict in plaintiff's favor for $138.46, and the special answers recited that deceased collected the note in January, 1884, and received thereon $138.46. Held, that the judgment should have been for the amount of the verdict, and not for that sum with interest from the date of filing claim, since any conflict between the general verdict and the special answers might have been removed by evidence of partial payment. Simons v. Beaver, 15 Ind. App. 510, 43 N. E. 478.

In an action for damages to plaintiff's land by overflow caused by defendant having placed a dam upon a certain creek, there was a general verdict for plaintiff, but the jury found, in answer to special interrogatories, that plaintiff's land would have been overflowed if the dam had not been built and that the overflow was caused by unusually heavy rain. Held, no such conflict between the general ver-the verdict; [67] nor will it prevent judgment on findings which, except as to it, are irreconcilable with the verdict.[68] Neither can irresponsive [69] or immaterial findings,[70] findings of evidentiary facts,[71] indefinite findings,[72] or findings outside the issues,[73] be permitted to control.

dict and the special findings as to warrant the court in entering judgment for defendant, since, notwithstanding the fact that the lands would have been overflowed though no dam were built, the jury may have considered that they were overflowed to a greater extent by reason of the dam. Todd v. Badger, 134 Ind. 204, 33 N. E. 963.

Failure to find all the facts essential to plaintiff's recovery does not render the general verdict in his favor inconsistent with the findings. In an action for personal injury, it is immaterial that the findings fail to show that the defendant was negligent or that plaintiff had not assumed the danger. American Tin Plate Co. v. Williams, 30 Ind. App. 46, 65 N. E. 304.

[67] Davis v. Reamer, 105 Ind. 318, 4 N. E. 857; Bechdolt v. Railroad Co., 113 Ind. 343, 15 N. E. 686; Board of Com'rs of Hamilton Co. v. Newlin, 132 Ind. 27, 31 N. E. 465; Chicago & E. Ry. Co. v. Cummings, 24 Ind. App. 192, 53 N. E. 1026; Fishbaugh v. Spunaugle, 118 Iowa, 337, 92 N. W. 58; Silsby v. Frost, 3 Wash. T. 388, 17 Pac. 887. So, too, general findings, which are simply conclusions by the jury from the facts found in answer to specific questions, should be ignored. Atchison, T. & S. F. R. Co. v. Brown, 2 Kan. App. 604, 42 Pac. 588; Geddes v. Blackmore, 132 Ind. 551, 32 N. E. 567.

[68] Bechdolt v. Railroad Co., 113 Ind. 343, 15 N. E. 686.

[69] Fromm v. Leonard, 21 Ind. 243.

[70] Edwards v. Applegate, 70 Ind. 325; West v. Cavins, 74 Ind. 265; Jewell v. Town of Sullivan, 5 Ind. App. 188, 31 N. E. 829; Liston v. Railroad Co., 70 Iowa, 714, 29 N. W. 445; Mays v. Foster, 26 Kan. 518; City of Topeka v. Noble, 9 Kan. App. 171, 58 Pac. 1015; Williams v. Eikenberry, 22 Neb. 210, 34 N. W. 373.

[71] Chicago & N. W. Ry. Co. v. Dunleavy, 129 Ill. 132, 22 N. E. 15;

[72] Adams v. Cosby, 48 Ind. 153; Comer v. Himes, 49 Ind. 482; West v. Cavins, 74 Ind. 265; Carver v. Leedy, 80 Ind. 335; Sanders v. Weelburg, 107 Ind. 266, 7 N. E. 573; Rice v. City of Evansville, 108 Ind. 7, 9 N. E. 139, 58 Am. Rep. 22; Rice v. Manford, 110 Ind. 596, 11 N. E. 283.

[73] Kullmann v. Greenebaum, 84 Cal. 98, 24 Pac. 49; Keesling v. Ryan, 84 Ind. 89; Blacker v. Slown, 114 Ind. 322, 16 N. E. 621.

**Sufficiency of Findings to Support Judgment.** It follows from the foregoing that to justify the court in rendering judgment on the findings notwithstanding the general verdict the former must be such as absolutely to determine the controversy in favor of the moving party. The pleadings may be looked to to determine the issues and to ascertain what if any facts are admitted, but no reference to the evidence taken on the trial may be had, and all presumptions must be indulged in favor of the general verdict. If the general verdict is for the defendant, all the facts necessary to entitle plaintiff to recover must clearly appear by the findings in order to authorize judgment for him.[74] In such case the findings must be as full and unambiguous as a special verdict, and with even stronger reason than when no general verdict is returned, but merely the naked facts, for in the case of motion by plaintiff for judgment on the findings non obstante veredicto the jury have drawn a conclusion which is within their province and entitled to weight, and that conclusion is known to be adverse to movant.[75]

Elgin, J. & E. Ry. Co. v. Raymond, 148 Ill. 241, 35 N. E. 729; Ohio & M. Ry. Co. v. Ramey, 39 Ill. App. 412; Farley v. Eller, 40 Ind. 319; Baltimore & O. C. Ry. Co. v. Rowan, 104 Ind. 88, 3 N. E. 627.

The ultimate facts having been found against plaintiff, no finding of probative facts will be permitted to control. Pico v. Cuyas, 47 Cal. 174; Wood v. Pendola, 78 Cal. 287, 20 Pac. 678; Gill v. Driver, 90 Cal. 72, 27 Pac. 64.

74 *Examples:* Bremmerman v. Jennings, 61 Ind. 334; McKinley v. Bank, 118 Ind. 375, 21 N. E. 36; Davis v. Campbell, 93 Iowa, 524; 61 N. W. 1053; Heyman v. Simmons, 4 Kan. App. 1, 45 Pac. 728.

75 "The plaintiff, who has the burden of proof, in a case where the general verdict is against him, is in a much worse situation than his adversary, for all the facts essential to a recovery must appear in the answer of the jury, and they must be irreconcilable with the general verdict, while in the case of the defendant all that need appear is enough to defeat the plaintiff's case, and make a reconciliation between the general verdict and the answers of the jury impossible."

"Where a plaintiff asks judgment on the special findings notwithstanding the general verdict, he will fail, unless all the findings are

Where the general verdict is for the plaintiff, to overthrow it and entitle defendant to judgment on the findings it need only appear that one or more of the necessary elements established by the general verdict does not exist or is untrue.[76] If the special findings contradict material facts necessarily found by the general verdict, the latter cannot stand, and the contradiction of any one material fact is as final to the general verdict as if the special findings refuted every averment necessary to the cause of action.[77] And it would seem that the effect should be the same, whether the findings show a fact inimical to recovery, or merely failure to prove an essential fact, the burden of proof being upon the plaintiff.[78]

If the findings are clearly antagonistic to the general verdict, judgment should be rendered upon them,[79] and the party in

favorable to him; for if some are favorable and some unfavorable he cannot escape the force of the general verdict." Rice v. City of Evansville, 108 Ind. 7, 9 N. E. 139, 58 Am. Rep. 22, and cases cited.

When the special findings cover every fact or issue in controversy, the right to recover becomes purely a question of law. It is then like determining the rights of the parties upon an agreed state of facts. Schulte v. Railroad Co., 114 Iowa, 89, 86 N. W. 63.

[76] Lake Erie & W. R. Co. v. Graver, 23 Ind. App. 678, 55 N. E. 968.

When a special finding is indispensable to the general verdict and is contrary thereto, it controls. Cleveland, C., C. & St. L. Ry. Co. v. Heine, 28 Ind. App. 163, 62 N. E. 455; Chicago & E. Ry. Co. v. Thomas, 155 Ind. 634, 58 N. E. 1040.

[77] Cleveland, C., C. & St. L. Ry. Co. v. Griffin, 26 Ind. App. 368, 58 N. E. 503; citing Ervin v. Evans, 24 Ind. App. 335, 56 N. E. 725.

[78] See Conners v. Railroad Co., 71 Iowa, 490, 32 N. W. 465, 60 Am. Rep. 814.

[79] In an action to recover goods sold, on the ground that the purchaser was insolvent when he bought them, upon a special finding that defendant was worth $5,000 over liabilities at the time of the purchase, and that he then did intend to pay for the goods, judgment should have been entered for him, notwithstanding that the jury returned a general verdict for plaintiff. Cortland Mfg. Co. v. Platt, 83 Mich. 419, 47 N. W. 330.

A general verdict was found in favor of plaintiff, but the answers to special interrogatories showed that it was based upon an oral con-

whose favor the general verdict is returned cannot escape in the manner attempted by ingenious counsel in Neimick v.

tract, which was barred by the statute of limitations, rather than on a written contract simply modified by parol and not barred. Held, that a motion for judgment in favor of defendant upon the special findings should have been sustained. Aldrich v. Price, 57 Iowa, 151, 9 N. W. 376.

The general verdict must remain on the record in the form in which it was rendered. U. S. Trust Co. v. Harris, 2 Bosw. (N. Y.) 75, 87.

**Negligence.** A special finding that plaintiff was a fellow servant of the person through whose negligence he was injured, being inconsistent with the general verdict, will control it. Egmann v. Railroad Co., 65 Ill. App. 345.

Where the general verdict is for plaintiff, and contributory negligence of plaintiff appears from the findings, judgment should be rendered on the latter. Miller v. Railroad Co., 110 Ill. App. 195; Chicago & E. I. Ry. Co. v. Hedges, 118 Ind. 5, 20 N. E. 530; Pennsylvania Co. v. Meyers, 136 Ind. 242, 36 N. E. 32; Ervin v. Evans, 24 Ind. App. 335, 56 N. E. 725; Cleveland, C., C. & St. L. Ry. Co. v. Griffin, 26 Ind. App. 368, 58 N. E. 503; Hill v. Railroad Co., 31 Ind. App. 98, 67 N. E. 276; Republic Iron & Steel Co. v. Jones, 32 Ind. App. 189, 69 N. E. 191; Lake Shore & M. S. R. Co. v. Graham, 162 Ind. 374, 70 N. E. 484; Coffman v. Railroad Co., 90 Iowa, 462, 57 N. W. 955; Norfolk Beet Sugar Co. v. Preuner, 55 Neb. 656, 75 N. W. 1097.

But a finding of contributory negligence will not warrant judgment on the findings, where they also find willful negligence. Wabash R. Co. v. Speer, 156 Ill. 244, 40 N. E. 835.

If the facts specially found show that appellant's negligence was not the proximate cause of appellee's injury, or that appellee's own negligence contributed to his injury, then in either event such facts would be in irreconcilable conflict with the general verdict and would control. Lake Erie & W. R. Co. v. Graver, 23 Ind. App. 678, 55 N. E. 968.

Where it is necessary for plaintiff to prove exercise of ordinary care, and to a question as to whether plaintiff's intestate did exercise ordinary care the jury answer, "In doubt for want of evidence," plaintiff has failed in an essential particular to establish his case, and a general verdict for plaintiff is in irreconcilable conflict with the special findings. Bryson v. Railroad Co., 89 Iowa, 677, 57 N. W. 430.

A finding of plaintiff's freedom from negligence is not a specific finding of an issuable fact, but is a general conclusion drawn from all

American Ins. Co.[80] In the case referred to, after motion for judgment on the findings had been made by his adversary, counsel sought to obviate the effect of irreconcilable findings by amending his complaint so as to make an issue (claimed to be consistent with the agreement alleged) upon which the jury might be said to have found their verdict, thus avoiding the inconsistency. But the trial court denied the motion, and the appellate court sustained its ruling, holding that the proposed amendment was inconsistent with the agreement alleged in the complaint as the basis of plaintiff's right to recover. And, furthermore, that if plaintiff desired to avail himself of the right to so amend, he should have made his offer at the close of the testimony, and asked for a finding thereon.

**Judgment Where Damages Not Found, or Found Only by Findings.** In Lamb v. Briggs [81] there was a bare general verdict "for the defendant," a guarantor, but the finding showed a certain amount due to plaintiff on the note sued upon. Plaintiff moved for judgment on the special findings, the motion was sustained, and judgment was rendered thereon. The Code provided that "when, by the verdict, either party is entitled to recover money of the adverse party, the jury, in their verdict, must assess the amount of the recovery." It was held on appeal that the findings might be taken as the verdict if they found all the facts necessary to entitle plaintiff to recover, but, as they did not negative the defense that plaintiff was co-guarantor, there was no verdict in the case, and to render judgment on the findings was error.

If there is neither assessment of damages in the special findings, nor facts found from which the court could, as matter of law, make such assessment, plaintiff's motion for judgment

the evidence upon the subject, which inheres in the general verdict and is no stronger than the general finding. Missouri, K. & T. R. Co. v. Bussey, 66 Kan. 735, 71 Pac. 261.

80 16 Mont. 318, 40 Pac. 597.

81 22 Neb. 138, 34 N. W. 217.

thereon should be overruled, even if the findings are irreconcilable with the general verdict.[82]

**Inconsistency Between Verdict and Findings as to Damages.** Where the findings show a party to be entitled to a greater sum than that awarded by the general verdict, he should move for judgment on the answers to the interrogatories.[83] Similarly, if the damages found by the verdict are greater than the findings authorize, judgment should be entered on the findings.[84] In such case it is error to overrule a motion to reduce

[82] Sievers v. Lumber Co., 151 Ind. 642, 50 N. E. 877.

[83] Brickley v. Weghorn, 71 Ind. 497; Froman v. Rous, 83 Ind. 94; Schaffner v. Kober, 2 Ind. App. 412, 28 N. E. 871; Wood v. Wack, 31 Ind. App. 252, 67 N. E. 562.

"We have no doubt that a plaintiff may be awarded a larger sum than that stated in the general verdict, if the answers show him entitled to it. Where the facts specially found clearly show that the jury have erred in computing the amount of recovery, there is a conflict between the answers and the general verdict, and the former must control. There may be an inconsistency between the general verdict and the answers to interrogatories, although the general verdict is favorable to the party who prays judgment on the answers." Froman v. Rous, 83 Ind. 94.

In an action to foreclose a lien and recover the value of a windmill erected by plaintiff on land of the defendant, the value of the improvements was expressly fixed, in an order admitted to have been executed by defendant, at $221.29. Such order required plaintiff, on notice of failure of the windmill to work well, to make it so work. The jury found specially that the mill was constructed according to the contract, and that, while it did not work well at first, the plaintiff

[84] Skillen v. Jones, 44 Ind. 136. Where in proceedings to condemn land for railroad purposes, the jury by their general verdict find the value of the land to be $350, and the damages otherwise sustained by the owner $170, and also find specially that the owner sustained no damages as to the balance of the land not taken, and that the value of what the railroad had appropriated was not diminished by any collateral benefits to the owner, the special finding must control; and the judgment will, on appeal, be modified by setting aside that part awarding $170 damages. Rio Grande Southern Ry. Co. v. Deasey, 3 Colo. App. 196, 32 Pac. 725.

the judgment to make it correspond with the findings.[85] But a motion for judgment upon answers for a specified amount less than the jury found in its verdict is properly overruled where the answers to the interrogatories are insufficient to warrant a judgment for so small an amount, even though they would warrant a judgment for less than the amount of the general verdict.[86]

**Effect of Erroneous Instructions.** Where the jury return a general verdict for plaintiff, when, under a special finding and one of the instructions, defendant is entitled to judgment, it is proper to set aside the general verdict, but the court is not bound by the instruction to render judgment for defendant. If the instruction is erroneous, it should grant a new trial. The general verdict being set aside, it still remains for the court to determine whether the finding entitles defendant to judgment, not under the instruction, but under the law.[87]

But where neither party complains of an instruction, on appeal it must be regarded as the law of the case, and, where the special findings show clearly that under the charge given the verdict should have been for the defendant, a judgment for plaintiff on the general verdict will be reversed, and

upon notice remedied the defects, and they found a general verdict for plaintiff for $98.44. Held, that on the special findings plaintiff was entitled to judgment for the full amount fixed by the order. Phelps & Bigelow Windmill Co. v. Buchanan, 46 Kan. 314, 26 Pac. 708. See, also, Taylor v. Lehman, 17 Ind. App. 585, 46 N. E. 84. But though the general verdict is for a smaller sum than that warranted by the findings, it will not be set aside as inconsistent with the latter, where, under the evidence, the jury may have based its verdict upon its findings of facts not covered by the findings returned. Kemper v. City of Burlington, 81 Iowa, 354, 47 N. W. 72.

85 Leavenworth, N. & S. Ry. Co. v. Wilkins, 45 Kan. 674, 26 Pac. 16.

86 Barley v. Brown, 13 Ind. App. 521, 41 N. E. 351.

87 Evans v. Harvester Works, 63 Iowa, 204, 18 N. W. 881. Instructions binding upon jury, see Felton v. Railroad Co., 69 Iowa, 577, 29 N. W. 618.

the cause remanded, with direction to enter judgment for defendant on the findings.[88]

[88] Krauskopf v. Krauskopf, 82 Iowa, 535, 48 N. W. 932. See, however, Baird v. Railroad Co., 55 Iowa, 121, 7 N. W. 460.

A motion for judgment notwithstanding the general verdict, on the ground of its inconsistency with a finding, will not be granted where the general verdict is warranted by law and the facts, and the sole inconsistency is a matter of deduction from an erroneous instruction procured by movant; and this is so regardless of whether the successful party objected to the erroneous instruction. "The Code provision that, when the special finding shall be inconsistent with the general verdict, the special finding shall control, was never designed to enable one party to convert an error, committed at his own instigation, into a weapon for the destruction of the rights of the other." Denver & R. G. R. Co. v. Bedell, 11 Colo. App. 139, 54 Pac. 280.

# CHAPTER IX.

## NEW TRIAL—VENIRE DE NOVO—APPEAL.

Many of the causes for a new trial have been mentioned in connection with other matters in preceding chapters. What follows is intended mainly as a recapitulation, the various grounds of the motion being collected under one heading for greater convenience to the practitioner.

**Insufficiency of Evidence to Support Findings.** The most common ground of the motion for a new trial is the insufficiency of the evidence to support the findings of the jury.[1] So far as is indicated by some of the decisions, no distinction is made between consistent and inconsistent findings. Apparently, if in either case the answers are not sustained by the evidence, the fact is regarded as proof that the jury has been moved by improper influences, such as passion or prejudice, and a new trial is awarded as of course.[2] But it is said in

[1] St. Louis Bridge Co. v. Fellows, 31 Ill. App. 282; Blew v. Hoover, 30 Ind. 450; Murray v. Phillips, 59 Ind. 56; Louisville, N. A. & C. Ry. Co. v. Thompson, 107 Ind. 442, 8 N. E. 18, 9 N. E. 357, 57 Am. Rep. 120; Board of Com'rs of Jackson County v. Nichols, 139 Ind. 611, 38 N. E. 526; McCarty v. James, 62 Iowa, 257, 17 N. W. 492; Heath v. Coal Co., 65 Iowa, 737, 23 N. W. 148; Howe v. Lincoln, 23 Kan. 468; Atchison, T. & S. F. R. Co. v. Cone, 37 Kan. 567, 15 Pac. 499; Stevens v. Matthewson, 45 Kan. 594, 26 Pac. 38; Chicago, K. & N. Ry. Co. v. Muncie, 56 Kan. 210, 42 Pac. 710; Atchison, T. & S. F. Ry. Co. v. Davis, 64 Kan. 127, 67 Pac. 441, and cases cited; Hill v. Ellis, 5 Kan. App. 532, 48 Pac. 204; Cronk v. Railway Co., 3 S. D. 93, 52 N. W. 420.

[2] Schulte v. Railway Co., 114 Iowa, 89, 86 N. W. 63, and cases cited; Missouri, K. & T. Ry. Co. v. Weaver, 16 Kan. 456; Atchison, T. & S. F. Ry. Co. v. Davis, 64 Kan. 127, 67 Pac. 441, and cases cited. Inaccurate answers do not afford ground for setting aside the general verdict and for a new trial, unless the facts called for are controlling, or of such importance that findings thereon against the weight of the testimony necessarily indicate passion or prejudice. Kuehl v. Rail-

*Indiana* that it is only when the answers to the interrogatories are so inconsistent with the general verdict that judgment should be rendered thereon notwithstanding the general verdict that it is proper to assign as cause for a new trial that the answers are not sustained by the evidence.[3] Where the answers are consistent with the verdict, the cause assigned for a new trial should be, not that the answers to the interrogatories are not sustained by the evidence, but that the verdict is not sustained by the evidence.[4] This is for the reason that, though the answers be not sustained by the evidence, unless they are in absolute conflict with the general verdict the latter may be supported by the evidence, for it may cover material facts and branches of the case not touched upon by the findings, and, in fact, will always do so unless the special findings are so full as to amount to a special verdict. So that a new trial will be granted for want of evidence to support special findings only when it would be granted for insufficiency of the evidence to support the general verdict.[5]

When an answer stands in irreconcilable conflict with the general verdict, it will not defeat it if such answer is not supported by the evidence. If the answer is consistent with the general verdict, it cannot overthrow the verdict because it is not supported by the evidence.[6] In the first case, judgment will not be rendered on the findings, but, on motion, the court will set aside the verdict (carrying the findings with it) and award a new trial.[7] In the second, if the verdict is not sus-

road Co. (Iowa) 102 N. W. 512, citing Pence v. Railway Co., 79 Iowa, 389, 44 N. W. 686.

3 Sievers v. Box Co., 151 Ind. 642, 50 N. E. 877.

4 Id.

5 Indianapolis & St. L. R. Co. v. Stout, 53 Ind. 143; Burkhart v. Gladish, 123 Ind. 337, 24 N. E. 118; Phœnix v. Lamb, 29 Iowa, 352.

6 Board of Com'rs of Jackson County v. Nichols, 139 Ind. 611, 38 N. E. 526; Insurance Co. of North America v. Osborn, 26 Ind. App. 88, 59 N. E. 181; Warren v. Railroad Co. (Cal.) 67 Pac. 1.

7 Burkhart v. Gladish, 123 Ind. 337, 24 N. E. 118, citing Staser v. Hogan, 120 Ind. 207, 21 N. E. 911, 22 N. E. 990.

tained by the evidence, a new trial will be granted. The court is not permitted to ignore the consistency or inconsistency and render judgment contrary to that which the verdict and findings, without regard to the evidence, justify, for on the motion for judgment on the findings they must be taken at face value—they are verities. The court may consider the evidence only for the purpose of determining whether or not the verdict should stand, and may not, either actually or in effect, substitute findings of its own for those made by the jury.

To justify the court in setting aside the verdict and granting a new trial, the fact or facts found by the jury contrary to or without warrant by the evidence must be indispensable to the support of the verdict.[8]

The motion should include the general verdict, as well as the special findings;[9] but a motion to "set aside the verdict and grant a new trial" is broad enough to cover both.[10]

**Inconsistency Between Findings.** The *Indiana* rule is that inconsistent findings cancel each other, and are without effect on the general verdict,[11] which also appears to be the view taken in *Colorado*.[12]

However, in a case where the findings were inconsistent with the general verdict and with each other, and it was evident that the jury had given an answer which they might not have

8 New York, C. & St. L. R. Co. v. Baltz, 141 Ind. 661, 38 N. E. 402.

Where a special finding is not supported by the evidence, and the fact so found is material, though not necessarily determinative, a new trial must be granted. Peck v. Hutchinson, 88 Iowa, 320, 55 N. W. 511, and cases cited. But see Young v. Lohr, 118 Iowa, 624, 92 N. W. 684.

The answer, "No evidence," is not ground for a new trial, if no answer that could have been given would necessarily have controlled the general verdict. Frank Bird Transfer Co. v. Krug, 30 Ind. App. 602, 65 N. E. 309.

9 Ohio & M. Ry. Co. v. Selby, 47 Ind. 471, 17 Am. Rep. 719.

10 McCrum v. Corby, 15 Kan. 112.

11 See chapter 8.

12 Drake v. Mining Co., 32 Colo. 259, 75 Pac. 912.

intended, an Indiana court considered that justice required that a new trial be had.[13]

In *Idaho, Kansas, Oklahoma,* and *Rhode Island* it is held that inconsistency between the findings prevents judgment being entered on the verdict, and is ground for a new trial.[14] The conflicting findings are considered as indicating that the jury did not give the case fair and intelligent consideration,[15] or were misled by the instructions.[16]

**Miscellaneous Grounds.** Failure to agree upon answers to material questions results in a mistrial. The jury should be discharged, and the case be submitted to a new jury.[17] Under such circumstances a general verdict cannot be accepted, and if one is returned it should be set aside and a new trial granted.[18]

[13] Van Hook v. Young's Estate, 29 Ind. App. 471, 64 N. E. 670.

[14] See chapter 8. But inconsistency between the findings and the general verdict is not ground for a new trial. Adamson v. Rose, 30 Ind. 380; Byram v. Galbraith, 75 Ind. 134; Anderson v. Hubble, 93 Ind. 570, 47 Am. Rep. 394; Louisville, N. A. & C. Ry. Co. v. Kane, 120 Ind. 140, 22 N. E. 80; Moffitt v. Albert, 97 Iowa, 213, 66 N. W. 162.

[15] Atchison, T. & S. F. R. Co. v. Holland, 58 Kan. 317, 49 Pac. 71.

[16] Chase v. Bank of Horton, 9 Kan. App. 186, 59 Pac. 39. The answer held to indicate either that the testimony was not properly understood, or that the jury was unwilling to fairly answer the questions submitted. Union Pac. Ry. Co. v. Sternbergh, 54 Kan. 410, 38 Pac. 486. Answers framed with reference to their effect on the general verdict. Atchison, T. & S. F. R. Co. v. Hamlin, 67 Kan. 476, 73 Pac. 58.

[17] Kansas Pac. Ry. Co. v. Reynolds, 8 Kan. 623; Clark v. Weir, 37 Kan. 98, 14 Pac. 533; Redford v. Railway Co., 9 Wash. 55, 36 Pac. 1085. See, also, Arkansas M. Ry. Co. v. Canman, 52 Ark. 517, 13 S. W. 280; Tourtelotte v. Brown, 1 Colo. App. 408, 29 Pac. 132; Leffel v. Leffel, 35 Ind. 76; Hardin v. Branner, 25 Iowa, 364; Elliott v. Village of Graceville, 76 Minn. 430, 79 N. W. 503; Doom v. Walker, 15 Neb. 339, 18 N. W. 138.

[18] Tourtelotte v. Brown, supra; Harbaugh v. People, 33 Mich. 241; Rathbun v. Parker, 113 Mich. 594, 72 N. W. 31; Nichols, Shepard & Co. v. Wadsworth, 40 Minn. 547, 42 N. W. 541; Eischen v. Railway Co., 81 Minn. 59, 83 N. W. 490.

If the jury give answers which cannot, by reason of the fact that they are ambiguous, indefinite, or evasive, be used as tests of the correctness of the general verdict [19] or which show want of intelligence or fairness,[20] or indicate passion and prejudice,[21] or which show that the jury based their verdict on a theory of the case not involved in the issues submitted,[22] or where the verdict and findings are returned in separate fractions and at different times,[23] a new trial should be granted.

A new trial may also be granted on account of refusal of proper interrogatories,[24] improper submission [25] or withdrawal,[26] or the giving of erroneous instructions either as to

19 Woodson v. McCune, 17 Cal. 304; Garfield v. Knight's Ferry, Id. 510; Hopkins v. Stanley, 43 Ind. 553; Astley v. Capron, 89 Ind. 167: Matchett v. Railway Co., 132 Ind. 344, 31 N. E. 792; Darling v. West, 51 Iowa, 259, 1 N. W. 531; Lytton v. Railroad Co., 69 Iowa, 338, 28 N. W. 628; Fisk v. Railway Co., 74 Iowa, 424, 38 N. W. 132; Atchison, T. & S. F. R. Co. v. Campbell, 16 Kan. 200; Same v. Cone, 37 Kan. 567, 15 Pac. 499; Wilson v. Railroad Co., 57 Mich. 155, 23 N. W. 627.

Where the general verdict appears to the court to be wrong, and it is shown by the special findings that the jury are unable to assign any certain or tangible grounds for their conclusion, the verdict should be set aside, and a new trial ordered. Ford v. Railroad Co., 69 Iowa, 627, 29 N. W. 755.

20 Southern Kan. Ry. Co. v. Gorsuch, 47 Kan. 583, 28 Pac. 703; Atchison, T. & S. F. R. Co. v. Wells, 56 Kan. 222, 42 Pac. 699.

21 Schulte v. Railway Co., 114 Iowa, 89, 86 N. W. 63; Missouri, K. & T. Ry. Co. v. Weaver, 16 Kan. 456; Csatlos v. Railroad Co., 78 App. Div. 635, 79 N. Y. Supp. 653.

22 Aultman & Taylor Mach. Co. v. Wier, 67 Kan. 674, 74 Pac. 227.

23 Ryan v. Insurance Co., 77 Wis. 611, 46 N. W. 885.

24 Astley v. Capron, 89 Ind. 167; Barnett v. Feary, 101 Ind. 95; City of Topeka v. Boutwell, 53 Kan. 20, 35 Pac. 819, 27 L. R. A. 593. See chapter IV.

25 Pittsburg, C., C. & St. L. R. Co. v. Smith, 207 Ill. 486, 69 N. E. 873; Wilson v. Phelps, 86 Iowa, 735, 53 N. W. 115; Beaudin v. Bay City (Mich.) 99 N. W. 285. See chapter 5.

26 Ermentraut v. Insurance Co., 67 Minn. 451, 70 N. W. 572; Sun Mut. Ins. Co. v. Dudley, 65 Ark. 240, 45 S. W. 539; McKelvey v. Railway Co., 35 W. Va. 500, 14 S. E. 261.

the answers to be made or as to the law of the case, which appear to have been prejudicial.[27]

**Waiver of Objections.** In order that error may be available on the motion to set aside the verdict and for a new trial, or on appeal, objection must be made in season, and an exception taken if it is overruled.

Objection to the form of interrogatories is waived unless taken at the time of submission,[28] and to the form of the answers unless made when the verdict is returned.[29]

That answers are indefinite or evasive, or that the jury returned a general verdict without answers to the interrogatories, or that for any reason the special findings do not respond sufficiently to requests therefor, is no ground for a new trial, and furnishes no point on appeal, where no motion was made to require the jury to answer more fully.[30] Permitting the jury to be discharged without giving specific answers precludes subsequent objection, and is a waiver of the right to answers.[31]

27 See chapter 6.

28 Morse v. Morse, 25 Ind. 156; Brooker v. Weber, 41 Ind. 426; Van Hook v. Young's Estate, 29 Ind. App. 471, 64 N. E. 670; Dupont v. Starring, 42 Mich. 492, 4 N. W. 190; Flannery v. Railway Co., 23 Mo. App. 120.

29 Alhambra Addition Water Co. v. Richardson, 72 Cal. 598, 14 Pac. 379; Reeves v. Plough, 41 Ind. 204; Byram v. Galbraith, 75 Ind. 134; Manny v. Griswold, 21 Minn. 506; Thompson v. Thompson, 49 Neb. 157, 68 N. W. 372; Moss v. Priest, 19 Abb. Prac. (N. Y.) 314; Evans & Howard Fire Brick Co. v. Railway Co., 21 Mo. App. 648; Menne v. Neumeister, 25 Mo. App. 300.

30 Brown v. Railroad Co., 72 Cal. 523, 14 Pac. 138; Id. (Cal.) 12 Pac. 512 (q. v); Elgin, J. & E. Ry. Co. v. Raymond, 148 Ill. 241, 35 N. E. 729; Chicago & A. R. Co. v. Johnson, 27 Ill. App. 351; Cleveland, C., C. & St. L. Ry. Co. v. Doerr, 41 Ill. App. 530; Bradley v. Bradley, 45 Ind. 67; Carpenter v. Galloway, 73 Ind. 418; Chicago & E. I. R. Co. v. Ostrander, 116 Ind. 259, 15 N. E. 227, 19 N. E. 110; Arthur v. Wallace, 8 Kan. 267; Kansas Pac. Ry. Co. v. Pointer, 14 Kan. 37; Morrow v. Commissioners, 21 Kan. 484; Varco v. Railway Co., 30 Minn. 18, 13 N. W. 921; Caldwell v. Brown, 9 Ohio Cir. Ct. R. 691; Carrico v. Railway Co., 39 W. Va. 86, 19 S. E. 571, 24 L. R. A. 50.

31 City of Guthrie v. Thistle, 5 Okl. 517, 49 Pac. 1003; McCormack

**How Motion for New Trial and for Judgment on Findings Affect Each Other.** The motion for a new trial does not take the place of a motion for judgment on the special findings,[32] and is not necessary in order to present the overruling of a motion for such judgment.[33]

The right to move for a new trial is not waived by motion for judgment on the special findings non obstante;[34] and though, according to approved practice, the motion for judgment should precede the other, yet the two may be filed together, and be disposed of in their proper order.[35]

By procuring a new trial a party waives any error there may be in overruling his motion for judgment on the findings.[36]

## VENIRE DE NOVO.

A venire facias de novo is an ancient process of the common law to obtain a new trial for defects in the proceedings appearing of record, such as a defective verdict or irregularities in selecting or impaneling the jury. It differs from a motion

v. Phillips, 4 Dak. 506, 34 N. W. 39; Chicago & N. W. Ry. Co. v. Dunleavy, 129 Ill. 132, 22 N. E. 15.

32 Brickley v. Weghorn, 71 Ind. 497; Byram v. Galbraith, 75 Ind. 134; Anderson v. Hubble, 93 Ind. 570, 47 Am. Rep. 394; Louisville, N. A. & C. Ry. Co. v. Kane, 120 Ind. 140, 22 N. E. 80; Drake v. Mining Co., 32 Colo. 259, 75 Pac. 912.

33 Horn v. Eberhart, 17 Ind. 118.

34 Brannon v. May, 42 Ind. 92; Murray v. Phillips, 59 Ind. 56; Nichols v. State, 65 Ind. 512; Leslie v. Merrick, 99 Ind. 180; Hollenbeck v. City of Marshalltown, 62 Iowa, 21, 17 N. W. 155; Pieart v. Railway Co., 82 Iowa, 148, 47 N. W. 1017; Atchison, T. & S. F. R. Co. v. Holland, 58 Kan. 317, 49 Pac. 71.

35 Diamond Plate Glass Co. v. De Hority, 143 Ind. 381, 40 N. E. 681; Pieart v. Railway Co., 82 Iowa, 148, 47 N. W. 1017; Luse v. Railway Co., 57 Kan. 361, 46 Pac. 768; Atchison, T. & S. F. R. Co. v. Holland, 58 Kan. 317, 49 Pac. 71; Davis v. Turner, 69 Ohio St. 101, 68 N. E. 819. But see Stein v. Railway Co., 41 Ill. App. 38.

36 Williams v. Frick, 71 Iowa, 362, 32 N. W. 382. See, also, Hollenbeck v. City of Marshalltown, 62 Iowa, 21, 17 N. W. 155; Fitzpatrick v. Papa, 89 Ind. 17.

for a new trial in that the propriety of granting it depends upon fixed rules of law, not permitting the exercise of discretion, and in that it is granted upon defects appearing in the record rather than upon extrinsic irregularities and errors occurring at the trial which do not appear of record.[37]

**Motion not Applicable to Cases under Interrogatory Statutes.** The answers to interrogatories do not constitute the verdict, and a venire de novo cannot be awarded because they are indefinite, evasive, contradictory, or improper in substance or form.[38] Where a special verdict is called for, the findings furnish the only basis of judgment, and a venire de novo should be awarded where the findings are so defective or ambiguous on their face that no judgment can be rendered thereon.[39] But judgment is rendered, if at all, on the general verdict, and not upon the special findings, in cases under the interrogatory statutes, and in no manner depends upon the special findings for support,[40] except where judgment notwithstanding the verdict is rendered. The judgment must be rendered either on the general verdict or upon sufficient findings absolutely irreconcilable with it. If the findings are improper or uncertain they

[37] 14 Enc. Pl. & Prac. 716, 717.

[38] Ogle v. Dill, 61 Ind. 438; Keesling v. Ryan, 84 Ind. 89; Bedford, S. O. & B. R. Co. v. Rainbolt, 99 Ind. 554; Chicago & E. I. R. Co. v. Ostrander, 116 Ind. 259, 15 N. E. 227, 19 N. E. 110. See, also, McElfresh v. Guard, 32 Ind. 408; West v. Cavins, 74 Ind. 265.

[39] Pittsburgh, C. & St. L. Ry. Co. v. Hixon, 110 Ind. 225, 11 N. E. 285; Buscher v. City of La Fayette, 8 Ind. App. 590, 36 N. E. 371; Chicago & E. R. Co. v. Branyan, 10 Ind. App. 570, 37 N. E. 190; Jones v. Casler, 139 Ind. 382, 38 N. E. 812, 47 Am. St. Rep. 274; Bellows v. Bank, 2 Mason, 31, Fed. Cas. No. 1,279; post, chapter 14.

[40] Bedford, S. O. & B. R. Co. v. Rainbolt, supra. "Where, as here, the general verdict of the jury is perfect and complete in every particular, and free from uncertainty or ambiguity, we are of opinion that a venire de novo ought not to be granted merely because the answers of the jury to the interrogatories were 'irregular, indefinite, improper, and uncertain.'" Pittsburgh, C. & St. L. Ry. Co. v. Hixon, 110 Ind. 225, 11 N. E. 285.

do not impair the general verdict, and the imperfection does not affect the rendition of judgment.

## Appeal.

**Record.** In *Indiana* it has been "uniformly held that the general verdict, the special findings of the jury on particular questions of fact, the motion for judgment on such special findings notwithstanding the general verdict, the ruling of the trial court on such motion, and the exceptions to such ruling, all constitute proper parts of the record of the cause, on an appeal * * * without any bill of exceptions or any order of the trial court." [41]

The statutes providing for special interrogatories generally provide that the findings shall be "filed with the clerk and entered upon the minutes," "recorded with the verdict," or similar expression.

—— **Presumptions.** Where the record shows that certain interrogatories, which are set out with their answers, were returned with the general verdict, but is silent as to their submission, it will be presumed that they were properly submitted and are properly part of the record. It cannot be presumed that the court received from the jury, and made part of the record in the case, interrogatories which had not been properly submitted to the jury, with correct instructions concerning them.[42] So, where the record does not disclose when the court was asked to submit interrogatories, it will be presumed

[41] Frank v. Grimes, 105 Ind. 346, 351, 4 N. E. 414; Salander v. Lockwood, 66 Ind. 285; Boots v. Griffiths, 97 Ind. 241; Redinbo v. Fretz, 99 Ind. 458; Schaffner v. Kober, 2 Ind. App. 409, 28 N. E. 871. See, also, Davis v. Turner, 69 Ohio St. 101, 68 N. E. 819.

[42] Frank v. Grimes, supra; Shoner v. Pennsylvania Co., 130 Ind. 170, 28 N. E. 616, 29 N. E. 775; Pennsylvania Co. v. Meyers, 136 Ind. 242, 36 N. E. 32; Byers v. Davis, 3 Ind. App. 387, 29 N. E. 798; Life Assur. Co. v. Haughton, 31 Ind. App. 626, 67 N. E. 950; Atchison, T. & S. F. R. Co. v. Johnson, 3 Okl. 41, 41 Pac. 641, and cases cited.

in support of the court's refusal that they were not presented at the proper time.†

Where the record fails to show that questions were submitted at request of counsel, or without the knowledge of opposing counsel, it will be presumed that the court submitted them of its own motion, in which case there was no requirement that they be submitted to counsel.[43]

It seems, however, that the interrogatories are not to be considered properly part of the record, where it appears that an unconditional request for submission was made, and there is nothing to show either that the court was requested to instruct, or did of its own motion instruct, the jurors that if they rendered a general verdict they should find specially upon the particular questions of fact stated in writing by the appellant in his request.[44]

—— **Bill of Exceptions—When Necessary.** The action of the court in overruling a motion to require the jury to make their answers to questions more specific cannot be brought into the record for review by assigning the ruling thereon as cause for a new trial. It can only be made part of the record by bill of exceptions or an order of the court.[45]

Where the record on appeal does not contain the testimony, the court will consider only the exceptions to the charge, and whether the general verdict is consistent with the special findings. The presumption is in such case that every fact necessary to sustain the allegations of the complaint and to justify the verdict of the jury was proven on the trial.[46] The

† Morris v. Morris, 119 Ind. 341, 21 N. E. 918; Cleveland Stone Co. v. Stone Co., 11 Ind. App. 423, 39 N. E. 172. Withdrawal presumed proper where interrogatories not in record. Groscop v. Rainier, 111 Ind. 361, 12 N. E. 694.

43 Briggs v. McEwen, 77 Iowa, 303, 42 N. W. 303.

44 Ogle v. Dill, 61 Ind. 438.

45 Pittsburg, C., C. & St. L. Ry. Co. v. Horseshoe Co., 154 Ind. 322, 56 N. E. 766.

46 Warner v. Association, 8 Utah, 431, 32 Pac. 696; Blew v. Hoover, 30 Ind. 450; Mershon v. Insurance Co., 34 Iowa, 87. The record

question of the sufficiency of the evidence to support the verdict cannot be ascertained in the absence of a bill of exceptions, and the answers to the interrogatories may not be used to determine the question.[47]

Refusal to submit interrogatories cannot be reviewed where the evidence is not in the record.[48] The record should also show that the party proposing the interrogatories had complied with the statute so as to impose upon the trial court the duty to submit them.[49]

In *Illinois,* submitting or refusing to submit a question of fact to the jury, when requested by a party as provided by statute, may be excepted to and be reviewed on appeal or writ of error as a ruling on a question of law.[50]

—— **Ruling on Motion for Judgment.** The ruling on the motion for judgment upon the answers, notwithstanding the general verdict, may be determined by inspection of the record without bill of exceptions, as in the case of demurrer to a pleading.[51] It is only necessary that the decision objected to be entered on the record, and that the ground of objection to

not setting out all the testimony, it must be presumed that evidence was given to support the findings. Stevens v. Rose, 69 Mich. 259, 37 N. W. 205.

47 Louisville, N. A. & C. Ry. Co. v. Kane, 120 Ind. 140, 22 N. E. 80. "The rule in this court is that, on assignment of grounds for a new trial which question merely the sufficiency or legal effect of the evidence, the court will not consider answers to interrogatories." Lake Erie & W. R. Co. v. McFall (Ind. Sup.) 72 N. E. 552, citing: Chicago, St. L. & P. R. Co. v. Kennington, 123 Ind. 409, 24 N. E. 137; Staser v. Hogan, 120 Ind. 207, 21 N. E. 911, 22 N. E. 990; Ohio & M. Ry. Co. v. Selby, 47 Ind. 471, 17 Am. Rep. 719; Sievers v. Peters Box Co., 151 Ind. 642, 50 N. E. 877, 52 N. E. 399.

48 Murphy v. Gould, 40 Neb. 728, 59 N. W. 383.

49 Byers v. Davis, 3 Ind. App. 387, 394, 29 N. E. 798.

50 Hurd's Rev. St. 1899, c. 110, § 58b.

51 Cargar v. Fee, 140 Ind. 572, 39 N. E. 93, and cases cited. See, also, Conners v. Railway Co., 71 Iowa, 490, 32 N. W. 465, 60 Am. Rep. 814.

the ruling of the court appear in the entry, with an exception noted.[52]

In determining the question whether the trial court erred in its ruling upon the motion for judgment on the findings, the appellate court cannot look to the evidence.[53]

**Action by Appellate Court.** The usual procedure where the appellate court reverses a judgment rendered on the findings notwithstanding the general verdict is to direct that judgment be rendered on the general verdict;[54] but, where the hypotheses by which the general verdict is upheld are unusual or remotely probable, a new trial will be ordered.[55] In *Kansas* it is the rule that, "if the verdict does not meet with the approval of the trial court, it should be set aside, and a new trial granted." Adhering thereto, in a case where the defendant filed two motions, one to set aside the verdict for plaintiff and for a new trial, and the other for judgment in its favor on the special findings, and the court granted the latter, and in the order stated that otherwise he should have awarded a new trial, as the verdict was contrary to the evidence, the appellate court reversed the judgment, and remanded the cause for a new trial.[56]

Ordinarily, when the lower court has erroneously overruled a motion for judgment on the special findings, the appellate court will reverse, with instructions to sustain the motion.[57]

[52] Under section 640, Burns' Ann. St. Ind. 1894, an exception is essential. Hill v. Railroad Co., 31 Ind. App. 98, 67 N. E. 276. And so in a specific assignment of error. Copeland v. Ferris, 118 Iowa, 554, 92 N. W. 699.

[53] Pennsylvania Co. v. Smith, 98 Ind. 42; Shuck v. State, 136 Ind. 63, 35 N. E. 993; Schulte v. Railway Co., 114 Iowa, 89, 86 N. W. 63. But see Newman v. Railway Co., 80 Iowa, 678, 45 N. W. 1054.

[54] Jewell v. Town of Sullivan, 5 Ind. App. 188, 31 N. E. 829; Shuck v. State, 136 Ind. 63, 35 N. E. 993.

[55] Jewell v. Town of Sullivan, supra.

[56] Luse v. Railway Co., 57 Kan. 361, 46 Pac. 768.

[57] See, e. g., Lake Erie & W. R. Co. v. Graver, 23 Ind. App. 678, 55

But it is not bound to do so, "but may, when justice requires, remand with instructions to award a venire de novo or grant a new trial." [58]

N. E. 968; Cleveland, C., C. & St. L. Ry. Co. v. Griffin, 26 Ind. App. 368, 58 N. E. 503; Lawrence v. Leathers, 31 Ind. App. 414, 68 N. E. 179; Republic Iron & Steel Co. v. Jones, 32 Ind. App. 189, 69 N. E. 191; Lake Shore & M. S. R. Co. v. Graham, 162 Ind. 374, 70 N. E. 484; Newman v. Railway Co., 80 Iowa, 678, 45 N. W. 1054.

[58] Matchett v. Railway Co., 132 Ind. 334, 31 N. E. 792; Stewart v. Patrick, 5 Ind. App. 50, 30 N. E. 814; McAfee v. Reynolds, 130 Ind. 33, 38 N. E. 423, 18 L. R. A. 211, 30 Am. St. Rep. 194; Chicago & E. R. Co. v. Thomas, 155 Ind. 634, 58 N. E. 1040.

# CHAPTER X.

## SPECIAL VERDICTS.

### Definition and Distinction—Statutory Regulation.

In chapter IV some attention was paid to the distinction between special verdicts and special findings on particular questions of fact, so that little time need here be spent on the matter. It may be well, however, to cite a few cases in which the phrase "special verdict" is defined, and to refer to some in which the difference between general verdicts and those that are special, in the proper sense, are indicated.

A general verdict is not made special merely by indicating the ground on which it is based,[1] nor should it be so construed because in connection therewith are returned answers to certain questions requested to be submitted for a special verdict; the court not being required by statute to direct a special verdict upon specific questions proposed by counsel, and what questions should be submitted to the jury in connection with the general verdict being a matter within the discretion of the trial court.[2]

Neither will answers to questions submitted by the court sua sponte be regarded as a special verdict, and their sufficiency alone to support judgment be considered, where a general verdict is also returned under instructions. In such case the findings should be regarded as made under the statute regulating interrogatories on particular questions of fact, which does not require that all the issues should be covered.[3]

[1] Shifflet v. Morelle, 68 Tex. 382, 4 S. W. 843.

[2] McDougall v. Sulphite-Fibre Co., 97 Wis. 382, 73 N. W. 327, citing Fenelon v. Butts, 53 Wis. 346, 10 N. W. 501.

[3] See Carroll v. Railroad Co., 99 Wis. 399, 75 N. W. 176, 67 Am. St. Rep. 872.

**"Special Verdict" Defined.** A special verdict is where the jury find the facts only, and leave the questions of law arising on them to the court.[4]

Where the jury respond affirmatively or negatively to the issues submitted to them, it is a general verdict, although there be several issues. When they state the facts, and leave the court to apply the law arising from them, it is a special verdict.[5]

[4] People v. Hill, 16 Cal. 113; Day v. Webb, 28 Conn. 144; Conner v. Railway Co., 105 Ind. 62, 4 N. E. 441, 55 Am. Rep. 177; La Frombois v. Jackson, 8 Cow. (N. Y.) 600, 18 Am. Dec. 463; Manning v. Monaghan, 23 N. Y. 539; Smith v. Ireland, 4 Utah, 187, 7 Pac. 749; Willey v. Morrow, 1 Wash. T. 474; Patnode v. Westenhaver. 114 Wis. 460, 483, 90 N. W. 467; Peterson v. U. S., 2 Wash. C. C. 36, Fed. Cas. No. 11,036; Mumford v. Wardwell, 6 Wall. 423, 18 L. Ed. 756; Suydam v. Williamson, 20 How. 427, 15 L. Ed. 978. See, also, Bird v. Lanius, 7 Ind. 615; Graham v. State, 66 Ind. 386.

[5] Porter v. Railroad Co., 97 N. C. 66, 2 S. E. 581, 2 Am. St. Rep. 272.

**North Carolina Practice.** The above case also holds that findings upon issues are not special findings upon particular questions of fact (under Code, § 409); that the particular questions of fact that may be called for are important, leading questions of fact, arising in the case, but which are not made issuable facts in the pleadings.

It is the writer's understanding that instead of taking a general verdict it is the practice in North Carolina to submit issues calling for categorical answers. This is done under Code, § 395, which is as follows: "The issues arising upon the pleadings, material to be tried, shall be made up by the attorneys appearing in the action and reduced to writing, or by the judge presiding, before or during the trial." See Tucker v. Satterthwaite, 120 N. C. 118, 27 S. E. 45; Witsell v. Railway Co., 120 N. C. 557, 27 S. E. 125; Bradley v. Railway Co., 126 N. C. 735, 36 S. E. 181; Vanderbilt v. Brown, 128 N. C. 498, 39 S. E. 36: Griffin v. Railroad Co., 134 N. C. 101, 46 S. E. 9.

Although Porter v. Railroad Co., supra, holds that such a verdict is not a special verdict, yet it corresponds closely to the special verdict as submitted in *Wisconsin* and *Texas*. Witness also the following cases:

"Upon the issues found, the court judges, as matter of law, whether the plaintiff shall recover judgment." Bradley v. Railway Co., 126 N. C. 735, 36 S. E. 181.

"It was found by experience that the old mode of submitting but one issue to the jury, where there were several issues of fact raised

A general verdict is a finding in favor of one of the parties to an action; a special verdict finds the facts, but is not in favor of either party until the court declares the law arising thereon.[6]

The special verdict reiterates all the facts alleged which are sustained by the proofs,[7] and these facts must be sufficiently numerous and explicit to leave nothing for the court to do but determine questions of law.[8]

—— **Statutory Definitions.** The statutes of *Arizona, Arkansas, California, Colorado, Idaho, Indiana, Iowa, Kansas, Minnesota, Missouri, Montana, Nebraska, New York, North Carolina, Oklahoma, Oregon, South Carolina, Texas, Utah, Wisconsin,* and *Wyoming* define the term "special verdict."

by the pleadings, was not satisfactory. The old mode of one issue, which means to find for the plaintiff or for the defendant, gave rise in many cases to what were called 'vicious verdicts.' If it could be so, the jury ought to find the issues submitted to them without knowing whether their findings were for the plaintiff or the defendant. * * * The trial judge should keep it in mind that the very object of submitting written issues to the jury is that they should find the facts, and then the court would apply the law." Elizabethton Shoe Co. v. Hughes, 122 N. C. 296, 29 S. E. 339.

6 Morrison v. Watson, 95 N. C. 479.

7 Darden v. Mathews, 22 Tex. 320; Handel v. Elliott, 60 Tex. 145; McKeen v. Sultenfuss, 61 Tex. 330.

8 Williams v. Love, 1 Ind. T. 585, 43 S. W. 856.

**General, not Special, Verdict.** Where a verdict in an action for waste found for plaintiff, and assessed damages, but subject to the opinion of the court whether, upon certain facts stated, the plaintiff could maintain the action, it was held that this was a general, and not a special, verdict. Dejarnatte v. Allen, 5 Grat. (Va.) 499.

Certain findings construed as a general verdict. McGuffie v. State, 17 Ga. 497; Gover v. Turner, 28 Md. 600; Ross v. Mather, 47 Barb. (N. Y.) 582.

When verdict general under *Georgia* Code, see Lynes v. State, 46 Ga. 208.

**Distinction between General and Special Verdict.** See People v. Bridge Co., 47 N. Y. 586; Louisville, N. A. & C. Ry. Co. v. Balch, 105 Ind. 93, 4 N. E. 288; Com. v. Call, 21 Pick. 509, 32 Am. Dec. 284.

Thus, *California:*[9] "The verdict of the jury is either general or special. A general verdict is that by which they pronounce generally upon all or any of the issues, either in favor of the plaintiff or defendant; a special verdict is that by which the jury find the facts only, leaving the judgment to the court. The special verdict must present the conclusions of fact as established by the evidence, and not the evidence to prove them; and those conclusions of fact must be so presented as that nothing shall remain to the court but to draw from them conclusions of law."

The Code of *Colorado*[10] is practically identical with the foregoing, and the definitions contained in the codes and statutes of other states mentioned do not differ materially, though few include so much as to requisites.[11]

Under these statutes the phrase is understood practically as at common law.[12]

**Special Verdicts Abolished.** In *Indiana, Kansas, Kentucky,* and *Oklahoma* special verdicts have been abolished.

*Indiana:* "In all actions hereafter tried by a jury, the jury shall render a general verdict. * * *"[13]

*Kansas:* "In all cases the jury shall render a general verdict. * * *"[14]

*Kentucky:* In this state, prior to 1886, the jury might find a special verdict, with or without a general, unless otherwise

9 Deering's Code Civ. Proc. § 624.

10 Mills' Ann. Code, § 198.

11 Requisites of Special Verdict. See 1 L. R. A. 303, note.

12 Eisemann v. Swan, 6 Bosw. (N. Y.) 668; Williams v. Willis, 7 Abb. Prac. (N. Y.) 90; Fraschieris v. Henriques, 6 Abb. Prac. N. S. (N. Y.) 251; Chicago & N. W. Ry. Co. v. Dunleavy, 129 Ill. 132, 22 N. E. 15; Collins v. Riley, 104 U. S. 324, 26 L. Ed. 752.

13 Burns' Ann. St. 1901, § 555; Thornton's Rev. 1897, § 560 (under act approved March 4, 1897). Prior thereto the provision was, "In all actions the jury, unless otherwise directed by the court, may, in their discretion, render a general or special verdict." See Burns' Ann. St. 1894, § 555.

14 Gen. St. 1889, par. 4381.

directed by the court; but the amendment of May 15, 1886, struck out the authorization for a special verdict. The only verdicts authorized are (1) general; or (2) general with separate-general; or (3) separate-general.[15]

*Oklahoma:* "In all cases the jury shall render a general verdict. * * *"[16]

**Form of Verdict Entirely in Jury's Discretion.** The statutes of *Arkansas, Illinois, Michigan,* and *New Jersey* provide that the jury, in their discretion, may render a general or special verdict.

The *Arkansas* statute contains no limitation, but the *Illinois*[17] law confines the right to "civil proceedings in this state in courts of record." In *Michigan* it is provided that "No jury shall be compelled in any case to give a general verdict, so that they may not find a special verdict showing the facts respecting which the issue is joined and thereon require the judgment of the court upon such facts"; and similar language is employed in the *New Jersey* law.

Formerly, in *Iowa,* the Code provided that "In all actions, the jury, in their discretion, may render a general or special verdict;"[18] and thereunder it was held error for the court to state to the jury that no general verdict need be returned, and to direct a special verdict only, against objection;[19] for, it was said, every party has the right to a general verdict if he de-

[15] Civ. Code Prac. §§ 317, subd. 5, 327 (Carroll's Rev. Codes 1900).

[16] St. 1893, par. 4176, § 298. But see Severy v. Railway Co., 6 Okl. 163, 50 Pac. 162.

[17] Hurd's Rev. St. 1899, c. 110, § 58a. The act of 1872 (repealed 1874) gave the trial court discretion to order, or refuse to order, a special verdict. Such decision was not reviewable. Kane v. Footh, 70 Ill. 587; Barnes v. Hamon, 71 Ill. 609; Toledo, W. & W. Ry. Co. v. Maxfield, 72 Ill. 95. The present statute, "so far as it relates to special verdicts, is merely declaratory of the common law." Chicago & N. W. Ry. Co. v. Dunleavy, 129 Ill. 132, 22 N. E. 15.

[18] Code 1873, § 2808.

[19] Schultz v. Cremer, 59 Iowa, 182, 13 N. W. 59; Heffner v. Brownell, 78 Iowa, 648, 43 N. W. 468.

mands it and the jury sees fit to render it. The court erred in depriving the jury of that discretion to which they were entitled.[20]

In the Code of 1897 the above-quoted provision is not found.

**Discretion of Jury Limited—To Cases Where Not Otherwise Directed.** The *Ohio* statute provides that "In all actions the jury, unless otherwise directed by the court, may, in its discretion, render either a general or special verdict." [21]

**—— To Cases for Recovery of Money Only, etc.** The statutes of *Idaho, Minnesota, Nebraska, Nevada, North Carolina, Oregon, South Dakota, Washington,* and *Wyoming* provide that "in an [or "every"] action for the recovery of money only, or specific real property, the jury, in their discretion, may render a general or special verdict"; while the laws of *Colorado* and *New York* extend the discretion, the former by omitting the word "real," and the latter by adding, after the words "real property," the phrase "or a chattel."

It is generally held that, in cases of the character mentioned by the statute, the discretion of the jury as to the form of the verdict is absolute.[22] But in *Minnesota* the provision referred to has been construed as meaning that in an action for the re-

[20] Schultz v. Cremer, supra; Hall v. Carter, 74 Iowa, 364, 37 N. W. 956.

In *Michigan* it is held that the jury may find a general or special verdict, but the judge cannot compel them to do either, nor to give reasons for a general finding. Peck v. Snyder, 13 Mich. 21.

[21] Bates' Ann. St. 1897, § 5201. Under Rev. St. 1880, the provision was the same as that of the states first mentioned in the succeeding paragraph.

[22] Thompson v. Gregor, 11 Colo. 531, 19 Pac. 461; Meyers v. Hart, 3 Colo. App. 392, 33 Pac. 647; Pickett v. Handy, 5 Colo. App. 295, 38 Pac. 606. See, also, Hunt v. Elliott, 77 Cal. 588, 20 Pac. 132. Under a former *Ohio* statute, containing provisions similar to the above, it was held that a party has a right to have the jury instructed that they may in their discretion render a special verdict, and that refusal to do so is error. Adams v. Pollock, 12 Ohio St. 618. See Rev. St. 1880, § 5201.

covery of money only, or specific real property, the judge may, in his discretion, instruct the jury that they may, in their discretion, render a general or special verdict.[23]

In *North Dakota* and *Wisconsin* the jury's discretion is restricted (1) to actions for the recovery of money only or specific real property, where (2) they are not otherwise directed by the court.

The provision of the *California* Code is: "In an action for the recovery of money only, or specific real property, the jury, unless instructed by the court to render a special verdict, may in their discretion render a general or special verdict."

In *Missouri* "in every issue for the recovery of money only, or specific real or personal property," it is required that "the jury shall render a general verdict."

**Discretion of Court as to Form of Verdict.** In *Idaho, Minnesota, Nebraska, Nevada, New York, North Carolina, Oregon, South Dakota, Washington,* and *Wyoming,* the statutes provide that, in cases other than those in which discretion is conferred upon the jury as to the form of their verdict (recovery of money only, etc.), "the court may direct the jury to find a special verdict in writing upon all or any of the issues." [24]

In *New York* there is an exception to this power, "where one or more specific questions of fact, stated under the direction of the court, are tried by the jury."

Apparently the discretion lodged in the court is not absolute. It must be soundly exercised. Where the issues are of a complicated nature, it has been held the duty of the court to submit special issues at the request of a party, and that refusal to do so was reversible error.[25]

In *Arizona,* "where the court does not instruct the jury to find a special verdict, the verdict shall be general."

The *Colorado* law contains no express provision as to when

[23] Morrow v. Railway Co., 74 Minn. 480, 77 N. W. 303.

[24] Quotation from *Idaho*. See, also, Thompson v. Gregor, 11 Colo. 531, 19 Pac. 461.

[25] Burke v. McDonald, 2 Idaho (Hasb.) 679, 33 Pac. 49.

the court may direct a special verdict; but, as it limits the jury's discretion, that of the court is implied in cases outside the limitation.

The *Montana* and *Utah* provisions permit the court in all cases to direct the jury to find a special verdict, while in *Missouri* the court may so direct except in issues for the recovery of money only, or specific real or personal property, which the statute requires shall be disposed of by a general verdict.

In *Vermont*, "the jury impaneled for the trial of any civil cause may find a special verdict agreeably to the usages of law." And it is held not a matter of exception for the court to order it.[26]

—— **Direction on Request of Party.** In *California, North Dakota, Ohio, Rhode Island,* and *Wisconsin* the jury must in all cases return a special verdict when so directed by the court, and the court must so direct upon proper request by a party.

In *Texas,* under Rev. St. 1879, art. 1333, the submission of a case upon special issues was in the discretion of the trial court, and it was held that the appellate court would not revise its action unless it clearly appeared that there had been an abuse of discretion.[27]

At the same session at which the above-mentioned statutes were adopted, article 1333 was amended (Laws 1879, p. 119), and has since been given in the revisions as follows: "The jury shall render a general or special verdict, as shall be directed by the court at the request of a party to the suit," etc.;[28] the revisers, however, overlooking a second amendment, by which the article was restored to its original form (Sp. Laws 1879, p. 38).

The statute as first amended was construed by the Supreme Court as meaning that "the jury shall render a general verdict,

26 Hogle v. Clark, 46 Vt. 418; Babcock v. Culver, Id. 715.

27 Cole v. Crawford, 69 Tex. 124, 5 S. W. 646; Texas & P. Ry. Co. v. Miller, 79 Tex. 78, 15 S. W. 264, 11 L. R. A. 395, 23 Am. St. Rep. 308.

28 See Appendix; Sayles' Ann. Civ. St. 1897; Rev. St. 1895, art. 1333.

or a special verdict which the court shall direct when so requested by a party to the suit"—"shall" being interpreted as a word of command.[29]

In Acts 1899, c. 111, p. 190, the article returns to its first form, making it discretionary with the court to submit the case on special issues;[30] and thereunder it is held that a refusal thus to submit furnishes no ground for reversing the judgment.[31] But there is added to the article the following: "Provided, that a case shall not be submitted on special issues by the court unless one or all of the parties to the suit request such submission."

The law now appears to stand thus: The court may not direct a special verdict without request; but neither need it grant such request, and apparently the discretion exercised in refusing a submission on special issues is not reviewable.[32]

**General Requirements.** It is uniformly provided that the special verdict shall be in writing, and be filed with the clerk and entered upon the mintutes.

In addition to the foregoing regulations, others prescribing the manner of preparation of questions, their form, the time when the request for a special verdict shall be made, etc., are occasionally found. These will be noticed later, under appropriate headings.

**In What Courts Special Verdicts may be Rendered.** It seems that the right to return special verdicts is confined to juries in courts proceeding according to the course of the common law, in the absence of express statutory authority.

[29] Galveston, H. & S. A. Ry. Co. v. Jackson, 92 Tex. 638, 50 S. W. 1012, which case gives a history of special-verdict legislation in Texas, and clears up some doubts as to the status of the law on the subject. See, also, Texas Loan Agency v. Fleming, 18 Tex. Civ. App. 668, 46 S. W. 63.

[30] See Appendix.

[31] Home Circle Soc. v. Shelton (Tex. Civ. App.) 85 S. W. 320; Galveston, H. & S. A. Ry. Co. v. Jackson, 93 Tex. 266, 54 S. W. 1023.

[32] Galveston, H. & S. A. Ry. Co. v. Jackson, 93 Tex. 266, 54 S. W. 1023.

No judgment can be rendered on a special verdict in a justice's court. In the leading opinion on this point, the Supreme Court of *New York* said: "This court have decided that a demurrer to evidence is a proceeding inapplicable to a justice's court, because justices are not, generally, acquainted with the science of law ([Reynolds v. Bedford] 3 Caines, 140); yet, should special verdicts be allowed in such a court, the same legal knowledge would be requisite to enable a justice to render judgment on such verdict, because in one instance the facts are admitted by the party, and in the other they are found by the jury; and the only question in either case is a question of law, to be determined by the justice. Besides, it might be attended with unavoidable injustice to a party, for a special verdict might be so defective that no judgment could be rendered thereon. In such cases the practice of other courts (Sellon, 495), having the power, is to award a venire facias de novo. This a justice cannot do. The party consequently would be without a remedy in that cause, and would be obliged to commence a new action. It therefore appears to be manifestly unfit and improper that special verdicts should be allowed in justices' courts." [33]

Special verdicts may be taken in federal courts; [34] but such courts are not bound to submit them in accordance with the rules of practice of a particular state.[35]

**Constitutionality of Statute.** In Udell v. Citizens' St. R. Co.[36] it was objected that the *Indiana* act of March 11, 1895, providing for special verdicts, violated the right of trial by jury guarantied by the Constitution. In reply to arguments of counsel, the court said:

"In civil actions, under the Constitution of this state, the

[33] Wylie v. Hyde, 13 Johns. 249, 250.

[34] Daube v. Iron Co., 46 U. S. App. 591, 23 C. C. A. 420, 77 Fed. 713. See, also, Baltimore & O. R. Co. v. Adams, 10 App. D. C. 97.

[35] United States Mut. Acc. Ass'n v. Barry, 131 U. S. 100, 9 Sup. Ct. 755, 33 L. Ed. 60.

[36] 152 Ind. 507, 52 N. E. 799, 71 Am. St. Rep. 336.

jury never possessed the right to decide questions of law. Their inquiries have always been confined to matters of fact. The scope of such inquiries is not abridged by the act of March 11, 1895. The argument of counsel, founded upon the distinction between primary facts and inferences or conclusions from facts, is unsound. If an inference or conclusion from a fact or facts is itself a fact proper to be found by the jury, it may be made the subject of an interrogatory. But if the proposed inference or conclusion from a fact or facts is not itself a fact, but a conclusion or inference of law, then the jury has no right to find such conclusion or inference. The statute in question authorized either party to submit to the jury every essential question of fact, together with every proper inference or conclusion of fact. If parties to actions did not avail themselves of this privilege, it was not because of any defect or prohibition in the law."

**Special Verdicts Where Not Regulated by Statute.** In states where no specific statutory provision on the subject exists, special verdicts may be found as at common law. The court is not justified in directing the jury to find a special verdict, though it may, in its discretion, in a proper case recommend one.[37] A jury has the right to decline finding any other than a general verdict.[38]

[37] Baltimore & O. R. Co. v. School Dist., 3 Penny. (Pa.) 518.

The jury may be directed to return a verdict upon each distinct count, or the required information may be obtained by framing special verdicts; but the former method is the one generally resorted to in practice. Johnson v. Higgins, 53 Conn. 236, 1 Atl. 616.

[38] Fuller v. Insurance Co., 31 Me. 325. But see Farr v. Thompson, 1 Speers (S. C.) 93.

The court cannot refuse to receive a special verdict. 1 Co. Litt. 228; 4 Bl. Comm. 361.

# CHAPTER XI.

## SPECIAL VERDICTS (Continued).

Request for, Preparation and Form of, Verdict—Submission and Refusal.

**Direction on Request Mandatory.** In *California, Ohio, North Dakota, Rhode Island,* and *Wisconsin,* the court is required, when counsel so requests, to direct the jury to find a special verdict. The provision of the statute is mandatory;[1] but it is held to apply only to cases triable by jury, and not to cases triable by the court alone, in which issues are submitted to the jury, since the verdict in the latter is simply advisory.[2]

The statute making a special verdict matter of right upon proper request "was not intended to take away the power which has been vested in and exercised by the judges of the common-law courts from time immemorial, of directing a nonsuit when the plaintiff fails to establish a cause of action by his proof, or of directing a verdict either for the plaintiff or defendant when, upon the evidence offered, it becomes a question of law as to which party is entitled to a verdict. Juries are called to determine questions of fact only, at least in civil actions;

1 Cleveland, C., C. & St. L. Ry. Co. v. Village of St. Bernard, 19 Ohio Cir. Ct. 299; Davis v. Town of Farmington, 42 Wis. 425, 431; Schumaker v. Heinemann, 99 Wis. 251, 74 N. W. 785; Gatzow v. Buening, 106 Wis. 1, 81 N. W. 1003, 49 L. R. A. 475, 80 Am. St. Rep. 1; Pearson v. Kelly (Wis.) 100 N. W. 1064. See, also, Bird v. Lanius, 7 Ind. 615; Noble v. Enos, 19 Ind. 73; Leavenworth, L. & G. R. Co. v. Rice, 10 Kan. 426; Bush v. Peake, 14 Kan. 290. Not error to deny request, unless the refusal was prejudicial. Gatzow v. Buening, supra.

2 Reddick v. Keesling, 129 Ind. 128, 28 N. E. 316 (under Rev. St. Ind. 1881, § 546, providing that the court shall, at the request of either party, direct the jury to give a special verdict); Taylor v. Collins, 51 Wis. 123. 8 N. W. 22; Adams v. Rodman, 102 Wis. 456, 78 N. W. 588, 759.

and when the facts are admitted, or not controverted, the rights of the parties are then fixed by the law applicable to the state of facts admitted or uncontroverted, and there is no function for the jury to perform in the case. This statute must receive a reasonable construction. It would be absurd to say that the Legislature intended that, when there is no proof to establish the facts necessary to make out a cause of action, the party against whom the verdict must go upon the law of the case may demand that the jury shall pass upon and find these facts in the form of a special verdict. * * * The true meaning of the statute is that, when the case is submitted to the jury upon the evidence, either party may demand that the jury shall find a special, instead of a general, verdict." [3]

**Request Necessary.** Whether a special verdict is matter of right, or is discretionary with the court, a proper request therefor is necessary. Evidently, there can be no error where the court does not do that which it is neither required by law nor asked to do.[4]

[3] Furlong v. Garrett, 44 Wis. 111, 125.

**Object of Statute.** "The right to a special verdict is a most valuable one. By requiring the jury to pass separately and specifically upon each controverted question of fact material to the issue, a more careful and methodical consideration of the testimony by the jury may be secured, and the precise grounds upon which the judgment is based will be disclosed." Davis v. Town of Farmington, 42 Wis. 425, 431.

"The statute authorizing special verdicts appears designed to guard against mistaken or willful verdicts, and to enable the court to review the precise grounds on which verdicts are found." Dorsey v. Phillips & Colby Const. Co., 42 Wis. 583, 603.

"The aim of the statute is to enable the court to focus the mental operations of the jury upon the turning points in a case, avoiding the danger present in taking a general verdict of the law being applied to facts in form, without any precedent finding of facts." Patnode v. Westenhaver, 114 Wis. 460, 483, 90 N. W. 467.

[4] See Louisville, N. A. & C. Ry. Co. v. Kane, 120 Ind. 140, 22 N. E. 80; Kalckhoff v. Zoehrlaut, 43 Wis. 373; Fenelon v. Butts, 53 Wis. 344, 10 N. W. 501; Kenyon v. Kenyon, 72 Wis. 234, 39 N. W. 361;

The *Texas* law provides that, "Upon appeal or writ of error, an issue not submitted and not requested by a party to the cause shall be deemed as found by the court in such manner as to support the judgment: provided, there be evidence to sustain such finding." [5]

**Time of Making Request.** The only statutes which specify the time at which the request shall be made are those of *North Dakota* and *Wisconsin*. The former requires it to be made "at or before the close of the testimony and before any argument to the jury is made or waived." This was also, until very recently, the language of the Wisconsin law. But by chapter 390, Laws 1903, the section (2858, Rev. St. 1898) was amended, so that it reads: "The court, in its discretion, may, and when either party, before the introduction of any testimony in his behalf, shall so request, the court shall, direct the jury to find a special verdict."

This amendment is evidently intended to give the court opportunity to frame questions with suitable care, instead of upon the spur of the moment, and is calculated to secure (if it were necessary) closer attention on the part of the trial judge to the issues and the testimony thereunder.

Under these statutes, if the demand is not made at the time prescribed, it comes too late to make it the duty of the court to direct a special verdict.[6] The matter then rests in the discretion of the trial judge, and to refuse the request is not error.[7]

McDougall v. Sulphite-Fibre Co., 97 Wis. 382, 73 N. W. 327; Smith v. Smith, 10 Tex. Civ. App. 485, 32 S. W. 28. When the record is silent as to a request for a special verdict, one will be presumed, the contrary not appearing. Stahl v. Askey (Tex. Civ. App.) 81 S. W. 79.

[5] See Brown v. Sovereign Camp, 20 Tex. Civ. App. 373, 49 S. W. 893; Galveston, H. & S. A. Ry. Co. v. Botts, 22 Tex. Civ. App. 609, 55 S. W. 514.

[6] United States Exp. Co. v. Jenkins, 73 Wis. 471, 41 N. W. 957.

[7] Id.; Pool v. Railway Co., 56 Wis. 227, 14 N. W. 46; Lockhart v. Fessenich, 58 Wis. 588, 17 N. W. 302.

A request for special verdict may be properly refused after a request to instruct the jury generally, and after the court has intimated to counsel the character of the instructions,[8] or after argument on requested instructions.[9] But it is not error for the court to grant a request for a special verdict made after argument, and after discussion by counsel of questions of law involved in the instructions, for the court might at such time direct the verdict of its own motion.[10]

Under the *Ohio* statute, which makes a special verdict matter of right on demand, but does not specify when the request shall be made, it is held that it comes in season if made at the close of the argument and before the charge.[11]

It would seem that in any case the request should come before instructions are given, as these will be materially different according to the understanding the court has as to the kind of verdict to be rendered. Instructions given on the supposition that the verdict is to be general will frequently, while proper in connection with a general verdict, be improper and involve reversible error when coupled with questions for a special verdict.

**Mode and Nature of Request.** The request for a special verdict need not be in writing, except in *California,* but questions proposed by counsel must be. In *Texas,* under the statute providing that failure to submit any issue shall not be deemed ground for reversal on appeal unless its submission has been requested in writing by the party complaining of the judgment, an assignment of error predicated upon the trial court's refusal to submit additional special issues, as requested, will not be con-

8 Ohio & M. Ry. Co. v. Wrape, 4 Ind. App. 100, 30 N. E. 428, citing inter alia, Hartlep v. Cole, 120 Ind. 253, 22 N. E. 130; Kopelke v. Kopelke, 112 Ind. 435, 13 N. E. 695.

9 Sandford Tool & Fork Co. v. Mullen, 1 Ind. App. 204, 27 N. E. 448.

10 Lowman v. Sheets, 124 Ind. 416, 24 N. E. 351, 7 L. R. A. 784. See, also, Johnson v. Culver, 116 Ind. 278, 19 N. E. 129.

11 Baltimore & O. R. Co. v. McCamey, 12 Ohio Cir. Ct. R. 543, 5 O. C. D. 631.

sidered where the record does not show that the request was in writing.[12]

It is generally held that the preparation and form of the special verdict, or, more accurately, of the questions to which answers are desired, is largely in the discretion of the trial court. Where, therefore, counsel requests the court to direct the jury to find a special verdict and to submit to them certain questions only, it is not error to refuse so to direct.[13] Such a request is not a request for a special verdict to which the court must accede under the statute; and if the court does submit questions so proposed, and the jury return answers thereto, accompanied by a general verdict, the answers will not be regarded as amenable to the rules governing the construction of special verdicts.[14]

**Request as Bar to Objection.** A party cannot complain of an answer directly responsive to a question submitted by him in a special verdict.[15]

12 Yeager v. Neil, 26 Tex. Civ. App. 414, 64 S. W. 701. See Stahl v. Askey (Tex. Civ. App.) 81 S. W. 79.

13 Fenelon v. Butts, 53 Wis. 344, 10 N. W. 501.

14 McDougall v. Sulphite-Fibre Co., 97 Wis. 382, 73 N. W. 327.

Merely presenting the draft of a special verdict is not equivalent to a request. Woollen v. Whitacre, 91 Ind. 502; Louisville, N. A. & C. Ry. Co. v. Kane, 120 Ind. 140, 22 N. E. 80.

Where, at the close of the evidence, defendant handed a paper to the court, reciting that it was a request to submit to the jury for answer, "and as a special verdict," certain questions, but the court treated the request as one for the submission of such questions only, and defendant's attorney did not further indicate that his intention was to request a special verdict, he could not thereafter contend that such was the effect of his application, and that it was therefore error to charge the jury generally as to the legal effect of their answers to the questions submitted. Schmitt v. Northern Pac. R. Co., 120 Wis. 397, 98 N. W. 202. An oral request is all that is necessary. Id.

A party requesting direction of a special verdict cannot also require that interrogatories be propounded, to be answered in the event of a general verdict being returned. If he does so, he waives his request for a special verdict. Noble v. Enos, 19 Ind. 73.

15 Pittsburgh, C., C. & St. L. R. Co. v. Beck, 152 Ind. 421, 53 N. E. 439; Gale v. Insurance Co., 33 Mo. App. 664.

The court has the right to understand that a question proposed by counsel includes everything the party requesting it desires to have submitted on the matter to which it relates, and he cannot on appeal be heard to allege the insufficiency of the question as ground for reversal.[16]

But failure to request submission of a proper question covering a material and controverted fact in issue is not a waiver of the defect in the verdict resulting from the omission.[17]

**Preparation and Form.** Mr. Stephen, in his work on Pleading,[18] says that "the jury have nothing to do with the formal preparation of the special verdict. When it is agreed that a verdict of that kind is to be given, the jury merely declare their opinion as to any fact remaining in doubt, and then the verdict is adjusted without their further interference. It is settled under the correction of the judge, by the counsel and attorneys on either side, according to the state of facts as found by the jury, with respect to all particulars on which they have delivered an opinion, and, with respect to other particulars, according to the state of facts which it is agreed that they *ought* to find upon the evidence before them. The special verdict, when its form is thus settled, is, together with the whole proceedings on the trial, then entered on *record*, and the question of law arising on facts found is argued before the court in bank, and decided by that court, as in case of demurrer." [19]

In *Indiana* the practice formerly existed of submitting to the jury two drafts, prepared by counsel for the respective parties, and subject to the approval of the court, which drafts set forth in narrative form such facts as counsel contended were established by the evidence. The jury adopted the draft which con-

16 Wright v. Mulvaney, 78 Wis. 89, 46 N. W. 1045, 9 L. R. A. 807, 23 Am. St. Rep. 393.

17 Hildman v. City of Phillips, 106 Wis. 611, 82 N. W. 566.

18 Page 91. "See the form of it. Wittersheim v. Lady Carlisle, 1 H. Bl. 631; Cook v. Gerrard, 1 Saund. 171a."

19 See, also, Suydam v. Williamson, 20 How. 427, 15 L. Ed. 978; Mumford v. Wardwell, 6 Wall. 423, 18 L. Ed. 756.

tained the facts according to their view of the weight of the evidence.[20] But they might alter a draft to correspond with their recollection of the testimony, or reject both forms, and prepare a special verdict for themselves.[21]

While this practice obtained, it was said that "the court should not be required to prepare a special verdict for many reasons. In the first place, the opinion of the court as to what had been proved would have undue influence with the jury. In the next place, the court is required to pass upon the form and sufficiency of the special verdict. And in the third place, after the verdict has been returned, the court is frequently required to pass upon motions for venire de novo, new trial, and in arrest of judgment; and this cannot be fairly and satisfactorily done if the judge has been required to prepare a draft of what he believed had been proved at the trial." [22]

On the other hand, "the counsel engaged in the trial of a cause understood the issues involved, the facts necessary to be found to cover the issues, the testimony in the cause, and the requisite form to be adopted. Nor do we think that there is any danger that an attorney would take advantage of his position to deceive or mislead the jury. An attorney acts under the solemnity of an oath, and the responsibility that he owes the court, the jury, his client, and the public; and all these weighty considerations would induce him to act fairly and truthfully in preparing a special verdict. Besides, he knows

[20] See Hopkins v. Stanley, 43 Ind. 553. See, also, Hammond, Whiting & E. C. Electric Ry. Co. v. Spyzchalski, 17 Ind. App. 7, 46 N. E. 47; Miller v. Shackleford, 4 Dana (Ky.) 264; Cleveland, C., C. & St. L. Ry. Co. v. Village of St. Bernard, 10 O. C. D. 415.

[21] Pittsburgh, Ft. W. & C. Ry. Co. v. Ruby, 38 Ind. 309, 10 Am. Rep. 111. Under section 286 of the Civil Code of Kansas, as it read from 1870 up to 1874, the jury themselves were required to prepare in writing and render the special verdict which they might agree upon, without any aid from either of the parties. Foster v. Turner, 31 Kan. 58, 1 Pac. 145.

[22] Pittsburgh, Ft. W. & C. Ry. Co. v. Ruby, 38 Ind. 309, 10 Am. Rep. 111.

that, if he does not state the facts correctly, the fraud would be discovered by the jury, and would operate to the prejudice of his client and the injury of his cause." [23]

The method above outlined was finally discarded in favor of a verdict upon interrogatories, each of which was to be answered by the jury, under the evidence, and each to be so framed as to require the finding thereon to embrace but a single fact. The statute, as amended, directed that counsel on each side should prepare such number of interrogatories as might be necessary to cover all of the facts material to the issues in the action, all of which interrogatories were to be submitted to the court, subject to its change, modification, and final approval. When so approved, the court caused them to be numbered, not in separate sets, but as an entirety from one to the close, and submitted them to the jury with the instruction that each be answered, and all returned as a special verdict in the cause.[24]

Under the old practice statute it was held that an assignment of error showing a refusal by the court to submit a form of special verdict prepared by counsel, on the ground that it was the province and duty of the court to prepare and submit to the jury the special verdict, is good on the ground of such assumption by the court being liable to affect and prejudice the finding of the jury.[25]

[23] Id. Under this practice "it was almost impossible for the jury to return an unbiased verdict." Town of Kentland v. Hagen, 17 Ind. App. 1, 46 N. E. 43, q. v.

[24] Acts 1895, p. 248, amending sec. 546, Rev. St. 1881 (sec. 555, Rev. St. 1894); Bower v. Bower, 146 Ind. 393, 45 N. E. 595. The court may, of its own motion, submit to the jury its own draft of a special verdict. Lauter v. Duckworth, 19 Ind. App. 535, 48 N. E. 864.

Under the present statute of *Indiana*, the jury is required to render a general verdict in all actions.

[25] Case v. Ellis, 4 Ind. App. 224, 30 N. E. 907. But in Town of Kentland v. Hagen, 17 Ind. App. 1, 46 N. E. 43, under the Act of 1895, it was said that, though counsel might propose interrogatories, the court should submit such as it thinks proper, rewritten and renumbered, as coming from the court.

Other cases in which the submission by counsel of forms for special verdicts is approved will be found in the footnote.[26]

**Special Verdict upon Interrogatories.** The prevailing practice under the statutes relating to special verdicts seems to be to submit a series of questions covering all the issues, and to require answers thereto, which, in connection with the questions, constitute the verdict; [27] and in *North Dakota* and *Wisconsin* it is expressly required that this method be followed.

The statutes of the states last mentioned specifically make it the duty of the court to prepare the questions.[28] This does not preclude counsel from suggesting amendments and additions. Only, they may not insist upon submission of the questions or form presented. Neither party can dictate the terms of any particular question to the jury,[29] and the court is justified in refusing to adopt and submit any questions which are improper or which are covered by others prepared by it. "The only legitimate purpose of suggestions from counsel, as to what particular questions shall be submitted, * * * is to direct the attention of the court to the issuable facts upon which the controversy depends." [30]

In *Texas* it is said that there is no uniform practice determining the mode of forming and submitting special issues to a jury. They may be prepared by counsel and sanctioned by the court; formulated by the judge at the request of counsel,

[26] Louisville, N. A. & C. Ry. Co. v. Flanagan, 113 Ind. 488, 14 N. E. 370, 3 Am. St. Rep. 674; Miller v. Shackleford, 4 Dana (Ky.) 264; Cleveland, C., C. & St. L. Ry. Co. v. Village of St. Bernard, 19 Ohio Cir. Ct. R. 299; Mumford v. Wardwell, 6 Wall. 423, 18 L. Ed. 756.

[27] In *Virginia* it is said that a special verdict upon interrogatories "is not known to our practice." Hall v. Ratliff, 93 Va. 327, 24 S. E. 1011.

[28] See Pratt v. Peck, 65 Wis. 463, 27 N. W. 180; Schumaker v. Heinemann, 99 Wis. 251, 74 N. W. 785; Gatzow v. Buening, 106 Wis. 1, 81 N. W. 1003, 49 L. R. A. 475, 80 Am. St. Rep. 1.

[29] American Co. v. Bradford, 27 Cal. 360.

[30] Gatzow v. Buening, supra.

or on his own motion, to meet the requirements of the case in furtherance of justice.[31]

The last statement doubtless gives the general rule of practice.

—— **Form of Verdict—Requisites of Questions.** The form of a special verdict is largely in the discretion of the trial court,[32] and, if the questions submitted cover all the controverted issues of fact and are reasonably specific, the Supreme Court will not interfere.[33] As in other cases of discretionary action, the ruling of the trial court will be sustained except where there has been a clear abuse of discretion.[34]

The questions should, so far as practicable, be framed so as

[31] Heflin v. Burns, 70 Tex. 347, 8 S. W. 48.

Answers to questions agreed upon by counsel, without a general verdict, must be regarded in the light of a special verdict. Carr v. Carr, 4 Lans. (N. Y.) 314.

[32] American Co. v. Bradford, 27 Cal. 360; McCormack v. Phillips, 4 Dak. 506, 34 N. W. 39; Louisville, N. A. & C. Ry. Co. v. Flanagan, 113 Ind. 488, 14 N. E. 370, 3 Am. St. Rep. 674; Jordan v. Farthing, 117 N. C. 181, 23 S. E. 244; Ward v. Busack, 46 Wis. 407, 1 N. W. 107; Pratt v. Peck, 65 Wis. 463, 27 N. W. 180; Heddles v. Railway Co., 74 Wis. 239, 42 N. W. 237; Bartlett v. Beardmore, 77 Wis. 356, 46 N. W. 494; Lindner v. Insurance Co., 93 Wis. 526, 67 N. W. 1125; Werner v. Railroad Co., 105 Wis. 300, 81 N. W. 416; Lee v. Railway Co., 101 Wis. 352, 77 N. W. 714; Hebbe v. Town of Maple Creek, 121 Wis. 668, 99 N. W. 442.

[33] Hoppe v. Railway Co., 61 Wis. 357, 21 N. W. 227; Bartlett v. Beardmore, 77 Wis. 356, 46 N. W. 494; Raymond v. Keseberg, 98 Wis. 317, 73 N. W. 1010; Dodge v. O'Dell's Estate, 106 Wis. 296, 82 N. W. 135. "As to what issues shall be submitted must depend upon the careful and intelligent consideration of the trial judge. There should never be an issue submitted as to a question of fact, as distinguished from an issue of fact. There should be only such issues of fact submitted as arise out of the pleadings. There should not be too many issues submitted, as this tends to confuse the jury. But there should always be such issues submitted as will plainly and intelligently present to the jury the contentions of the parties." Elizabethon Shoe Co. v. Hughes, 122 N. C. 296, 29 S. E. 339.

[34] Zimmer v. Railroad Co., 118 Wis. 614, 95 N. W. 959, and cases cited.

to secure intelligent consideration, on the evidence, of the issues made by the pleadings and controverted on the evidence, separately, and a decision thereof without reference to the final result on the rights of the parties.[35]

All questions of fact raised by the pleadings, and necessary to determine the case, should be separately and distinctly stated,[36] and those facts from which an issuable fact may be inferred are properly omitted, though questions covering such evidentiary facts may be added in the discretion of the court for the purpose of "tying the jury down to the precise question in controversy." [37] But the object of a special verdict is solely to obtain a decision of issues of fact, not to decide disputes between witnesses as to minor facts, even if such minor facts are essential to establish, by inference or otherwise, the main fact.[38]

Rules governing the form and content of questions are largely corollaries of the settled requisites of special verdicts, which are reserved for consideration in another place; but a few essentials and desirable qualities in interrogatories are the following:

Questions which suggest the answers desired by the party preparing them should not be submitted by the court as his own, since they are calculated to impress the jury with the belief that the judge is of opinion that they should be given the answers they suggest.[39] They should be single,[40] for other-

35 Mauch v. City of Hartford, 112 Wis. 40, 87 N. W. 816; Byington v. City of Merrill, 112 Wis. 211, 88 N. W. 26.

36 Phœnix Water Co. v. Fletcher, 23 Cal. 482; Brewster v. Bours, 8 Cal. 501; Baxter v. Railway Co., 104 Wis. 307, 80 N. W. 644. See, also, Coolidge v. Ayers, 76 Vt. 405, 57 Atl. 970.

37 Baxter v. Railroad Co., 104 Wis. 307, 80 N. W. 644.

38 Id., and cases cited.

39 Q. "Is it not a fact," etc. Oaks v. West (Tex. Civ. App.) 64 S. W. 1033. Or which embody the law applicable to the fact to be determined. Lyon v. City of Grand Rapids, 121 Wis. 609, 99 N. W. 311.

40 Peake v. City of Superior, 106 Wis. 403, 82 N. W. 306; Phœnix Water Co. v. Fletcher, 23 Cal. 481; Riske v. Grocery Co. (Tex. Civ. App.) 84 S. W. 243.

wise the answers may be ambiguous. Issues should not be subdivided and covered by several questions, nor should questions be so framed as to require the jury to decide a single issue by viewing it in various aspects.[41] But the objection that a special verdict does not comply with the statute requiring interrogatories to be so framed that the jury will be required to find only a single fact in answer to each, will not be sustained where it is admitted that the verdict contains all material facts necessary to sustain the judgment thereon, and no request was made to the court to exercise its statutory authority to modify the interrogatories prepared by counsel.[42]

The inclusion in a question of the special verdict of several inquiries capable of answer in different ways is not necessarily erroneous and prejudicial. It is so only when, measured by its answer, it leaves the decision of the jury ambiguous and uncertain. "If a jury be asked whether three separate propositions be true, all joined by the conjunctive, and answer in the affirmative, there is no uncertainty or ambiguity about any one of them. By declaring that all are true, they have declared that each is. The same question, answered in the negative, might constitute reversible error, if more than one proposition submitted were material; for then the jury, by answering in the negative to the inquiry whether all are true, have not necessarily declared their decision as to any one of them." [43]

The statutes of *North Dakota* and *Wisconsin* expressly require that the questions submitted shall relate to material [44]

[41] Mauch v. City of Hartford, 112 Wis. 40, 87 N. W. 816.

**Elements of Damages.** The jury cannot be required to itemize damages. Blesch v. Railway Co., 48 Wis. 168, 2 N. W. 113. See, also, Keller v. Gaskill, 20 Ind. App. 502, 50 N. E. 363; Ohio & M. Ry. Co. v. Judy, 120 Ind. 397, 22 N. E. 252.

[42] Chicago & S. E. Ry. Co. v. Coulter, 18 Ind. App. 512, 48 N. E. 388.

[43] Shaw v. Gilbert, 111 Wis. 165, 183, 86 N. W. 188; Hebbe v. Town of Maple Creek, 121 Wis. 668, 99 N. W. 442.

[44] The ends of justice will, no doubt, often be promoted by questions not strictly necessary, which guide the jury by a logical process

issues and admit a direct answer. They should be so framed as to call for an affirmative or negative reply.[45] It is evident that, the shorter and simpler the answer required, the less the liability to mistake and confusion on the part of the jury, and of ambiguity in the verdict.[46]

As a general rule, a question for a special verdict should not be framed in the alternative or disjunctive,[47] as tending to render the answer indefinite; and a compound question in which the parts are connected by the conjunctive "and" may be obnoxious for the same reason.[48] However, the answer to a question in the alternative may be sufficient, where the testimony proving one branch also proves the other,[49] or where the legal result is the same, to whichever part the answer is applied.[50]

of reasoning to the proper conclusion as to the real subject of inquiry. Baxter v. Railroad Co., 104 Wis. 307, 80 N. W. 644.

45 Mauch v. City of Hartford, 112 Wis. 40, 87 N. W. 816; Russell v. Meyer, 7 N. D. 335, 75 N. W. 262, 47 L. R. A. 637.

46 See Marshall v. Blackshire, 44 Iowa, 475; Jackson v. Insurance Co., 27 Mo. App. 77; Wilkie v. Chandon, 1 Wash. St. 355, 25 Pac. 464; Redford v. Railway Co., 9 Wash. 55, 36 Pac. 1085; Jewell v. Railway Co., 54 Wis. 610, 12 N. W. 83, 41 Am. Rep. 63; Murray v. Abbot, 61 Wis. 198, 20 N. W. 910.

47 Sherman v. Lumber Co., 77 Wis. 14, 45 N. W. 1079; Geisinger v. Beyl, 80 Wis. 443, 50 N. W. 501; Gunther v. Ullrich, 82 Wis. 222, 52 N. W. 88, 33 Am. St. Rep. 32; Klochinski v. Lumber Co., 93 Wis. 417, 67 N. W. 934; Goesel v. Davis, 100 Wis. 678, 76 N. W. 768; Lowe v. Ring (Wis.) 101 N. W. 698. Error in submitting question so framed cured by answers to other questions. Spille v. Iron Co., 105 Wis. 340, 81 N. W. 397.

48 Dugal v. City of Chippewa Falls, 101 Wis. 533, 77 N. W. 878. Question held not to be compound. Nauman v. Ullman, 102 Wis. 92, 78 N. W. 159.

49 Geisinger v. Beyl, 80 Wis. 443, 50 N. W. 501. Two propositions in the disjunctive form, requiring but one affirmative answer, may properly be submitted if the jury would be justified in giving an affirmative answer, if either proposition, taken separately, would justify such answer. Gerhardt v. Swaty, 57 Wis. 24, 40, 14 N. W. 851.

50 Patry v. Railway Co., 82 Wis. 408, 52 N. W. 312. A question submitted for a special verdict, "Did the defendant or his author-

Questions not based upon testimony,[51] or concerning which there is no controversy,[52] or proper answers to which would be inconclusive [53] and would not support a judgment,[54] need not be submitted.

—— **Objections to form** must be made at the time of submission; otherwise it will be presumed that there was assent to the submission of questions as drawn by the court.[55]

ized agent ever make the alleged agreement?" is not objectionable because in the alternative. Goodland v. Le Clair, 78 Wis. 176, 47 N. W. 268.

[51] Lauter v. Duckworth, 19 Ind. App. 535, 48 N. E. 864; Reed v. City of Madison, 85 Wis. 667, 56 N. W. 182; Mueller v. Iron Co. (Wis.) 104 N. W. 67. It is not necessary to find upon issues as to which no evidence has been given. Jones v. Insurance Co., 61 N. Y. 79.

[52] Schrubbe v. Connell, 69 Wis. 476, 34 N. W. 503; Heddles v. Railway Co., 74 Wis. 239, 42 N. W. 237.

Where the evidence is uncontradicted, the court need not submit questions (Weisel v. Spence, 59 Wis. 301, 18 N. W. 165; Coggswell v. Davis, 65 Wis. 191, 26 N. W. 557; Stringham v. Cook, 75 Wis. 589, 44 N. W. 777; Schaefer v. City of Ashland, 117 Wis. 553, 94 N. W. 303), but may consider the undisputed facts as part of the special verdict in rendering judgment (see post, chapter 12, "Uncontroverted Facts"). Or the court may direct the jury to find the facts which the court holds established beyond controversy. Harriman v. Insurance Co., 49 Wis. 71, 5 N. W. 12; Gammon v. Abrams, 53 Wis. 323, 10 N. W. 479; Schaefer v. City of Ashland, supra.

[53] Coggswell v. Davis, supra; Goesel v. Davis, 100 Wis. 678, 76 N. W. 768.

[54] Texas & P. Ry. Co. v. Miller, 79 Tex. 78, 15 S. W. 264, 11 L. R. A. 395, 23 Am. St. Rep. 308.

Improper interrogatories are not prejudicial, where under others plaintiff is enabled to develop his whole case. Andrews v. Telegraph Co., 119 N. C. 403, 25 S. E. 955.

[55] Gerhardt v. Swaty, 57 Wis. 24, 14 N. W. 851. Where no exceptions to the phraseology of questions in a special verdict are reserved, such exceptions cannot be considered on appeal. Dodge v. O'Dell's Estate, 106 Wis. 296, 82 N. W. 135.

—— **Number of Questions.** In Ward v. Busack,[56] the Supreme Court of *Wisconsin* remarked: "From our knowledge of the nature of the special verdicts which have come under the consideration of this court, we believe we are justified in saying that the tendency of some of the profession, in making use of the law which requires that a special verdict shall be rendered whenever demanded, to abuse it by demanding that the jury shall answer an infinite series of questions, the object and tendency of which is to confuse, embarrass, and confound the jury, needs the restraining hand of the judges presiding at the circuits; and that this court will take pleasure in sustaining such judges in every proper effort to make a special verdict a concise statement of the real facts at issue in the case." And in a later decision it is suggested that the trial judges "discountenance a minute cross-examination of the jury, and insist that a few questions should be framed, covering all material and controverted questions of fact, * * *" and "see to it that the right to a special verdict is not used to entrap the jury into error, as it sometimes is by defendants in desperate or doubtful cases." [57]

Similarly, the Supreme Court of *North Dakota* has said: "By a special verdict a jury set forth their findings on each point in issue, but they are not to find anything except the ultimate facts in controversy. If there are, for instance, three questions of fact in a case which should be submitted to the jury, either party may ask that the jury be required to answer categorically each one of these questions in the form of a special verdict. But the jury cannot be further requested to answer, in addition, any number of special interrogatories which the ingenuity of counsel may frame." [58]

56 46 Wis. 407, 411, 1 N. W. 107, 109.

57 Haley v. Lumber Co., 81 Wis. 412, 427, 51 N. W. 956. The number of questions should be sufficient to at least cover, singly, every fact in issue under the pleadings. Baxter v. Railroad Co., 104 Wis. 307, 80 N. W. 644.

58 Russell v. Meyer, 7 N. D. 335, 75 N. W. 262, 47 L. R. A. 637.

It is doubtless the case that, under the general supervision the court exercises over the preparation and form of special verdicts, there is a wide discretion as to the number of questions that shall be submitted. But clear abuse of this discretion, in putting a multitude of unnecessary interrogatories, where a few would cover all the issues without embarrassing the jury, is reversible error.[59] The discretion of the court "goes to the manner of submitting questions covering the issues which the statute requires to be presented by the verdict, not to obscuring them by joining with them a mass of questions, which the statute expressly prohibits. A violation of the statute by including irrelevant matters in the verdict is not necessarily reversible error. * * * But when such errors go to the extent of denying the privilege of the special-verdict statute they affect substantial rights, and constitute reversible error."[60]

**Submission and Refusal.** Whether the court submits questions for a special verdict of its own motion, or on request of counsel, and whoever may prepare the form of verdict, counsel have certain rights to be heard upon the submission. It is usual for the trial judge, where he prepares the draft, to submit it to counsel before argument. If counsel have

[59] Oaks v. West (Tex. Civ. App.) 64 S. W. 1033. See, also, Eberhardt v. Sanger, 51 Wis. 72, 8 N. W. 113; Burns v. Rolling Mill Co., 60 Wis. 541, 19 N. W. 380; Doran v. Ryan, 81 Wis. 63, 51 N. W. 259; Fromer & Co. v. Stanley, 95 Wis. 56, 69 N. W. 820; Patnode v. Westenhaver, 114 Wis. 460, 480, 90 N. W. 467, with full citation of Wisconsin cases on number of questions.

In Bower v. Bower, 146 Ind. 393, 45 N. E. 595, three hundred and ninety-five interrogatories were submitted.

[60] Patnode v. Westenhaver, 114 Wis. 460, 483, 484, 90 N. W. 467.

The statute which authorizes the submission of special issues to the jury does not contemplate that the jury shall be called upon to specially find every material fact in evidence, and such practice should not be allowed. Hartford Fire Ins. Co. v. Post, 25 Tex. Civ. App. 428, 62 S. W. 140.

Criticism that a large number of confusing questions were submitted, where a few would have sufficed, is not obviated by the fact that

suggestions to make in the way of amendments or additions, whereby defects may be remedied, the judge should give them attention. Clearly, if questions prepared by the court do not cover all the material controverted facts, refusal to embody additional questions proposed by counsel, which will cure the fault, is reversible error.[61] At least, the refusal will necessarily

appellant requested submission of a still greater number. Louis F. Fromer & Co. v. Stanley, 95 Wis. 56, 69 N. W. 820.

In Mauch v. City of Hartford, 112 Wis. 40, 62, 87 N. W. 816—an action for damages for injuries alleged to have been sustained by reason of the defective condition of a sidewalk—the trial court is criticised for ignoring the repeated suggestions of the Supreme Court in respect to the form of special verdicts, in submitting a mass of unnecessary and confusing questions.

The opinion, by Marshall, J., states that the following questions are all that would have been necessary or in the least helpful:

(1) Was the sidewalk, at the place where and time when plaintiff was injured, insufficient for public use?

(2) If the jury answer "Yes" to the first question, did the defendant have notice of such insufficiency, so that, by the exercise of reasonable diligence, it might have remedied it before the plaintiff was injured?

(3) If the jury say "Yes" to the first aud second questions, was such insufficient condition of the sidewalk the proximate cause of plaintiff's injury?

(4) Was plaintiff guilty of want of ordinary care which contributed to produce her injury?

(5) What sum of money will compensate plaintiff for her injury?

61 See Ward v. Busack, 46 Wis. 407, 1 N. W. 107; F. Dohmen Co. v. Insurance Co., 96 Wis. 38, 71 N. W. 69; Andrews v. Railroad Co., 96 Wis. 348, 71 N. W. 372.

Where a case is submitted on special issues, failure to submit a material issue is reversible error, though the question proposed by counsel was not in proper form. It was the duty of the court to put it in proper form, and then submit it. Richards v. Minster, 29 Tex. Civ. App. 85, 70 S. W. 98.

**Proximate Cause.** In an action to recover for personal injuries it being a disputed question whether the injuries were the proximate result of the negligence complained of, or of some independent and intervening cause for which defendant was not responsible, it was error to refuse to submit that question to the jury for a special

result in a verdict upon which a valid judgment cannot be rendered. It is evident, as well, that substitution by the court for a question proposed by counsel, of another which does not cover substantially the same ground, the former being proper, would have the same result. The trial judge has a large discretion as to the form of the verdict or questions, but it may be properly exercised only within the limits of an accurate presentation of all the issues. In other words, it goes to form rather than substance. In every case there are certain controverted points or facts, which the jury must determine in order that judgment may be rendered. It is the court's duty to see that these disputed essential facts are clearly and accurately set before the jury for findings. The language of questions proposed by counsel may be changed by the court, or the questions may be rejected altogether, as the court may deem best, providing all facts in issue are distinctly stated; but beyond this discretion does not go.

It is, therefore, not error to refuse to submit questions substantially included in others submitted;[62] or dependent upon

finding. Kreuziger v. Railway Co., 73 Wis. 158, 40 N. W. 657. See, also, McGowan v. Railway Co., 91 Wis. 147, 64 N. W. 891; Klatt v. Lumber Co., 92 Wis. 622, 66 N. W. 791.

[62] Coleman v. Slade, 75 Ga. 61; Powell v. Chittick, 89 Iowa, 513, 56 N. W. 652; Hamilton v. Buchanan, 112 N. C. 463, 17 S. E. 159; Sun Ins. Office v. Beneke (Tex. Civ. App.) 53 S. W. 98; Berg v. Railway Co., 50 Wis. 419, 7 N. W. 347; Reed v. City of Madison, 85 Wis. 667, 56 N. W. 182; Raymond v. Keseberg, 98 Wis. 317, 73 N. W. 1010; Schumaker v. Heinemann, 99 Wis. 251, 74 N. W. 785; Werner v. Railroad Co., 105 Wis. 300, 81 N. W. 416; Hildman v. City of Phillips, 106 Wis. 611, 82 N. W. 566; Tesch v. Light Co., 108 Wis. 593, 84 N. W. 823, 53 L. R. A. 618; Boyce v. Lumber Co., 119 Wis. 642, 97 N. W. 563; Wunderlich v. Insurance Co., 104 Wis. 382, 80 N. W. 467; Gatzow v. Buening, 106 Wis. 1, 81 N. W. 1003, 49 L. R. A. 475, 80 Am. St. Rep. 1.

It is proper to refuse to submit the question whether plaintiff could have heard the engine, etc., had he stopped and listened, which is fully included in the inquiry whether he was guilty of contributory negligence. Moreover, the fact, if found, would be inconclusive, if

others which the court has rightly refused to submit;[63] or introducing mere elements of issues.[64] No practice is better calculated to defeat the very object of a special verdict than that of submitting questions differing in form, each covering in its entirety a particular issue, or one of the questions so covering a material and controverted issue, and others covering some element thereof.[65]

Refusal to embody certain interrogatories in the special verdict is not error where the special verdict is so framed, by means of the interrogatories submitted, that the jury could find all the material facts;[66] or where the questions propounded by counsel, however answered, would not be conclusive of the right of either party to a verdict.[67] Nor is it reversible error to neglect or refuse to submit questions which upon the evidence could receive but one legitimate answer, where such answer would have sustained the judgment rendered in the case.[68]

If the issues submitted are such as to enable the parties to

not immaterial. Schroeder v. Railroad Co., 117 Wis. 33, 93 N. W. 837.

63 Pier v. Railway Co., 94 Wis. 357, 68 N. W. 464.

64 Schumaker v. Heinemann, 99 Wis. 251, 74 N. W. 785; Horne v. Bank, 108 N. C. 109, 12 S. E. 840.

65 Byington v. City of Merrill, 112 Wis. 211, 225, 88 N. W. 26.

66 Illinois Cent. R. Co. v. Cheek, 152 Ind. 663, 53 N. E. 641; Hocutt v. Railroad Co., 124 N. C. 214, 32 S. E. 681; Watson v. Railway Co., 57 Wis. 332, 15 N. W. 468; Wright v. Mulvaney, 78 Wis. 89, 46 N. W. 1045, 9 L. R. A. 807, 23 Am. St. Rep. 393; Kenyon v. City of Mondovi, 98 Wis. 50, 73 N. W. 314; Crouse v. Railroad Co., 102 Wis. 196, 78 N. W. 446.

67 Kalbus v. Abbot, 77 Wis. 621, 46 N. W. 810; Gulf, C. & S. F. Ry. Co. v. Anderson, 76 Tex. 244, 13 S. W. 196. Refusal to submit immaterial issues not error. Gilmore v. Bright, 101 N. C. 382, 7 S. E. 751.

68 McNarra v. Railway Co., 41 Wis. 69; Williams v. Porter, Id. 422, 430; Hutchinson v. Railway Co., Id. 541; Ward v. Busack, 46 Wis. 407, 1 N. W. 107; Fick v. Mulholland, 48 Wis. 413, 4 N. W. 346; Berg v. Railway Co., 50 Wis. 419, 7 N. W. 347; Ault v. Manufacturing Co., 54 Wis. 300, 11 N. W. 545; Pool v. Railway Co., 56 Wis. 227, 14 N. W. 46; Weisel v. Spence, 59 Wis. 301, 18 N. W. 165;

present every phase of the contention, no objection can be sustained either for issues submitted or for refusing to submit other or different issues.[69] It is enough if the facts found are sufficient to sustain the judgment, and it does not appear that the law applicable to any material testimony was not fairly presented to the jury.[70]

**Failure to Object.** Where a special verdict is required, it becomes the duty of the court to submit to the jury questions of fact in writing, covering all of the material issues in the case upon which there is any conflict of evidence. In Schultz v. Chicago, M. & St. P. Ry. Co.[71] the defendant demanded a special verdict at the proper time, and upon the request the court submitted but one question, to which counsel objected generally. No specific objection, however, was made or exception taken to the failure of the court to submit questions covering

Wright v. City of Ft. Howard, 60 Wis. 119, 18 N. W. 750, 50 Am. Rep. 350.

69 Coley v. City of Statesville, 121 N. C. 301, 28 S. E. 482; Bradsher v. Hightower, 118 N. C. 399, 24 S. E. 120; Ricks v. Stancill, 119 N. C. 99, 25 S. E. 721; Rittenhouse v. Railway Co., 120 N. C. 544, 26 S. E. 922.

Error in submitting a question is immaterial when the findings upon the questions properly submitted sustain the judgment. Johnson v. Railway Co., 64 Wis. 425, 25 N. W. 223.

70 Brown v. Mitchell (N. C.) 9 S. E. 702, 11 Am. St. Rep. 748.

"It must be left to the sound discretion of the nisi prius judge to determine, when required or allowed to settle the issues, whether the action can be tried more intelligently and satisfactorily by the jury upon specific issues submitted for the purpose of eliciting distinct findings in the nature of a special verdict, or by confining the inquiry, in imitation of the old method, to a single issue, or a small number of issues, and pointing out, by instruction, how the conflicting evidence, controverted in the pleadings and on trial, though not involved in the terms of the issues submitted, bears upon the verdict to be rendered in response to them, provided, always, that the issues submitted are raised by the pleadings." Emery v. Railroad Co., 102 N. C. 209, 9 S. E. 139, 11 Am. St. Rep. 727.

71 48 Wis. 375, 378, 4 N. W. 399. See York v. Hilger (Tex. Civ. App.) 84 S. W. 1117.

all the issues. The jury returned an answer to the question, with a general verdict for plaintiff.

On appeal, Lyon, J., said: "The court attempted to comply with the statute. The objection only informed the court that counsel thought the question submitted an improper one. No suggestion was made that counsel thought or desired that other questions should be submitted. All other issues were in fact submitted to the jury in the general charge, and we are unable to discover any erroneous statement of law therein. It seems that under such circumstances it was the duty of counsel then and there to make specific objection that the question submitted was not the only one in issue, and that they desired a special submission of other issues. Failing to do so, but standing by during the whole proceeding without objection or exception reaching to the irregularity, we think, and so hold, that they waived the irregularity, and cannot afterwards be heard to complain of it. Any other rule would or might render the statute giving the right to a special verdict an instrument of wrong and injustice."

But it is not to be understood that, where a judgment is based upon the special findings alone, failure to request submission of material questions is a waiver of defects in the verdict. The special verdict must determine every material question, must find every controverted fact, and there can be no waiver of this requisite. It is possible that, where the special verdict is accompanied by a general verdict, the latter may cure and supply defects and omissions in the former,[72] the so-called "special verdict" really being treated as a finding upon particular questions of fact under the interrogatory statute. Only upon such construction can the decision from which the quotation is taken be sustained. But it has recently been questioned whether the position of the court therein was sound, and it is conceded that *Wisconsin* decisions regarding the association of general and

[72] See Hutchinson v. Railway Co., 41 Wis. 541; Sherman v. Lumber Co., 77 Wis. 14, 45 N. W. 1079; Klatt v. Lumber Co., 92 Wis. 622, 66 N. W. 791.

special verdicts in the same action are (or, at least, until very recently have been) inconsistent.[73]

The quotation, and the citations below, are given because, in its latest pronouncement, the Wisconsin court has not expressly determined whether there can be a waiver of irregularity under the circumstances of the Schultz Case, though it has cleared up other difficulties connected with the subject. It would certainly appear that there cannot be such waiver, under a statute which makes the right to a special verdict absolute upon proper demand, which requires that the verdict shall be prepared by the court, and which plainly distinguishes findings upon particular questions of fact from special verdicts, and mentions general verdicts only in connection with the former. The special verdict provided for by the statute evidently intends special findings on all material facts.[74] The court is not, therefore, complying with the statute when the questions submitted do not cover all the issues, and taking a general verdict does not excuse the nonobservance; rather, it emphasizes it. It is expressly made the duty of the judge to prepare the questions, and counsel has done everything necessary to entitle him thereto when he seasonably demands a special verdict. It is no part of his duty to frame or suggest questions. But to hold that counsel waives defects in the verdict by failing to object that all the issues are not covered by the questions prepared by the judge (which objection must necessarily be specific) may be practically to require counsel to himself prepare the form of verdict, on penalty of losing his right thereto, or on pain of being required to accept a general verdict, improperly returned with the special findings, as covering all the issues not found by the special verdict, which would completely destroy the right and benefit which the statute sought to confer.

[73] See opinion by Winslow, J., in Ward v. Railroad Co., 102 Wis. 215, 78 N. W. 442. See, also, post, chapter 13.

[74] Davis v. Town of Farmington, 42 Wis. 425; F. Dohmen Co. v. Insurance Co., 96 Wis. 38, 71 N. W. 69.

Where there is no general verdict, no question of waiver can arise. If the special verdict omits to pass upon essentials, there is nothing to help it out by presumption. It has no prop, and if its own legs are missing it cannot stand.[75]

**Equity Cases.** Where the case is one of equitable jurisdiction, the court is not bound to submit any issues, and, if it does so, may disregard the findings either by setting them aside, or by letting them stand, and allowing them more or less weight in its final hearing and decree, according to its own view of the evidence in the case.[76]

The verdict is merely advisory,[77] and errors in submission of questions are not prejudicial.[78]

In *Georgia,* however, the act of February 23, 1876 (Acts 1876, p. 105), now embraced in section 4849, Civ. Code, renders it compulsory upon the judge, in the trial of proceedings for equitable relief, upon the request of either party, made after the case has been called for trial and before the beginning of the introduction of evidence, to require the jury "to find a special verdict of the facts only" in the cause. But even before the passage of this act, the law declaring that in equity cases "special verdicts may be found by the jury" (now found in section 4850, Civ. Code) had long been in force.[79]

Under the act aforesaid, the judge, without a request, may

[75] A special verdict which does not determine all material and controverted facts in issue is defective, and such defect is not waived by failure to object to the questions submitted, or to request the submission of other questions. Jenewein v. Town of Irving (Wis.) 99 N. W. 346, 348, and cases cited.

[76] W. H. Taggart Mercantile Co. v. Clack (Ariz.) 71 Pac. 925, and cases cited. See ante, chapter 4.

[77] Taylor v. Collins, 51 Wis. 123, 8 N. W. 22; Delaney v. Hartwig, 91 Wis. 412, 64 N. W. 1035; Kammermeyer v. Hilz, 116 Wis. 313, 92 N. W. 1107. See, also, Warring v. Freear, 64 Cal. 54, 28 Pac. 115.

[78] Adams v. Rodman, 102 Wis. 456, 78 N. W. 759.

[79] Hardin v. Foster, 102 Ga. 180, 29 S. E. 174, citing Lake v. Hardee, 57 Ga. 459. See Appendix.

properly exercise his discretion in framing and submitting to the jury specific questions, and directing them to render a special verdict upon the issues of fact involved. And it seems that whether the submission is by the court sua sponte, or upon request, the decree must accord with the findings.[80]

[80] Id.

## CHAPTER XII.

### SPECIAL VERDICTS (Continued).

Requisites of Special Verdict—Remedy for Defects—Amendment.

**Must Find Every Material Fact.** The special verdict must pass upon all the material issues,[1] so as to enable the court to say upon the pleadings and verdict, without reference to the evidence, which party is entitled to judgment.

1 *Alabama.* Lee v. Campbell, 4 Port. 198.

*California.* Garfield v. Water Co., 17 Cal. 510; Phœnix Water Co. v. Fletcher, 23 Cal. 482; Montgomery v. Sayre, 91 Cal. 206, 27 Pac. 648; Id. (Cal.) 25 Pac. 552; Cox v. Delmas, 99 Cal. 104, 33 Pac. 836.

*Indiana.* Goldsby v. Robertson, 1 Blackf. 247; Schmitz v. Lauferty, 29 Ind. 400; Gulick v. Connelly, 42 Ind. 134; Housworth v. Bloomhuff, 54 Ind. 488; Kealing v. Voss, 61 Ind. 466; Dixon v. Duke, 85 Ind. 434; Vinton v. Baldwin, 95 Ind. 433; Louisville, N. A. & C. Ry. Co. v. Frawley, 110 Ind. 18, 9 N. E. 594; Waymire v. Lank, 121 Ind. 1, 22 N. E. 735; Toledo, St. L. & K. C. R. Co. v. Trimble, 8 Ind. App. 333, 35 N. E. 716; Louisville, N. A. & C. Ry. Co. v. Costello, 9 Ind. App. 462, 36 N. E. 299; Schellenbeck v. Studebaker, 13 Ind. App. 437, 41 N. E. 845, 55 Am. St. Rep. 240; City of Ft. Wayne v. Durnell, 13 Ind. App. 669, 42 N. E. 242; Id. (Ind. App.) 39 N. E. 1049; Hoppes v. Chapin, 15 Ind. App. 258, 43 N. E. 1014; Pacific Mut. Life Ins. Co. v. Turner, 17 Ind. App. 644, 47 N. E. 231. But see post, "Omitted Findings."

*Iowa.* Crouch v. Deremore, 59 Iowa, 43, 12 N. W. 759.

*Kansas.* McGonigle v. Gordon, 11 Kan. 174.

*Kentucky.* Witty v. Railroad Co., 83 Ky. 21; Louisville & N. R. Co. v. Brice, 84 Ky. 298, 1 S. W. 483.

*Massachusetts.* Clarke v. Lamb, 6 Pick. 516; Walker v. Dewing, 8 Pick. 520; Stiles v. Granville, 6 Cush. 458.

*Michigan.* Buckley v. Great Western Ry. Co., 18 Mich. 121.

*Minnesota.* Lowell v. North, 4 Minn. 32 (Gil. 15); Meighen v. Strong, 6 Minn. 177 (Gil. 111), 80 Am. Dec. 441; Armstrong v. Hinds, 9 Minn. 356 (Gil. 341); Pint v. Bauer, 31 Minn. 4, 16 N. W. 425; Coleman v. Railroad Co., 38 Minn. 260, 36 N. W. 638; Lane v. Lanfest,

The rule requiring the verdict to contain findings on all material issues being uniform, it remains to inquire what are the facts which the verdict must determine in order to support a

40 Minn. 375, 42 N. W. 84; Crich v. Insurance Co., 45 Minn. 441, 48 N. W. 198.

*Mississippi.* State v. Allen, 69 Miss. 508, 10 South. 473, 30 Am. St. Rep. 563.

*Nevada.* Knickerbocker & N. Silver Min. Co. v. Hall, 3 Nev. 194.

*New York.* Sisson v. Barrett, 2 N. Y. 406; Langley v. Warner, 3 N. Y. 327; Merwan v. Ingersol, 3 Cow. 367; Seward v. Jackson, 8 Cow. 406; Eisemann v. Swan, 6 Bosw. 668; Williams v. Jackson, 5 Johns. 489; Williams v. Willis, 7 Abb. Prac. (N. Y.) 90.

*North Carolina.* State v. Watts, 32 N. C. 369; State v. Curtis, 71 N. C. 56; Hilliard v. Outlaw, 92 N. C. 266; State v. Yount, 110 N. C. 597, 15 S. E. 231.

*Ohio.* Blake's Lessee v. Davis, 20 Ohio, 231; Hambleton v. Dempsey, 20 Ohio, 168.

*Pennsylvania.* Wallingford v. Dunlap, 14 Pa. 31; Pittsburgh, Ft. W. & C. R. Co. v. Evans, 53 Pa. 250; Loew v. Stocker, 61 Pa. 347; McCormick v. Insurance Co., 163 Pa. 184, 29 Atl. 747; Standard Sewing Mach. Co. v. Insurance Co., 201 Pa. 645, 51 Atl. 354.

*South Carolina.* Farr v. Thompson, 1 Speers, 93; Lawrence v. Beaubien, 2 Bailey, 623, 23 Am. Dec. 155; Allen v. Fogler, 6 Rich. Law, 54.

*Texas.* Paschal v. Cushman, 26 Tex. 74; Frost v. Frost, 45 Tex. 324; Moore v. Moore, 67 Tex. 294, 3 S. W. 284; Heflin v. Burns, 70 Tex. 347, 8 S. W. 48; Dodd v. Gaines, 82 Tex. 429, 18 S. W. 618; Michon v. Ayalla, 84 Tex. 685, 19 S. W. 878; Newbolt v. Lancaster, 83 Tex. 272, 18 S. W. 740; Stephenson v. Chappell, 12 Tex. Civ. App. 296, 36 S. W. 482; Thomas v. Salmons (Tex. Civ. App.) 39 S. W. 1094.

*United States.* Chesapeake Ins. Co. v. Stark, 6 Cranch, 268, 3 L. Ed. 220; Bank of Alexandria v. Swann, 4 Cranch, C. C. 136, Fed. Cas. No. 853; Daube v. Coal & Iron Co., 46 U. S. App. 591, 23 C. C. A. 420, 77 Fed. 713; Harden v. Fisher, 1 Wheat. 300, 4 L. Ed. 96; Patterson v. U. S., 2 Wheat. 221, 4 L. Ed. 224; Barnes v. Williams, 11 Wheat. 415, 6 L. Ed. 508; Prentice v. Zane's Adm'r, 8 How. 470, 12 L. Ed. 1160; Suydam v. Williamson, 20 How. 441, 15 L. Ed. 978; Bellows v. Bank, 2 Mason, 31, Fed. Cas. No. 1,279; Ward v. Cochran, 150 U. S. 608, 14 Sup. Ct. 230, 37 L. Ed. 1195.

*Virginia.* Robinson's Adm'r v. Brock, 1 Hen. & M. 213; Tunnell v. Watson, 2 Munf. 283; Brown v. Ferguson, 4 Leigh, 37, 24 Am. Dec. 707; Hall v. Ratliff, 93 Va. 327, 24 S. E. 1011.

*Wisconsin.* Bell v. Shafer, 58 Wis. 223, 16 N. W. 628; Cartright

judgment? The special verdict should not find facts that are immaterial.[2] What facts, then, are material?

v. Town of Belmont, 58 Wis. 370, 17 N. W. 237; Knowlton v. Railroad Co., 59 Wis. 278, 18 N. W. 17; Hoppe v. Railroad Co., 61 Wis. 357, 21 N. W. 227; McLimans v. City of Lancaster, 63 Wis. 596, 23 N. W. 689; Pratt v. Peck, 65 Wis. 463, 27 N. W. 180; Kerkhof v. Paper Co., 68 Wis. 674, 32 N. W. 766; Kreuziger v. Railroad Co., 73 Wis. 158, 40 N. W. 657; Conroe v. Case, 74 Wis. 85, 41 N. W. 1064; Geisinger v. Beyl, 80 Wis. 443, 50 N. W. 501; Deisenrieter v. Malting Co., 92 Wis. 164, 66 N. W. 112; Haley v. Lumber Co., 81 Wis. 412, 51 N. W. 956; Kutchera v. Goodwillie, 93 Wis. 448, 67 N. W. 729; Hildman v. City of Phillips, 106 Wis. 611, 82 N. W. 566; Missinskie v. McMurdo, 107 Wis. 578, 83 N. W. 758.

See also, Coolidge v. Ayers, 76 Vt. 405, 57 Atl. 970.

**Setting out Documents.** The verdict should set forth such documentary evidence as may be matter for judicial construction. Ross v. United States, 12 Ct. Cl. 565.

If the jury find a deed specially, they ought to find it in hæc verba; but, if the deed be lost, it is the duty of the jury to find the substance of it, if this be proved. Miller v. Shackleford, 4 Dana (Ky.) 274.

In setting forth deeds they should be set out, not in hæc verba, but merely in substance, unless the question is one of construction. 1 Chit. Arch. (8th Ed.) 439.

If not set out either literally or substantially, a document cannot be considered in aid of the verdict, notwithstanding a corresponding instrument is found in the record. McArthur v. Porter's Lessee, 1 Pet. (U. S.) 626, 7 L. Ed. 290.

**Defective Verdicts.** A special verdict finding that defendant does not appear or offer any evidence in support of his plea is a nullity. Merwan v. Ingersol, 3 Cow. (N. Y.) 367.

"We of the jury find for the plaintiff one hundred and eight dollars and thirty-three cents damages, if the law be for him; if not we find for the defendant," is not a special verdict, and is wholly insufficient to render judgment upon. Hann v. Field, Litt. Sel. Cas. (Ky.) 376. A special verdict presenting no other question than the relevancy of testimony adduced on trial was held to be irregular. The judge should have decided the question, and his decision then

---

[2] Brazil Block Coal Co. v. Hoodlet, 129 Ind. 327, 27 N. E. 741; Wabash R. Co. v. Miller, 18 Ind. App. 549, 48 N. E. 663; Erwin v. Clark, 13 Mich. 10; Bentley v. Insurance Co., 40 W. Va. 729, 23 S. E. 584.

**Responsiveness to Pleadings.** The facts to be found in a special verdict are the issuable facts presented by the pleadings,[3] or, at least, facts that might properly have been put in issue

might have been reviewed on case made by a bill of exceptions. Welland Canal Co. v. Hathaway, 8 Wend. (N. Y.) 480, 24 Am. Dec. 51.

**Negligence—Proximate Cause.** Where it is a disputed question whether the injuries were the proximate result of the negligence complained of, the special verdict must find specifically both negligence, and that such negligence was the proximate cause of the injury, or it is fatally defective.

McGowan v. Railroad Co., 91 Wis. 147, 64 N. W. 891; Kucera v. Lumber Co., 91 Wis. 637, 65 N. W. 374; Deisenrieter v. Kraus-Merkel Malting Co., 92 Wis. 164, 66 N. W. 112; Klatt v. Lumber Co., 92 Wis. 622, 66 N. W. 791; Kutchera v. Goodwillie, 93 Wis. 448, 67 N. W. 729; Davis v. Railroad Co., 93 Wis. 470, 67 N. W. 16, 33 L. R. A. 654, 57 Am. St. Rep. 935; Bagnowski v. Linderman & Hoverson Co., 93 Wis. 592, 67 N. W. 1131; Rysdorp v. Lumber Co., 95 Wis. 622, 70 N. W. 677; Andrews v. Railroad Co., 96 Wis. 348, 71 N. W. 372; Beyersdorf v. Sash & Door Co., 109 Wis. 456, 84 N. W. 860.

"The verdict is fatally defective for want of any finding on the subject of proximate cause. It finds specially that defendants did not exercise ordinary care in the operation of their train and in keeping

[3] Phœnix Water Co. v. Fletcher, 23 Cal. 481; Chicago, St. L. & P. R. Co. v. Burger, 124 Ind. 275, 24 N. E. 981; Neutz v. Coal & Coke Co., 139 Ind. 411, 38 N. E. 324; Hatfield v. Lockwood, 18 Iowa, 296; Tew v. Young, 134 N. C. 493, 47 S. E. 23; Eisemann v. Swan, 6 Bosw. (N. Y.) 668; Cole v. Crawford, 69 Tex. 124, 5 S. W. 646; Stephenson v. Chappell, 12 Tex. Civ. App. 296, 36 S. W. 482; Kenyon v. Kenyon, 72 Wis. 234, 39 N. W. 361; Heddles v. Railroad Co., 74 Wis. 239, 42 N. W. 237; Baxter v. Railroad Co., 104 Wis. 307, 80 N. W. 644; Sladky v. Lumber Co., 107 Wis. 250, 83 N. W. 514; Daube v. Coal & Iron Co., 46 U. S. App. 591, 23 C. C. A. 420, 77 Fed. 713. There need be no finding upon immaterial facts, nor upon facts proven but not within the issues. Brazil Block Coal Co. v. Hoodlet, 129 Ind. 327, 27 N. E. 741. The jury have nothing to do with the legal requisites of the plea. Richmond v. Tallmadge, 16 Johns. (N. Y.) 307.

It is the duty of the trial court to frame the special verdict, and to include therein every material issue raised by the pleadings and evidence. Orttel v. Railroad Co., 89 Wis. 127, 61 N. W. 289. It is not error to fail to submit an issue not made by the pleadings. Kenyon v. Kenyon, 72 Wis. 234, 39 N. W. 361.

by the pleadings.[4] The facts found by the jury need not be set out in the precise language of the pleading. If the substance

the track free from obstructions; that plaintiff was injured, and was not guilty of any want of ordinary care which contributed to produce such injury. But that is not sufficient to cast upon defendants the consequences of such injury. It should not be forgotten, in such cases, that the mere fact that one person is injured by the failure to exercise ordinary care on the part of another in respect to some duty which such other owes to such person does not render such other liable therefor, unless such injury was the natural and probable result of such negligence, and one which, in the light of attending circumstances, such other ought reasonably to have foreseen might occur as a result of such negligence. This is absolutely an essential element of proximate cause, requisite to actionable negligence; and, where there is no general verdict, and such element does not appear conclusively from the evidence, and is not found by the special verdict, no valid judgment can be given upon it." Sheridan v. Bigelow, 93 Wis. 426. 428, 67 N. W. 732, and cases cited; Groth v. Thomann, 110 Wis. 488, 86 N. W. 178. See, also, Hallum v. Village of Omro (Wis.) 99 N. W. 1051.

The question whether the negligent act relied on was the proximate cause of the injury may be submitted by a question in substance in that form, and the court should instruct the jury as to what will constitute proximate cause, in view of the facts and circumstances; or it may be submitted to the jury to find the facts which show that (within the rule adopted by the court) the negligence was, in a legal as well as a natural sense, the proximate cause of the injury, and was therefore actionable. Andrews v. Railroad Co., 96 Wis. 348, 359, 71 N. W. 372. See, also, as to form of question, Bigelow v. Danielson, 102 Wis. 470, 78 N. W. 599; Baxter v. Railroad Co., 104 Wis. 307, 80 N. W. 644.

In an action for injuries the better practice is to include in the verdict in every case a question covering the subject of proximate cause, and to explain it so that the jury may not needlessly fail to answer it intelligently. Hallum v. Village of Omro (Wis.) 99 N. W. 1051.

**Special Verdicts in Replevin.** Wegner v. Bank, 76 Wis. 242, 44 N. W. 1096; Feder v. Daniels, 79 Wis. 578, 48 N. W. 799; Herbst Importing Co. v. Burnham, 81 Wis. 408, 51 N. W. 262; Strasser v. Goldberg, 120 Wis. 621, 98 N. W. 554. See, also, Singer Mfg. Co. v. Sammons, 49 Wis. 316, 320, 5 N. W. 788.

---

[4] Eberhardt v. Sanger, 51 Wis. 72, 8 N. W. 111.

of the issues be found it is sufficient,[5] and there need be no greater minuteness in the verdict than in the pleadings.[6] Nor need all the allegations of the complaint be found, providing enough facts are found to constitute a cause of action within the averments made.[7] It is also said that a special verdict which disposes of all the litigated issues is sufficient.[8]

A special verdict must cover all the issues. But this does not mean that it should be so framed as to cover each particular matter of dispute between witnesses. The only proper test to which a special verdict should be subjected is the pleadings. If it covers all the facts therein put in issue, in respect to which the evidence is conflicting, it is sufficient.[9]

It is to be borne in mind that an issue must be made by the evidence as well as the pleadings, to authorize its submission to the jury. Where there is no testimony tending to support an allegation upon which a party seeks to recover judgment, but the undisputed evidence demonstrates that such allegation is not true, a charge which authorizes the jury to find that such allegation is proven is palpably erroneous.[10]

Judgment cannot be supported by a special verdict that is

[5] Puterbaugh v. Puterbaugh, 131 Ind. 288, 30 N. E. 519, 15 L. R. A. 341; Becknell v. Hosier, 10 Ind. App. 5, 37 N. E. 580; Railsback v. Railsback, 12 Ind. App. 659, 40 N. E. 276, 1119; Commonwealth v. Chathams, 50 Pa. 181, 88 Am. Dec. 539; Alhambra Addition Water Co. v. Richardson, 72 Cal. 598, 14 Pac. 379.

[6] First Nat. Bank v. Peck, 8 Kan. 660; Murdock v. Clarke (Cal.) 24 Pac. 272. See, also, Western Union Tel. Co. v. Stratemeier, 11 Ind. App. 601, 39 N. E. 527.

[7] Bower v. Bower, 146 Ind. 393, 45 N. E. 595. A special verdict need not find surplusage contained in the complaint. Tucker v. Hyatt, 151 Ind. 332, 51 N. E. 469, 44 L. R. A. 129.

[8] Ward v. Busack, 46 Wis. 407, 1 N. W. 107. See, also, Jones v. Insurance Co., 61 N. Y. 79.

[9] Wisconsin Farm Land Co. v. Bullard, 119 Wis. 320, 96 N. W. 833. See post, "Uncontroverted Facts."

[10] Texas & P. Ry. Co. v. Hightower, 12 Tex. Civ. App. 41, 33 S. W. 541; Houston & T. C. Ry. Co. v. Tierney, 72 Tex. 312, 12 S. W. 586; Willis v. Whitsitt, 67 Tex. 676, 4 S. W. 253. See, also, City of

not complete with reference to the object of the suit,[11] and not responsive to the pleadings in so far as material controverted matters are concerned.[12]

As to findings embracing facts not within the issues presented by the pleadings, they cannot form the basis for a conclusion of law; [13] but they are not an obstacle to the rendition of such judgment as is warranted by the remaining findings properly returned under the issues.[14] They are to be treated as surplusage and ignored.[15]

Where the material facts stated in the verdict are wholly outside of the issues, defendant is entitled to judgment, for the plaintiff can alone recover according to the allegations of his complaint.[16]

La Fayette v. Allen, 81 Ind. 166; Gibbons v. Railroad Co., 62 Wis. 546, 22 N. W. 533.

Findings of a special verdict, not based on the evidence, are properly stricken out as surplusage. Rahr v. Assur. Co., 93 Wis. 355, 67 N. W. 725.

It is not necessary for the jury to find upon the issues as to which no evidence was given. Jones v. Insurance Co., 61 N. Y. 79.

11 Thompson v. Tinnin, 25 Tex. Supp. 56.

12 Ehlers v. Wannack, 118 Cal. 310, 50 Pac. 433; Warring v. Freear, 64 Cal. 54, 28 Pac. 115; Howard v. Brower, 37 Ohio St. 402; Thompson v. Tinnin, supra.

13 Cincinnati Barbed-Wire Fence Co. v. Chenoweth, 22 Ind. App. 685, 54 N. E. 403; Hardy v. De Leon, 5 Tex. 211. See, also, Gehl v. Produce Co., 105 Wis. 573, 81 N. W. 666.

Where the special verdict finds that the defendant's negligence consisted of acts different from those alleged in the complaint, it will not support a judgment. Chicago, St. L. & P. Ry. Co. v. Burger, 124 Ind. 275, 24 N. E. 981.

If the finding is different from the issue, no judgment can be rendered on the verdict. Patterson v. U. S., 2 Wheat. (U. S.) 225, 4 L. Ed. 224.

14 Van Valkenburgh v. Dean, 15 Ind. App. 693, 44 N. E. 652. It is likewise immaterial that the special verdict does not show a fact not in issue. Alexandria Mining & Exploring Co. v. Irish, 16 Ind. App. 534, 44 N. E. 680.

15 Kearney v. Wurdeman, 33 Mo. App. 447; Bowlus v. Insurance Co., 133 Ind. 106, 32 N. E. 319, 20 L. R. A. 400.

16 Puterbaugh v. Puterbaugh, 131 Ind. 288, 30 N. E. 519, 15 L. R.

In a leading case the Supreme Court of *Kansas* admitted that to prevent wrong it is often necessary to go back of the issuable facts and ascertain the truth in regard to some item of testimony, and continued: "For instance, a matter in dispute might be whether a party accepted certain work under a contract. The general allegation would be that he accepted. The special verdict following it might be that he accepted. Yet, if what he actually did was found, the law would say that there was no acceptance. And as truth is the object of all investigation, that which he did ought in some way to be ascertained and presented. In other words, we must go back of the issues to the testimony or those subdivided facts and circumstances which combine to make the general facts alleged. This, it is claimed, is the scope and purpose of a special verdict, and construing the statute (Code, § 286) as we have simply emasculates it. It is shorn of its strength, and a special verdict becomes of but little more advantage than a general verdict. It applies the law to the facts with but little greater exactness. We concede the necessity for such procedure, and think provision is made for it by another clause of the statute. After the provision for a special verdict, the statute (section 7, c. 87, Laws 1870) reads: 'And upon like request to instruct the jury if they shall render a general verdict to find upon particular questions of fact, to be stated in writing, and shall direct a written finding thereon.' Under this clause full scope is given for ascertaining any fact in the case which may affect its determination, whether one of the main essential facts, or any minute subdivision thereof. And in order to give full force to these findings, the next section of the Code (section 287) provides that, 'when the special finding of facts is inconsistent with the general verdict, the former controls the latter, and the court may give judgment accordingly.'" [17]

A. 341. The question is properly presented by motion for judgment on the special verdict. Dixon v. Duke, 85 Ind. 434; Johnson v. Culver, 116 Ind. 278, 19 N. E. 129. See, also, Boardman v. Griffin, 52 Ind. 101; Elliott, App. Proc. § 767.

[17] First Nat. Bank v. Peck, 8 Kan. 660, 667. (The special verdict

**Must Find Facts, Not Evidence.** Upon the trial of an issue of fact, a special verdict should find facts to which the law gives a determinate effect, conclusive of the issue, and no judgment can be rendered on findings of facts which are in the nature of evidence only, and are not, in law, conclusive of the questions at issue.[18] The verdict must be a statement of the ultimate facts, not of the evidence on which they rest.[19] This follows from the requirement that nothing further shall remain but for

statute was in force in Kansas 1870–1874.) This is construing the interrogatory statute more liberally than it is interpreted by most courts. Elsewhere the particular facts that may be called for under the statute are held to be the "ultimate" or "controlling" facts, and even "the ultimate facts presented in a special verdict." See chapter 5, and City of Wyandotte v. White, 13 Kan. 191.

[18] Boyer v. Robertson, 144 Ind. 604, 43 N. E. 879; Seward v. Jackson, 8 Cow. (N. Y.) 406; Leach v. Church, 10 Ohio St. 148; Blank's Adm'r v. Foushee, 4 Munf. (Va.) 61; Barnes v. Williams, 11 Wheat. (U. S.) 415, 6 L. Ed. 508.

In Hambleton v. Dempsey, 20 Ohio, 168, the jury, instead of setting out the facts in their special verdict, referred the court to the items of testimony, written and oral, produced on the trial. Judgment was rendered on the verdict, but was reversed on appeal, the court saying: "The jury have found no one fact to be true, but have simply referred the court to the evidence, and told them that if, upon that evidence, they are of opinion the law of the case is with the plaintiffs, then the jury find for the plaintiffs, etc. It is the game of 'hide and go seek' between the court and jury. The evidence is laid before the jury, and they are told to find the facts. The jury lay the same evidence before the court, and tell them to find the facts and law together. Such practice as this we cannot sanction."

[19] Lanagin v. Nowland, 44 Ark. 84; Vincent v. Morrison, Breese (Ill.) 227; Germania Fire Ins. Co. v. Tile Co., 11 Ind. App. 385, 39 N. E. 304; State v. Griffin, 16 Ind. App. 555, 45 N. E. 935; Hill v. Covell, 1 N. Y. 522; Sisson v. Barrett, 2 N. Y. 406; Langley v. Warner, 3 N. Y. 327; Birckhead v. Brown, 5 Hill (N. Y.) 634; La Frombois v. Jackson, 8 Cow. (N. Y.) 589, 18 Am. Dec. 463; Rogers v. Insurance Co., 9 Wend. (N. Y.) 611; State v. Watts, 32 N. C. 369; Russell v. Meyer, 7 N. D. 335, 75 N. W. 262, 47 L. R. A. 637; Leach v. Church, 10 Ohio St. 148; Kinsley v. Coyle, 58 Pa. 461; Farr v. Thompson, 1 Speers (S. C.) 93; Brown v. Ralston, 4 Rand. (Va.) 504; Prentice v. Zane's Adm'r, 8 How. (U. S.) 470, 12 L. Ed. 1160; Suydam v. Williamson, 20 How. 427, 15 L. Ed. 978; Monticello Bank v. Bost-

the court to draw the proper conclusions of law from the facts found. The judge cannot usurp the functions of the jury, draw inferences from the evidence presented by them, and then proceed to render judgment upon the facts so found. The jury would play no part in such a proceeding except to say what evidence they believed, without stating what facts it established. They are the exclusive judges of the facts, and have defeated the only object of the submission when they fail to return, as their conclusions from the testimony, the ultimate facts in the case.

But it is said that if the verdict find probative facts from which the court can declare that the ultimate facts necessarily result, it is sufficient.[20] However, finding evidence sufficient prima facie to establish such facts is not enough.[21] If the ver-

wick, 40 U. S. App. 721, 77 Fed. 123, 23 C. C. A. 73; Rex v. Huggins, 2 Ld. Raym. 1574; Bird v. Appleton, 1 East, 111.

A special verdict in an action for personal injuries, stating that plaintiff suffered severe permanent injuries, and was thereby rendered unable to perform physical labor, is sufficient, without stating the evidentiary facts on which it is based. Louisville, N. A. & C. Ry. Co. v. Miller, 141 Ind. 533, 37 N. E. 343.

It is the duty of the jury to consider the evidentiary facts, but to find the inferential. Locke v. Bank, 66 Ind. 353.

The facts in issue must be so found "that the law will irresistibly infer a certain result." Gordon v. Stockdale, 89 Ind. 240.

A history of the case in the nature of a recital of the testimony, or a detail of the various steps of the transaction, is not the function of a special verdict. First Nat. Bank v. Peck, 8 Kan. 660; Jackson v. Insurance Co., 27 Mo. App. 62.

Evidence contained in answers to questions is not part of the record and cannot be considered on appeal. Tucker v. Conrad, 103 Ind. 349, 2 N. E. 803.

20 Alhambra Addition Water Co. v. Richardson, 72 Cal. 598, 14 Pac. 379; Coveny v. Hale, 49 Cal. 552; Rowley v. Sanns, 141 Ind. 179, 40 N. E. 674.

21 Chicago & N. W. Ry. Co. v. Dunleavy, 129 Ill. 132, 22 N. E. 15; Blake's Lessee v. Davis, 20 Ohio, 231; Rogers v. Insurance Co., 9 Wend. (N. Y.) 611. See, also, Graham v. Bayne, 18 How. (U. S.) 60, 15 L. Ed. 265; Barnes v. Williams, 11 Wheat. (U. S.) 415, 6 L. Ed. 508; Prentice v. Zane's Adm'r, 8 How. 470, 12 L. Ed. 1160.

dict simply sets out the evidence, the court cannot find the omitted conclusions of fact, even with the consent of the parties.[22] It is only where the evidentiary facts returned are such as the law has made conclusive evidence of the ultimate facts that they are tantamount to finding the latter, and will support judgment.[23]

Special verdicts are not designed to elicit from the jury an abstract of the evidence,[24] or to decide disputes between witnesses over evidentiary facts.[25] Questions calling for findings on purely evidentiary matters are therefore improper, and to refuse to submit them is not error.[26] But the presence of evi-

[22] Seward v. Jackson, 8 Cow. (N. Y.) 406. Where a special verdict finds many facts which are badges of fraud, but does not find the ultimate fact of fraud, the court cannot supply the omission and find the fraud, since fraud is a question of fact, and cannot be inferred as a matter of law. Alberts v. Baker, 21 Ind. App. 373, 52 N. E. 469. See, also, Stix v. Sadler, 109 Ind. 254, 9 N. E. 905; Caldwell v. Boyd, 109 Ind. 447, 9 N. E. 912.

[23] John v. Bates, Litt. Sel. Cas. (Ky.) 106; Chicago & N. W. Ry. Co. v. Dunleavy, 129 Ill. 132, 22 N. E. 15.

[24] McKeon v. Railroad Co., 94 Wis. 477, 69 N. W. 175, 35 L. R. A. 252, 59 Am. St. Rep. 910; Pratt v. Peck, 65 Wis. 463, 27 N. W. 180; Zimmer v. Electric R. Co., 118 Wis. 614, 95 N. W. 957, and cases cited.

[25] Baxter v. Railroad Co., 104 Wis. 307, 80 N. W. 644.

[26] Kohler v. Railroad Co., 99 Wis. 33, 74 N. W. 568; Lyle v. Machine Co., 108 Wis. 81, 84 N. W. 18, 51 L. R. A. 906; Cullen v. Hanisch, 114 Wis. 24, 89 N. W. 900.

An interrogatory assuming as true an evidentiary fact is properly refused. Gundlach v. Schott, 192 Ill. 509, 61 N. E. 332, 85 Am. St. Rep. 348.

**Negligence.** The question, "If you should answer the foregoing question [as to whether the negligence of the defendant was the proximate cause of the injury], in what did that negligence consist?" is properly refused, as it calls upon the jury to state evidentiary facts from which it drew its conclusion of the issuable facts. McCoy v. Railroad Co., 88 Wis. 56, 59 N. W. 453; Illinois Cent. R. Co. v. Scheffner, 209 Ill. 9, 70 N. E. 619. See, also, Cummings v. Furnace Co., 60 Wis. 603, 18 N. W. 742; Caswell v. Railroad Co., 42 Wis. 193. But in *Indiana*, under the rule that the verdict should set out both the primary and inferential facts, in order that the court

dence in a special verdict will not render it defective if there are enough facts properly found to warrant judgment for either party.[27] And if there are facts well stated, and judgment in the court below be rendered contrary to the facts so properly found, the judgment will be reversed, though the evidence stated in the special verdict might have warranted a verdict and judgment the other way.[28]

**Must Find Facts, Not Conclusions of Law.** In a special verdict the jury must find only the facts, without applying to them their opinion of the law.[29] Hundreds of cases might be cited to this proposition, did not the very definition and purpose of a special verdict render such citation superfluous. If the special verdict amounts merely to a conclusion of law, it must be set aside.[30] But, as in the case of evidentiary matters improperly included in the verdict, conclusions of law do not destroy the effect of facts properly found, and, if these be sufficient to sustain a judgment, the verdict should stand.[31] The

may determine whether the question of negligence is for court or jury (see Shirk v. Railroad Co., 14 Ind. App. 126, 42 N. E. 656), such a question would apparently be proper. See post, "Conclusions of Law—Negligence."

Refusal to submit the question whether plaintiff could have heard the engine coming if he had stopped and listened before reaching the track was proper, since such question presents only an evidentiary and inconclusive fact, and was fully covered by the inquiry whether he was guilty of contributory negligence. Schroeder v. Railroad Co., 117 Wis. 33, 93 N. W. 837.

27 **"Utile per inutile non vitiatur."** 2 Co. Litt. 227a; Locke v. Bank, 66 Ind. 353; Kealing v. Vansickle, 74 Ind. 529, 39 Am. Rep. 101; Whitcomb v. Smith, 123 Ind. 329, 24 N. E. 109; Railsback v. Railsback, 12 Ind. App. 659, 40 N. E. 276.

28 Seward v. Jackson, 8 Cow. (N. Y.) 406; La Frombois v. Jackson, 8 Cow. (N. Y.) 589, 18 Am. Dec. 463.

29 Aurelius v. Railroad Co., 19 Ind. App. 584, 49 N. E. 857, and cases cited; Hatfield v. Lockwood, 18 Iowa, 296; Erwin v. Clark, 13 Mich. 10; Commonwealth v. Chathams, 50 Pa. 181, 88 Am. Dec. 539; U. S. v. Collier, 3 Blatchf. (U. S.) 325, Fed. Cas. No. 14,833.

30 Keller v. Boatman, 49 Ind. 104.

31 Terre Haute & I. R. Co. v. Brunker, 128 Ind. 542, 26 N. E. 178;

conclusions are regarded as surplusage,[32] and it is not error to refuse to strike them from the verdict.[33]

—— **Negligence.** There is considerable confusion in the *Indiana* decisions as to whether negligence and contributory negligence are facts to be set out and determined in a special verdict.

Louisville, N. A. & C. Ry. Co. v. Berkey, 136 Ind. 181, 35 N. E. 3; Island Coal Co. v. Risher, 13 Ind. App. 98, 40 N. E. 158; Voris v. Association, 20 Ind. App. 630, 50 N. E. 779; Dull v. Railroad Co., 21 Ind. App. 571, 52 N. E. 1013.

32 Miller v. Shackleford, 4 Dana (Ky.) 274; Louisville, N. A. & C. Ry. Co. v. Miller, 141 Ind. 533, 37 N. E. 343; Toledo, St. L. & K. C. R. Co. v. Tapp, 6 Ind. App. 304, 33 N. E. 462; Butler v. Hopper, 1 Wash. C. C. 499, Fed. Cas. No. 2241; Hogan v. Railroad Co., 59 Wis. 139, 17 N. W. 632; Fick v. Railroad Co., 68 Wis. 469, 32 N. W. 527, 60 Am. Rep. 878; Winchell v. Abbot, 77 Wis. 371, 46 N. W. 665; MacCarthy v. Whitcomb, 110 Wis. 113, 85 N. W. 707.

33 Louisville, N. A. & C. Ry. Co. v. Frawley, 110 Ind. 18, 9 N. E. 594; Same v. Flanagan, 113 Ind. 488, 14 N. E. 370, 3 Am. St. Rep. 674.

*Examples:* A conclusion is not one of law because it is reached by a process of reasoning from many primary circumstances. Baxter v. Railroad Co., 104 Wis. 307, 312, 80 N. W. 644.

In a special verdict in a cause where usury is pleaded, the jury need not find the usury. They find the facts, and the law infers the usury. Brummel v. Enders, 18 Grat. (Va.) 873.

In trover, a verdict finding that the defendant "took and converted all of said property to its own use," etc., is a mere conclusion of law. Louisville, N. A. & C. Ry. Co. v. Balch, 105 Ind. 93, 4 N. E. 288.

On an issue as to whether a donor had sufficient mental capacity to make a valid gift inter vivos, a finding that donor was of "unsound mind" is a mere conclusion of law. Teegarden v. Lewis, 145 Ind. 98, 40 N. E. 1047. *Contra:* Unsoundness of mind is an ultimate fact, while intemperate habits, etc., are evidentiary facts. In re Gharky's Estate, 57 Cal. 279; Clements v. McGinn (Cal.) 33 Pac. 920.

In an action for malicious prosecution, a finding in the special verdict that there was not "any probable cause for the prosecution" is but a conclusion. Terre Haute & I. R. Co. v. Mason, 148 Ind. 578, 46 N. E. 332. The verdict need not state that the prosecution was without probable cause, since that is a question for the court.

In Toledo & W. Ry. Co. v. Goddard,[34] the court submitted to the jury the question, "Was not the defendant guilty of negligence in placing the freight car on the side track on the street, thereby obstructing the same?" Answer: "Yes." And, "Was not the defendant guilty of negligence in not placing some visible signal at or near the southwest corner of the woodshed, to indicate the approach of the backing train, to prevent collision?" Answer: "Yes." These interrogatories were held improper because they did not ask the jury to find upon any particular question of fact, but simply assumed that certain facts existed, and asked the jury if they did not constitute negligence. It was said that, when the facts are found, then their legal consequences constitute purely a question of law for the court;[35] that the jury should have been asked whether the defendant had placed a freight car on the side track, etc., and whether the company had placed a visible sig-

Tucker v. Hyatt, 151 Ind. 332, 51 N. E. 469, 44 L. R. A. 129; Helwig v. Beckner, 149 Ind. 131, 133, 46 N. E. 644, and cases cited.

A special verdict finding that defendant was a principal on a note is not objectionable as being a conclusion of law. Devine v. Mortgage Co. (Tex. Civ. App.) 48 S. W. 585. Nor is a finding that a note was paid before action brought. Wipperman v. Hardy, 17 Ind. App. 142, 46 N. E. 537.

Whether or not the facts exist which make two or more persons fellow servants, in the legal sense, is a question of fact. When the facts have been put beyond dispute by the findings of the jury, it then becomes a question for the court to determine whether or not the facts found bring the matter within the legal definition of a "fellow servant." Keller v. Gaskill, 20 Ind. App. 502, 50 N. E. 363.

See, also, MacCarthy v. Whitcomb, 110 Wis. 113, 120, 85 N. W. 707.

An interrogatory, "Is there any evidence in this case tending to show that the plan upon which this bridge was built was not a good one," with its answer, "Yes," will be disregarded. Whether there is any evidence tending to prove an alleged fact is a question of law for the court, not of fact for the jury. Bowen v. Railroad Co., 95 Mo. 268, 8 S. W. 230; Id., 75 Mo. 426.

[34] 25 Ind. 185.

[35] To same effect, Doggett v. Railroad Co., 78 N. C. 305; Brannen v. Gravel Road Co., 115 Ind. 115, 17 N. E. 202, 7 Am. St. Rep. 411.

nal at or near the southwest corner of the woodshed, etc., and that upon the jury's answers the court should then have determined, as a question of law, whether the facts so found constituted such negligence as to make the defendant liable for the injury.[36]

In Pittsburgh, C. & St. L. R. Co. v. Spencer,[37] it was said that conclusions of law in a special verdict are without force, and a general statement that an act was negligently done is but a conclusion of law. The facts showing how the act was done are essential, for without them the court cannot ascertain or pronounce the law. All the authorities agree that the law is exclusively for the court in cases where special verdicts are returned. But if it be held that a general statement of negligence is good, then nothing at all is left to the court, for the jury have determined both the law and the facts. Where a general verdict is sought, the court instructs the jury on the law of negligence, and thus pronounces the law of the case; but, in cases where a special verdict is asked, the law is pronounced, not in the instructions, but upon the facts stated by the jury. If the jury themselves state the law, then the court is a mere passive spectator, or at most a mere moderator.

In Indianapolis, P. & C. Ry. Co. v. Bush [38] it was held that the principle that where the evidence is conflicting, and more than one inference can be drawn from the facts, the question of negligence is generally for the jury, has no application in the case of a special verdict. Negligence, it was said, is never purely a question of fact, and therefore cannot be found as a fact in a special verdict. A finding that one party was not guilty of negligence, and the other was, is a mere conclusion of law.[39]

[36] See, also, Bellefontaine Ry. Co. v. Hunter, 33 Ind. 335, 5 Am. Rep. 201.

[37] 98 Ind. 186.

[38] 101 Ind. 582.

[39] Pennsylvania Co. v. Marion, 104 Ind. 239, 3 N. E. 874; Conner v. Railroad Co., 105 Ind. 62, 4 N. E. 441, 55 Am. Rep. 177; Woolery v.

In accordance with this view, a number of *Indiana* cases hold that, where the jury is to return a special verdict, the court should not instruct them as to what does or does not constitute negligence or contributory negligence, because they have no right to apply the law to the facts to determine whether or not negligence exists, nor have they the right to know that, if a given state of facts is found, the court, in applying the law, will infer negligence.[40]

In Cincinnati, I., St. L. & C. Ry. Co. v. Grames,[41] the deci-

Railroad Co., 107 Ind. 381, 8 N. E. 226, 57 Am. Rep. 114; Chicago, St. L. & P. R. Co. v. Burger, 124 Ind. 275, 24 N. E. 981; Korrady v. Railroad Co., 131 Ind. 261, 29 N. E. 1069; Louisville & N. R. Co. v. Eves, 1 Ind. App. 224, 27 N. E. 580; Hankey v. Downey, 3 Ind. App. 325, 29 N. E. 606.

Findings of a jury that defendant was guilty of negligence, or that defendant could have discovered defects in the machinery, and that plaintiff could not discover such defects; that defendant did not exercise ordinary care under the circumstances, or that the plaintiff did exercise such care as an ordinarily prudent person would have exercised under like circumstances—are findings of mere conclusions, and must be disregarded in considering the sufficiency of the facts found to make a case in favor of plaintiff. Shirk v. Railroad Co., 14 Ind. App. 126, 42 N. E. 656, and cases cited.

**Contributory Negligence.** The court alone can draw the inference as to whether or not the plaintiff exercised ordinary care under the particular circumstances. Geddes v. Blackmore, 132 Ind. 551, 32 N. E. 567. But in Terre Haute & I. R. Co. v. Brunker, 128 Ind. 542, 26 N. E. 178, it is held that, if it is proper to allege in a complaint that plaintiff was without fault, no harm can result from the jury so finding.

A finding in a personal injury case that plaintiff was "exercising due and proper care" is merely an inference from the facts, which the appellate court will disregard unless the facts are also found. Gaston v. Bailey, 14 Ind. App. 581, 43 N. E. 254.

40 Toler v. Keiher, 81 Ind. 383; Louisville, N. A. & C. Ry. Co. v Frawley, 110 Ind. 18, 9 N. E. 594; Louisville, N. A. & C. Ry. Co. v. Hart, 119 Ind. 273, 21 N. E. 753, 4 L. R. A. 549; Stayner v. Joyce, 120 Ind. 99, 22 N. E. 89.

41 8 Ind. App. 112, 34 N. E. 613.

sions are reviewed by the Court of Appeals, and the following conclusions are reached:

(1) That in case where negligence is the issue, and the facts are undisputed, and but one inference can be drawn therefrom, the court may draw that inference; but where the facts are controverted, or where more than one inference may reasonably be drawn from the facts, the question is generally one for the jury under proper instructions from the court.

(2) This principle is applicable to cases in which a general verdict is returned, but has no application where a special verdict is taken, in which

(3) The jury should find the facts only. Negligence is not an inference, and cannot be so found by the jury.

It is argued that if the court must determine, as a question of law, whether or not the facts pleaded constitute negligence, it is also the duty of the court to determine, when those same facts are found in a special verdict, whether or not negligence shall be inferred.[42]

But on the same facts the Supreme Court held [43] that the special verdict before them was insufficient to warrant judgment for plaintiff because it failed to find that he exercised ordinary care under the circumstances; and this notwithstanding that the facts found by the jury would authorize the inference that he did exercise such care, for such inference must be drawn by the jury.[44] The court says: "In reaching this conclusion we have not overlooked the cases of Pittsburgh, C. & St. L. R. Co. v. Spencer, 98 Ind. 186, Indianapolis, P. & C. Ry. Co. v. Bush, 101 Ind. 582, and Conner v. Railroad Co., 105

[42] Citing Faris v. Hoberg, 134 Ind. 269, 33 N. E. 1028, 39 Am. St. Rep. 261.

[43] Cincinnati, I., St. L. & C. R. Co. v. Grames, 136 Ind. 39, 34 N. E. 714.

[44] At the date of this decision it was incumbent upon plaintiff to prove that he was free from contributory negligence, or that the injury was in no degree attributable to any want of ordinary care. This need no longer be alleged or proved in Indiana.

Ind. 62, 4 N. E. 441, 55 Am. Rep. 177. The first two cases hold—and we think correctly—that a general statement of the jury in a special verdict to the effect that a particular act was or was not negligent is the statement of a mere conclusion, and will be ignored by this court. But there is a very broad distinction between that kind of a statement and the finding of an inferential fact from the existence of other stated facts. These cases in no wise conflict with the conclusion at which we have arrived in this case." Conner v. Railroad Co.,[45] which denied the right of the jury to infer negligence, is declared to be unsupported by authority.

The same view is taken in Louisville, N. A. & C. Ry. Co. v. Miller,[46] and Louisville, N. A. & C. Ry. Co. v. Costello.[47] In the latter case it is said that, when but one reasonable inference can be drawn from the facts found in the special verdict, the question involved, either as to the negligence of the defendant or as to whether plaintiff was without fault, is for the court; but whenever, on either the question of negligence or contributory negligence, there may reasonably be differences of opinion as to the inference or conclusion which may be fairly drawn from such facts, such question is then one of fact—an ultimate fact—to be determined by the jury.[48]

The rule ultimately adopted in *Indiana,* as understood by the writer, may be stated as follows: The jury must find the ultimate facts, and may not find the inferences without the facts.[49]

45 105 Ind. 62, 4 N. E. 441, 55 Am. Rep. 177.

46 141 Ind. 533, 37 N. E. 343.

47 9 Ind. App. 462, 36 N. E. 299.

48 Citing Cincinnati, I., St. L. & C. R. Co. v. Grames, 136 Ind. 39, 34 N. E. 714; Rush v. Mining Co., 131 Ind. 135, 30 N. E. 904; Woolery v. Railroad Co., 107 Ind. 381, 8 N. E. 226, 57 Am. Rep. 114.

It is essential that the jury should set out in their verdict both the primary and the final inferential facts, in order that the court may determine whether or not different conclusions may be drawn from them. Shirk v. Railroad Co., 14 Ind. App. 126, 42 N. E. 656.

49 The jury were asked, "What effort did plaintiff make to prevent his hay and land from being burnt?" etc., and answered, "Done all he

If the facts so found are such that only one inference may be drawn from them, viz., negligence or no negligence, the jury need not find the inferential fact also,[50] and the court will determine as matter of law, from such facts found, whether there was or was not negligence. If, however, the ultimate facts are such that reasonable men of equal intelligence may honestly and rationally differ as to the inferences, it is for the jury to determine the inferences also; and in such cases these must be stated in the verdict.[51] They are not to be treated, under such circumstances, as conclusions of law, which the court can or

could." This was held to be a conclusion of the jury, which could not be accepted as equivalent to find that plaintiff did all that an ordinarily prudent man would have done under the circumstances, in the absence of the primary facts leading up to such conclusion. Louisville, N. A. & C. Ry. Co. v. Roberts, 18 Ind. App. 538, 47 N. E. 839.

Q. "Was the plaintiff guilty of any negligence in the setting or in the escape of said fire?" etc. Answer: "No." Q. "Was the plaintiff guilty of any negligence or carelessness in or about the burning or setting fire on his land?" Answer: "No." These questions call for and the answers are, conclusions of law. Louisville, N. A. & C. Ry. Co. v. Carmon, 20 Ind. App. 471, 50 N. E. 893; Id. (Ind. App.) 48 N. E. 1047. Nor, if these answers were not objectionable otherwise, would they show freedom from fault, since negligence may consist in omission as well as commission. Id.

The questions submitted should not call purely for conclusions of fact, but should cover as well the physical facts put in issue by the pleadings. Lee v. Railroad Co., 101 Wis. 352, 77 N. W. 714. But see Mauch v. City of Hartford, 112 Wis. 40, 87 N. W. 816, and Patnode v. Westenhaver, 114 Wis. 483, 90 N. W. 467, which require the verdict to be a mere skeleton, made up of the most general inferences. See, also, First Nat. Bank v. Peck, 8 Kan. 660.

50 If a special verdict on a mixed question of law and fact find facts from which the court can draw clear conclusions, it is no objection that the jury have not themselves drawn such conclusions, and stated them as facts in the case. Monkhouse v. Hay, 8 Price, (Exch.) 256. See, also, Winchell v. Abbot, 77 Wis. 371, 46 N. W. 665.

51 Louisville, N. A. & C. Ry. Co. v. Miller, 141 Ind. 550, 37 N. E. 348; Cleveland, C., C. & St. L. Ry. Co. v. Dugan, 18 Ind. App. 440, 48 N. E. 238; Keller v. Gaskill, 20 Ind. App. 502, 50 N. E. 363; Citi-

will ignore. They are conclusions of fact, which none but the jury may draw.

On the other hand, where the facts found lead irresistibly to the conclusion of negligence or the absence of it, the inference of negligence or the want of it is purely a conclusion of law, which it is exclusively the province of the court to determine. Hence a finding of negligence or want of negligence, if inconsistent with other findings, is to be disregarded.[52] Where such finding is in harmony with the others, and sets forth the conclusion which the law would reach upon the facts found, the verdict is good, though the inference was not properly for the jury.[53]

"Where a question of negligence arises in a case, the jury cannot be allowed to say conclusively, after finding certain special facts, that these facts constitute negligence, when in fact

zens' St. R. Co. v. Hoffbauer, 23 Ind. App. 614, 56 N. E. 54; Republic Iron & Steel Co. v. Jones, 32 Ind. App. 189, 69 N. E. 191. See, also, Hogan v. Railroad Co., 59 Wis. 139, 17 N. W. 632.

Where the plaintiff, to recover, must show absence of contributory negligence, it is as necessary that the special verdict should show freedom from negligence on the part of plaintiff as that it should show negligence on the part of defendant. Cleveland, C., C. & St. L. Ry. Co. v. Hadley, 12 Ind. App. 516, 40 N. E. 760; Louisville, N. A. & C. Ry. Co. v. Carmon, 20 Ind. App. 471, 50 N. E. 893; Id. (Ind. App.) 48 N. E. 1047.

The jury may not return the primary facts on evenly balanced evidence, where the burden of establishing the ultimate fact rests on the party in whose favor the primary facts are found. Citizens' St. R. Co. v. Reed, 151 Ind. 396, 51 N. E. 477.

52 See Hogan v. Railroad Co., 59 Wis. 139, 17 N. W. 632; Martin v. Bishop, 59 Wis. 417, 18 N. W. 337; Fick v. Railroad Co., 68 Wis. 469, 32 N. W. 527, 60 Am. Rep. 878; Bibby v. Lumber Co., 80 Wis. 367, 50 N. W. 337; and particularly Stafford v. Railroad Co., 110 Wis. 331, 345, 346, 85 N. W. 1036; Dummer v. Light Co., 108 Wis. 589, 84 N. W. 853.

53 Terre Haute & I. R. Co. v. Brunker, 128 Ind. 542, 26 N. E. 178; Pittsburgh, C. C. & St. L. Ry. Co. v. Burton, 139 Ind. 357, 37 N. E. 150.

and manifestly they do not constitute negligence. But in order to disregard the general conclusion of the jury it is necessary that it may be seen that they are only general conclusions from the facts which have already been sufficiently ascertained or found. Otherwise, it would be necessary to regard such general conclusions as general findings of fact." [54]

**Uncontroverted Facts.** It is not necessary that a special verdict should contain facts admitted by the pleadings.[55] It need find only such facts as are alleged in the pleadings upon one side and denied on the other.[56]

But as to facts concerning which the evidence is undisputed, there is a difference of opinion. On the one hand, it has been held that undisputed facts should be included in the verdict, which otherwise does not find facts sufficient to warrant a judgment.[57] It must be self-sustaining—must stand or fall according to its own inherent qualities [58]—and is defective though the evidence shows beyond controversy the existence of the material facts omitted therefrom.[59] However clear and undisputed the evidence upon the issues not found, the court cannot render judgment without usurping in part the functions

[54] Atchison, T. & S. F. R. Co. v. Plunkett, 25 Kan. 188, 198.

[55] Powell v. Bank of Lemoore, 125 Cal. 468, 58 Pac. 83; Burton v. Boyd, 7 Kan. 28; McGonigle v. Gordon, 11 Kan. 167; Fenske v. Nelson, 74 Minn. 1, 76 N. W. 785; Barto v. Himrod, 8 N. Y. 485, 59 Am. Dec. 506; Ward v. Busack, 46 Wis. 407, 1 N. W. 107; Carpenter v. Town of Rolling, 107 Wis. 559, 83 N. W. 953.

But it should find facts admitted upon the trial. Wabash R. Co. v. Miller, 18 Ind. App. 549, 48 N. E. 663.

[56] Cole v. Crawford, 69 Tex. 124, 5 S. W. 646.

[57] Wallingford v. Dunlap, 14 Pa. 33; Spath v. Bryan, 18 Pittsb. Leg. J. O. S. (Pa.) 79; Craven v. Gearhart, 1 Wkly. Notes Cas. (Pa.) 257. And see Daube v. Coal & Iron Co., 46 U. S. App. 591, 23 C. C. A. 420, 77 Fed. 713.

[58] Vansyckel v. Stewart, 77 Pa. 124.

[59] Ledyard v. Brown, 27 Tex. 393; Smith v. Warren, 60 Tex. 462; Stephenson v. Chappell, 12 Tex. Civ. App. 296, 36 S. W. 482; Thomas v. Salmons (Tex. Civ. App.) 39 S. W. 1094.

of the jury, thereby infringing a right guarantied by the Constitution and laws.[60]

In *Wisconsin,* on the other hand, it is held that any fact established by undisputed evidence may be considered as part of the special verdict,[61] and the court may make a formal finding covering it,[62] thus completing the foundation for judgment as shown by the record. The "material issues" of fact to which the statute requires the questions propounded to relate are the controverted issues, and to require the jury to determine whether or not an undisputed fact exists is an absurdity. "A finding

[60] Moore v. Moore, 67 Tex. 293, 3 S. W. 285. But see Texas statute, Appendix, as to presumption on appeal.

[61] Williams v. Porter, 41 Wis. 422; McNarra v. Railroad Co., Id. 69; Eberhardt v. Sanger, 51 Wis. 72, 8 N. W. 111; Farwell v. Warren, 76 Wis. 527, 45 N. W. 217; Stringham v. Cook, 75 Wis. 589, 44 N. W. 777; Winchell v. Abbot, 77 Wis. 371, 46 N. W. 665; Bush v. Maxwell, 79 Wis. 114, 48 N. W. 250; Montreal River Lumber Co. v. Mihills, 80 Wis. 540, 50 N. W. 507; Hart v. Railroad Co., 86 Wis. 483, 57 N. W. 91; Murphey v. Weil, 89 Wis. 146, 61 N. W. 315; Mills & Le Clair Lumber Co. v. Railroad Co., 94 Wis. 336, 68 N. W. 996; Cooper v. Insurance Co., 96 Wis. 362, 71 N. W. 606.

Where the evidence shows conclusively that the plaintiff is not entitled to recover, and the special verdict contains no finding of fact which interferes with the rendition of judgment for the defendant, the court may give judgment for the latter. Munkwitz v. Uhlig, 64 Wis. 380, 25 N. W. 424.

In Ward v. Busack, 46 Wis. 407, 414, 1 N. W. 107, Ryan, C. J., concurs in the judgment, but dissents from the dictum "that the court may eke out the failure of a special verdict to pass on all the issues, by holding that the evidence on the question omitted appears to the court to be uncontradicted and satisfactory. That is invading the province of the jury, and violating the rule that a verdict must pass upon all the issues. * * * It is essential to the right administration of justice that a sharp line should always be drawn between the functions of the jury and the functions of the court. And I fear that, among the many laxities induced by the Code, there is a tendency to relax this rule, creating vicious confusion of function."

But the rule has long been firmly established in Wisconsin practice. See Berg v. Railroad Co., 50 Wis. 419, 425, 7 N. W. 347.

[62] Mayhew v. Mather, 82 Wis. 355, 52 N. W. 436; Murphey v. Weil,

upon the [uncontroverted] issue is matter of form rather than substance; for certainly there can be no substantial difference between directing the jury to find that the title was in the plaintiff, and then giving judgment for him on such finding, and rendering the same judgment without such finding."[63]

89 Wis. 146, 61 N. W. 315. See, also, Hart v. Railroad Co., 86 Wis. 483, 57 N. W. 91; McDermott v. Railway Co., 91 Wis. 38, 64 N. W. 430.

[63] Hutchinson v. Railroad Co., 41 Wis. 541, 553.

**Negligence.** Where there is no express finding of fault or negligence, the verdict is defective, and plaintiff is not entitled to judgment unless the court can say, as a matter of law, that negligence is clearly and decisively shown by the uncontradicted evidence. Orttel v. Railroad Co., 89 Wis. 127, 61 N. W. 289.

A judgment cannot be entered upon a verdict which fails to include every material issue raised by the pleadings and evidence, if the omitted issue might have been so resolved as to prevent such judgment. Id.

**Proximate Cause.** Where, in an action for injuries, the element of responsible causation appears as a matter of law from the evidence and the other facts found, no special finding on the question of proximate cause is necessary. Hallum v. Village of Omro (Wis.) 99 N. W. 1051.

**Wisconsin Rule Invoked in United States Supreme Court.** In Hodges v. Easton, 106 U. S. 408, 1 Sup. Ct. 307, 27 L. Ed. 169 (in error to the Circuit Court of the United States for the Eastern District of Wisconsin), the court propounded to the jury certain questions covering only a part of the material issues. The questions, with the answers thereto, were returned as a special verdict.

Plaintiffs moved for judgment on the special verdict, while defendants moved to set aside the verdict and for a new trial upon the ground, among others, that the special verdict "does not contain findings upon the material issues in the case." These motions were heard together, and it was ordered by the court "that the motion of defendants for a new trial be and is hereby overruled, and that the motion of the plaintiffs for judgment upon the special verdict of the jury and facts conceded or not disputed upon the trial be and is hereby granted."

The damages were assessed by the court, and judgment was entered against defendants.

Defendants in error contended that the decisions of the Supreme Court of Wisconsin were conclusive that undisputed facts need not

This is in accordance with the practice in English courts of law. An exception to the rule that the court would not intend anything upon a special verdict existed in favor of the power of amendment to this extent: that where the jury had omitted to find an essential fact, and the evidence of this fact was clear

appear in the special verdict, and that the judgment upon its face showed that it was not based exclusively on answers to the special questions, but also upon conceded and undisputed facts.

There was no general verdict, nor was there a bill of exceptions showing the evidence adduced.

Held, that as the facts set out in the special verdict were insufficient to sustain the judgment, and as without a waiver of trial by jury—against which every reasonable presumption should be indulged—it was the constitutional right of the defendants to have the jury pass upon all the material facts in issue, the judgment must be reversed, and a new trial had.

In the conrse of the opinion by Mr. Justice Harlan, it is said:

"But it is suggested that the final judgment, upon its face, shows that it was not based exclusively on answers to the special questions and the stipulation of the parties, * * * but also 'upon facts conceded or not disputed upon the trial.' Although this court is not informed by the record as to what those conceded and undisputed facts are, it is insisted that we should presume, in support of the judgment, that they were, in connection with the facts specially found, sufficient to justify the action of the court below. This position, it is contended, is sustained by numerous decisions of the Supreme Court of Wisconsin upon the subject of general and special verdicts, as defined and regulated by the laws of that state in force when this action was tried.

"It is not necessary, in this opinion, to enter upon an examination of those decisions, nor to consider how far local law controls in determining either the essential requisites of a special verdict in the courts of the United States, or the conditions under which a judgment will be presumed to have been supported by facts other than those set out in the special verdict. The difficulty we have arises from other considerations. The record discloses that the defendants had a determination, by the jury, of a part of the facts, while other facts, upon which the final judgment was rested, were found by the court to have been conceded or not disputed. If we should presume that there were no material facts considered by the court beyond those found in the answers to special questions, then, as we have seen,

and undoubted, the court would supply the deficiency in the verdict by amending it. An early instance of this kind was in trover, where the jury had omitted to find the quantity of goods

the facts found do not authorize the judgment. If, on the other hand, we should adjudge it to have been defendants' duty to preserve the evidence in a bill of exceptions, and that, in deference to the decisions of the state court, it should be presumed that the 'facts conceded or not disputed on the trial' were, in connection with the facts ascertained by the jury, ample to support the judgment, we have then a case, at law, which the jury was sworn to try, determined, as to certain material facts, by the court alone, without a waiver of jury trial as to such facts. It was the province of the jury to pass upon the issues of fact, and it was the right of the defendants, secured by the Constitution of the United States, to have them do so. That right could have been waived, but it could not be taken from them by the court. If, upon the trial, all the facts essential to recovery had been undisputed, or so conclusively established the cause of action as to have authorized the withdrawal of the case altogether from the jury, by a peremptory instruction to find for plaintiffs, it would still have been necessary that the jury make its verdict, albeit in conformity with the order of the court. The court could not, consistently with the constitutional right of trial by jury, submit part of the facts to the jury, and itself determine the remainder, without a waiver by the defendants of a verdict by the jury. In civil cases, other than those in equity and admiralty, and except where it is otherwise provided in bankruptcy proceedings, 'the trial of issues of fact' —that is, of all the material issues of fact—'in the circuit courts shall be by jury,' unless the parties, or their attorneys of record, stipulate in writing for the waiver of a jury. Rev. St. §§ 648, 649 [U. S. Comp. St. 1901, p. 525]. There is no such stipulation in this case, and there is nothing in the record from which such a stipulation or waiver may be inferred. It has been often said by this court that the trial by jury is a fundamental guaranty of the rights and liberties of the people. Cousequently, every reasonable presumption should be indulged against its waiver. For these reasons, the judgment below must be reversed."

**Nonlitigated Matter.** Where a fact at the trial of a cause is not controverted, nor litigated before the jury, the court will order a venire de novo to determine it, unless the opposing party will consent to amend the special verdict by inserting it. Watson v. Delafield, 1 Johns. (N. Y.) 150.

Where a fact, proved by documentary evidence, is not controverted on the trial, but both parties take it for granted, and it is, however,

converted, but, as the quantities were proved at the trial, the court refused to award a venire de novo, but supplied the defect by amending the verdict in that respect.[64]

**Definiteness and Certainty Essential.** An indefinite or uncertain verdict will not sustain a judgment.[65] The facts must be found expressly and specifically, not generally and impliedly,[66] nor upon an hypothesis.[67] The verdict should be the end of the controversy, and not result in its continuance.[68]

But it is sufficient if the substance of the issues be found;[69] and though the verdict be not as clear and full as desirable, yet if, when taken as a whole, in connection with inferences fairly arising from the facts specially found, a sufficient basis to support a judgment is disclosed, judgment thereon will not be disturbed.[70]

omitted in the special verdict, the court may direct the verdict to be amended by inserting that such fact was admitted on the trial. Sleght v Hartshorne, 1 Johns. (N. Y.) 149.

64 2 Thomp. Tr. § 2656, citing Mayo v. Archer, 1 Strange, 531, 514.

65 Stodder v. Powell, 1 Stew. (Ala.) 287; Tisdale v. Lumber Co., 131 Ala. 456, 31 South. 729; Louisville, N. A. & C. Ry. Co. v. Frawley, 110 Ind. 18, 9 N. E. 594; Becknell v. Hosier, 10 Ind. App. 5, 37 N. E. 580; Pint v. Bauer, 31 Minn. 4, 16 N. W. 425; State v. Curtis, 71 N. C. 56; Puffer v. Lucas, 107 N. C. 322, 12 S. E. 130, 464; Bottoms v. Railroad Co., 109 N. C. 72, 13 S. E. 738; Loew v. Stocker, 61 Pa. 347; Kyser v. Cannon, 29 Ohio St. 360; State v. Duncan, 2 McCord (S. C.) 129; Moore v. Moore, 67 Tex. 293, 3 S. W. 285; Scottish-American Mortg. Co. v. Scripture (Tex. Civ. App.) 40 S. W. 210; Schwartzman v. Cabell (Tex. Civ. App.) 49 S. W. 113; Clay v. Ransome, 1 Munf. (Va.) 454; Brown v. Ralston, 4 Rand. (Va.) 504; Hall v. Ratliff, 93 Va. 327, 24 S. E. 1011; Carroll v. Bohan, 43 Wis. 218; McGowan v. Railroad Co., 91 Wis. 147, 64 N. W. 891.

66 Breeze v. Doyle, 19 Cal. 101.

67 Woodson v. McCune, 17 Cal. 304; Carroll v. Bohan, 43 Wis. 218.

68 Moore v. Moore, 67 Tex. 293, 3 S. W. 285.

69 Puterbaugh v. Puterbaugh, 131 Ind. 288, 30 N. E. 519, 15 L. R. A. 341; Evansville & T. H. R. Co. v. Taft, 2 Ind. App. 237, 28 N. E. 443.

70 Brinson-Judd Grain Co. v. Becker, 76 Mo. App. 375. Reference may always be had to the context to clear up obscurity in a particular part. Alhambra Addition Water Co. v. Richardson, 72 Cal. 598, 14 Pac. 379.

Answers which indicate only how the jury leans, such as, "We think not," etc., are quite insufficient to base a judgment upon;[71] as is also an answer that plaintiff "done all that he could," to a question inquiring what efforts plaintiff made to protect his property from a fire for which he claimed damages.[72]

When none but indirect and evasive answers can be drawn from the jury, the verdict should not stand.[73] Thus, in an action to recover damages for injuries received upon a highway, caused, as was alleged, by defects in such highway, among the questions submitted for a special verdict was the following: "Under all the evidence, was it an exercise of ordinary care and caution for the plaintiff's wife to attempt to drive across from the Burr Oak road onto the Lewis Valley road in the darkness?" Answer: "Under all of the circumstances, she was justified in doing as she did." In respect to this question and answer, the Supreme Court said: "What the jury meant by saying that she was justified in doing as she did, we cannot say. They may have thought that the circumstances would justify some negligence on her part. Whether such was or was not their view is a matter of mere conjecture. The question admitted of a categorical answer, and the defendant was clearly entitled to such an answer. Because it was not so answered, there must be another trial." [74]

But an answer, "He might not," to the question, "Could

71 Hopkins v. Stanley, 43 Ind. 553. A special finding in form, "We, the jury, believe," etc., held sufficient. McGuire v. Railroad Co., 23 Mo. App. 325. See, also, Evans & Howard Fire Brick Co. v. Railroad Co., 21 Mo. App. 648.

72 Louisville, N. A. & C. Ry. Co. v. Roberts, 18 Ind. App. 538, 47 N. E. 839.

73 Carroll v. Bohan, 43 Wis. 218; McGowan v. Railroad Co., 91 Wis. 147, 64 N. W. 891.

74 Davis v. Town of Farmington, 42 Wis. 425, 433. See, also, Fitzgerald v. Insurance Co., 64 Wis. 463, 25 N. W. 785.

**Don't Know.** When, on a proper submission, the jury answer that they do not know, or cannot tell from the evidence, it is equivalent to

plaintiff have heard the whistle?" is not evasive, where there was lack of proof upon which a more definite answer could have been given. It is merely expressive of the inability of the jury to answer the question at all.[75] While the answer, "We have no proof that she did," in reply to a question as to whether plaintiff, before the injury, knew of the defect in the walk, is equivalent to an answer in the negative, the burden of proving contributory negligence being on the defendant.[76]

In *Wisconsin* it is held that where an answer is evasive, if the uncontradicted evidence answers it clearly, the court will consider it as properly answered, in determining the judgment to be rendered.[77]

A special verdict, uncertain by reason of inconsistent and confused findings, cannot be cured by disregarding the uncertain portions, though the verdict is sufficient without them.[78] But inconsistent parts become immaterial where, e. g., the findings acquit the defendant of fault in causing the accident, and judgment must be rendered on it in any case.[79]

Where the verdict is so imperfect that no judgment can be rendered upon it, and is not susceptible of amendment, a venire de novo should be awarded.[80]

a finding that the fact is not proved. Turner v. Railroad Co., 23 Mo. App. 12.

**Cannot Answer,** as to material facts, necessitates a new trial. Tew v. Young, 134 N. C. 493, 47 S. E. 23.

75 Urbanek v. Railroad Co., 47 Wis. 59, 1 N. W. 464.

76 McLimans v. City of Lancaster, 63 Wis. 596, 23 N. W. 689.

77 Nelson v. Railroad Co., 60 Wis. 320, 19 N. W. 52. Answer, "Don't know," to question as to whether engine was properly managed, set aside, and, in effect, answered by court in the affirmative upon the undisputed evidence. Menominee River Sash & Door Co. v. Railroad Co., 91 Wis. 447, 65 N. W. 176.

78 Becknell v. Hosier, 10 Ind. App. 5, 37 N. E. 580.

79 Robinson v. Town of Washburn, 81 Wis. 404, 51 N. W. 578.

80 Whitesides v. Russell, 8 Watts & S. (Pa.) 44; Wallingford v. Dunlap, 14 Pa. 31; Seward v. Jackson, 8 Cow. (N. Y.) 406; State v. Wallace, 25 N. C. 195; Lawrence v. Beaubien, 2 Bailey (S. C.) 623, 23 Am. Dec. 155; Robinson's Adm'r v. Brock, 1 Hen. & M. (Va.) 213;

**Omitted Findings—Failure to Answer.** As has been seen, where a special verdict is returned, all the facts essential to support the judgment rendered must be found.[81] By this, however, is not meant that no judgment can be rendered on a verdict failing to pass upon all facts in issue. If the jury return facts which show no right of recovery, or which show a good cause of action, without available defense, the verdict is sufficient to sustain a judgment.[82] Silence in regard to a material fact raises the presumption that the fact has not been proved and does not exist,[83] and the omission will therefore be regarded as equivalent to an express finding against the party having the burden of proof on such issue,[84] which may entitle the opposite

Pegram v. Isabell, Id. 387; Bellows v. Bank, 2 Mason (U. S.) 31, Fed. Cas. No. 1,279. See "Omitted Findings," and post, chapter 14, "Venire de Novo."

[81] Ante, p. 204; Waymire v. Lank, 121 Ind. 1, 22 N. E. 735; Lake Shore & M. S. Ry. Co. v. Van Auken, 1 Ind. App. 492, 27 N. E. 119; Walkup v. May, 9 Ind. App. 412, 36 N. E. 917; Meyer v. Green, 21 Ind. App. 138, 51 N. E. 942, 69 Am. St. Rep. 344; State v. Crump, 104 N. C. 763, 10 S. E. 468; Moore v. Moore, 67 Tex. 293, 3 S. W. 285; Hildman v. City of Phillips, 106 Wis. 611, 82 N. W. 566; Ward v. Cochran, 150 U. S. 597, 14 Sup. Ct. 230, 37 L. Ed. 1195.

Mandamus will not lie to compel a court to receive a special verdict until the jury have found on all the issues submitted to them. Rose v. Harvey, 18 R. I. 527, 30 Atl. 459.

[82] Lee v. Campbell's Heirs, 4 Port. (Ala.) 198.

[83] Glantz v. City of South Bend, 106 Ind. 305, 6 N. E. 632; Louisville, N. A. & C. Ry. Co. v. Buck, 116 Ind. 566, 19 N. E. 453, 2 L. R. A. 520, 9 Am. St. Rep. 883. The following cases hold that what is not found is nonexistent for the purpose of a decision. No presumption is to be indulged on account of the omission. The verdict is defective. Thayer v. Society, 20 Pa. 60; Pittsburgh, Ft. W. & C. R. Co. v. Evans, 53 Pa. 250; Loew v. Stocker, 61 Pa. 347; Tuigg v. Treacy, 31 Pittsb. Leg. J. (Pa.) 226; Lawrence v. Beaubien, 2 Bailey (S. C.) 623, 23 Am. Dec. 155; Collins v. Riley, 104 U. S. 327, 26 L. Ed. 752.

[84] Noblesville Gas & Improvement Co. v. Loehr, 124 Ind. 79, 24 N. E. 579; Evansville & R. R. Co. v. Maddux, 134 Ind. 571, 33 N. E. 345; Mitchell v. Bain, 142 Ind. 604, 42 N. E. 230; Archibald v. Long, 144 Ind. 451, 43 N. E. 439; Boyer v. Robertson, 144 Ind. 604, 43 N. E. 879; Banner Cigar Co. v. Brewing Co., 145 Ind. 266, 44

party to judgment.[85] When the party having the onus in a case asks judgment upon a special verdict, the material facts therein found within the issues must establish his right under the law to a judgment; but, where the moving party is not the one upon whom the burden of the issue rests, his right to be awarded a judgment does not depend alone upon the presence of material facts—he may be entitled to the judgment by reason of the absence of some essential fact which it was incumbent upon his adversary to establish.[86] But the omission to find an essential fact raises the presumption that such fact was not proven, only when the facts found are inferential. In such case the verdict is not defective. Where, however, the jury finds only the

N. E. 455; Evansville & R. R. Co. v. Charlton, 6 Ind. App. 56, 33 N. E. 129; Western Union Tel. Co. v. Newhouse, 6 Ind. App. 422, 33 N. E. 800; Shipps v. Atkinson, 8 Ind. App. 505, 36 N. E. 375; Cooper v. Forgey, 14 Ind. App. 151, 42 N. E. 651; Louisville, N. A. & C. Ry. Co. v. Quinn, 14 Ind. App. 554, 43 N. E. 240; Fireman's Ins. Co. v. Dunn, 22 Ind. App. 332, 53 N. E. 251.

See chapter 14, "Venire de Novo."

[85] Where the special verdict fails to find any fact essential to entitle the plaintiff to judgment, the defendant's motion for judgment should be sustained, unless the case is one where the burden is on the defendant. Dixon v. Duke, 85 Ind. 434; Trittipo v. Morgan, 99 Ind. 269; Waymire v. Lank, 121 Ind. 2, 22 N. E. 735; Louisville, N. A. & C. Ry. Co. v. Miller, 141 Ind. 533, 37 N. E. 343; Helwig v. Beckner, 149 Ind. 131, 46 N. E. 644. See, also, McGonigle v. Gordon, 11 Kan. 167.

**Texas Statute.** When a special verdict does not find all the facts necessary to form the basis of a judgment, but does answer all the questions submitted, the court is presumed to have found from the evidence the omitted facts necessary to support the judgment, if the evidence is present to authorize the finding thus presumed. Southern Cotton Oil Co. v. Wallace, 23 Tex. Civ. App. 12, 54 S. W. 638. See, also, City of San Antonio v. L. A. Marshall Co. (Tex. Civ. App.) 85 S. W. 315; chapter 14, "Appeal."

It is immaterial that there is no finding by the jury upon a fact, if neither party requested submission of the issue (under Sayles' Ann. Civ. St. 1897, art. 1331). Holly & Co. v. Simmons (Tex. Civ. App.) 85 S. W. 325.

[86] Wabash R. Co. v. Ray, 152 Ind. 392, 51 N. E. 920.

evidentiary facts, the verdict is fatally defective, no judgment can be rendered thereon, and a venire de novo must be awarded.[87]

The writer's understanding of the procedure under the foregoing, which may be called the *"Indiana Rule,"* is as follows: If the verdict fails to find upon a point or points essential to plaintiff's case, judgment for plaintiff cannot be entered. Under such circumstances defendant's motion for judgment should be sustained, since the issues concerning which no facts are found are regarded as not proved by the party on whom rests the burden of proof. Such judgment should be rendered, however, only where the facts returned are ultimate, and the omission is not contrary to the evidence. If there is, in fact, evidence upon which findings could have been made, a new trial should be granted.[88]

Under the common law no presumption either way can be indulged upon such an omission. Nothing must remain for the

[87] Boyer v. Robertson, 144 Ind. 604, 43 N. E. 879 (because the verdict shows that facts sufficient to establish the inferential facts have been proved; there can be, therefore, no presumption against the party having the burden of proof; but as the inferential facts have not been found, the verdict will not support a judgment). See collection of authorities in this decision.

Where failure to find facts is contrary to the evidence, it may furnish sufficient reason for a new trial, but not for a venire de novo. Louisville, N. A. & C. Ry. Co. v. Buck, 116 Ind. 566, 19 N. E. 453, 2 L. R. A. 520, 9 Am. St. Rep. 883.

[88] See Ex parte Walls, 73 Ind. 95; Louisville, N. A. & C. Ry. Co. v. Buck, supra; City of Ft. Wayne v. Durnell, 13 Ind. App. 669, 42 N. E. 242.

When no judgment in favor of the party having the burden of proof can properly be based on the verdict, the adverse party may move for a new trial, or for judgment on the verdict, or may except to the sustaining of a motion for judgment against him. Germania Fire Ins. Co. v. Tile Co., 11 Ind. App. 385, 39 N. E. 304.

In a special finding or verdict, every fact necessary to the plaintiff's recovery must be found and stated, or the judgment must be for the defendant. Toledo, St. L. & K. C. R. Co. v. Trimble, 8 Ind. App. 333, 35 N. E. 716, citing Kehr v. Hall, 117 Ind. 405, 20 N. E. 279.

court but to draw the conclusions of law.[89] The verdict must respond to all the issues, or it is defective.[90] Where, as in Indiana, the court assumes that facts not returned were not proved by the party having the burden of the issues, it distinctly makes a finding of fact which the jury have not made. The Messrs. Elliott, in their work on Appellate Procedure, deplore the casting aside of the common-law rule by the courts of their state, and remark: "It is difficult, we may add, to conceive how the court could consistently incorporate the common-law rule into our system (for it was not incorporated by legislation), and yet leave out an essential and commendable element." [91] Judge Thompson calls the principle upheld in Indiana a "modern development" of the rule that nothing can be supplied by intendment; [92] rather a "modern reversal," we would think. But the fact is that such intendments have been made elsewhere, and weighty authority sustains the rule applied in Indiana while special verdicts were in use.[93] The rule is based on the idea that the facts to be stated in a special verdict are those that have been *proved on the trial,* and none other; that it is not the office of a special verdict to find specially upon all the issues, but only to find the facts proven within the issues. "The inevitable corollary proposition is that, if the special finding or verdict is silent in reference to any issue or facts, such silence is not an

[89] Langley v. Warner, 3 N. Y. 327; Sisson v. Barrett, 2 N. Y. 406; Till v. Covell, 1 N. Y. 522; Seward v. Jackson, 8 Cow. (N. Y.) 406.

[90] 2 Tidd's Pr. 922. The Code has made no alteration in the requisites of a special verdict. Eisemann v. Swan, 6 Bosw. (N. Y.) 668; Williams v. Willis, 7 Abb. Prac. (N. Y.) 90; Fraschieris v. Henriques, 6 Abb. Prac. N. S. (N. Y.) 251.

[91] Section 758.

[92] 2 Thomp. Tr. § 2651, note 5.

[93] Wesson v. Saline Co., 34 U. S. App. 680, 20 C. C. A. 227, 73 Fed. 917; Sneed v. Milling Co., 20 C. C. A. 230, 73 Fed. 925; Daube v. Coal & Iron Co., 46 U. S. App. 591, 77 Fed. 713, 23 C. C. A. 420; United States v. Harris, 46 U. S. App. 653, 77 Fed. 821, 23 C. C. A. 483. See, also, Sisson v. Barrett, 2 N. Y. 406; La Frombois v. Jackson, 8 Cow. (N. Y.) 589, 18 Am. Dec. 463.

omission apparent on the record which can be ground for granting a venire de novo." [94]

The omission of a special finding does not render the verdict insufficient to support judgment where the omitted fact may be fairly inferred from the facts found,[95] or where there is no controversy as to the omitted fact.[96] Nor will failure to find upon some issue, a finding upon which would merely have the effect of invalidating a judgment fully supported by the findings made, be held ground for reversal unless it is shown by statement or bill of exceptions that evidence was submitted in relation to such issue.[97]

Failure of the jury to answer some of the questions submitted will not be fatal to the judgment unless an answer to such questions favorable to the party against whom judgment is rendered would necessarily make such judgment erroneous; [98] nor will failure of the verdict to assess the amount of damages sustained by plaintiff prevent entry of judgment thereon, where the damages are assessed in the formal conclusion of the verdict.[99]

Where the jury return a special verdict which omits to pass upon certain issues, failure to object to the questions submitted, or to request others, or to take exceptions to the reception of the verdict, is not a waiver of the right to attack the verdict.[100]

[94] Ex parte Walls, 73 Ind. 95, 110. See, also, Graham v. State, 66 Ind. 386; Glantz v. City of South Bend, 106 Ind. 305, 6 N. E. 632.

[95] Jones v. Foster, 67 Wis. 296, 30 N. W. 697; Abbot v. Gore, 74 Wis. 509, 43 N. W. 365. See, also, Brinson-Judd Grain Co. v. Becker, 76 Mo. App. 375. Contra, 2 Hawk. P. C. 622; Tancred v. Christy, 12 M. & W. 316.

[96] Stringham v. Cook, 75 Wis. 589, 44 N. W. 777; Winchell v. Abbot, 77 Wis. 371, 46 N. W. 665; Trapp v. New Birdsall Co., 109 Wis. 543, 85 N. W. 478. See ante, "Uncontroverted Facts."

[97] Himmelman v. Henry, 84 Cal. 104, 23 Pac. 1098.

[98] Bush v. Maxwell, 79 Wis. 114, 48 N. W. 250.

[99] Cole v. Powell, 17 Ind. App. 438, 46 N. E. 1006. See, also, Imperial Fire Ins. Co. v. Kiernan, 83 Ky. 468.

[100] Sherman v. Lumber Co., 77 Wis. 14, 45 N. W. 1079; Crich v. Insurance Co., 45 Minn. 441, 48 N. W. 198.

There would be a waiver where the special verdict was accom-

**Inconsistency.** If the findings of the jury are contradictory, no judgment can be rendered on the verdict, which should be set aside, and a new trial granted.[101] The legal conclusion must follow as a necessary consequence from the facts stated, which cannot happen either where the facts are doubtful, or where distinct facts are set in opposition to each other.[102] But

panied by a general. Sherman v. Lumber Co., supra, citing Kelley v. Railroad Co., 53 Wis. 74, 9 N. W. 816. But see Cook v. McNaughton, 128 Ind. 410, 24 N. E. 361, 28 N. E. 74; Bohr v. Neuenschwander, 120 Ind. 449, 22 N. E. 416.

[101] Where repugnancy between material findings cannot be overcome by reasonable interpretation, it needs no citation of authority to enforce the proposition that the verdict determines no facts to which the court can apply the law. Among a great number of cases so holding, are the following:

Pint v. Bauer, 31 Minn. 4, 16 N. W. 425; Smyth v. Marsich, 4 App. Div. 171, 38 N. Y. Supp. 932; Porter v. Railroad Co., 97 N. C. 66, 2 S. E. 581, 2 Am. St. Rep. 272; Puffer v. Lucas, 107 N. C. 322, 12 S. E. 130; Bottoms v. Railroad Co., 109 N. C. 72, 13 S. E. 738; Cushman v. Masterson (Tex. Civ. App.) 64 S. W. 1031; Waller v. Liles, 96 Tex. 21, 70 S. W. 17; Commerce Milling & Grain Co. v. Morris & Parker (Tex. Civ. App.) 86 S. W. 73; Montreal River Lumber Co. v. Mihills, 80 Wis. 540, 50 N. W. 507; Goff v. Railroad Co., 86 Wis. 237, 56 N. W. 465; Darcey v. Lumber Co., 87 Wis. 245, 58 N. W. 382; Benson v. City of Madison, 101 Wis. 312, 77 N. W. 161; Pautz v. Packing Co., 118 Wis. 47, 94 N. W. 654; Fehrman v. Pine River, 118 Wis. 150, 95 N. W. 105; McBride v. Railroad Co., 3 Wyo. 247, 21 Pac. 687. For effect of inconsistency between a general conclusion and special facts found, see Selleck v. Griswold, 49 Wis. 39, 5 N. W. 213.

The finding of a specific fact inconsistent with a more general finding upon the same subject will, to the extent of such specific fact, cut down and limit such more general finding. Shenners v. Railway Co., 78 Wis. 382, 47 N. W. 622.

[102] State v. Duncan, 2 McCord (S. C.) 129.

A special verdict in an action of libel, finding facts which would justify the giving of exemplary damages, but awarding nominal damages only, should be set aside as inconsistent. Cottrill v. Cramer, 59 Wis. 231, 18 N. W. 12.

Where the jury found that the injury was proximately caused by the master's negligence, that plaintiff knew the condition of the appliance, that the danger was apparent to one in plaintiff's position using

there is no real inconsistency where the conflict is only between material findings and immaterial matters improperly included in the verdict, for the latter are to be disregarded in rendering judgment.[103]

The effort should always be made to harmonize the several parts of the verdict. The court will not strain the language of a finding to make out a case of conflict.[104] On the contrary, it will endeavor by a practicable construction to make the verdict the end of the controversy, and, where the repugnancy of answers to each other will prevent a judgment being entered, may send the jury back for further deliberation.[105]

Inconsistencies are immaterial where the inconsistent findings do not and cannot in any way qualify or limit the answers upon which the right of either party to a judgment in his favor are made clear. Thus, in an action for damages for personal injuries claimed to have been sustained by reason of a defective sidewalk, the jury returned a special verdict, finding, among other facts: (1) That plaintiff did not suffer any injuries as alleged in her complaint by reason of the alleged negligence of

ordinary care and observation, but that he was not guilty of contributory negligence, judgment for plaintiff cannot stand. Darcey v. Lumber Co., 87 Wis. 245, 58 N. W. 382. See, also, Bottoms v. Railroad Co., 109 N. C. 72, 13 S. E. 738.

103 Jonas v. Hirshburg, 18 Ind. App. 581, 48 N. E. 656. See, also, Gottschalk v. Witter, 25 Ohio St. 76.

Where the jury, in returning a special verdict, were requested to answer a certain question if they answered the previous question in the affirmative, and, though they answered the preceding question negatively, nevertheless answered the conditional question, any inconsistency in the verdict thereby produced is immaterial, since, as the question was never submitted to them, it and the answer thereto drop entirely out of the case. McGeehan v. Gaar, Scott & Co. (Wis.) 100 N. W. 1072.

104 Alhambra Addition Water Co. v. Richardson, 72 Cal. 598, 14 Pac. 379.

105 Oriental Investment Co. v. Barclay, 25 Tex. Civ. App. 543, 64 S. W. 80. And see Wightman v. Railroad Co., 73 Wis. 169, 40 N. W. 689, 2 L. R. A. 185, 9 Am. St. Rep. 778.

the defendant; (2) that the defendant did not have any notice, either actual or constructive, of the alleged defect before the accident happened. It also found (3) that plaintiff was injured, by reason of said alleged defect in the highway, in the hip, and her other diseases were aggravated; and (4) that plaintiff had sustained no damages by such injury. It was held that by findings here numbered 1 and 2 the defendant was clearly acquitted of all fault, and that the inconsistency between findings 3 and 4 became utterly immaterial.[106]

In *Wisconsin*, since a fact established by the undisputed evidence may be considered a part of the special verdict, if a finding in the verdict is inconsistent with such fact, it is proper to grant a new trial.[107]

The court should not refuse to receive and record a verdict because of inconsistent findings, where it is not obvious that no judgment can be rendered upon it. It should be received and filed, so that any action of the court based upon it may be reviewed on appeal.[108]

**Remedy for Defects—Amendment.** The jury may be required by the court to correct their insufficient and irregular answers,[109] and put their verdict in proper form,[110] as by adding a conditional conclusion,[111] or amending the verdict by stating that they "find" a certain fact, instead of stating that they "believe" such fact.[112]

But in an action for injuries, where the jury returned a spe-

[106] Robinson v. Town of Washburn, 81 Wis. 404, 51 N. W. 578.

[107] Murphey v. Weil, 89 Wis. 146, 61 N. W. 315.

[108] Robinson v. Town of Washburn, 81 Wis. 404, 51 N. W. 578.

[109] Bowman v. Phillips, 47 Ind. 341; City of Lebanon v. Twiford, 13 Ind. App. 384, 41 N. E. 844; Kansas Pac. R. Co. v. Pointer, 14 Kan. 37; Fick v. Mulholland, 48 Wis. 413, 4 N. W. 346; Coats v. Town of Stanton, 90 Wis. 130, 62 N. W. 619.

[110] Quinn v. State, 123 Ind. 59, 23 N. E. 977; Sleght v. Hartshorne, 1 Johns. (N. Y.) 149; Herbst Importing Co. v. Burnham, 81 Wis. 408, 51 N. W. 262.

[111] Toler v. Keiher, 81 Ind. 383.

[112] Hirsch v. Jones (Tex. Civ. App.) 42 S. W. 604.

cial verdict stating the amount to be recovered for each injury which they found the plaintiff had sustained, except that they found he had endured great pain, and was damaged thereby "in the sum of ——— dollars," and the court called the attention of the jury to the blank, and sent them out to correct their verdict, which they did by inserting $500 in the blank, the court's action was held a direction to assess damages for the pain of plaintiff, and hence error.[113] However, later, in the same case and by the same court, the trial judge's action in this respect was held proper.†

Where the jury's attention is called to such a blank, and, being again sent out, they fail to fill it, the intention to find no damages is shown. The verdict is, therefore, not defective, and a venire de novo should not be awarded.[114]

Where the defect is merely one of form, the court may amend the verdict of its own motion, or direct the jury to do so under its supervision. "It is believed that the power of amending special verdicts in matters of form exists as broadly, and is supported on the same grounds, as the power to amend general verdicts."[115] The court may direct the jury to retire and complete their verdict by answering questions which, under the instructions, they had mistakenly considered it unnecessary to answer; and this even after separation of the jury.[116] So, too,

[113] City of Ft. Wayne v. Durnell (Ind. App.) 39 N. E. 1049.

† City of Ft. Wayne v. Durnell, 13 Ind. App. 669, 42 N. E. 242.

[114] City of Lebanon v. Twiford, 13 Ind. App. 384, 41 N. E. 844.

[115] 2 Thomp. Trials, § 2656. Mere formal defects in the verdict may be cured by sending jury back to correct. Salem-Bedford Stone Co. v. O'Brien, 150 Ind. 656, 49 N. E. 457, citing Chicago & E. I. R. Co. v. Ostrander, 116 Ind. 259, 15 N. E. 227, 19 N. E. 110.

It is improper to send the jury out for further consideration, except to correct an omission. The verdict may not be changed. Sutliff v. Gilbert, 8 Ohio, 405.

[116] Olwell v. Railroad Co., 92 Wis. 330, 66 N. W. 362, and cases cited. See, also, State v. Arthur, 21 Iowa, 322; Rush v. Pedigo, 63 Ind. 479. But in Pittsburgh, C., C. & St. L. R. Co. v. Montgomery, 152 Ind. 1, 49 N. E. 582, 71 Am. St. Rep. 301, Brazil Block Coal Co. v. Hoodlet, 129 Ind. 327, 27 N. E. 741, Vinton v. Baldwin, 95 Ind. 433,

where findings are manifestly made under misapprehension of the instructions, the court may decline to receive the verdict, and direct the jury to retire for further consultation;[117] and, if the special verdict find such facts as leave nothing for the court to do but make a mathematical calculation, the court may fix the amount of damages or recovery without usurping the functions of the jury.[118]

The verdict may be amended by adding undisputed or non-litigated matters in cases where there appears to be no doubt or dispute as to what actually occurred on the trial,[119] such amendments being regarded as of form rather than of substance.[120] But amendments which amount to an actual change in the substance of the verdict cannot be made without the consent of both parties;[121] nor can the court substitute its finding for one made by the jury, where there is any evidence to support the latter.[122] To permit this would have the effect

and City of La Fayette v. Allen, 81 Ind. 166, it is held that, if a special verdict fails to find material facts, the remedy is not by motion to coerce the jury into making such finding, which would be an invasion by the court of the jury's province, but by motion for a new trial.

117 Wightman v. Railroad Co., 73 Wis. 169, 174, 40 N. W. 689, 2 L. R. A. 185, 9 Am. St. Rep. 778, and cases cited.

118 Knight v. Fisher, 15 Colo. 176, 25 Pac. 78; Wainwright v. Burroughs, 1 Ind. App. 393, 27 N. E. 591; Johnson v. Bucklen, 9 Ind. App. 154, 36 N. E. 176; City of Lebanon v. Twiford, 13 Ind. App. 384, 41 N. E. 844; City of Ft. Wayne v. Durnell, 13 Ind. App. 669, 42 N. E. 242; Id. (Ind. App.) 39 N. E. 1049, q. v.; Plano Mfg. Co. v. Kesler, 15 Ind. App. 110, 43 N. E. 925; Hoppes v. Chapin, 15 Ind. App. 258, 43 N. E. 1014. See, also, Dawson v. Shirk, 102 Ind. 184, 1 N. E. 292; Doran v. Ryan, 81 Wis. 63, 51 N. W. 259.

119 Crich v. Insurance Co., 45 Minn. 441, 48 N. W. 198; Mayhew v. Mather, 82 Wis. 355, 52 N. W. 436.

120 Hutchinson v. Railroad Co., 41 Wis. 541.

121 Walker v. Dewing, 8 Pick. (Mass.) 520; United States v. Bird's Creditors, 2 Brev. (S. C.) 85. And see Mitchell v. Mitchell, 122 N. C. 332, 29 S. E. 367; Coke & Reardon v. Ikard (Tex. Civ. App.) 87 S. W. 869.

122 Ohlweiler v. Lohmann, 82 Wis. 198, 52 N. W. 172; Sheehy v. Duffy, 89 Wis. 6, 61 N. W. 295. See, also, Conover v. Knight, 91 Wis.

of placing special verdicts in legal actions substantially on the footing of verdicts in equitable actions, making them merely advisory.[123]

The exercise of the power to refer the verdict of a jury back to them for further consideration is jealously scrutinized by appellate courts. It has always been looked upon with disfavor except where its purpose is to allow the jury to perfect a verdict in mere matter of form, as to supply an omission to make some computation of interest, the amount due upon some contract, or similar defect.[124] "It is only such a palpable error, mistake, or omission which can be corrected in this way—something which is a mere clerical or formal mistake. * * * Where the jury have found upon all the issues submitted to them, the court is not empowered to call their attention to real or supposed inconsistencies in their answers, and again send them out to change their answers or to make them consistent." [125]

—— **Setting Aside Findings.** A motion to strike out portions of a special verdict is not proper practice. If the matter objected to is immaterial, the court will treat it as surplusage; if material, and it be stricken out, the verdict is no longer the verdict of the jury, but the verdict or finding of the court.[126]

569, 65 N. W. 371. The jury's finding must be contrary to the undisputed, credible evidence to justify a court in directing a verdict or changing the jury's answer from the affirmative to the negative. Blohowak v. Grochoski, 119 Wis. 189, 96 N. W. 551.

"If there is any credible evidence which to a reasonable mind can support an inference in favor of a party, the question is for the jury, and the court cannot assume to answer it, either upon motion for nonsuit or direction of verdict, or by substituting other answers after the verdict is returned. At that stage the court has nothing to do with the preponderance of fairly conflicting evidence." Beyer v. Insurance Co., 112 Wis. 138, 141, 88 N. W. 57.

123 Sheehy v. Duffy, 89 Wis. 6, 61 N. W. 295.

124 Blesch v. Railroad Co., 48 Wis. 168, 2 N. W. 113.

125 Blesch v. Railroad Co., 48 Wis. 168, 194, 2 N. W. 113; Stricker v. Town of Reedsburg, 101 Wis. 457, 77 N. W. 897.

126 Louisville, N. A. & C. Ry. Co. v. Hart, 119 Ind. 273, 21 N. E. 753,

If some of the findings are not sustained by the evidence, the proper mode of bringing the question up for review is by motion for a new trial.[127]

But where, as in *Wisconsin,* the court may take into consideration the undisputed testimony, it is proper practice to move to set aside the parts not sustained by the evidence, and for judgment on the remainder and on the uncontradicted evidence.[128] If, upon the remaining findings and the uncontradicted evidence, the law is with the moving party, there is no ground for a new trial. If, however, there is any conflict of evidence as to the facts involved in the findings which it asks shall be set aside, the motion should be denied, and a new trial granted. It is only where there is no evidence to support a material finding that it can be stricken from the record.[129]

Where findings are stricken out, as above, the approved practice is to include in the order proper findings, so that the record will show a foundation of fact for the judgment without any bill of exceptions. Otherwise, until such bill, the judgment would have no support in the record.

Where findings are contrary to the undisputed evidence, it is not proper practice to move for judgment notwithstanding the objectionable findings. The trial court cannot render judg-

4 L. R. A. 549. It is improper for the court to strike out a finding which is inconsistent with others, and give effect to the latter, for this would be making a new verdict. McBride v. Railroad Co., 3 Wyo. 247, 21 Pac. 687.

127 Tarkington v. Purvis, 128 Ind. 182, 25 N. E. 879, 9 L. R. A. 607; Louisville, N. A. & C. Ry. Co. v. Hart, supra.

128 Conroy v. Railroad Co., 96 Wis. 243, 70 N. W. 486, 38 L. R. A. 419; Menominee River Sash & Door Co. v. Railroad Co., 91 Wis. 447, 65 N. W. 176.

129 Menominee River Sash & Door Co. v. Railroad Co., supra.

Where a finding is merely against the preponderance of the evidence, upon setting it aside a new trial should be granted. Ohlweiler v. Lohmann, 82 Wis. 198, 52 N. W. 172; Id., 88 Wis. 75, 59 N. W. 678; Dahl v. Railroad Co., 65 Wis. 371, 27 N. W. 185; Schweickhart v. Stuewe, 75 Wis. 157, 43 N. W. 722; Sheehy v. Duffy, 89 Wis. 13, 61 N. W. 295.

ment until these findings are set aside. As a consequence, the appellate court having no original power to correct or set aside any part of a special verdict, appellant is not entitled to a direction that judgment be entered in his favor, where he has made no application to the trial court to set aside the parts of the verdict not sustained by the evidence, and for judgment on the remainder and on the undisputed evidence. The appellate court, under such circumstances, can only award a new trial.[130]

—— **Mistake in Answer—Affidavit of Jurors—New Trial.** In Wolfgram v. Town of Schoepke,[131] an action for damages for personal injuries, a special verdict was returned, finding all material facts in favor of plaintiff except that to the question, "Was plaintiff guilty of any want of ordinary care which contributed to the injury he received?" the jury answered, "Yes."

Plaintiff produced affidavits of all twelve jurors to the effect that all the jurors agreed that plaintiff was not guilty of want of ordinary care, and that the insertion of the answer "Yes," instead of the word "No," was a mistake. The foreman, agreeing with these facts, stated that he intended to write the answer to the question so as to find that plaintiff was not guilty of any want of ordinary care which contributed to his injury.

Upon these affidavits the plaintiff moved that the answer "Yes" be stricken out, and the answer "No" inserted in lieu thereof. The motion was denied, from which denial plaintiff appealed. The plaintiff also moved on the minutes and affidavits for a new trial. Defendant moved to strike out the jurors' affidavits. The court granted plaintiff's motion to set aside the verdict and award a new trial, and denied defendant's motion to strike out the affidavits, "excepting that said affidavits be received and considered only as tending to show that there was a mistrial by reason of a mistake by the jury in writing the answer to question No. 16," but rejecting said affidavits in so

130 Conroy v. Railroad Co., 96 Wis. 243, 70 N. W. 486, 38 L. R. A. 419; Keller v. Schmidt, 104 Wis. 596, 80 N. W. 935. See, also, Schwelckhart v. Stuewe, 75 Wis. 157, 43 N. W. 722.

131 (Wis.) 100 N. W. 1054, 1056.

far as they "tend, generally, to impeach or contradict said special verdict." No costs were imposed on either party. From that order defendant appealed.

The following extract from the opinion is justified by the clarity of the reasoning therein contained as to what, in fact, constitutes the verdict:

"The general rule is very ancient, and often reiterated, that the statements of the jurors will not be received to establish their own misconduct or to impeach their verdict. Edmiston v. Garrison, 18 Wis. 595, 603. An excellent collection and analysis of decided cases will be found in Woodward v. Leavitt, 107 Mass. 453, 9 Am. Rep. 49. From this it appears that the early idea was that of secrecy in their deliberations, and, further, the impropriety of receiving jurors' statements as to their mental processes, whether to impeach or support their verdict. This rule, in its application, has been subjected to much of refinement and qualification by different courts, involving conflict of dicta and of actual decision which it would not be profitable to review in detail nor possible to harmonize. The necessity of some limitation to the general rule against receiving statements of the jurors is declared in McBean v. State, 83 Wis. 206, 209, 53 N. W. 497. In some cases the rule is limited to things which transpire in the jury room or in court, but it will be found in most of those cases also limited to matters involved in reaching the verdict. The limitation was recognized and applied in Hempton v. State, 111 Wis. 127, 145, 86 N. W. 596; Roman v. State, 41 Wis. 312; Schissler v. State (Wis.) 99 N. W. 593; Peppercorn v. City of Black River Falls, 89 Wis. 38, 41, 61 N. W. 79, 46 Am. St. Rep. 818; Mattox v. United States, 146 U. S. 140, 13 Sup. Ct. 50, 36 L. Ed. 917. In line with the same idea are a number of decisions drawing a distinction between the proceedings involved in reaching and agreeing upon the verdict and the mere act of expressing it, either orally or in writing. The following cases recognize such distinction, and hold that the reasons excluding jurors' testimony as to their conduct in the former stage do not exclude their evidence as to what really was the verdict agreed on in order to prove that it has not been correctly expressed, through mistake or otherwise: Egan v. Ebden, 1 Burrows, 383; Roberts v. Hughes, 7 Mees. & W. 399; Little v. Larrabee, 2 Greenl. (Me.) 37, 11 Am. Dec. 43; Weston v. Gilmore, 63 Me. 493; Peters v. Fogarty, 55 N. J. Law, 386, 26 Atl. 855; Jackson v. Dickenson, 15 Johns. (N. Y.) 309, 8 Am. Dec. 236; Dalrymple v. Williams, 63 N. Y. 361, 20 Am. Rep. 544; Hodgkins v. Mead, 119 N. Y. 166, 23 N. E. 559; Capen v. Inhabitants of Stoughton, 16 Gray (Mass.) 364; Pelzer Mfg. Co. v. Insurance Co. (C. C.) 71 Fed. 830. Several of these cases were cited with approval of this very distinction in McBean v. State, supra. Against this doctrine we find Polhemus v. Heiman, 50 Cal. 438; Murphy v. Murphy, 1 S. D. 316, 47 N. W. 142, 9 L. R. A. 820; and McKinley v. Bank, 118 Ind. 375, 21 N. E. 36. Of these, the first two seem to be controlled by local statutes, and are therefore not persuasive. The Indiana case, however, squarely denies the admissibility of jurors' testimony to prove that the written answer to a special question was the reverse of the agreement in fact reached. This view is based on the rule that jurors cannot 'impeach their own verdict.' But is it an attempt to impeach their own verdict? That depends on the sense in which that word is used. Is the written paper filed, or the agreement which the jury reach, the verdict? We think the latter is what is intended when we say the jurors cannot impeach it. The former, like most records, is but the expression or evidence of some mental conception. Hence it may well be said that a showing that such writing is not correct is not impeachment of the verdict itself. The repudiation of written expressions, when, by mistake, they fail to express the intention or mental concept, is familiar in the law. A writing is not a contract when it fails to express that on which the minds of the parties met, and courts freely exercise the power to correct mistakes when the proof leaves no doubt that the real contract was something else. That which decides the rights of parties litigant is the harmonious agreement of the jurors. Each party is entitled to such judgment as results from that agreement. Any other is presumptively unjust, and any rule that necessitates it is unreasonable, unless supported by considerations of public policy, or of such danger from opening the door to investigation that wrong is likely to be done oftener than right promoted. We are persuaded that the reasons which should exclude a juror from showing that he made a mistake in reaching his conclusion (see Murdock v. Sumner, 22 Pick. [Mass.] 156) do not extend to a showing that the words used in conveying it to the court, or enrolling it on the records, by mistake of the person uttering or writing them, fail to express the conclusion reached by all the jurymen. Of course, the showing of the latter fact must be clear beyond peradventure; at least, to warrant a change in the written verdict and final judgment thereon. If the slightest doubt lurks in the mind of the court, he should confine relief to the granting of a new trial, which, of course, he may always order when there is reasonable cause to believe that the judgment will do injustice. Some courts incline to the view that a new trial is the only relief after the jury have separated. Little v. Larrabee, supra; Weston v. Gilmore, 63 Me. 493. But the clear weight of authority is that, upon sufficiently clear showing of the mistake, and of what was the verdict agreed on and intended to be expressed, the court may substitute a true expression for the incorrect one, and enter judgment accordingly. See Egan v. Ebden, supra; Peters v. Fogarty, supra; Dalrymple v. Williams, supra; Hodgkins v. Mead, supra; Pelzer Mfg. Co. v. Insurance Co., supra.

"We conclude, therefore, that the trial court properly received and considered the affidavits of the jurors in this case; that they at least sufficed to satisfy the court of great danger of injustice being done by entry of judgment in accordance with the written verdict, and therefore justified him in exercising his discretion to relieve plaintiff from the predicament in which he stood by awarding him another trial. Whether such affidavits made so plain a case as to entitle plaintiff to correction of the verdict and judgment in his favor is a question not open to defendant on this appeal. Plaintiff might probably have raised it had he refrained from motion for a new trial, and appealed from a judgment in defendant's favor." [132]

**Signing Verdict.** The special verdict is required by statute to be in writing, and should therefore be signed by the foreman of the jury. But irregularity in the return for failure of the foreman to sign the answers is waived, where no objection is made at the time the verdict is returned.[133]

**Formal Conclusion.** In *North Carolina* it was until recently held that where the jury in a special verdict do not say that they find one way or the other, according as the opinion of the court may be upon the law, the verdict is imperfect.[134] It is now settled, however, that no formal conclusion is necessary,[135] and the general opinion is that its omission will not vitiate the verdict.[136] In finding the facts the jury finds by necessary implication for the party who should prevail on the facts,

132 Plaintiff's appeal dismissed, on the ground that the order denying his motion to correct the verdict was not appealable, as it did not determine the action, nor prevent a judgment from which plaintiff might have appealed (under Rev. St. Wis. 1898, § 3069). Upon defendant's appeal the order was reversed, and cause remanded, with directions to embody in the order granting a new trial the payment of reasonable terms by plaintiff as a condition.

133 Mounts v. Goranson, 29 Wash. 261, 69 Pac. 740. As to proper signature under California Code, see In re Keithley's Estate, 134 Cal. 9, 66 Pac. 5.

134 State v. Wallace, 25 N. C. 195; State v. Stewart, 91 N. C. 566; State v. Morris, 104 N. C. 837, 10 S. E. 454; State v. Moore, 107 N. C. 770, 12 S. E. 249. See, also, Mumford v. Wardwell, 6 Wall. (U. S.) 423, 18 L. Ed. 756.

135 State v. Ewing, 108 N. C. 755, 13 S. E. 10; State v. Spray, 113 N. C. 686, 18 S. E. 700.

136 Bower v. Bower, 146 Ind. 393, 45 N. E. 595, and cases cited; Helwig v. Beckner, 149 Ind. 131, 46 N. E. 644; Illinois Cent. R. Co. v. Cheek, 152 Ind. 663, 53 N. E. 641. See cases cited in succeeding notes

and he is entitled to judgment.[137] The verdict need not find for either plaintiff or defendant, so long as it determines all matters at issue between them.[138]

[137] Hendrickson v. Walker, 32 Mich. 68.

[138] Knight v. Fisher, 15 Colo. 176, 25 Pac. 78. The rule that the conclusion should be conditional is mentioned in Baxter v. Railroad Co., 104 Wis. 307, 315, 80 N. W. 644, on authority of Suydam v. Williamson, 20 How. 427, 15 L. Ed. 978, but the former case holds that such finding may be either "express or implied."

The formal conclusion, for plaintiff or defendant, is not absolutely necessary to the validity of a special verdict, and cannot be considered in determining whether the law, on the facts found, is with plaintiff or defendant. Helwig v. Beckner, 149 Ind. 131, 46 N. E. 644, citing Hendrickson v. Walker, 32 Mich. 68; Louisville, N. A. & C. Ry. Co. v. Lucas, 119 Ind. 583, 21 N. E. 968, 6 L. R. A. 193; Evansville & T. H. R. Co. v. Taft, 2 Ind. App. 237, 242, 28 N. E. 443.

# CHAPTER XIII.

## SPECIAL VERDICTS (Continued).

### General and Special Verdict—Instructions—Argument—Construction.

In *Indiana*, under a former statute, it was held that a general verdict was not contemplated where a special verdict passing upon all the issues was demanded,[1] and that to take both, and give any effect to the general verdict, tended to defeat the object of the special verdict statute.[2]

In the case last cited it was said: "The purpose of a special verdict is to avoid the mistakes that the jury may make in the application of the law to the facts; and hence a demand for a special verdict is a demand that there shall be no general verdict." "A special verdict was returned, and, being the verdict demanded, it was the verdict, and the only verdict, that could be considered in the rendition of the final judgment. The general verdict returned with it had no office to perform."

In *Kentucky* it was held that under Civ. Code Prac. § 317, subdiv. 5 (as it existed prior to the amendment of 1886), which provided that either party may require the court to direct the jury to find a special verdict, and that, if so required, the questions of law may be reserved by the court until after verdict,

[1] Bower v. Bower, 146 Ind. 393, 45 N. E. 595. See, also, Toler v. Keiher, 81 Ind. 383; Todd v. Fenton, 66 Ind. 25; McCormack v. Phillips, 4 Dak. 506, 34 N. W. 39.

[2] Louisville, N. A. & C. Ry. Co. v. Balch, 105 Ind. 93, 4 N. E. 288. Not error for jury to return both general and special verdicts, when not instructed as to form. Hershman v. Hershman, 63 Ind. 451. But see Webster v. Bebinger, 70 Ind. 9, which holds, in effect, that it would be error to give judgment on the general verdict where antagonistic. See, also, Louisville, N. A. & C. Ry. Co. v. Balch, supra, distinguishing these cases.

the court may also, in its discretion, direct a general verdict, but is not compelled to do so.[3]

In *Texas* the court cannot be required to submit the general issue when the case has been submitted on special issues. Such procedure is not warranted by statute [4] and is irregular.[5] Yet where the verdicts are consistent, and the same judgment would follow upon each, the irregularity of taking both general and special verdicts is of no consequence.[6] But where the finding upon special issues is contradicted by the general verdict no judgment can be rendered, and the verdict should be set aside.[7]

In *Wisconsin* it was formerly held that it was not error, though unnecessary, to take a general verdict not inconsistent with the special,[8] though in Kelley v. Chicago, M. & St. P. Ry. Co.[9] grave doubts as to the propriety of the practice were expressed. But it is now settled that it is error, in a case where objection is taken, to submit a general in connection with a special verdict, where the court gives full instructions on the gen-

[3] Witty v. Railroad Co., 83 Ky. 21.

[4] Dwyer v. Kalteyer, 68 Tex. 564, 5 S. W. 75; Southern Cotton-Oil Co. v. Wallace, 23 Tex. Civ. App. 12, 54 S. W. 638; Belknap v. Groover (Tex. Civ. App.) 56 S. W. 249.

[5] Heflin v. Burns, 70 Tex. 347, 8 S. W. 48; Blum v. Rogers, 71 Tex. 676, 9 S. W. 595.

[6] Id.

[7] Blum v. Rogers, supra.

[8] Hoppe v. Railway Co., 61 Wis. 357, 21 N. W. 227; Cooper v. Insurance Co., 96 Wis. 362, 71 N. W. 606. In the case last cited it is said: "In such case the general verdict is merely a correct conclusion of law from the special findings, and neither benefits nor harms either party."

Where there is a general as well as a special verdict, and they are inconsistent, the latter prevails; and, if the latter is defective, the former will not cure it. Davis v. Town of Farmington, 42 Wis. 425. See, also, Lemke v. Railway Co., 39 Wis. 449; Ryan v. Insurance Co., 46 Wis. 671, 1 N. W. 426; Kelley v. Railway Co., 53 Wis. 74, 9 N. W. 816.

[9] 53 Wis. 74, 77, 9 N. W. 816.

eral propositions of law involved, especially where exception is taken to such general instructions; [10] for this plainly informs the jury of the effect of their answers to the special questions, and how to make such answers consistent with the general verdict.[11]

Whether or not it is error to submit a general verdict with a special, where no objection is made and no general charge given, is not decided.

When neither party has requested a special verdict, and the jury unequivocally disagree on a general verdict, the court may afterwards submit questions calling for a special verdict alone.[12] The objection that a general charge, which might inform the jury of the effect of their answers, has been given, should have little force in such case. Inability to agree upon a general verdict would indicate absence of any general prejudice or particular leaning on the part of the jury, and simplifying the jury's duty would be calculated to secure a consistent verdict where otherwise a mistrial would result.

Conversely, if the jury cannot agree upon the special issues, and by consent they are withdrawn and a general verdict rendered, it is not error.[13] But the jury cannot withdraw a special verdict and render a general because the legal effect of the former was not what they expected.[14]

When the jury render a general verdict, accompanied by a

[10] See post, "Instructions."

[11] Ward v. Railway Co., 102 Wis. 215, 225, 78 N. W. 442. See, also, Crouse v. Railway Co., 102 Wis. 196, 78 N. W. 778; Schaidler v. Railway Co., 102 Wis. 564, 78 N. W. 732; Wills v. Railway Co., 108 Wis. 255, 84 N. W. 998.

[12] Williams v. Love, 1 Ind. T. 585, 43 S. W. 856.

[13] Mitchell v. Hockett, 25 Cal. 538, 85 Am. Dec. 151. "It is very remarkable, when we consider the questions submitted, that they could not agree upon the special issues, but did agree upon a general verdict." Id. After the jury has returned a special verdict, the court should not resubmit the cause for a general verdict, with instructions. Spalding v. Mayhall, 27 Mo. 377.

[14] Fitzpatrick v. Himmelmann, 48 Cal. 589.

special, they may be sent back under instructions to correct their verdict by striking out the general finding.[15]

### INSTRUCTIONS.

When a special verdict is required, the jury are to find the facts only. Beyond this they have no concern. They may draw no conclusions. If they do they are to be disregarded, and if the verdict amounts to nothing but conclusions no judgment can be rendered upon it. It is for the court alone to say what is the legal significance of the facts found, and it may neither trespass upon the jury's province nor permit invasion of its own.

This sharp distinction of functions was designed largely to prevent miscarriage of justice by reason of hasty, prejudiced, or ignorant application of legal principles by the jury in the case of a general verdict. That is the reason behind the statute, if not behind the common-law origin of special verdicts. An appreciative use of the statute will, therefore, recognize that the less the jury is permitted to see the effect of its answers on the rights of the parties the more fully and satisfactorily will it be likely to discharge its duty.

But general instructions on the law applicable to the case defeat the very object of the provisions relating to this form of verdict. They are calculated, and in most cases cannot fail, to apprise the jury of the effect of their answers. If the jurors be painstaking and conscientious, they will endeavor, doubtless, to shut their eyes to the necessary consequences of their findings, especially when cautioned by the court, and will try to make them solely on the evidence as it appeals to their intelligence. But at best, the glimpse of the judgment which will follow this answer or that will tend to incline the juror's mind so to answer as to assist the side which has his sympathy, and in respect to that sentiment one or the other party must al-

15 City of Ft. Wayne v. Duryee, 9 Ind. App. 620, 37 N. E. 299.

ways have the advantage. Moreover, granted a willful jury, and its members will directly frame the answers so as to support the judgment they wish to see rendered, without regard to the weight of the evidence, the issues under the pleadings, or the burden of proof.

It is accordingly settled that the court need not and should not give general instructions as to the law applicable to the case, nor even state the rules of law by which the facts are to be weighed.[16] A special verdict dispenses with instructions except as to rules of evidence and the frame of the verdict.

**Request for General Instructions should be Refused,**[17] though it is not necessarily reversible error to comply [18] where the instructions do not "indicate how the jury should find upon any given question of fact, or interfere with the proper consideration and determination of each question submitted, independently of all others." [19]

[16] Toler v. Keiher, 81 Ind. 383; Indianapolis, P. & C. Ry. Co. v. Bush, 101 Ind. 582; Johnson v. Culver, 116 Ind. 278, 19 N. E. 129; Bower v. Bower, 146 Ind. 393, 45 N. E. 595; Louisville, N. A. & C. Ry. Co. v. Lynch, 147 Ind. 165, 44 N. E. 997, 34 L. R. A. 293; Town of Kentland v. Hagan, 17 Ind. App. 1, 46 N. E. 43; Cole v. Crawford, 69 Tex. 124, 5 S. W. 646; Goesel v. Davis, 100 Wis. 678, 76 N. W. 768; Ward v. Cochran, 18 C. C. A. 1, 71 Fed. 127.

It is only where the case is submitted to the jury on a general charge for a general verdict, or when the special issue submitted involves a mixed question of law and fact, that it becomes necessary to advise them (the jury) of the law governing in any given state of facts. York v. Hilger (Tex. Civ. App.) 84 S. W. 1117.

The prayer, "cannot recover," is not applicable to the *North Carolina* system of submitting a case upon issues. Farrell v. Railroad Co., 102 N. C. 390, 9 S. E. 302, 3 L. R. A. 647, 11 Am. St. Rep. 760; Bottoms v. Railroad Co., 109 N. C. 72, 13 S. E. 738; Witsell v. Railroad Co., 120 N. C. 557, 27 S. E. 125; Vanderbilt v. Brown, 128 N. C. 498, 39 S. E. 36.

[17] Stayner v. Joyce, 120 Ind. 99, 22 N. E. 89; Southern Cotton Oil Co. v. Wallace, 23 Tex. Civ. App. 12, 54 S. W. 638.

[18] Louisville, N. A. & C. Ry. Co. v. Frawley, 110 Ind. 18, 9 N. E. 594.

[19] Reed v. City of Madison, 85 Wis. 667, 680, 56 N. W. 182.

The court should explain to the jury distinctly what facts are material to be found within the issues, and give them such instructions as will enable them to find and settle the facts, so that the law may be applied by the court to the facts found.[20] No instructions are proper except such as are necessary to inform the jury as to the issues made by the pleadings; the rules for weighing and reconciling testimony; who has the burden of proof; with whatever else may be necessary to enable the jury clearly to understand their duties concerning the special verdict.[21] And it is always both proper and necessary, where it is the duty of the jury to assess damages, to instruct them as to the law governing the measure of damages.[22]

Such instructions as are given should be limited to the issues covered by the questions, and be given in connection with the questions seriatim,[23] in order to aid the jury in giving proper

[20] Louisville, N. A. & C. Ry. Co. v. Flanagan, 113 Ind. 488, 14 N. E. 370, 3 Am. St. Rep. 674; Same v. Buck, 116 Ind. 566, 19 N. E. 453, 2 L. R. A. 520, 9 Am. St. Rep. 883.

[21] Udell v. Railroad Co., 152 Ind. 507, 52 N. E. 799, 71 Am. St. Rep. 336; Louisville, N. A. & C. Ry. Co. v. Frawley, 110 Ind. 18, 9 N. E. 594; Woollen v. Wire, 110 Ind. 251, 11 N. E. 236; Johnson v. Culver, 116 Ind. 278, 19 N. E. 129; Swaler v. Grubbs, 126 Ind. 106, 25 N. E. 877; Roller v. Kling, 150 Ind. 159, 49 N. E. 948. See, also, Lyle v. McCormick, 108 Wis. 81, 84 N. W. 18, 51 L. R. A. 906.

When the court instructs the jury on the subject of the burden of proof, it should instruct them as to which side the burden of proof lies as to each of the issues covered by the special questions. Siebrecht v. Hogan, 99 Wis. 437, 445, 75 N. W. 71.

[22] Western Union Telegraph Co. v. Newhouse, 6 Ind. App. 422, 33 N. E. 800.

[23] Burns v. Mill Co., 60 Wis. 541, 19 N. W. 380; Kohler v. Railroad Co., 99 Wis. 33, 74 N. W. 568; Goesel v. Davis, 100 Wis. 678, 76 N. W. 768; McDermott v. Jackson, 102 Wis. 419, 78 N. W. 598; Fox v. Martin, 104 Wis. 581, 80 N. W. 921; Rhyner v. City of Menasha, 107 Wis. 201, 83 N. W. 303; Warden v. Reser, 38 Kan. 86, 16 Pac. 60.

The court should confine the instructions to an explanation of the questions, one by one, so as to enable the jury to understand the same and intelligently make answer thereto. Lyon v. City of Grand Rap-

answers.[24] The statement of mere abstract principles of law should be wholly omitted;[25] to give such is error.[26]

But the giving of general instructions in connection with a special verdict will not be held error unless exceptions are preserved;[27] and the exceptions must directly raise the impropriety of giving general instructions without indicating their applicability, if any, to the questions of the special verdict. Ex-

ids, 121 Wis. 609, 99 N. W. 311; Schrunk v. Town of St. Joseph, 120 Wis. 223, 97 N. W. 946.

24 It is error to refuse to give instructions requested as to each question submitted that may be reasonably necessary to enable the jury to answer it intelligently and according to the law governing the subject. Baxter v. Railroad Co., 104 Wis. 307, 80 N. W. 644.

If requested, the court should give to the jury the rules and definitions applicable to the various issues and necessary for them to understand in order to render their verdict intelligently. The better practice is to furnish them with such instruction, whether requested or not. Southern Cotton Oil Co. v. Wallace, 23 Tex. Civ. App. 12, 54 S. W. 638.

Where the special verdict was plain and unambiguous, and called for the jury's conclusion on a certain question, but the jury were instructed to answer the question "Yes" or "No," according as they were convinced as to a wholly different subject, it was held that it could not be presumed either that all the jury ignored the question put, and answered a different one in accordance with the instruction of the court, or that all of them ignored the instruction of the court, and answered the question as written, and that therefore there was no acceptable finding by the jury. Hebbe v. Town of Maple Creek, 111 Wis. 480, 87 N. W. 459.

25 Mauch v. City of Hartford, 112 Wis. 40, 87 N. W. 816. See particularly Ward v. Railroad Co., 102 Wis. 215, 78 N. W. 442; Cullen v. Hanisch, 114 Wis. 24, 89 N. W. 900, which contain numerous citations on points of practice connected with special verdicts.

26 See Lyon v. City of Grand Rapids, 121 Wis. 609, 625, 99 N. W. 311, 317, and cases collected; Morrison v. Lee (N. D.) 102 N. W. 223. But not where the request for a special verdict is insufficient. See particularly Schmitt v. Railroad Co., 120 Wis. 397, 98 N. W. 202.

27 Brunette v. Town of Gagen, 106 Wis. 618, 82 N. W. 564; Sheppard v. Rosenkrans, 109 Wis. 58, 85 N. W. 199, 83 Am. St. Rep. 886.

ceptions taken to general instructions upon the ground that they are "contrary to law" are insufficient.[28]

—— **In Negligence Cases.** Though the giving of general instructions upon the law of the case is generally disapproved, it is not to be understood that the statutory right to a special verdict is only satisfied by questions that do not need to be considered in the light of legal principles given to the jury by the court. Often, whether certain conduct complained of is negligence, where the evidentiary facts are well established, is a question of fact, in respect to which different minds may reasonably come to different conclusions. "In that situation it is necessary to carefully instruct the jury regarding the standard of care necessary to the performance of the duty alleged to have been violated, leaving it to them to determine whether the alleged wrongdoer came up to the legal standard in the particular instance complained of. The questions of contributory negligence, of proximate cause, and what is reasonable, are only, ordinarily, determinable by viewing evidentiary facts in the light of legal principles. The ultimate fact being only properly determinable by viewing evidentiary facts in the light of legal standards, instructions by the court in regard to such standards are necessary." [29]

**Indicating Effect of Answers.** It is error to tell or indicate in the instructions the legal effect that an answer or answers will have,[30] and a general charge is well calculated to

[28] Gutzman v. Clancy, 114 Wis. 589, 90 N. W. 1081, 58 L. R. A. 744.

[29] Baxter v. Railroad Co., 104 Wis. 307, 314, 80 N. W. 644. See, also, Mauch v. City of Hartford, 112 Wis. 40, 87 N. W. 816, as to proper form of question on contributory negligence and instructions therewith.

[30] Kohler v. Railroad Co., 99 Wis. 33, 74 N. W. 568; Ward v. Railroad Co., 102 Wis. 215, 78 N. W. 442; New Home Sewing Mach. Co. v. Simon, 104 Wis. 120, 80 N. W. 71; Baxter v. Railroad Co., 104 Wis. 307, 80 N. W. 644; Mushach v. Chair Co., 108 Wis. 57, 84 N. W. 36; Sheppard v. Rosenkrans, 109 Wis. 58, 85 N. W. 199, 83 Am. St. Rep. 886; Byington v. City of Merrill, 112 Wis. 211, 88 N. W. 26; Gerrard

afford such information.[31] The jury has no right to be informed how any particular answer to a question would affect the case, or what judgment would follow in consequence of it; for to impart such information would almost necessarily defeat the object intended to be secured by a special verdict.[32]

But the rule evidently applies especially to the instructions given in connection with the questions or to the general charge. It is not error not to so frame questions as to disguise the effect of certain questions upon the final result.[33]

It has also been held that it is not error to instruct the jury that if they answer special questions in a certain way they need go no further, though the instruction indicates the effect their answers would have, especially where the trial judge cautioned the jury that they had nothing to do with the effect of their answers, but that their sworn duty was to answer the questions correctly and honestly from the evidence, leaving the result out of the case entirely, as that belonged to the court.[34]

In the case last cited the court said: "It would seem to be an unreasonable waste of time and labor to require the jury, after disposing of the case by an affirmative answer (to a certain crucial question), to spend hours, perhaps days, in endeavoring

v. Railway Co., 113 Wis. 258, 89 N. W. 125, 57 L. R. A. 465; Patnode v. Westenhaver, 114 Wis. 460, 90 N. W. 467. See, also, Schrunk v. Town of St. Joseph, 120 Wis. 223, 97 N. W. 946; Bauer v. Richter, 103 Wis. 412, 79 N. W. 404.

31 Byington v. City of Merrill, 112 Wis. 211, 88 N. W. 26.

32 Coats v. Town of Stanton, 90 Wis. 130, 62 N. W. 619.

33 Baumann v. Coal Co., 118 Wis. 330, 95 N. W. 139. See, also, Louisville & N. R. Co. v. Mitchell, 87 Ky. 327, 8 S. W. 706. But see Morrison v. Lee (N. D.) 102 N. W. 223.

34 Chopin v. Paper Co., 83 Wis. 192, 199, 52 N. W. 452. Nor is it error, where several questions are submitted, each seeking to determine by an affirmative or negative answer the existence or nonexistence of a particular fact, to instruct the jury that if they answer any one of the questions in the affirmative they must necessarily answer the others in the negative. Fox v. Association, 96 Wis. 390, 71 N. W. 363.

to arrive at an agreement on a question which had thus become perfectly immaterial."

**Designating Party Requesting Instruction.** It is not ordinarily reversible error to characterize instructions as requested by one party or the other or to fail to so characterize them. It is not, however, advisable practice to state at whose instance the instructions are given. The province of the court is to inform the jury only of their duty in answering the specific questions, with such definition of the terms used in those questions as may be necessary to that end. It is of no importance to the jury whether such information is given in words selected by either counsel or by the court. The instruction, when given, is that of the court, and the better practice is to make no distinction between that portion which originates with the judge and that which originates with either counsel.[35]

**Directing Answers, Etc.** The court may include questions covering undisputed matters and direct proper answers. "It has not yet been held error for a trial court to include in a special verdict undisputed matters, and direct answers to be made, or not to frame the verdict so as to disguise the effect of particular questions upon the final result. Doubtless the court may so frame a special verdict as to cover all the facts vital to the cause of action and defense, if it sees fit, whether controverted on the evidence or not. If the result is to inform the jury how particular questions must be answered to enable plaintiff to recover, that is the result of the law, not the abuse of it." [36]

Nor is it error to admonish the jury to make their answers consistent with one another. "It certainly cannot be error to

[35] Gutzman v. Clancy, 114 Wis. 589, 598, 90 N. W. 1081, 58 L. R. A. 744. See, also, Stevenson v. Railway Co., 94 Iowa, 719, 61 N. W. 964. For a case in which a question was given as "propounded by counsel for the defendant," with instructions prejudicial to defendant, see Conway v. Mitchell, 97 Wis. 290, 72 N. W. 752.

[36] Baumann v. Coal Co., 118 Wis. 330, 335, 95 N. W. 139.

direct a jury to do a certain thing, when the judgment based upon their verdict would be reversed were they to disobey the direction." [37]

## ARGUMENT.

The real legislative purpose of the special verdict statute is to secure a decision by the jury of "each material issue made by the pleadings and controverted on the evidence, separate from any other issue, and entirely uninfluenced by any thought as to the final result to be reached by an application of the law to the facts requiring a general finding, or any general consideration by the jury at all of the case as a whole, including the law and the facts, and entirely uninfluenced, so far as practicable, by any knowledge of the law in respect to the result of their findings." [38] But will enforcement of the inferential prohibition of the law against the court indicating the effect of the answers by instructions assure unbiased action on the part of the jury, if counsel are permitted in argument to treat the case in its legal aspects? In *Wisconsin,* the draft of the special verdict is often prepared in advance of argument and submitted to the inspection of counsel, who discuss the questions seriatim, and advise the jury as to their replies. There is no reason to think that the effect of their answers will be brought to the jury's attention less forcibly by counsel than by the court. Indeed, the average argument is addressed to the very point of impressing upon the jury just what effect this or that answer will have. It seems absurd that counsel may impart objectionable information which the court may not.[39]

[37] Hoppe v. Railway Co., 61 Wis. 357, 368, 21 N. W. 227.

[38] Byington v. City of Merrill, 112 Wis. 211, 228, 88 N. W. 26.

[39] Objection to such conduct being sustained by the trial court, there is no prejudicial error. Lyon v. City of Grand Rapids, 121 Wis. 609, 99 N. W. 311. See, ante, chapter 6, "Discussion of Interrogatories in Argument."

### Construction.

In determining whether the findings of a special verdict will support a judgment, and what judgment should be rendered, certain rules of construction are followed which result either from the nature of the procedure or are dictated by the modern policy of courts to construe with liberality and to regard substance rather than form.[40]

**Surplusage.** It has been seen that mere evidentiary matters and conclusions of law, improperly included in the verdict, are to be disregarded,[41] as also findings outside the issues.[42]

[40] Reqnisites of special verdict discussed. Housworth v. Bloomhuff, 54 Ind. 487; State v. Belk, 76 N. C. 10; Ross v. U. S., 12 Ct. Cl. 565. Rules of construction, see Shenners v. Railway Co., 78 Wis. 382, 47 N. W. 622.

[41] See chapter 12; Kealing v. Vansickle, 74 Ind. 529, 39 Am. Rep. 101; Conner v. Railway Co., 105 Ind. 62, 4 N. E. 441, 55 Am. Rep. 177; Louisville, N. A. & C. Ry. Co. v. Frawley, 110 Ind. 18, 9 N. E. 594; Indiana, B. & W. Ry. Co. v. Finnell, 116 Ind. 414, 19 N. E. 204; Reeves v. Grottendick, 131 Ind. 107, 30 N. E. 889; Parks v. Satterthwaite, 132 Ind. 411, 32 N. E. 82; Branson v. Studabaker, 133 Ind. 147, 33 N. E. 98, and cases cited; Louisville, N. A. & C. Ry. Co. v. Berkey, 136 Ind. 181, 35 N. E. 3; Jones v. Casler, 139 Ind. 382, 38 N. E. 812. 47 Am. St. Rep. 274; Louisville, N. A. & C. Ry. Co. v. Bates, 146 Ind. 564, 45 N. E. 108; Buscher v. City of Lafayette, 8 Ind. App. 590, 36 N. E. 371; Nelson v. Railway Co., 60 Wis. 320, 19 N. W. 52; Rahr v. Assurance Co., 93 Wis. 355, 67 N. W. 725; Krause v. Busacker, 105 Wis. 350, 81 N. W. 406; United States v. Collier, 3 Blatchf. 325, Fed. Cas. No. 14,833; Butler v. Hopper, 1 Wash. C. C. 499, Fed. Cas. No. 2,241; Peterson v. U. S., 2 Wash. C. C. 36, Fed. Cas. No. 11,036.

An improper interrogatory and answer in a special verdict are immaterial where the special verdict is sufficient regardless of them. Pittsburgh, C., C. & St. L. R. Co. v. Beck, 152 Ind. 421, 53 N. E. 439.

The jury have no right to find specially what a person might or would have done in a certain event, and such finding, though not objected to, is not conclusive of the matter found. Smith v. Telegraph Co., 83 Ky. 104, 4 Am. St. Rep. 126.

[42] Richmond v. Tallmadge, 16 Johns. (N. Y.) 307.

If the findings upon material matters are sufficient to warrant the rendition of judgment for either party, it is enough. As the rule is stated in one case, if, after eliminating conclusions of law, evidentiary matters, etc., there are substantive facts sufficient to authorize a judgment, appeal will be fruitless.[43]

**Findings Liberally Construed.** The special verdict is to be reasonably and fairly construed,[44] in the light of the issues under the pleadings.[45] It is to be treated as an entirety,[46] and not

[43] Puterbaugh v. Puterbaugh, 131 Ind. 288, 30 N. E. 519, 15 L. R. A. 341. See, also, Hammann v. Mink, 99 Ind. 279; Bartholomew v. Pierson, 112 Ind. 430, 14 N. E. 249; Terre Haute & I. R. Co. v. Brunker, 128 Ind. 542, 26 N. E. 178.

[44] Daniels v. McGinnis, 97 Ind. 549; Woodward v. Davis, 127 Ind. 172, 26 N. E. 687; Branson v. Studabaker, 133 Ind. 147, 33 N. E. 98; Becknell v. Hosier, 10 Ind. App. 5, 37 N. E. 580; City of Elwood v. Carpenter, 12 Ind. App. 459, 40 N. E. 548; Wipperman v. Hardy, 17 Ind. App. 142, 46 N. E. 537; Jonas v. Hirshburg, 18 Ind. App. 581. 48 N. E. 656; State v. Stanton's Liquors, 38 Conn. 237; Miller v. Shackleford, 4 Dana (Ky.) 271; Plummer v. Currier, 52 N. H. 287; Ruscher v. Stanley, 120 Wis. 380, 98 N. W. 223; Plano Mfg. Co. v. Bergmann, 102 Wis. 21, 78 N. W. 157. See, also, Graham v. Battery Co., 186 Mass. 226, 71 N. E. 532.

[45] Eisemann v. Swan, 6 Bosw. (N. Y.) 668; Barto v. Himrod, 8 N. Y. 483, 59 Am. Dec. 506; Mack v. Bensley, 74 Wis. 112, 42 N. W. 215. The question is whether the facts found establish the defense pleaded, not whether they establish a defense. McCarty v. Hudsons, 24 Wend. (N. Y.) 291; Richmond v. Tallmadge, 16 Johns. (N. Y.) 307.

Answers of a special verdict will not be held uncertain if they are sufficiently certain when construed with reference to the issues in the action and the parties properly before the court. Bartlett v. Clough, 94 Wis. 196, 68 N. W. 875. To discover the real points at issue, resort must be had to the pleadings. Rudiger v. Railroad Co., 101 Wis. 292, 77 N. W. 169.

[46] Dixon v. Duke, 85 Ind. 434; Steves v. Fraze, 19 Ind. App. 284, 49 N. E. 385; Voris v. Association, 20 Ind. App. 630, 50 N. E. 779; Seekel v. Norman, 78 Iowa, 254, 43 N. W. 190; Brinson-Judd Grain Co. v. Becker, 76 Mo. App. 375; Burns v. Mill Co., 60 Wis. 541, 19 N. W. 380; Raymond v. Keseberg, 84 Wis. 302, 54 N. W. 612, 19 L. R. A. 643; Innes v. City of Milwaukee, 96 Wis. 170, 70 N. W. 1064.

as though its findings "were dug up from the ruins of ancient cities at different epochs." [47]

The verdict will support judgment if it passes on all the issues, however inartificially it may be worded [48] or illogically put together. The only essential is that all the facts necessary to support a judgment appear or necessarily result from those found.[49]

It is sufficient though the amount of the recovery is shown only in the formal conclusion,[50] or though there is no formal assessment of damages, where the findings plainly show the amount intended.[51] If from the finding the court can determine the amount of the recovery by simple computation, the verdict should stand.[52] It is sufficient if it can be ascertained from undisputed facts for what amount judgment should be rendered.[53]

[47] Alhambra Addition Water Co. v. Richardson, 72 Cal. 598, 14 Pac. 379. There is no requirement that facts in a special verdict shall be stated in logical or consecutive order. The findings should be construed as an entirety, and not in fragmentary parts. Louisville, N. A. & C. Ry. Co. v. Lynch, 147 Ind. 165, 44 N. E. 997, 46 N. E. 471, 34 L. R. A. 293.

[48] Fenn v. Blanchard, 2 Yeates (Pa.) 543; Evansville & T. H. R. Co. v. Taft, 2 Ind. App. 237, 28 N. E. 443.

[49] See Miller v. Shackleford, 4 Dana (Ky.) 274; Worford v. Isbel, 1 Bibb (Ky.) 251, 4 Am. Dec. 633; Picket v. Richet, 2 Bibb (Ky.) 178; Leftwich v. Day, 32 Minn. 512, 21 N. W. 731; Brinson-Judd Grain Co. v. Becker, 76 Mo. App. 375; O'Brien v. Hilburn, 22 Tex. 616.

"Falsa orthographia sive falsa grammatica non vitiat concessionem." Neither will bad grammar vitiate a special verdict when its meaning is apparent. Reynolds v. Lighting Co. (R. I.) 59 Atl. 393.

[50] Cole v. Powell, 17 Ind. App. 438, 46 N. E. 1006; Carthage Turnpike Co. v. Overman, 19 Ind. App. 309, 48 N. E. 874.

[51] Imperial Fire Ins. Co. v. Kiernan, 83 Ky. 468. Otherwise a venire de novo must be awarded. Whitesides v. Russell, 8 Watts & S. (Pa.) 44.

[52] Roberts v. Roberts, 122 N. C. 782, 30 S. E. 347; Hoppes v. Chapin, 15 Ind. App. 258, 43 N. E. 1014. See, also, Wainwright v. Burroughs, 1 Ind. App. 393, 27 N. E. 591.

[53] Sheehy v. Duffy, 89 Wis. 6, 61 N. W. 295. Contra, Galveston, Etc.,

**No Aider by Intendment.** A special verdict must find all the essential facts in the case; it cannot be aided by intendment or extrinsic facts appearing upon the record.[54] It does not

H. & S. A. Ry. Co. v. Botts, 22 Tex. Civ. App. 609, 55 S. W. 514, where it is held that a special verdict finding that a consignment of live stock was damaged $2 per head, without finding the number of cattle or the aggregate damage, is insufficient to base judgment upon, although the number of cattle shipped is not controverted.

The court cannot take into consideration undisputed facts. Wallingford v. Dunlap, 14 Pa. 31.

[54] *Alabama.* Lee v. Campbell's Heirs, 4 Port. 198; Sewall v. Glidden, 1 Ala. 52.

*Indiana.* Gordon v. Stockdale, 89 Ind. 240; Pittsburgh, C. & St. L. R. Co. v. Spencer, 98 Ind. 186; Louisville, N. A. & C. Ry. Co. v. Costello, 9 Ind. App. 462, 36 N. E. 299; Becknell v. Hosier, 10 Ind. App. 5, 37 N. E. 580.

*Kentucky.* Hann v. Field, Litt. Sel. Cas. (Ky.) 376; Carson v. Osborn, 10 B. Mon. 155.

*Louisiana.* State v. Ritchie, 3 La. Ann. 511.

*Michigan.* People v. Wells, 8 Mich. 104.

*Nevada.* Knickerbocker & N. Silver Min. Co. v. Hall, 3 Nev. 194.

*New York.* Jenks v. Hallet, 1 Caines, 60; Richmond v. Tallmadge, 16 Johns. 307; La Frombois v. Jackson, 8 Cow. 600, 18 Am. Dec. 463; People v. Thompson, 21 Wend. 235; McCarty v. Hudsons, 24 Wend. (N. Y.) 291; Fuller v. Van Geesen, 4 Hill, 171; Birckhead v. Brown, 5 Hill, 645; Miller v. People, 25 Hun, 473.

*Ohio.* Blake's Lessee v. Davis, 20 Ohio, 231.

*Pennsylvania.* Fenn v. Blanchard, 2 Yeates, 543; Wallingford v. Dunlap, 14 Pa. 31; Loew v. Stocker, 61 Pa. 347.

*South Carolina.* Lawrence v. Beauhien, 2 Bailey (S. C.) 623, 23 Am. Dec. 155.

*Tennessee.* Jones v. State, 2 Swan, 399.

*Texas.* Kuhlman v. Medlinka, 29 Tex. 385; Smith v. Warren, 60 Tex. 462; Heflin v. Burns, 70 Tex. 347, 8 S. W. 48; Stephenson v. Chappell, 12 Tex. Civ. App. 296, 36 S. W. 482; Thomas v. Salmons (Tex. Civ. App.) 39 S. W. 1094.

*Virginia.* Tunnell v. Watson, 2 Munf. 283; McMichen v. Amos, 4 Rand. 137.

*Wisconsin.* Everit v. Bank, 13 Wis. 419; Cotzhausen v. Simon, 47 Wis. 103, 1 N. W. 473; Murphey v. Weil, 89 Wis. 146, 61 N. W. 315.

*United States.* Prentice v. Zane's Adm'r, 8 How. 470, 12 L. Ed. 1160; Collins v. Riley, 104 U. S. 327, 26 L. Ed. 752; Distilling & Cattle Feed-

stand on the same footing with the findings of a court or referee. The court or referee renders the judgment, and may be presumed to have found facts not expressly stated. But where the verdict is special, the jury cannot be presumed to have found more than is specified in their verdict.[55] In fact, whatever is not found therein is presumed not to exist.[56] The verdict is to be construed, however, in connection with the pleadings, and need not contain any facts admitted by them.[57]

The rule that no fact not stated can be inferred from the facts found [58] has been relaxed in *Wisconsin,* at least, where it

ing Co. v. Gottschalk Co., 24 U. S. App. 638, 13 C. C. A. 618, 66 Fed. 609; U. S. v. Arnold, 34 U. S. App. 177, 16 C. C. A. 575, 69 Fed. 987; Daube v. Iron Co., 46 U. S. App. 591, 23 C. C. A. 420, 77 Fed. 713.

*England.* Bird v. Appleton, 1 East (K. B.) 111; Hubbard v. Johnstone, 3 Taunt. (C. P.) 209.

Where the existence of a deed is material to the case of the party sustaining the burden of proof, and the jury have not found its existence, the court will not help out the verdict by the presumption of a deed. Bolling v. Mayor, etc., 3 Rand. (Va.) 563. And a deed referred to, but not set out in the verdict, cannot be considered in aid of the verdict, though found in the record. McArthur v. Porter's Lessee, 1 Pet. (U. S.) 626, 7 L. Ed. 290.

[55] People v. Bridge Co., 47 N. Y. 586. See, also, Sun Mut. Ins. Co. v. Insurance Co., 107 U. S. 485, 1 Sup. Ct. 582, 27 L. Ed. 337. But the general rule is that findings by the court are in the nature of a special verdict, and are to be similarly construed. See Sisson v. Barrett, 2 N. Y. 406; Burk v. Webb, 32 Mich. 173; Knox v. Trafalet, 94 Ind. 348; Raimond v. Parish of Terrebonne, 132 U. S. 192, 10 Sup. Ct. 57, 33 L. Ed. 309, and cases cited; Elliott, App. Proc. § 757; 2 Thomp. Trials, § 2658.

[56] Vausyckel v. Stewart, 77 Pa. 124; Pittsburgh, Ft. W. & C. R. Co. v. Evans, 53 Pa. 250; Thayer v. Society, 20 Pa. 60; Lee v. Campbell's Heirs, 4 Port. (Ala.) 198; Lawrence v. Beaubien, 2 Bailey (S. C.) 623, 23 Am. Dec. 155; Collins v. Riley, 104 U. S. 322, 26 L. Ed. 752.

[57] Barto v. Himrod, 8 N. Y. 483, 59 Am. Dec. 506; Blakeley v. Association (Tex. Civ. App.) 26 S. W. 292.

[58] Tien v. Railway Co., 15 Ind. App. 304, 44 N. E. 45; Allen v. Folger, 6 Rich. Law (S. C.) 54; Turner v. Smith, 18 Grat. (Va.) 831; Hall v. Ratliff, 93 Va. 327, 24 S. E. 1011; Bank of Alexandria v. Swann, 4 Cranch, C. C. 136, Fed. Cas. No. 853; Collins v. Riley, 104 U. S. 327,

is held that an omitted fact may be inferred from the facts found, if the deduction is "fair," [59] and it certainly can be so supplied when deducible as matter of law from other findings returned.[60]

**No Reference to Evidence.** The general rule is that a special verdict cannot be aided by reference to the evidence.[61] It must find all the facts controverted by the pleadings, and not admitted by the parties, necessary to support the judgment, and the court cannot look to the evidence for facts on which to base the judgment,[62] which cannot be supported in part by the verdict and in part by the court's conclusions of fact, even though the latter are based upon the undisputed evidence.[63]

26 L. Ed. 752; Tancred v. Christy, 12 M. & W. 316; 2 Hawk. P. C. 622. But see, United States v. Collier, 3 Blatchf. 325, Fed. Cas. No. 14,833. Where negligence is a question of fact, the court may not infer it even though the facts found warrant the inference, unless no other reasonable inference can be drawn. Cincinnati, I. & St. L. & C. R. Co. v. Grames, 136 Ind. 39, 34 N. E. 714.

59 Jones v. Foster, 67 Wis. 296, 30 N. W. 697; Abbot v. Gore, 74 Wis. 509, 43 N. W. 365; Lyman v. City of Green Bay, 91 Wis. 488, 65 N. W. 167; Martin v. Martin's Estate, 108 Wis. 284, 84 N. W. 439, 81 Am. St. Rep. 895. See, also, State v. Fuller, 1 Bay (S. C.) 245, 1 Am. Dec. 610.

60 John v. Bates, Litt. Sel. Cas. (Ky.) 106; Teegarden v. Lewis, 145 Ind. 98, 40 N. E. 1047, 44 N. E. 9; Id. (Ind. Sup.) 35 N. E. 24. See, also, Ruscher v. Stanley, 120 Wis. 380, 98 N. W. 223; Eldred v. Oconto Co., 33 Wis. 133; Hutchinson v. Railway Co., 41 Wis. 541.

61 Boyer v. Robertson, 144 Ind. 604, 43 N. E. 879; Jenks v. Hallet, 1 Caines (N. Y.) 60; Eisemann v. Swan, 6 Bosw. (N. Y.) 668; Behring v. Somerville, 63 N. J. Law, 568, 44 Atl. 641, 49 L. R. A. 578; Wallingford v. Dunlap, 14 Pa. 33; Commonwealth v. Grimes, 116 Pa. 450. 9 Atl. 665; Claiborne v. Tanner's Heirs, 18 Tex. 68; Maxwell v. Bank (Tex. Civ. App.) 23 S. W. 342; Barnes v. Williams, 11 Wheat. 415. 6 L. Ed. 508; Prentice v. Zane's Adm'r, 8 How. 470, 12 L. Ed. 1160; Monticello Bank v. Bostwick, 40 U. S. App. 721, 23 C. C. A. 73, 77 Fed. 123; United States v. Harris, 46 U. S. App. 653, 77 Fed. 821, 23 C. C. A. 483.

62 Texas & P. Ry. Co. v. Watson & Richardson, 13 Tex. Civ. App. 555. 36 S. W. 290; Maxwell v. Bank (Tex. Civ. App.) 23 S. W. 342.

63 Texas Brewing Co. v. Meyer (Tex. Civ. App.) 38 S. W. 263.

In *Wisconsin,* however, it is held that in rendering judgment the court may take account of matters omitted from the verdict, but established by the undisputed evidence. In Murphey v. Weil [64] the court says: "A special verdict must find all the facts essential to a recovery, and nothing can be supplied by way of intendment. This is the rule. * * * The rule is satisfied if all the facts essential to a recovery, which are controverted by evidence upon the trial, are specially found in the verdict. So the formal verdict may be sufficient, although it does not find specially facts which, although put in issue by the pleadings, are yet not controverted on the trial, or are established by the undisputed evidence.[65] No doubt the trial court, in passing on the sufficiency of the special verdict, must treat material facts so established by the undisputed evidence in the same manner and to the same effect as if they were formally incorporated into the verdict. Or may formally incorporate them into the verdict by amendment. 2 Thomp. Trials, § 2656. The difference is of form merely. In either case, facts so established by the undisputed evidence go to support or defeat the verdict or the judgment founded on it, whether they are formally incorporated into the verdict or not. * * * For every purpose of review they are equivalent to a special finding of the fact so undisputed in the case."

**Burden of Proof.** A special verdict will be construed most strongly against the party upon whom rests the burden of proof, applying the same rule as in the construction of a pleading.[66] Silence in respect to an essential fact not specially

[64] 89 Wis. 146, 150, 151, 61 N. W. 315.

[65] Citing Stringham v. Cook, 75 Wis. 589, 594, 44 N. W. 777; Montreal River Lumber Co. v. Mihills, 80 Wis. 540, 551, 50 N. W. 507; Hart v. Railroad Co., 86 Wis. 483, 489, 57 N. W. 91. See chapter 12, "Uncontroverted Facts." Contra, Claiborne v. Tanner, 18 Tex. 68; Moore v. Moore, 67 Tex. 293, 3 S. W. 285; Stephenson v. Chappell, 12 Tex. Civ. App. 296, 36 S. W. 482; Galveston, H. & S. A. Ry. Co. v. Botts, 22 Tex. Civ. App. 609, 55 S. W. 514.

[66] Louisville, N. A. & C. Ry. Co. v. Costello, 9 Ind. App. 462, 36 N. E. 299; Citizens' St. R. Co. v. Reed, 151 Ind. 396, 51 N. E. 477.

found or necessarily included in the verdict is equivalent to an express finding against such party.[67]

[67] Louisville, N. A. & C. Ry. Co. v. Costello, supra; Bell v. Corbin, 136 Ind. 269, 36 N. E. 23; Belshaw v. Chitwood, 141 Ind. 377, 40 N. E. 908; City of New Albany v. Endres, 143 Ind. 192, 42 N. E. 683; Relender v. State, 149 Ind. 283, 49 N. E. 30; Louisville, N. A. & C. Ry. Co. v. Quinn, 14 Ind. App. 554, 43 N. E. 240; Austin v. McMains, 14 Ind. App. 514, 43 N. E. 141; Daube v. Iron Co., 23 C. C. A. 420, 77 Fed. 713; United States v. Harris, 23 C. C. A. 483, 77 Fed. 821. See chapter 12, "Omitted Findings,"—"Indiana Rule."

# CHAPTER XIV.

## SPECIAL VERDICTS (Continued).

### New Trial—Venire De Novo—Appeal.

**New Trial.** A new trial may be granted, among other reasons, for refusal to submit a special verdict when properly requested under a mandatory statute;[1] and for submission against objection after the time limited by statute;[2] because of the withdrawal of interrogatories over objection;[3] for abuse of the court's discretion in submitting a large number of unnecessary and confusing questions,[4] or for refusal to submit questions proposed by counsel covering material disputed points;[5] because the questions are so framed as to suggest the answers desired,[6] are double and produce ambiguous answers,[7] or are otherwise objectionable.[8]

It may be ordered because the instructions are so framed as to tell or indicate the legal effect that an answer or answers will have,[9] or because abstract principles of law are laid down for the jury's guidance,[10] there being no general verdict; because

1 Pearson v. Kelly (Wis.) 100 N. W. 1064; Case v. Ellis, 4 Ind. App. 224, 30 N. E. 907. Ante, chapter 11.

2 Siebrecht v. Hogan, 99 Wis. 437, 75 N. W. 71.

3 Duesterberg v. State, 116 Ind. 144, 17 N. E. 624.

4 Patnode v. Westenhaver, 114 Wis. 460, 90 N. W. 467; Oaks v. West (Tex. Civ. App.) 64 S. W. 1033.

5 Kreuziger v. Railway Co., 73 Wis. 158, 40 N. W. 659. See, also, Town of Kentland v. Hagan, 17 Ind. App. 1, 46 N. E. 43.

6 Oaks v. West, supra.

7 Peake v. City of Superior, 106 Wis. 403, 82 N. W. 306.

8 Brown v. Lumber Co., 117 N. C. 287, 23 S. E. 253. Ante, chapter 11.

9 Sheppard v. Rosenkrans, 109 Wis. 58, 85 N. W. 199, 83 Am. St. Rep. 886. Ante, chapter 13.

10 Ante, chapter 13.

of erroneous amendment of the verdict by the court;[11] for the reason that the verdict fails to find all the material facts,[12] or is indefinite, evasive, or irresponsive.[13] It is also ground for a new trial that the verdict amounts merely to a conclusion of law,[14] or returns the evidence instead of the ultimate facts.[15]

[11] Conover v. Knight, 91 Wis. 569, 65 N. W. 371. But see Ellis v. Railroad Co., 120 Wis. 645, 98 N. W. 942.

[12] City of La Fayette v. Allen, 81 Ind. 166; Vinton v. Baldwin, 95 Ind. 433; Brazil Block Coal Co. v. Hoodlet, 129 Ind. 327, 27 N. E. 741; Pittsburgh, C., C. & St. L. R. Co. v. Montgomery, 152 Ind. 1, 49 N. E. 582, 71 Am. St. Rep. 301; Meighen v. Strong, 6 Minn. 177 (Gil. 111), 80 Am. Dec. 441; Hill v. Covell, 1 N. Y. 522; People v. Bridge Co., 47 N. Y. 586; State v. Oakley, 103 N. C. 408, 9 S. E. 575; State v. Crump, 104 N. C. 763, 10 S. E. 468; Moore v. Moore, 67 Tex. 294, 3 S. W. 284; Newbolt v. Lancaster, 83 Tex. 272, 18 S. W. 740; Bell v. Shafer, 58 Wis. 223, 16 N. W. 628; Conroe v. Case, 74 Wis. 85, 41 N. W. 1064; Kutchera v. Goodwillie, 93 Wis. 448, 67 N. W. 729; Rysdorp v. Lumber Co., 95 Wis. 622, 70 N. W. 677. Ante, chapter 12.

In *Indiana* while special verdicts were in use it was the rule that failure to find all the material facts would not prevent judgment being entered on the verdict (for the omission was held equivalent to a finding against the party having the burden of the issues) unless the failure to find was contrary to the evidence, in which case a new trial was proper. See Louisville, N. A. & C. Ry. Co. v. Buck, 116 Ind. 566, 19 N. E. 453, 2 L. R. A. 520, 9 Am. St. Rep. 883; Ex parte Walls, 73 Ind. 95.

Under the common law a venire facias de novo was the proper remedy where the verdict returned was too uncertain to sustain a judgment, as, e. g., where it failed to find all material facts. See, post, "Venire de Novo."

[13] Hopkins v. Stanley, 43 Ind. 553; Louisville, N. A. & C. Ry. Co. v. Roberts, 18 Ind. App. 538, 47 N. E. 839; Woodson v. McCune, 17 Cal. 304; Jones v. Brinkley, 122 N. C. 62, 29 S. E. 221; Tew v. Young, 134 N. C. 493, 47 S. E. 23; McGowan v. Railway Co., 91 Wis. 147, 64 N. W. 891.

[14] Keller v. Boatman, 49 Ind. 104. Ante, chapter 12.

[15] Hambleton v. Dempsey, 20 Ohio, 168; Clark v. Halberstadt, 1 Miles (Pa.) 26; Porter v. Coleman, 1 Pittsb. R. (Pa.) 252; Oaks v. West (Tex. Civ. App.) 64 S. W. 1033; First Nat. Bank v. Peck, 8 Kan. 660. Ante, chapter 12.

Where findings are inconsistent they will not support a judgment, and a new trial should be ordered.[16]

The ground most commonly presented for setting aside the verdict and granting a new trial is that findings are not sustained by the evidence.[17] But the verdict will not be disturbed unless the objectionable finding is material[18] and flagrantly against the evidence.[19]

The foregoing grounds are intended to serve merely as suggestions, and by no means comprehend all the reasons which may be adduced in support of the motion. But as the circumstances under which a new trial should be granted have been so often referred to in connection with the subjects of the request for, form, and requisites of interrogatories and verdict,

[16] First Nat. Bank of Charlotte v. Alexander, 84 N. C. 30, 39 Am. Rep. 702; Hilliard v. Outlaw, 92 N. C. 266; Porter v. Railroad Co., 97 N. C. 66, 2 S. E. 581, 2 Am. St. Rep. 272; Johnson v. Townsend, 122 N. C. 442, 29 S. E. 419; Cushman v. Masterson, 3 Tex. Ct. Rep. 143, 64 S. W. 1031; Karger v. Rich, 81 Wis. 177, 51 N. W. 424; Darcey v. Lumber Co., 87 Wis. 245, 58 N. W. 382. Ante, chapter 12.

[17] Louisville, N. A. & C. Ry. Co. v. Hart, 119 Ind. 273, 21 N. E. 753, 4 L. R. A. 549; Tarkington v. Purvis, 128 Ind. 182, 25 N. E. 879, 9 L. R. A. 607; Casey's Adm'r v. Railroad Co., 84 Ky. 79; Louisville & N. R. R. Co. v. Brice, 84 Ky. 298, 1 S. W. 483; Cronk v. Railway Co., 3 S. D. 93, 52 N. W. 420; Schweickhart v. Stuewe, 75 Wis. 157, 43 N. W. 722; Ohlweiler v. Lohmann, 82 Wis. 198, 52 N. W. 172; Id., 88 Wis. 75, 59 N. W. 678; Sheehy v. Duffy, 89 Wis. 6, 61 N. W. 295; Menominee River Sash & Door Co. v. Railroad Co., 91 Wis. 447, 65 N. W. 176; Keller v. Schmidt, 104 Wis. 596, 80 N. W. 935; Dummer v. Light Co., 108 Wis. 589, 84 N. W. 853. Where the trial court has failed to state in the order the reasons for granting a new trial, the presumption is that it was granted because that court thought the verdict was against the weight of evidence. Mills v. Conley, 110 Wis. 525, 86 N. W. 203.

Judgment notwithstanding verdict, on the ground that the verdict is not supported by testimony, cannot be asked, because (1) such a motion concedes the facts to be as found by the verdict; and (2) under the statute the judgment must accord with the verdict. Scott v. Bank (Tex. Civ. App.) 66 S. W. 485, 493.

[18] Boos v. State, 11 Ind. App. 257, 39 N. E. 197.

[19] Empire Coal & Mining Co. v. McIntosh, 82 Ky. 554.

the instructions which may properly be given when a special verdict is taken, and other matters already fully treated, a summary of the principal errors for which the verdict may be set aside and a retrial had must here suffice.

The necessity of the motion for a new trial as a foundation for review is considered in the subdivison of this chapter on "Appeal."

## VENIRE DE NOVO.

At common law and under the system of some of our states, a venire facias de novo is the proper remedy when a special verdict has been returned which is so ambiguous or uncertain that a judgment cannot be pronounced upon it and it is not susceptible of amendment;[20] e. g., because of omitted facts,[21]

[20] Lee v. Campbell's Heirs, 4 Port. (Ala.) 429; Sewall v. Glidden, 1 Ala. 52; Salem-Bedford Stone Co. v. O'Brien, 150 Ind. 656, 49 N. E. 457; Buscher v. City of La Fayette, 8 Ind. App. 590, 36 N. E. 371; Boos v. State, 11 Ind. App. 257, 39 N. E. 197; Jonas v. Hirshburg, 18 Ind. App. 581, 48 N. E. 656; Carthage Turnpike Co. v. Overman, 19 Ind. App. 309, 48 N. E. 874; Trustees of Christian Church v. Shoemaker's Estate, 20 Ind. App. 319, 50 N. E. 594; Hadley v. Railway Co., 21 Ind. App. 675, 51 N. E. 337; Seward v. Jackson, 8 Cow. (N. Y.) 406; State v. Wallace, 25 N. C. 195; State v. Bray, 89 N. C. 480; State v. Finlayson, 113 N. C. 628, 18 S. E. 200; Whitesides v. Russell, 8 Watts & S. (Pa.) 44; Loew v. Stocker, 61 Pa. 347; Union Sav. Bank v. Fife, 101 Pa. 388; Lawrence v. Beaubien, 2 Bailey (S. C.) 623, 23 Am. Dec. 155; Tunnell v. Watson, 2 Munf. (Va.) 283; Prentice v. Zane's Adm'r, 8 How. 470, 12 L. Ed. 1160; Suydam v. Williamson, 20 How. 427, 15 L. Ed. 978; Bellows v. Bank, 2 Mason, 31, Fed. Cas. No. 1,279; Auncelme v. Auncelme, Cro. Jac. 31; Woolmer v. Caston, Cro. Jac. 113; Treswell v. Middleton, Cro. Jac. 653; Rex v. Hayes, 2 Ld. Raym. 1518; Bird v. Appleton, 1 East, 111; 2 Tidd, Pr. 922.

Where in a special verdict the essential facts are not distinctly found by the jury, although there is sufficient evidence to establish them, the court will not render judgment, but will remand the cause to the court below, with direction to award a venire de novo. Prentice v. Zane's Adm'r, 8 How. 470, 12 L. Ed. 1160.

[21] Kintz v. McNeal, 1 Denio (N. Y.) 436; Robinson's Adm'r v. Brock, 1 Hen. & M. (Va.) 213; Peterson v. U. S., 2 Wash. C. C. 36, Fed. Cas.

or because it finds the evidence instead of the facts.[22] But if the verdict is not uncertain, but the plaintiff's case, as thereby shown, is a defective case or a defective title, there should not be a venire de novo, but judgment should be given for the defendant.[23]

The result attained by the motion is the same as that secured by motion for a new trial, the difference being merely in the mode of procedure.[24]

In strictness the defect in the verdict for which a venire de novo will be granted must be one of form, apparent on the face of the verdict.[25] It was formerly held in *Indiana* that failure to find upon all the issues was good cause for a venire de novo,[26] as it is at common law; but the later cases decide that, if the verdict does not cover all the issues, this is not a defect appearing on its face.[27] A special verdict will not be consid-

No. 11,036; Shrewsbury v. Kynaston, 7 Brown, Parl. Cas. 396. A v. d. n. will not be granted where the amount of the damages is so fully stated in the findings that the amount of the recovery may be determined by mathematical calculation. Smith v. Barber, 153 Ind. 322, 53 N. E. 1014.

[22] Barnes v. Williams, 11 Wheat. 415, 6 L. Ed. 508; Chesapeake Ins. Co. v. Stark, 6 Cranch, 268, 3 L. Ed. 220.

[23] Brown v. Ferguson, 4 Leigh (Va.) 37; Bellows v. Bank, 2 Mason, 31, Fed. Cas. No. 1,279. See, also, Wood v. Luttrel, 1 Call (Va.) 232.

[24] Elliott, App. Proc. § 761; United States v. Hawkins, 10 Pet. 125, 9 L. Ed. 369. While the office of a venire de novo "cannot be supplied by a motion for a new trial, yet the sustaining of a motion for a venire de novo is as far-reaching in its effect as sustaining a motion for a new trial. In either case the issues are to be submitted to another jury for trial." Carthage Turnpike Co. v. Overman, 19 Ind. App. 309, 48 N. E. 874.

[25] Bowen v. Swander, 121 Ind. 164, 22 N. E. 725; Adams v. Main, 3 Ind. App. 232, 29 N. E. 792, 50 Am. St. Rep. 266; Bellows v. Bank, 2 Mason, 31, Fed. Cas. No. 1,279.

[26] Housworth v. Bloomhuff, 54 Ind. 487; Cincinnati & C. R. Co. v. Washburn, 25 Ind. 259.

[27] Deeter v. Sellers, 102 Ind. 458, 1 N. E. 854; Pittsburgh, C. & St. L. Ry. Co. v. Adams, 105 Ind. 151, 5 N. E. 187; Glantz v. City of South Bend, 106 Ind. 305, 6 N. E. 632; Hoosier Stone Co. v. McCain, 133 Ind. 231, 31 N. E. 956; Equitable Acc. Ins. Co. v. Stout, 135 Ind.

ered as so uncertain, ambiguous, or defective that no judgment can be rendered thereon, because some of the issues in the case are not affirmatively or expressly settled or determined therein one way or the other. If the verdict is silent concerning any of the facts in issue, the court will assume, upon motion for a venire de novo, that the party upon whom rested the burden of proof in respect to these facts failed to prove them. If the failure to find the facts was contrary to the evidence, it may furnish a sufficient reason for a new trial, but the failure does not render the special verdict objectionable, nor does it afford ground for a venire de novo.[28]

The remedy, as above indicated, for failure to cover the issues, is by motion for a new trial,[29] or the question of the insufficiency may be raised by motion for judgment on the verdict.[30]

The rule as to omitted facts which was applied in *Indiana* while special verdicts were employed was practically the only divergence in that state from the common-law principles governing the award of a venire de novo.[31]

Motion for a venire de novo reaches a defect in a verdict which fails to assess damages;[32] but there is no defect where

444, 33 N. E. 623; Jones v. Casler, 139 Ind. 382, 38 N. E. 812, 47 Am. St. Rep. 274; Bower v. Bower, 146 Ind. 393, 45 N. E. 595; Zimmerman v. Gaumer, 152 Ind. 552, 53 N. E. 829; Crawfordsville Music Hall Ass'n v. Clements (Ind. App.) 38 N. E. 226.

28 Louisville, N. A. & C. Ry. Co. v. Buck, 116 Ind. 566, 19 N. E. 453, 2 L. R. A. 520, 9 Am. St. Rep. 883. See, also, Meyer v. Green, 21 Ind. App. 138, 51 N. E. 942, 69 Am. St. Rep. 344.

29 Louisville, N. A. & C. Ry. Co. v. Buck, supra; Heiney v. Lontz, 147 Ind. 417, 46 N. E. 665.

30 Louisville, N. A. & C. Ry. Co. v. Hart, 119 Ind. 273, 21 N. E. 753, 4 L. R. A. 549. But the motion for judgment does not serve the purpose of a motion for a new trial. See post, p. 279; Elliott, App. Proc. p. 716, and note 1.

31 Elliott, App. Proc. § 759.

32 Brickley v. Weghorn, 71 Ind. 497; Wainwright v. Burroughs, 1 Ind. App. 393, 27 N. E. 591; Whitesides v. Russell, 8 Watts & S. (Pa.) 44; Miller v. Hower, 2 Rawle (Pa.) 53.

the verdict supplies data from which the court can calculate with certainty the amount of the recovery.[33] It should also be granted where the verdict, without finding the facts necessary to determine the issue, states legal conclusions.[34] But a venire de novo will not be awarded because the jury's answers are evasive,[35] or contain evidence, conclusions of law, or matters without the issues,[36] if, notwithstanding, the verdict is sufficient to support a judgment. Whatever the verdict may contain outside the facts essential to sustain a judgment is surplusage and is to be disregarded. The motion for a venire de novo will prevail only when the findings are so uncertain, ambiguous, or contradictory that it cannot be determined which way the jury intended to find upon material issues.[37] But where the special verdict shows that the jury have found the evidence of the facts necessary to a recovery, instead of the facts themselves, a venire de novo should be granted, for the verdict is incurably defective.[38]

## Appeal.

**When Appeal Lies.** Until the court has entered judgment on the special verdict [39] or ordered a new trial no appeal lies.

[33] Smith v. Barber, 153 Ind. 322, 53 N. E. 1014. See, also, Knight v. Fisher, 15 Colo. 176, 25 Pac. 78.

[34] Wysong v. Nealis, 13 Ind. App. 165, 41 N. E. 388.

[35] Miller v. Stevens, 23 Ind. App. 365, 55 N. E. 262.

[36] Conner v. Railway Co., 105 Ind. 62, 4 N. E. 441, 5 Am. St. Rep. 177; Lake Shore & M. S. Ry. Co. v. Stupak, 123 Ind. 210, 23 N. E. 246; Jones v. Casler, 139 Ind. 382, 38 N. E. 812, 47 Am. St. Rep. 274; Chicago & E. R. Co. v. Branyan, 10 Ind. App. 570, 37 N. E. 190; German Fire Ins. Co. v. Tile Co., 11 Ind. App. 385, 39 N. E. 304.

[37] Jones v. Casler, 139 Ind. 382, 38 N. E. 812, 47 Am. St. Rep. 274; Louisville, N. A. & C. Ry. Co. v. Frawley, 110 Ind. 18, 9 N. E. 594; Same v. Flanagan, 113 Ind. 488, 14 N. E. 370, 3 Am. St. Rep. 674.

[38] Boyer v. Robertson, 144 Ind. 604, 43 N. E. 879; Kinsley v. Coyle, 58 Pa. 461; Barnes v. Williams, 11 Wheat. 415, 6 L. Ed. 508.

[39] State v. Nash, 97 N. C. 514, 2 S. E. 645; State v. Hazell, 95 N. C. 623.

An appeal from an order denying a motion to correct the verdict or for judgment should be dismissed. The appeal should be from the judgment entered for the adversary or from an order for a new trial.[40]

**Verdict Part of Record.** A special verdict has the effect of incorporating facts into the record, and a bill of exceptions is not necessary to make it a part thereof.[41]

**Bill of Exceptions.** In the absence of a bill of exceptions, the questions presented must be determined upon the pleadings, the special verdict, and the orders and judgment of the trial court. The facts found by the verdict, and additional findings on the undisputed evidence by the court, must be regarded as verities in the case.[42] The presumption is that every averment of the complaint not negatived by the verdict was proven on the trial;[43] but it cannot be presumed that facts not stated in the complaint were proved.[44]

[40] Treat v. Hiles, 75 Wis. 265, 44 N. W. 1088; Mills v. Conley, 110 Wis. 525, 86 N. W. 203; Wolfgram v. Town of Schoepke (Wis.) 100 N. W. 1054. See, also, Murray v. Scribner, 70 Wis. 228, 35 N. W. 311. (Under Rev. St. Wis. 1898, § 3069, subd. 1 [Sanb. & B. Ann. St.], which provides that "the following orders, when made by the court, may be carried by appeal to the supreme court. (1) An order affecting a substantial right, made in any action, when such order in effect determines the action and prevents a judgment from which an appeal might be taken.")

[41] 2 "Cyc." 1068, citing Suydam v. Williamson, 20 How. 427, 15 L. Ed. 978; Daube v. Coal & Iron Co., 46 U. S. App. 591, 23 C. C. A. 420, 77 Fed. 713. See, also, Hart v. Railroad Co., 86 Wis. 483, 57 N. W. 91.

[42] Hart v. Railroad Co., 86 Wis. 483, 57 N. W. 91; Cooper v. Insurance Co., 96 Wis. 362, 71 N. W. 606.

[43] McHugh v. Railway Co., 41 Wis. 75; McDermott v. Railway Co., 91 Wis. 38, 64 N. W. 430. In the absence of a bill of exceptions the appellate court can only determine whether the law was correctly pronounced by the trial court. It cannot revise the evidence. Prentice v. Zane's Adm'r, 8 How. 470, 12 L. Ed. 1160; Martin v. Martin's Estate, 108 Wis. 284, 84 N. W. 439, 81 Am. St. Rep. 895.

[44] Where the findings demonstrate that the defendant was not chargeable with the negligence alleged in the complaint, it will not be presumed that a valid cause of action upon some other act of neg-

Error will not be presumed, but must be affirmatively shown, and where there is no bill of exceptions making the evidence a part of the record it is impossible for the appellant to maintain or for the appellate court to say, where material issues are omitted from the verdict, that the trial court erred in refusing to give judgment for plaintiff or in rendering judgment for defendant.[45] This conclusion results from the *Wisconsin* rule that, where the verdict fails to find on all the issues, the court may supply the defect by acting on the uncontradicted evidence in the case in rendering judgment. The evidence not being before the supreme court, it will presume that there was undisputed evidence taken into account by the trial court, which supplied the defects in such manner as to warrant its action. Such action "must be considered as based on the record and *minutes of the trial.*"

In *Indiana*, on the other hand, and wherever the rule may obtain that a fact not found is presumed to have been found against the party having the burden of proof, on appeal from the judgment rendered on a special verdict which omitted to pass upon an issue, the appellate court would have before it all the data necessary to enable it to determine whether, as matter of law, the judgment should stand, to wit, exactly the same facts upon which the trial court acted.

The appellate court cannot determine whether findings are contrary to law or not sustained by the evidence, in the absence of a bill of exceptions.[46] Nor, without it, can the court review the action of the trial court in submitting or refusing questions. The propounding or refusal to propound an interrogatory, and

ligence was proved at the trial. See Hogan v. Railroad Co., 59 Wis. 139, 17 N. W. 632. Where judgment on the special verdict and the minutes of the judge was entered for defendant, whether, in the absence of a bill of exceptions preserving the testimony, it must be presumed that the undisputed testimony, independently of the questions submitted to the jury, establishes defendant's right to judgment, not determined. Id. See Barnes v. Burns, 81 Wis. 232, 51 N. W. 419.

[45] Barnes v. Burns, 81 Wis. 232, 51 N. W. 419.

[46] Kessler v. Railroad Co., 20 Ind. App. 427, 50 N. E. 891.

the changing or modification of an interrogatory, by the court, should be objected to by counsel, and the exception to the ruling saved by bill of exceptions, and is properly presented by the motion for a new trial.[47]

Where the bill of exceptions does not contain all the evidence, and the findings appear inconsistent, the opinion of the trial judge, included in the bill and containing a statement of facts which clears up the findings, may be regarded as a verity in the case.[48]

**Reservation of Grounds of Review.** "Proper practice does not require the person against whom a judgment is rendered upon a special verdict to object to the judgment in order to entitle him to show upon an appeal that the judgment is not supported by the verdict. If neither the facts found nor the undisputed evidence in the case support the judgment, it must be reversed, whether objections or exceptions to the judgment be taken by the losing party or not. A judgment entered upon a special verdict is to be treated in this respect the same as a judgment entered upon findings of fact when the case is tried by the court without a jury; and in such case * * * if the conclusions of law which are embodied in the judgment are not supported by the findings of fact, the judgment will be reversed on appeal, though no exceptions be taken either to the findings of facts, conclusions of law, or judgment." [49]

But while the losing party may secure a reversal without objecting and taking exceptions to the judgment for his adversary, he will not be entitled to a direction that judgment be entered in his favor unless he has moved therefor in the court below.[50] However, it has been held in *Indiana* that a formal motion for judgment on a special verdict is not necessary, as it is the duty of the court to pronounce judgment in favor of

[47] Town of Kentland v. Hagan, 17 Ind. App. 1, 46 N. E. 43; Jonas v. Hirshburg, 18 Ind. App. 581, 48 N. E. 656.

[48] Jones v. Foster, 67 Wis. 296, 30 N. W. 697.

[49] Tyson v. City of Milwaukee, 50 Wis. 78, 93, 94, 5 N. W. 914.

[50] See Elliott, App. Proc. § 756; post, "Disposition of Cause."

the party shown by the verdict to be entitled to it,[51] and, if the rule is followed that the appellant is entitled to have done that which the trial court ought to have done, it would seem that appellant should be entitled to a direction that judgment be entered in his favor, where the facts determined by the verdict entitled him thereto, whether he moved therefor or not.

—— **Necessity of Motion Below for New Trial.** A special verdict settles the facts, and the court by its judgment pronounces the conclusion of law upon such facts. If the court errs in this respect, the error may be reviewed without a motion for a new trial.[52] But the appellate court cannot properly review the evidence to determine whether or not it supports the verdict and judgment, unless a motion for a new trial was submitted to the trial court. "In the absence of such motion the verdict must be taken as sustained by the evidence, and the only questions to be inquired into are the errors, if any, arising upon the trial in the admission or rejection of evidence, in the instructions of the court to the jury, or otherwise in the conduct of the trial." [53] The verdict is conclusive as to the facts.[54] In

[51] Carthage Turnpike Co. v. Overman, 19 Ind. App. 309, 48 N. E. 874.

[52] People v. Hill, 16 Cal. 113.

[53] Reed v. City of Madison, 85 Wis. 667, 673, 56 N. W. 182; Jonas v. Hirshburg, 18 Ind. App. 581, 48 N. E. 656. See, also, Prentice v. Zane's Adm'r, 8 How. 470, 12 L. Ed. 1160; Scott v. Bank (Tex. Civ. App.) 66 S. W. 485. The fact that a motion for a new trial was made at the trial term, but after judgment, and denied, is of no importance on appeal from the judgment alone, for such appeal does not bring up for review proceedings after judgment. Reed v. City of Madison, supra. Where the court set aside a finding of the special verdict, and rendered judgment for plaintiff on the remaining findings and the undisputed evidence, and defendant appealed from the judgment, it was held that by not asking for a new trial he had waived it, and could not on appeal urge that after setting the finding aside the court should have awarded a new trial. Gammon v. Abrams, 53 Wis. 323, 10 N. W. 479.

[54] Garwood v. Simpson, 8 Cal. 108; Duff v. Fisher, 15 Cal. 380; Wheeler v. Pereles, 43 Wis. 332. Each fact found therein is presumed

Seybold v. Terre Haute & I. R. Co.[55] it is said to be well settled that "when a party moves for a judgment in his favor on a special verdict, and excepts to the overruling of his motion, or where a party excepts to the action of the court in rendering judgment upon a special verdict, he thereby admits, so far as such action of the court is concerned, that the special verdict states the facts fully and correctly."

Motion for a new trial is also necessary to present by assignment of error on appeal the question of the trial court's error in refusing to submit interrogatories.[56]

—— **New Trial as Waiver.** By moving for and obtaining an order for a new trial, movant waives the right to have the appellate court review the trial court's denial of a previous motion for judgment on the verdict. It is inconsistent for a party to ask for and obtain an order setting aside the verdict and granting a new trial, and at the same time claim that no new trial should be had because he is entitled to judgment in his favor on the first trial. The court will not reverse an order asked for and obtained from the court below by the appellant himself.[57]

**Disposition of Cause—New Trial.** "Where a special verdict is returned, and a new trial is demanded on the ground that the verdict is not sustained by the evidence, such special verdict is entitled to the same presumptions in its favor as are extended to a general verdict. In such cases the court will not weigh the evidence, nor attempt to decide a conflict in the testimony. The jury trying the case are evidently the exclusive judges of

to have been supported by a preponderance of the evidence, and to have been established to the satisfaction of the jury. Shenners v. Railway Co., 78 Wis. 382, 47 N. W. 622.

55 18 Ind. App. 367, 46 N. E. 1054.

56 Aurelius v. Railroad Co., 19 Ind. App. 584, 49 N. E. 857; Town of Kentland v. Hagan, 17 Ind. App. 1, 46 N. E. 43.

57 Schweickhart v. Stuewe, 75 Wis. 157, 43 N. W. 722. See, also, Louisville, N. A. & C. Ry. Co. v. Miller, 141 Ind. 533, 37 N. E. 343; Wolfgram v. Town of Schoepke (Wis.) 100 N. W. 1054.

the credibility of the witnesses and of the weight of the evidence, and it is their province to determine what facts are found. They are presumed to have performed the duty imposed upon them by law impartially, conscientiously, and intelligently. The verdict comes here with the approval and indorsement of the judge of the court in which the case was tried. Great deference ought to be paid to a verdict so obtained and so sanctioned and approved. It is only where there is a failure of proof on some point material to the issues, and which is necessary to support the verdict, that this court will reverse the judgment, and send the case back for another trial." [58]

The appellate court will not render judgment, but will only grant a new trial, when the evidence is insufficient to sustain certain findings, and the appellant has not moved in the court below to set aside the insufficient findings and for judgment on the remainder and on the uncontradicted evidence; [59] for it has no original power to set aside any part of a special verdict. Its jurisdiction of such matters is appellate only.[60]

When judgment of reversal is rendered on the ground of an erroneous amendment to a special verdict in a material respect, the appellate court will award a new trial, as the lower court should have done, if the verdict was not in accordance with the merits, instead of amending the verdict.[61] In all cases where

[58] Pittsburgh, C., C. & St. L. R. Co. v. Beck, 152 Ind. 421, 53 N. E. 439.

Judgment will not be reversed because a special finding is contrary to the evidence, unless such finding is material. Douglas v. Baker, 79 Tex. 499, 15 S. W. 801.

To warrant reversal the finding must be flagrantly against the evidence. Empire Coal & Mining Co. v. McIntosh, 82 Ky. 554.

The verdict, when sustained by the trial court, is entitled to the most favorable construction warranted by the record. Plano Mfg. Co. v. Bergmann, 102 Wis. 21, 78 N. W. 157.

[59] Conroy v. Railroad Co., 96 Wis. 243, 70 N. W. 486, 38 L. R. A. 419; Keller v. Schmidt, 104 Wis. 596, 80 N. W. 935; Muenchow v. Zschetzsche & Son Co., 113 Wis. 8, 88 N. W. 909.

[60] Conroy v. Railroad Co., supra.

[61] Sheehy v. Duffy, 89 Wis. 6, 61 N. W. 295; Ohlweiler v. Lohmann,

the lower court undertakes to set aside a finding in a special verdict, a new trial should be ordered unless it clearly appears that the finding is wholly immaterial.[62]

Inconsistency between findings is, of course, ground for reversal, and upon such findings it will manifestly be impossible for the appellate court to direct judgment. But contradictory findings warrant reversal only when they relate to material facts, and are so repugnant to each other that it is beyond the ability of the court to render an intelligent judgment.[63]

The appellate court will not pass on issues omitted from a special verdict, but will simply order a new trial. It is timely to reverse a judgment on the merits of the case only after the jury have considered and found a verdict upon all the merits.[64] But, of course, under the *Indiana* rule as to the presumption against the party having the burden of proof, arising from the omission, the foregoing would not apply.

It seems that where particular issues not passed upon by the jury are entirely distinct from those found, the omission does not necessarily involve a retrial of all the issues in the case, but

82 Wis. 198, 52 N. W. 172; Annas v. Railroad Co., 67 Wis. 46, 30 N. W. 282, 58 Am. Rep. 848.

62 Annas v. Railroad Co., supra. But where the jury's findings showed actionable negligence, and the trial court, by a misapplication of legal principles to the evidence, set them aside and rendered judgment dismissing the complaint, it was held that a new trial was unnecessary. The judgment was reversed and the cause remanded with directions to render judgment on the verdict for plaintiff. Ellis v. Railroad Co., 120 Wis. 645, 98 N. W. 942.

63 German Ins. Co. v. Smelker, 38 Kan. 285, 16 Pac. 735. See, also, Murray v. Scribner, 70 Wis. 228, 35 N. W. 311; Shenners v. Railway Co., 78 Wis. 382, 47 N. W. 622; Darcey v. Lumber Co., 98 Wis. 573, 74 N. W. 337.

64 Steinke v. Match Co., 87 Wis. 477, 58 N. W. 842. But see McGonigle v. Gordon, 11 Kan. 167, in which the special verdict failed to find a fact necessary to support the judgment for plaintiff. There being no exceptions to the verdict, no motion for further findings or for a new trial, the supreme court reluctantly reversed the judgment and directed judgment for defendant.

the court may order a retrial only of the issues not passed upon.[65]

*Texas Statute.* The Texas statute provides that "the failure to submit any issue shall not be deemed a ground for reversal of the judgment upon appeal or writ of error, unless its submission has been requested in writing by the party complaining of the judgment. Upon appeal or writ of error, an issue not submitted and not requested by a party to the cause shall be deemed as found by the court in such manner as to support the judgment: provided, there be evidence to sustain such finding." [66]

—— **When Judgment Directed.** Upon appeal, reversal, with direction to enter judgment in accordance with the opinion of the appellate court, can be had only where the appellant has taken such steps in the lower court as entitled him to judgment there. The appellant is entitled to have done that which ought to have been done. Thus, where to the question, "Was the plaintiff guilty of any want of ordinary care?" etc., the jury answered, "No," and defendant's counsel moved the court to strike out the answer and insert in place thereof an affirmative answer, and for judgment on the verdict as so corrected, which motion was denied, and the ruling excepted to, if upon the undisputed evidence the question should have been answered, "Yes," the appellate court will remand the case, with direction to correct the verdict by changing the answer from "No" to "Yes," so as, in form, to find the plaintiff guilty of contributory negligence in accordance with the facts, and to render judg-

[65] Crich v. Insurance Co., 45 Minn. 441, 48 N. W. 198. See Treat v. Hiles, 75 Wis. 265, 278, 44 N. W. 1088, in which the court says: "Neither do we determine whether in an action at law the court may properly grant a new trial of a part only of the issues, leaving the verdict to stand as to other issues, or the cases in which that practice may be adopted, if there are such cases."

[66] See Galveston, H. & S. A. Ry. Co. v. Botts, 22 Tex. Civ. App. 609, 55 S. W. 514; Brown v. Sovereign Camp, 20 Tex. Civ. App. 373, 49 S. W. 893; Southern Cotton-Oil Co. v. Wallace (Tex. Civ. App.) 54 S. W. 638; Holly & Co. v. Simmons (Tex. Civ. App.) 85 S. W. 325.

ment on the verdict as so corrected in favor of the defendant.[67] So, in an action to recover for personal injuries due to the breaking of an iron hook, where the jury found that the hook was in a defective condition when the defendant delivered it to plaintiff and when it broke, and that plaintiff used it properly and was not guilty of any ordinary neglect in the use of the hook that contributed to the injury, and that the defendant did not use ordinary care in the selection of the iron for the hook, but also found that "up to the time the hook was delivered to plaintiff there was a defect in it that could be observed by the owner of the hook, or parties that used it, if they were exercising ordinary care in using or taking care of it," and both parties moved for judgment on the verdict, which was entered for plaintiff, the judgment of the lower court was reversed, and the cause remanded with direction to render judgment for defendant, the legal conclusion being that plaintiff was guilty of contributory negligence.[68] But where, in an action for injuries, the findings show plaintiff guilty of contributory negligence as matter of law, but the defendant made no motion for judgment on the verdict in the trial court, a judgment will not be directed on appeal, but a new trial will be ordered.[69]

A mere motion for judgment notwithstanding the verdict is no more than a motion for a directed verdict or a motion for a nonsuit, or a motion to set aside the verdict and grant a new trial, as regards a final disposition of the case without a new trial, upon the judgment entered adverse to such motion being reversed upon appeal. The proper practice, where the evidence warrants findings contrary to those returned, is to move the trial court to change the answers so as to conform to the evidence, and for judgment upon the substituted findings.

67 Stafford v. Railroad Co., 110 Wis. 331, 362, 85 N. W. 1036; Goldmann v. Light Co. (Wis.) 101 N. W. 384. See, also, Ellis v. Railroad Co., 120 Wis. 645, 98 N. W. 942.

68 Goltz v. Railway Co., 76 Wis. 136, 44 N. W. 752.

69 Dummer v. Light Co., 108 Wis. 589, 84 N. W. 853.

This having been done, the case may go back for judgment in appellant's favor.[70]

Granting a new trial is very much in the discretion of the trial court, and will not be reversed unless there clearly appears to have been an abuse of discretion. It is not the absolute duty of the trial court to set aside a special verdict not supported by the evidence, and to render judgment in accordance with the undisputed evidence. It may do so, or it may grant a new trial.[71] Where the trial court has refused to enter judgment on the special verdict on motion of plaintiff, and has set aside the verdict and granted a new trial on motion of defendant, the appellate court cannot, in the exercise of its discretion, direct that judgment be entered on the findings, for it has no such discretionary authority as the trial court.[72]

—— **Directing Amount of Recovery.** "Where the facts appear in a special finding or in a special verdict, it is proper for the appellate tribunal to rectify an error in the assessment of damages by directing the specific amount for which judgment shall be entered in cases where the damages are severable, and the verdict or finding supplies the data for determining what part is justly assessed and what part is wrongly awarded. But even in cases where the facts appear in special verdicts or findings, the specific amount cannot * * * be directly fixed by the appellate tribunal unless the items included in the sum named as damages are susceptible of severance." [73]

**Cure of Errors.** Elsewhere [74] the effect of special findings to cure errors in submitting or refusing instructions has been

[70] See Standard Mfg. Co. v. Slot, 121 Wis. 14, 98 N. W. 923.

[71] Schweickhart v. Stuewe, 75 Wis. 157, 43 N. W. 722; Gammon v. Abrams, 53 Wis. 323, 10 N. W. 479; McLimans v. City of Lancaster, 63 Wis. 596, 23 N. W. 689; Munkwitz v. Uhlig, 64 Wis. 380, 25 N. W. 424; Annas v. Railroad Co., 67 Wis. 46, 30 N. W. 282, 58 Am. Rep. 848; Schillinger v. Town of Verona, 85 Wis. 589, 55 N. W. 1040.

[72] J. & H. Clasgens Co. v. Silber, 87 Wis. 357, 58 N. W. 756.

[73] Elliott, App. Proc. p. 485, § 572.

[74] Chapter 6.

noticed. There remains to be considered their occasional operation to show that erroneous rulings on the evidence and pleadings were without prejudice.

—— **Improper Admission or Exclusion of Evidence.** The admission of improper evidence is not ground of reversal, where the special findings show the testimony elicited to have been immaterial.[75]

Thus, where the court erred in receiving evidence as to benefits to the defendant accruing by reason of the location of a railroad upon his land, a finding that there were no benefits renders the error of no consequence.[76]

So, error in the admission of evidence as to how an engine was operated is immaterial, where the jury finds that it was properly managed and operated;[77] and the improper admission of testimony as to the rate of speed of a locomotive is harmless, where there is a special finding on that subject which clearly was not based on the objectionable testimony.[78]

Similarly, error in rejecting evidence as to the extent of plaintiff's damages is without prejudice, where the jury find that plaintiff is not entitled to damages.[79]

But it should affirmatively appear or be fairly inferable that the admission of improper evidence did not influence the verdict, and where answers to interrogatories are uncertain they cannot remove the presumption of prejudicial effect. Thus, where the court erred in admitting evidence to show fraud, the error was held not to be cured by an answer that the jury could not say whether or not the sale and conveyance were fraudulent in fact. The appellate court regarded the guarded form of the finding as indicating that the improper testimony had some influence on the minds of the jurors.[80]

75 Southern Kan. Ry. Co. v. Walsh, 45 Kan. 653, 26 Pac. 45.
76 San Jose & A. R. Co. v. Mayne, 83 Cal. 566, 23 Pac. 522.
77 Abbot v. Gore, 74 Wis. 509, 43 N. W. 365.
78 Annas v. Railroad Co., 67 Wis. 46, 30 N. W. 282, 58 Am. Rep. 848.
79 Schrubbe v. Connell, 69 Wis. 476, 34 N. W. 503.
80 Crane v. Reeder, 25 Mich. 304.

**Rulings on Demurrer.** If error has been committed in overruling a demurrer to a bad paragraph of a complaint, it may be cured by showing that the verdict is not founded upon such paragraph, but is based on other and good paragraphs; [81] and a similar rule applies where a demurrer to a bad paragraph of the answer is overruled.[82]

But sustaining a demurrer to a good pleading is a different matter, for if the pleading is overthrown the party is not entitled to give evidence in support of the theory which it asserts, and he is therefore necessarily and materially injured by the rule striking it down.[83]

Where there is a special verdict an error in overruling a demurrer to a pleading is not material, as a correct statement or declaration of the law upon the facts found corrects the error in the ruling.[84] If the findings supply or find the existence of a fact missing or wanting in the complaint, or fail to so find, in either case the overruling of a demurrer to the complaint is harmless, because, in either event, a correct declaration of the law upon the facts found reaches the same legal result as would have been reached with a correct ruling on the demurrer, or with the defect in the complaint obviated by an amendment. The rule which forbids consideration of facts in a special verdict that are outside of the issues does not conflict. Facts in a special verdict may, in a case of this kind, be said to be outside of the

81 Barnett v. Feary, 101 Ind. 95; Evansville & R. R. Co. v. Maddux, 134 Ind. 578, 33 N. E. 345; Taylor v. Wootan, 1 Ind. App. 188, 27 N. E. 502, 50 Am. St. Rep. 200; Knight v. Knight, 6 Ind. App. 268, 33 N. E. 456.

82 Terrell v. Frazier, 79 Ind. 473; Coffeen v. McCord, 83 Ind. 593; Olds v. Moderwell, 87 Ind. 582; McComas v. Haas, 93 Ind. 276; Burgett v. Teal, 91 Ind. 260.

83 New v. Walker, 108 Ind. 365, 9 N. E. 386, 58 Am. Rep. 40.

84 State v. Vogel, 117 Ind. 188, 19 N. E. 773; Walling v. Burgess, 122 Ind. 299, 22 N. E. 419, 23 N. E. 1076, 7 L. R. A. 481; Scanlin v. Stewart, 138 Ind. 574, 37 N. E. 401, 38 N. E. 401; Ross v. Banta, 140 Ind. 120, 34 N. E. 865, 39 N. E. 732; Woodward v. Mitchell, 140 Ind. 406, 39 N. E. 437; Louisville, N. A. & C. Ry. Co. v. Downey, 18 Ind. App. 140, 47 N. E. 494; Tulley v. Bank, 18 Ind. App. 240, 47 N. E. 850.

issues only when they are outside of the scope of the issues; otherwise there could be no such thing as a verdict curing a defective complaint.[85]

Where a good pleading is held bad, a different result must follow. A special verdict could not either cure or render the error harmless, because the facts in such pleading cannot get into the verdict legitimately, and if they do appear cannot be considered in rendering judgment.[86] Such facts would not only be outside the issues, but outside the scope of the issues.[87]

To have the effect of curing errors, the special verdict or findings must be full and definite. The record must affirmatively show, as the case may be, that the judgment rests upon a good paragraph or paragraphs, or that the admission or rejection of evidence, or the submission or refusal of instructions, did not operate to the prejudice of the party complaining.[88]

85 Ross v. Banta, 140 Ind. 120, 34 N. E. 865, 39 N. E. 732.

86 Woodward v. Mitchell, 140 Ind. 406, 39 N. E. 437.

87 Ross v. Banta, supra.

88 See Crane v. Reeder, 25 Mich. 304; Bowlus v. Insurance Co., 133 Ind. 106, 32 N. E. 319, 20 L. R. A. 400.

# CHAPTER XV.

## SPECIAL VERDICTS IN CRIMINAL CASES.

Statutes providing for special verdicts by direction of the court have been held not to apply to criminal cases, in which the jury cannot be compelled to find any but a general verdict.[1] But the jury is at liberty to include special findings in its verdict,[2] and need not in terms find the accused guilty, but may declare certain facts to be established, and conclude that if upon these the court be of opinion that the defendant is guilty the jury so find; otherwise they find him not guilty.[3]

1 See People v. Marion, 29 Mich. 32, Reg. v. Allday, 8 Car. & P. 136. Whether a special verdict is allowable in criminal cases, quære. Dutcher v. State, 16 Neb. 32, 19 N. W. 612.

A general verdict on an indictment is equivalent to a special verdict finding all the facts which are well pleaded therein. Fitzgerald v. People, 49 Barb. (N. Y.) 122.

2 Underwood v. People, 32 Mich. 2, 20 Am. Rep. 633. And if the findings conflict with the general verdict, they control it, at least where the general verdict is "guilty" and a special finding warrants acquittal. See People v. Piper, 50 Mich. 390, 15 N. W. 523.

3 See Commonwealth v. Call, 21 Pick. (Mass.) 509, 32 Am. Dec. 284; State v. Wallace, 25 N. C. 195; State v. Moore, 29 N. C. 228; State v. Watts, 32 N. C. 369; State v. Curtis, 71 N. C. 56; State v. Bray, 89 N. C. 480; State v. Stewart, 91 N. C. 566; State v. Robinson, 116 N. C. 1046, 21 S. E. 701; State v. Savage, 36 Or. 191, 60 Pac. 610; Lewer v. Com., 15 Serg. & R. (Pa.) 93; Commonwealth v. Chathams, 50 Pa. 181, 88 Am. Dec. 539; Commonwealth v. Eichelberger, 119 Pa. 254, 13 Atl. 422, 4 Am. St. Rep. 642; City Council of Charleston v. Gadsden, 8 Rich. Law (S. C.) 180; Short v. State, 7 Yerg. (Tenn.) 510; Jackson v. State, 21 Tex. 668, 4 Bl. Comm. 361.

A special verdict is where the jury find certain facts to exist, and leave the court to say whether or not, by the law controlling such facts, the prisoner is guilty.

A verdict in the following words: "We, the jury, find from the evidence produced that the prisoner A. is guilty of the murder of B."—is a general verdict. McGuffie v. State, 17 Ga. 497.

On the trial of an indictment for an assault on M. with intent to

In *Louisiana,* on the contrary, it is held that the only verdict which a jury can render in a criminal case is a general verdict of guilty or not guilty, by which they pass on both the law and the facts.[4]

In *North Carolina,* where special verdicts in criminal cases are most frequently to be found, it was formerly held that a verdict of "guilty" or "not guilty," according to the opinion of the court upon the facts found, would not support a judgment by the court. The proper practice, as indicated, was for the court, upon its view of the conclusion the law would reach upon the facts found, to instruct the jury to render a verdict corresponding to such conclusion.[5] But it was later said, and it is now the law of that state, that a formal verdict of "guilty" or "not guilty" need not be rendered by the jury, the court having the power so to adjudge upon the findings.[6]

ravish, the jury returned a verdict that defendant was "not guilty of an assault with an attempt to commit rape, in manner and form," etc., but that he was "guilty of an assault upon, and improper and unlawful intercourse with, the said M.," at the time and place in the indictment mentioned. Held, that this was not a special verdict, and that it warranted judgment against defendant for a simple assault. Commonwealth v. Fischblatt, 4 Metc. (Mass.) 354.

A verdict, "We, the jury in the above-entitled action, find the defendant guilty of receiving stolen money, goods, and chattels, in manner and form as charged in the information," is a general verdict, and is sufficient. State v. Jenkins, 60 Wis. 599, 19 N. W. 406.

Where a general verdict of guilty appears of record, the supreme court cannot consider it a special verdict, although the presiding judge reports the case as such. State v. Cox, 28 N. C. 440.

4 State v. Jurche, 17 La. Ann. 71.

5 State v. Monger, 107 N. C. 771, 12 S. E. 250; State v. Moore, 107 N. C. 770, 12 S. E. 249; State v. Nies, 107 N. C. 820, 12 S. E. 443. See, also, as to necessity for conditional conclusion, State v. Wallace, 25 N. C. 195; State v. Stewart, 91 N. C. 566; State v. Divine, 98 N. C. 778, 4 S. E. 477.

6 State v. Ewing, 108 N. C. 755, 13 S. E. 10; State v. Spray, 113 N. C. 686, 18 S. E. 700; State v. Robinson, 116 N. C. 1046, 21 S. E. 701.

The state may appeal, in a criminal case, from the verdict of "not guilty" entered by the court upon the jury's findings. State v. Ewing, supra.

In *England,* according to Mr. Chitty, "the jury have a right in all cases, whether capital or otherwise, to find a special verdict, by which the facts of the case are put on the record, and the law is submitted to the judges." [7]

"It does not seem necessary that the jury, after stating the facts, should draw any legal conclusion. Thus, in case of murder, they need not find any malice aforethought, or show that the killing was felonious; for it is the province of the court to judge of the legal complexion of the offense from the facts stated in the verdict. And if they exceed their duty, and in so doing draw an erroneous inference, the court will pronounce that judgment which they think warranted by the facts, and reject the conclusion as superfluous." [8]

**Requisites.** The verdict must include all the essential elements of the offense charged or there can be no conviction.[9] Thus, "where the indictment set forth that the defendant discharged a gun against the deceased, and thereby gave him a

[7] 1 Chit. Cr. Law, 642, citing 1 Bulst. 87; 9 Co. 12, b. 63; Hawk. b. 2, c. 47, § 3; Bac. Abr. Verdict, D; 2 Hale, 302; 4 Bl. Comm. 361.

[8] 1 Chit. 645, citing 2 Ld. Raym. 1493, 1494; Strange, 773; Palm. 545; 12 Co. 87; 9 Co. 69; 4 Co. 42 b; 2 Hale, 302.

[9] Huffman v. State, 89 Ala. 33, 8 South. 28; State v. Arthur, 21 Iowa, 322; State v. Ritchie, 3 La. Ann. 511; Hunter v. Com., 2 Serg. & R. (Pa.) 298; Commonwealth v. Dooly, 6 Gray (Mass.) 360; Dyer v. Com., 23 Pick. (Mass.) 402; People v. Wells, 8 Mich. 104; State v. Curtis, 71 N. C. 56; State v. Blue, 84 N. C. 807; State v. Bray, 89 N. C. 480; State v. Oakley, 103 N. C. 408, 9 S. E. 575; State v. Crump, 104 N. C. 763, 10 S. E. 468; State v. Finlayson, 113 N. C. 628, 18 S. E. 200; Jones v. State, 2 Swan (Tenn.) 399; McEntee v. State, 24 Wis. 43, 47; Sullivan v. State, 44 Wis. 595; United States v. Buzzo, 18 Wall. 125, 21 L. Ed. 812.

"It is not sufficient that a special verdict finds simply the facts that raise the particular question or questions of law intended to be submitted to the court. It must find, unequivocally and explicitly, all the material facts that might warrant the court in adjudging the guilt or innocence of the defendant; otherwise the court could not adjudge that he is guilty or not guilty, and in that case it would direct a venire de novo." State v. Yount, 110 N. C. 597, 15 S. E. 231.

mortal wound, and the jury only stated that he discharged a gun, and thereby killed him, omitting that it was against him, although from the other circumstances stated that averment was amply supplied to common reason, it was adjudged that the court could not give any judgment against the prisoner. So where the defendants were indicted for a robbery from the person, and the special verdict stated facts that amounted to a simple larceny, and referred it to the court whether the prisoners were guilty of the crime stated in the indictment, the judges thought they could not pass sentence for the real offense upon such a proceeding. And in an information on the statute of usury, if the jury find the corrupt agreement, but take no notice of the loan, the finding will be altogether ineffectual." [10] And while, generally, negatives need not be found in a special verdict, they must be found when it is necessary to show that a person or thing does not come within a particular exception.[11]

But the verdict need not follow the technical language of the indictment. It is sufficient if it includes the substantial requisites of the charge; [12] "as where a defendant is charged with forging and counterfeiting a bank note, and the jury state that he erased and altered it, by changing the word 'two' into 'five,' this was holden to be a sufficient description of the offense." [13] "So where, on a charge of homicide, the indictment mentioned

[10] 1 Chit. Cr. Law, 644, citing: Kel. 111 (Rex v. Plummer); 2 Stra. 1015 (Rex v. Francis); Cro. Jac. 210 (Cook v. Laneday).

[11] Commonwealth v. Dooly, 6 Gray (Mass.) 360. A special verdict finding defendant guilty of the same facts as those charged in the indictment, but not finding him guilty in the county where the offense is laid, cannot be supported. Commonwealth v. Call, 21 Pick. (Mass.) 509, 32 Am. Dec. 284.

A verdict finding defendant "guilty as charged in the information, with the malicious intent as implied by law," does not find malicious intent as a fact, and will not support judgment for mayhem. State v. Blœdow, 45 Wis. 279.

[12] Commonwealth v. Chathams, 50 Pa. 181, 88 Am. Dec. 539.

[13] 1 Chit. 644, citing 1 Stra. (Rex v. Dawson) 19.

three wounds, and the special verdict found but one, the variance was not considered as fatal." [14]

If the verdict is not responsive to the charge, it will not sustain a judgment.[15] It must find the facts, and not the evidence to prove them; [16] and if the jury draw legal inferences from the facts returned by them, the court will disregard them.[17]

If findings on essential questions are irreconcilable, the verdict should be set aside and a venire de novo awarded,[18] as in all cases where the verdict is so imperfect that no judgment can be rendered upon it.[19] But it is also within the power of the court to order the jury to retire for further deliberation, for the purpose of remedying defects in the verdict.[20]

It is said that there are decisions to the effect that a special

[14] Id., citing 1 Bulst. (Rex v. Morgan) 87, 88; Hawk. b. 2, c. 47, § 4.

[15] People v. Olcott, 2 Johns. Cas. (N. Y.) 301, 1 Am. Dec. 168; State v. Heas, 10 La. Ann. 195. Where a special verdict applies to only a portion of the counts, leaving others undisposed of, and sentence is awarded on the whole indictment, judgment will be reversed. Baron v. People, 1 Parker, Cr. R. (N. Y.) 246.

Chitty gives the following: "For printed forms in treason, see Kel. 72, 73, 74; in murder, 1 Leach, 368; 5 Burr. 2794; 2 Ld. Raym. 1485, 1575; manslaughter, Cowp. 830; arson, Cald. 220; 1 Leach, 243; Robbery, 2 Stra. 1015; Com. Rep. 478; larceny, 1 Leach, 498, 499; on riot act, 4 Burr. 2073; assisting prisoner sentenced to escape, 3 P. Wms. 441; for false imprisonment, 3 T. Rep. 735, 736; Mr. J. Ashurst's Paper Books, 1; not repairing a way, 7 East, 588; 5 Taunt. 285; 3 Ld. Raym. 24; not executing the office of constable, 5 Burr. 2788; against overseer's disobedience of order of justice, 5 T. R. 159."

[16] State v. Watts, 32 N. C. 369; 2 Hawk. c. 47, § 9; Rex v. Royce, 4 Burr. 2077; 1 Wils. 56; Kel. 78; 2 East P. C. 708, 784.

[17] 1 Chit. 645.

[18] State v. River Corp., 111 N. C. 661, 16 S. E. 331.

[19] State v. Bray, 89 N. C. 480; Commonwealth v. Call, 21 Pick. (Mass.) 509, 32 Am. Dec. 284; State v. Duncan, 2 McCord (S. C.) 129; City Council of Charleston v. Gadsden, 8 Rich. Law (S. C.) 180; Rex v. Woodfall, 5 Burr. 2661; Campbell v. Rex, 11 Q. B. 799.

Chitty says that it seems doubtful whether a venire de novo ought to be awarded in capital cases. 1 Chit. 646.

[20] State v. Arthur, 21 Iowa, 322; State v. Maxwell, 42 Iowa, 208.

verdict in capital cases cannot be amended by the court, but that the better opinion is that though a verdict cannot be amended in matters of fact, yet the court may amend a mere error of form, even in capital cases, and that where the alteration is merely to fulfill the evident intention of the jury the court will in all cases allow it to be effected.[21]

**Construction.** As in the case of special verdicts in civil actions, and for even weightier reasons, there can be no aider of the verdict by intendment,[22] or reference to extrinsic facts appearing in the record; and this is so even though the circumstances stated may be sufficient to warrant an inference or presumption of the existence of the matter omitted.[23]

But it is said that if the verdict do not state the time when the facts occurred, the court will intend them to have happened in the order in which the jury have stated them.[24] It is also held that the special verdict need not follow the indictment in a trial for manslaughter, by finding that the killing was done voluntarily; for, if it be found that the defendant did the act, it is intended that he did it voluntarily unless the contrary appear.[25] Intent resulting by necessary implication from the facts found is sufficient.[26]

**Effect of Defective Verdict.** Applying the rule against inferences by the court, it has been held in *North Carolina* that

[21] 1 Chit. 645, 646, citing 5 Burr. 2663; 1 Leach, 383; 1 Stra. 515; 2 Stra. 844; 1 Doug. 375, in notes; Hawk. b. 2, c. 47, § 9.

[22] People v. Wells, 8 Mich. 104, 106; Clay v. State, 43 Ala. 350; Commonwealth v. Call, 21 Pick. (Mass.) 509, 32 Am. Dec. 284; State v. Custer, 65 N. C. 339; State v. Duncan, 2 McCord (S. C.) 129; Langley v. Paine, Palm. 192; Com. Rep. 480; 2 East, P. C. 708, 784, 4 Burr. 2073. See, also, Miller v. People, 25 Hun (N. Y.) 473.

[23] Jones v. State, 2 Swan (Tenn.) 399; Rex v. Plummer, Kel. 111.

[24] 1 Chit. Cr. Law, 645; Rex v. Keite, 1 Ld. Raym. 138.

[25] Rex v. Plummer, Kel. 111, 12 Mod. 627.

[26] State v. Fuller, 1 Bay (S. C.) 245, 1 Am. Dec. 610. "The defendant need not be in court on arguing a special verdict, as he must on motion in arrest of judgment. Rex v. Hayes, T. 3. G. 2. Stra. 843." Com. Dig. "Indictment," N.

where the verdict omits to set forth any fact essential to constitute the offense charged it is defective, and the defendant must be held acquitted.[27]

In *England* it is said that where the verdict is imperfect the court may either enter judgment of acquittal,[28] which is not, however, a bar to a second prosecution for the same felony,[29] or (at least in case of misdemeanors)[30] award a venire de novo.[31] The prisoner is not entitled to a discharge, for he might have had the verdict perfected, and, having failed to do so, he is deemed to have waived his objection to being again put in jeopardy.

The jury may not by a special verdict find the defendant guilty of a misdemeanor, where the indictment charges a felony.[32] But where it clearly appears from the findings that the defendant has been guilty of a crime, though not of the degree charged, the court will not discharge him, but will direct a fresh indictment to be preferred.[33]

In *Iowa* a defective finding in a criminal case does not entitle the defendant to a discharge.[34] And in *Massachusetts* an omitted essential fact is not available either to the government as a verdict of guilty, or to the accused as a verdict of acquittal. It neither affirms nor denies as to the truth of any allegation

27 State v. Belk, 76 N. C. 10. But the usual practice seems to be to grant a new trial. State v. Curtis, 71 N. C. 56; State v. Blue, 84 N. C. 807.

28 Rex v. Huggins, 2 Ld. Raym. 1585.

29 Rex v. Burridge, 3 P. Wms. 439. "In all cases where the indictment does not well charge a felony nor the special verdict certainly find any on the facts therein stated, or where the prisoner demurs, which is allowed, or where, on a general verdict of guilty, judgment is arrested for defects in an indictment, judgment of acquittal must be given; and this will be no bar to another indictment, constituting another offense." Com. Dig. "Indictment," N.

30 1 Chitty, 646.

31 Rex v. Hayes, 2 Ld. Raym. 1518; Rex v. Woodfall, 5 Burr. 2661.

32 1 Chitty, 646, citing 2 Stra. 1133; 1 Leach, 12; Cro. C. C. 33.

33 Rex v. Francis, 2 Stra. 1015.

34 State v. Arthur, 21 Iowa, 322.

of the indictment, other than as to facts specially stated, and should be set aside and a new trial ordered.[35]

[35] Commonwealth v. Call, 21 Pick. (Mass.) 509, 514, 32 Am. Dec. 284.

**Special Verdicts in Cases of:**

*Adultery:* Commonwealth v. Call, 21 Pick. (Mass.) 509, 32 Am. Dec. 284.
*Assault with Intent to Murder:* Waddill v. State, 33 Tex. 343.
*Burglary:* State v. Maxwell, 42 Iowa, 208.
*Conspiracy:* Commonwealth v. Judd, 2 Mass. 329, 3 Am. Dec. 54.
*Cruelty to Animals:* State v. Porter, 112 N. C. 887, 16 S. E. 915.
*Embezzlement:* Huffman v. State, 89 Ala. 33, 8 South. 28.
*Evading Rev. Act:* United States v. Buzzo, 18 Wall. 125, 21 L. Ed. 812.
*False Pretenses:* State v. Oakley, 103 N. C. 408, 9 S. E. 575.
*Forgery:* State v. Fuller, 1 Bay (S. C.) 245, 1 Am. Dec. 610.
*Fraud:* People v. Olcott, 2 Johns. Cas. (N. Y.) 301, 1 Am. Dec. 168; State v. Blue, 84 N. C. 807.
*Issuing Bank Bills:* People v. Wells, 8 Mich. 104.
*Keeping Disorderly House:* Hunter v. Com., 2 Serg. & R. (Pa.) 298.
*Larceny:* State v. Bray, 89 N. C. 480; State v. Savage, 36 Or. 191, 60 Pac. 610; Rex v. York, 1 Den. C. C. R. 335.
*Manslaughter and Murder:* Rex v. Plummer, Kel. 111; Rex v. Hazel, 1 Leach, 372.
*Obstructing Road:* State v. Stewart, 91 N. C. 566.
*Peddling without License:* State v. Crump, 104 N. C. 763, 10 S. E. 468. See, also, State v. Yount, 110 N. C. 597, 15 S. E. 231.
*Receiving Stolen Goods:* Dyer v. Com., 23 Pick. (Mass.) 402.
*Robbery:* State v. Curtis, 71 N. C. 56.
*Selling Liquor without License:* Commonwealth v. Dooly, 6 Gray (Mass.) 360.
*Vagrancy:* State v. Custer, 65 N. C. 339.

# APPENDIX.

## STATUTES RELATING TO SPECIAL VERDICTS, AND SPECIAL FINDINGS ON PARTICULAR QUESTIONS OF FACT.

[Note. Almost all of the following statutes define the phrase "special verdict"; but as the definitions are substantially the same, and differ not at all from the common-law acceptation of the term, for brevity they are omitted where possible. Similarly, the provision for control of the general verdict by the special findings, when the two are inconsistent, is indicated, but not given in full (except in the case of Arkansas, which will stand for all), wherever it forms a separate section of the law.]

### ARIZONA.

(Rev. Stat. 1901.)

**Sec. 209, Par. 1418:** (Defines special verdict.)

**Sec. 211, Par. 1420:** A special verdict so found, as between the parties, shall be conclusive as to the facts found.

**Sec. 212, Par. 1421:** Where the court does not instruct the jury to find a special verdict, the verdict shall be general.

**Sec. 218, Par. 1427:** In all cases, whether law or chancery, where more than one material issue of fact is joined, interrogatories may, under proper instructions, be submitted to the jury by the court in writing, and they shall be answered by the jury: provided, that such interrogatories shall be plain, terse, direct and simple, shall each be confined to a single question of fact, and shall be so framed as to be answered by yes or no, and shall be so answered.

## ARKANSAS.

(DIGEST, SANDEL & HILL, 1894.)

**Sec. 5830**: (Defines special verdict.)

**Sec. 5831**: In all actions the jury, in their discretion, may render a general or special verdict, but may be required by the court, in any case in which they render a general verdict, to find specially upon particular questions of fact to be stated in writing. This special finding is to be recorded with the verdict.

**Sec. 5832**: When the special finding of facts is inconsistent with the general verdict, the former controls the latter, and the court may give judgment accordingly.

## CALIFORNIA.

(CODE CIV. PROC., DEERING'S ANN. CODES & STAT. 1886.)

**Sec. 624**: The verdict of the jury is either general or special. A general verdict is that by which they pronounce generally upon all or any of the issues, either in favor of the plaintiff or defendant; a special verdict is that by which the jury find the facts only, leaving the judgment to the court. The special verdict must present the conclusions of fact as established by the evidence, and not the evidence to prove them; and those conclusions of fact must be so presented as that nothing shall remain to the court but to draw from them conclusions of law.

Sec. **625**: (As amended by Laws of 1905; previous form follows.) In an action for the recovery of money only, or specific real property, the jury, unless instructed by the court to render a special verdict, may in their discretion render a general or special verdict. In all cases the court must, upon the request in writing of any of the parties, direct the jury to find a special verdict in writing upon all or any of the issues and in all cases must instruct them upon the request in writing of any of the parties, if they render a general verdict, to find upon particular questions of fact, to be stated in writing, and must direct a written finding thereon. The special verdict or finding must be filed with the clerk and entered upon the minutes. Where a special finding of facts is inconsistent with the general verdict, the former controls the latter and the court must give judgment accordingly.

(**Sec. 625:** In an action for the recovery of money only, or specific real property, the jury, in their discretion, may render a general or special verdict. In all other cases the court may direct the jury to find a special verdict in writing upon all or any of the issues, and in all cases may instruct them, if they render a general verdict, to find upon particular questions of fact, to be stated in writing, and may direct a written finding thereon. The special verdict or finding must be filed with the clerk and entered upon the minutes. Where a special finding of facts is inconsistent with the general verdict, the former controls the latter and the court must give judgment accordingly.)

## COLORADO.

(MILLS' ANN. CODE.)

**Sec. 198:** (Practically identical with sec. 624, Cal.)

**Sec. 199:** In an action for the recovery of money only, or specific property, the jury in their discretion may render a general or special verdict. In any case in which the jury render a general verdict, they may be required by the court to find specially upon any particular questions of fact to be stated to them in writing, which questions of fact shall be submitted to the attorneys of the adverse party before the argument to the jury is commenced. The special verdict or finding shall be filed with the clerk and entered upon the minutes. Where a special finding of facts shall be inconsistent with the general verdict, the former shall control the latter, and the court shall give judgment accordingly.

## GEORGIA.

(Civ. Code 1895.)

**Sec. 4849:** When any question of fact is involved, the same shall be decided by a jury. If there is no such question, or the auditor's report, unexcepted to, covers all such questions, the judge may render a decree without the verdict of a jury. And in the trial of any proceedings for equitable relief in this state, upon the request of either party to said cause, made after the same is called for trial, and before the beginning of the introduction of evidence in the same, the presiding judge shall, when charging the jury, instruct and require them to find a special verdict of the facts only in said cause, and shall inform the jury what issues of fact are made by the pleadings in said cause. Upon the special verdict of facts so rendered, the presiding judge shall make a written judgment and decree in said cause under the law applicable to the same.

**Sec. 4850:** Special verdicts may be found by the jury, and they may recommend to the court the assessment of costs upon the respective parties. It is the province of the judge, however, to determine upon whom the costs shall fall.

(*Above sections under title "Extraordinary and Equitable Remedies," etc. Sec. 4849 is Act Feb. 23, 1876, Acts 1876, p. 105.*)

## IDAHO.

(Rev. Stat. 1887.)

**Sec. 4396:** (Defines general and special verdicts.)

**Sec. 4397:** In an action for the recovery of money only, or specific real property, the jury, in their discretion, may render a general or special verdict. In all other cases the court may direct a jury to find a special verdict in writing upon all or any of the issues, and in all cases may instruct them, if they render a general verdict, to find upon particular questions of fact, to be stated in writing, and may direct a written finding thereon.

The special verdict or finding must be filed with the clerk and entered upon the minutes. Where a special finding of facts is inconsistent with the general verdict, the former controls the latter, and the court must give judgment accordingly.

(*Same, Ann. Codes 1901, secs. 3477–8, Code Civ. Proc.*)

## ILLINOIS.

(REV. STAT., HURD, 1899.)

**Chap. 110**, sec. **58a**: In all trials by jury in civil proceedings in this state in courts of record, the jury may render, in their discretion, either a general or a special verdict; and in any case in which they render a general verdict they may be required by the court, and must be so required on request of any party to the action, to find specially upon any material question or questions of fact which shall be stated to them in writing, which questions of fact shall be submitted by the party requesting the same to the adverse party before the commencement of the argument to the jury.

(*In force July 1, 1887, L. 1887, p. 251.*)

Sec. **58b**: Submitting or refusing to submit a question of fact to the jury when requested by a party as provided by the first section hereof may be excepted to and be reviewed on appeal or writ of error as a ruling on a question of law.

Sec. **58c**: (For control.)

NOTE. Prior to 1872 special verdicts were not governed by statute in Ill. By provision contained in Practice Act, passed February 22, 1872 (L. 1871–2, p. 346, sec. 51), the court might, in its unreviewable discretion, require the jury, on request of either party, to render a special verdict. This provision was in force from July 1, 1872, to July 1, 1874. The act of 1887 differs from former provisions chiefly by making the demand for a special verdict mandatory on court and jury.

## INDIANA.

(REV. STAT., BURNS, 1901.)

**Sec. 554:** (Defines general and special verdicts.)

**Sec. 555:** In all actions hereafter tried by a jury, the jury shall render a general verdict, but in all cases when requested by either party, the court shall instruct them when they render a general verdict to find specially upon particular questions of fact to be stated to them in writing in the form of interrogatories on any or all of the issues in the cause, and this shall be the only form of verdict submitted to or rendered by the jury in the cause: provided, the provisions in this section shall not apply to cases in equity. These interrogatories are to be recorded with the verdict.

**Sec. 556:** (For control.)

(*Id., Rev. Stat., Thornton, 1897, secs. 560, 561. Act approved and in force March 4, 1897.*)

(REV. STAT., BURNS, 1894.)

**Sec. 554:** (Defines general and special verdicts.)

**Sec. 555:** In all actions the jury, unless otherwise directed by the court, may, in their discretion, render a general or special verdict; but the court shall, at the request of either party, direct them to give a special verdict in writing upon all or any of the issues; and in all cases, when requested by either party, shall instruct them, if they render a general verdict, to find specially upon particular questions of fact, to be stated in writing. This special finding is recorded with the verdict.

**Sec. 556:** (For control.)

*(Id., Ann. Prac. Code, Thornton & Ballard, 1889, secs. 546, 547; Rev. Stat. 1881, sec. 546.)*

NOTE. Sec. 555 was amended by Acts 1895, p. 248 [Horner's Rev. Stat. sec. 546], to provide that "the special verdict shall be prepared by counsel on either side of the cause, and submitted to the court, and be subject to change and modification of the court."

## IOWA.

(CODE 1897.)

**Sec. 3726:** (Defines special verdict.)

**Sec. 3727:** The jury in any case in which it renders a general verdict may be requested by the court, and must be so required on the request of any party to the action, to find specially upon any particular questions of fact, to be stated to it in writing, which questions of fact shall be submitted to the attorneys of the adverse party before the argument to the jury is commenced.

*(C. '73, sec. 2808; R. sec. 3079; C. '51, secs. 1786–1787.)*

**Sec. 3728:** When the special finding of facts is inconsistent with the general verdict, the former controls the latter, and the court may give judgment accordingly, or set aside the verdict and findings, as justice may require.

## KANSAS.

(GEN. STAT. 1889.)

**Par. 4380:** (Defines general and special verdicts.)

**Par. 4381:** In all cases the jury shall render a general verdict, and the court shall in any case at the request of the parties thereto, or either of them, in addition to the general verdict, direct the jury to find upon particular questions of fact, to be stated in writing by the party or parties requesting the same.

(*Gen. Stat. 1868, c. 80, sec. 286, as amended by Laws 1874, c. 91, sec. 1, and Laws 1870, c. 87, sec. 7.*)

**Par. 4382:** (For control.)

(*Id., Gen. Stat., Webb, 1897, c. 95, secs. 295–297; Dassler, 1899, secs. 4548–4550; Dassler, 1901, secs. 4732–4733.*)

## KENTUCKY.

(CIV. CODE.)

**Sec. 317, subdiv. 5:** When the evidence is concluded, but before the argument to the jury, either party may require the court to direct the jury to find a separate-general verdict with the general verdict. If a general verdict be required, either party may ask written instructions to the jury on points of law, which shall be given or refused by the court before the commencement of the argument to the jury.

**Sec. 327:** Unless otherwise directed, the jury may find a general, or a general and separate-general, verdict, or a separate-general verdict; but the court may, without motion, or upon motion of a party, direct the jury to find:

1. A separate-general verdict as to any issue; and with such finding the jury shall also return a general verdict; and, if the separate-general verdict be inconsistent with the general verdict, judgment shall be rendered pursuant to the former.

NOTE. Prior to 1886 the jury might find a special verdict, with or without a general, unless otherwise directed by the court; but the amendment of May 15, 1886, struck out the authorization for a special verdict, leaving the statute as above.

## MAINE.

(REV. STAT. 1903, CH. 84.)

**Sec. 99:** The traverse jury may, in all cases, find a special or general verdict, subject to the opinion of the court on a case agreed on by the parties and reserved, or on the facts as reported by the justice presiding at the trial.

## MARYLAND.

(L. 1894, C. 185; SUPP. TO PUB. GEN. L., POE, 1890–1898, P. 498.)

[In all cases where issues of fact are submitted to a jury, the court may in its own discretion, or shall at the request of either party, require the jury, in addition to rendering a general verdict for the plaintiff or defendant, to find specially upon any particular questions of facts, material to the issues on trial, which questions shall be in writing. * * *

All such special findings of facts * * * shall be in writing, and must be filed with the clerk as part of the record in the case, and in civil cases where a special finding of facts shall be inconsistent with the general verdict rendered at the same trial, the former shall control the latter and the court must give judgment accordingly; but nothing herein contained shall limit the court's power to grant a new trial or to arrest judgment on motion. *Repealed by Act of 1900, ch. 641.*]

## MICHIGAN.

(COMP. LAWS.)

**Sec. 10,237:** No jury shall be compelled, in any case to give a general verdict, so that they may not find a special verdict, showing the facts respecting which the issue is joined, and thereon require the judgment of the court upon such facts, and in all cases where an issue of fact is tried before any court of record, the court shall, at the request in writing, of the counsel of either party, instruct the jury if they return a general verdict, also to find upon particular questions of fact, to be stated in writing, and shall direct a written finding thereon: provided, such special questions shall not exceed five in number, and shall be each in single, short sentences, readily answered by yes or no. The special verdict, or finding, shall be filed with the clerk, and entered upon the minutes, and when any special finding of fact shall be inconsistent with a general verdict, the former shall control the latter and the court give judgment accordingly.

*(Comp. L. 1857, c. 128, sec. 57, amended by Act March 29, 1871, which added the provision for special interrogatories. The Act of 1885, L. 1885, Act No. 15, amended the section by adding the proviso as to number and form of questions. Howell's Ann. Stat. 1882, sec. 7606, same with exception of proviso.)*

## MINNESOTA.

(GEN. STAT. 1894.)

**Sec. 5379:** (Defines special and general verdicts.)

**Sec. 5380:** In every action for the recovery of money only, or specific real property, the jury, in their discretion, may render a general or special verdict; in all other cases the court may direct the jury to find a special verdict in writing upon all or any of the issues, and in all cases may instruct them, if they render a general verdict, to find upon particular questions of fact, to be stated in writing, and may direct a written finding thereon. The special verdict or finding shall be filed with the clerk, and entered upon the minutes.

Sec. **5382**: (For control.)

(*G. S. 1866, c. 66, sec. 218; G. S. 1878, c. 66, sec. 236.*)

(L. 1895, c. 324.)

Sec. **1.** In any action where a verdict is hereafter rendered awarding damages on account of the negligence of a co-employé or co-employés, fellow servant or fellow servants of the injured party, the court, upon the request of either party, made before the case is submitted to the jury, shall direct the jury to name and it shall be their duty to name in their verdict such co-employé or co-employés, fellow servant or fellow servants, if the evidence shall disclose their name or names; and if the evidence does not disclose the name or names, then such co-employé or co-employés, fellow servant or fellow servants shall be designated by words of description, having reference to class of service, nature of employment or otherwise, so as to identify them as far as possible under the evidence.

Provided further that this act shall not apply to cases where the name or description of such person or persons is not disclosed by the evidence.

(See Crane v. Chicago, M. & St. P. Ry. Co., 83 Minn. 278, 86 N. W. 328.)

## MISSOURI.

(REV. STAT. 1899.)

Sec. **720**: (Defines general and special verdicts.)

Sec. **721**: In every issue for the recovery of money only, or specific real or personal property, the jury shall render a general verdict. (*R. S. 1889, sec. 2161c.*)

Sec. **722**: In all other cases, if at any time during the progress of any cause, it shall, in the opinion of the court, become necessary to determine any fact in controversy by the verdict of a jury, the court may direct an issue or issues to be made. (*R. S. 1889, sec. 2162d.*)

**Sec. 723:** No issue shall be made, except such as shall be directed by the court.

**Sec. 724:** The trial of such issues shall be by jury, and the issues shall be disposed of by a general or special verdict before a final judgment shall be made therein. (*R. S. 1889, sec. 2164e.*)

(*Same, Burns' Ann. Prac. Code 1901, secs. 534–538.*)

## MONTANA.

(Code Civ. Proc.)

**Sec. 1100:** (Defines general and special verdicts.)

**Sec. 1101:** In all cases the court may direct the jury to find a special verdict in writing, upon all or any of the issues, and in all cases may instruct them, if they render a general verdict, to find upon particular questions of fact, to be stated in writing, and may direct a written finding thereon. (With usual provision as to filing and control.)

## NEBRASKA.

(Comp. Stat. 1899.)

**Par. 5864,** sec. **292:** (Defines general and special verdicts.)

**Par. 5865, sec. 293:** In every action for the recovery of money only, or specific real property, the jury, in their discretion, may render a general or special verdict. In all other cases the court may direct the jury to find a special verdict, in writing, upon all or any of the issues; and in all cases may instruct them, if they render a general verdict, to find upon particular questions of fact to be stated in writing, and may direct a written finding thereon. The special verdict or finding must be filed with the clerk and entered on the journal.

**Par. 5866, sec. 294:** (For control.)

(*Same, Cobbey's Ann. Stat. 1903, secs. 1277–1278.*)

## NEVADA.

(GEN. STAT. 1885.)

**Sec. 3199:** In an action for the recovery of money only, or specific real property, the jury, in their discretion, may render a general or special verdict. In all other cases the court may direct the jury to find a special verdict in writing upon all or any of the issues; and, in all cases, may instruct them, if they render a general verdict, to find upon particular questions of fact, to be stated in writing, and may direct a written finding thereon. The special verdict or finding shall be filed with the clerk and entered upon the minutes. Where a special finding of facts shall be inconsistent with the general verdict, the former shall control the latter, and the court shall give judgment accordingly.

## NEW JERSEY.

(GEN. STAT. 1895.)

**Par. 184, p. 2563:** No jury shall in any case be compelled to give a general verdict, so that they find a special verdict and show the truth of the fact, and require the aid of the court; but if of their own will they give a general verdict, the same shall be received. (*Incorporated in Practice Act of 1903, L. 1903, p. 537, sec. 159, p. 580.*)

## NEW MEXICO.

(COMP. LAWS 1897.)

Sec. **2993**: In all trials by jury in the district courts, the court shall at the request of the parties, or either of them, or their counsel, in addition to the general verdict, direct the jury to find upon particular questions of fact, to be stated in writing by the party or parties requesting the same. When the special finding of facts is inconsistent with the general verdict, the former shall control the latter, and the court shall give judgment accordingly.

## NEW YORK.

(CODE CIV. PROC.)

Sec. **1186**: (Defines special and general verdicts.)

Sec. **1187**: In an action to recover a sum of money only, or real property or a chattel, the jury may render a general or special verdict, in its discretion. In any other action, except where one or more specific questions of fact, stated under the direction of the court, are tried by a jury, the court may direct the jury to find a special verdict, upon all or any of the issues. Where the jury finds a general verdict, the court may instruct it to find also specially upon one or more questions of fact, stated in writing. The special verdict or special finding must be in writing; it must be filed with the clerk, and entered in the minutes. When a motion is made to nonsuit the plaintiffs or for the direction of a verdict, the court may, pending the decision of such motion, submit any question of fact raised by the pleadings to the jury or require the jury to assess the damage. After the jury shall have rendered a special verdict upon such submission or shall have assessed the damage, the court may then pass upon the motion to nonsuit or direct such general verdict as either party may be entitled to. On an appeal from the judgment entered upon such nonsuit or general verdict, such special verdict, or general verdict, shall form a part of the record and the appellate division or the court of appeals may direct such judgment thereon as either party may be entitled to.

**Sec. 1188:** (For control.)

## NORTH CAROLINA.

(Code Civ. Proc. 1883.)

**Sec. 408:** (Defines general and special verdicts.)

**Sec. 409:** * * * In every action for the recovery of money only, or specific real property, the jury, in their discretion, may render a general or special verdict. In all other cases the court may direct the jury to find a special verdict, in writing, upon all or any of the issues, and, in all cases, may instruct them, if they render a general verdict, to find upon particular questions of fact, to be stated in writing, and may direct a written finding thereon. The special verdict or finding shall be filed with the clerk and entered upon the minutes.

**Sec. 410:** (For control.)

Note. The writer is informed that the above will be secs. 510–512 of the new Code about to be published.

## NORTH DAKOTA.

(Rev. Codes 1899.)

**Sec. 5445:** The court in its discretion may, and when either party at or before the close of the testimony and before any argument to the jury is made or waived shall so request, shall direct the jury to find a special verdict. Such verdict shall be prepared by the court in the form of questions in writing, which shall be confined to matters involving the merits of the case and shall admit of direct answer and the jury shall make their answer thereto in writing. The court may also direct the jury, if they render a general verdict, to find in writing upon any particular questions of fact, to be stated as aforesaid. In every action for the recovery of money only, or specific real property, the jury may in their discretion, when not otherwise directed by the court, render a general or a special verdict. The special verdict or finding must be filed with the clerk and entered upon the minutes. When the special findings of fact are inconsistent with the general verdict, the former controls the latter and the court must give judgment accordingly.

## OHIO.

(ANN. STAT., BATES, 1897.)

**Sec 5201:** In all actions the jury, unless otherwise directed by the court, may, in its discretion, render either a general or special verdict; but the court shall, at the request of either party, direct them to give a special verdict in writing upon all or any of the issues, and in all cases, when requested by either party, the court shall instruct the jurors if they render a general verdict to find specially upon particular questions of fact, to be stated in writing, and shall direct a written finding thereon, and the verdict and finding must be filed with the clerk and entered on the journal.

**Sec. 5202:** (For control.)

(*Rev. Stat. 1880, secs. 5201–2: In actions for the recovery of money only, or specific real property, the jury may render either a general or special verdict, etc.*)

(*Foregoing sections correspond to Bates' Ann. Stat. 1900, secs. 5201, 5202.*)

## OKLAHOMA.

(STAT. 1893.)

**Par. 4175, sec. 297:** (Defines general and special verdicts.)

**Par. 4176, sec. 298:** In all cases the jury shall render a general verdict, and the court shall in any case at the request of the parties thereto, or either of them, in addition to the general verdict, direct the jury to find upon particular questions of fact to be stated in writing by the party or parties requesting the same.

**Par. 4177, sec. 299:** (For control.)

## OREGON.

(ANN. STAT., BELLINGER & COTTON, 1902.)

**Sec. 152:** (Defines general and special verdicts.)

**Sec. 154:** In every action for the recovery of money only, or specific real property, the jury, at their discretion, may render a general or special verdict. In all other cases the court may direct the jury to find a special verdict upon all or any of the issues; and in all cases may instruct them, if they render a general verdict, to find upon particular questions of fact, to be stated in writing. The special verdict or finding shall be filed with the clerk and entered in the journal, as provided in chapter III of this title.

**Sec. 155:** (For control.)

*(Same as Hill's Ann. L. 1887, secs. 215–216.)*

## RHODE ISLAND.

(COURT AND PRACTICE ACT 1905.)

**Sec. 353:** In any case the court may, and upon request of either party shall, direct the jury to return a special verdict upon any issue submitted to the jury. Such issues shall be settled by the justice presiding at the trial, and either party may except to his rulings thereon. In addition to such special findings on the issues submitted, the jury shall in each case return a general verdict, and shall assess such damages, if any, therein as they may deem just.

**Sec. 485:** Within seven days after verdict any person or party entitled to except in a cause or proceeding tried by a jury in the superior court may file in the office of the clerk of said court a motion for a new trial for any reason for which a new trial is usually granted at common law, other than error of law occurring at the trial. Such motion shall state the grounds relied upon in its support. The court, after hearing the parties, may set aside the verdict and order a new trial, with or without terms. A verdict shall not be set aside as excessive by the supreme court until the prevailing party has been given opportunity to remit so much thereof as the court adjudges excessive.

(GEN. LAWS 1896.)

(Superseded by the foregoing.)

(**Ch. 243, sec. 7:** In any case, the common pleas division of the supreme court may, and upon request of either party shall, direct the jury to return a special verdict upon any issue submitted to the jury. Such issue may be settled by the justice presiding at the trial, and either party may except to his rulings thereon. In addition to such special findings on the issues submitted, the jury shall in each case return a general verdict, and shall assess such damages, if any, therein as they may deem just. The appellate division of the supreme court may, on motion of any party made and filed, together with a statement of the evidence in such cause at said trial in manner as is elsewhere provided in case of petitions for new trial, set aside any general verdict and order judgment to be entered by the common pleas division in favor of either party upon any special verdict found in any cause; or it may order a new trial generally, or upon any issue submitted at such trial, as upon an inspection of all the evidence adduced, and the general or special verdicts found therein, to it shall seem just.)

## SOUTH CAROLINA.

(CODE.)

**Sec. 282:** A general verdict is that by which the jury pronounce generally upon all or any of the issues, either in favor of the plaintiff or defendant. A special verdict is that by which the jury find the facts only, leaving the judgment to the court.

## SOUTH DAKOTA.

(REV. CODE CIV. PROC. 1903.)

**Sec. 271:** In an action for the recovery of money only, or specific real property, the jury, in their discretion, may render a general or special verdict. In all other cases the court may direct the jury to find a special verdict in writing upon all or any of the issues, and in all cases may instruct them, if they render a general verdict, to find upon particular questions of fact, to be stated in writing, and may direct a written finding thereon. The special verdict or finding must be filed with the clerk and entered upon the minutes. Where a special finding of facts is inconsistent with the general verdict, the former controls the latter, and the court must give judgment accordingly.

*(Ann. Stat., Grantham, sec. 6270.)*

## TEXAS.

(SAYLES' CIV. STAT. 1897.)

(Part in brackets superseded by the article which follows it.)

**Art. 1330:** (Defines special verdict.)

**Art. 1331:** The special verdict must find the facts established by the evidence and not the evidence by which they are established; and it shall be the duty of the court when it submits a case to the jury upon special issues to submit all the issues made by the pleading. But the failure to submit any issue shall not be deemed a ground for reversal of the judgment upon appeal or writ of error unless its submission has been requested in writing by the party complaining of the judgment. Upon appeal or writ of error, an issue not submitted and not requested by a party to the cause, shall be deemed as found by the court in such manner as to support the judgment; provided, there be evidence to sustain such finding.

[**Art. 1333.** The jury shall render a general or special verdict, as shall be directed by the court at the request of a party to the suit, and the verdict shall comprehend the whole issue or all the issues submitted to them; * * * and in all cases where a special verdict is rendered * * * the court shall, unless the same be set aside and a new trial granted, render judgment thereon, and it shall be sufficient for the party excepting to the conclusions of law or judgment of the court to cause to be noted on the record in the judgment entry that he excepts thereto, and such party may thereupon take his appeal or writ of error without a statement of facts or further exceptions in the transcript, but the transcript shall in such case contain the special verdict or conclusions of fact and law aforesaid and the judgment rendered thereon.] (*Acts 1879, p. 119.*)

(SAYLES' CIV. STAT. SUPP. 1903.)

**Art. 1333:** The jury shall render a general or special verdict as may be directed by the court, and the verdict shall comprehend the whole issue or all the issues submitted to them; and upon a trial by the court the judge shall, at the request of either of the parties, also state in writing the conclusions of facts found by him separately from the conclusions of law, which conclusions of fact and law shall be filed with the clerk and shall constitute a part of the record; and in all cases where a special verdict of the jury is rendered or the conclusions of fact found by the judge are separately stated the court shall, unless the same be set aside and a new trial granted, render the judgment thereon, and it shall be sufficient for the party excepting to the conclusions of law or judgment of the court to cause it to be noted on the record in the judgment entry that he excepts thereto, and such party may thereupon take his appeal or writ of error without a statement of facts or further exceptions in the transcript, but the transcript shall in such case contain the special verdict or conclusions of fact and law aforesaid and the judgment rendered thereon; provided, that a case shall not be submitted on special issues by the court unless one or all of the parties to the suit request such submission. (*Acts 1899, p. 190, c. 111.*)

## UTAH.

(REV. STAT. 1898.)

**Sec. 3162:** (Defines special and general verdicts.)

**Sec. 3163:** In all cases, the court may direct the jury to find a special verdict in writing upon all or any of the issues, or may instruct them, if they render a general verdict, to find upon particular questions of fact, to be stated in writing, and may direct a written finding thereon. The special verdict or finding must be filed with the clerk and entered upon the minutes. When a special finding of facts is inconsistent with the general verdict, the former controls the latter, and the court must give judgment accordingly.

## VERMONT.

(Vermont Statutes.)

**Sec. 1231:** The jury, impanelled for the trial of any civil cause, may find a special verdict agreeably to the usages of law.

## WASHINGTON.

(Ballinger's Ann. Codes & Stat. 1897.)

**Sec. 5021:** In every action for the recovery of money only, or specific real property, the jury, in their discretion, may render a general or special verdict.

In all other cases the court may direct the jury to find a special verdict in writing upon all or any of the issues, and in all cases may instruct them, if they render a general verdict, to find upon particular questions of fact, to be stated in writing, and may direct a written finding thereon.

The special verdict or finding shall be filed with the clerk and entered in the minutes.

**Sec. 5022:** (For control.)

## WEST VIRGINIA.

(Code 1899.)

**Ch. 131, sec. 5:** * * * Upon the trial of any issues by a jury, whether under this section or not, the court may on motion of any party, direct the jury, in addition to rendering a general verdict, to render separate verdicts upon any one or more of the issues, or to find in writing upon particular questions of fact to be stated in writing. The action of the court upon such motion shall be subject to review as in other cases. Where any such separate verdict or special findings shall be inconsistent with the general verdict, the former shall control the latter, and the court shall give judgment accordingly.

## WISCONSIN.

(LAWS 1903, CH. 390.)

**Sec. 2858**, Wis. Stat. 1898, amended to read as follows: The court, in its discretion, may, and when either party, before the introduction of any testimony in his behalf, shall so request, the court shall, direct the jury to find a special verdict. Such verdict shall be prepared by the court in the form of questions, in writing, relating only to material issues of fact and admitting a direct answer, to which the jury shall make answer in writing. The court may also direct the jury, if they render a general verdict, to find in writing upon any particular questions of fact, to be stated as aforesaid. In every action for the recovery of money only or specific real property the jury may, in their discretion, when not otherwise directed by the court, render a general or a special verdict.

(WISCONSIN STAT. 1898, SANBORN & BERRYMAN.)

**Sec. 2857:** (Defines general and special verdicts.)

**Sec. 2858:** The court, in its discretion, may, and when either party, at or before the close of the testimony and before any argument to the jury is made or waived, shall so request, the court shall, direct, etc. (as above).

**Sec. 2860:** Every verdict and special finding of facts shall be entered on the minutes and when in writing be filed with the clerk. When a special finding of facts shall be inconsistent with the general verdict the former shall control the latter, and the court shall give judgment accordingly.

(Sec. 2858: Code, sec. 171; "last part of sec. 11, ch. 132, R. S. 1858, with the new provision of sec. 1, ch. 194, 1874, as amended by ch. 21, 1875, amended to designate more clearly the mode of taking a special verdict, and put it under the direction of the court." Sec. 2860: Code, secs. 171, 172; part of sec. 11, and sec. 14, ch. 132, R. S. 1858.)

## WYOMING.

(Rev. Stat. 1899.)

**Sec. 3655:** (Defines special and general verdicts.)

**Sec. 3656:** In actions for the recovery of money only, or specific real property, the jury may render either a general or special verdict; in all other cases the court may direct the jury to find a special verdict in writing upon all or any of the issues; in all cases the court may instruct the jurors, if they render a general verdict, to find upon particular questions of fact to be stated in writing, and may direct a written finding thereon; and the verdict or finding must be filed with the clerk and entered on the journal.

**Sec. 3657:** (For control.)

# INDEX.

## A

## B

## D

## E

## G



## H



## I

## N

## O

## P



## Q



## R

WEST PUBLISHING CO., PRINTERS AND STEREOTYPERS, ST. PAUL, MINN.